FICTION AS HISTORY

VASUDHA DALMIA

Fiction as History

The Novel and the City in Modern North India

Fiction as History: The Novel and the City in Modern North India by Vasudha Dalmia was first published by Permanent Black D-28 Oxford Apts, 11 IP Extension, Delhi 110092 INDIA, for the territory of SOUTH ASIA.

Not for sale in South Asia

Cover design by Anuradha Roy

Published by State University of New York Press, Albany

© 2019 Vasudha Dalmia

All rights reserved

No part of this book may be used or reproduced in any manner whatsoever without written permission. No part of this book may be stored in a retrieval system or transmitted in any form or by any means including electronic, electrostatic, magnetic tape, mechanical, photocopying, recording, or otherwise without the prior permission in writing of the publisher.

For information, contact State University of New York Press, Albany, NY
www.sunypress.edu

Library of Congress Cataloging-in-Publication Data

Names: Dalmia, Vasudha, author
Title: Fiction as history : the novel and the city in modern north India
Description: Albany : State University of New York Press, 2019 | Includes bibliographical references.
Identifiers: ISBN 9781438476056 (hardcover) | ISBN 9781438476070 (e-book) | ISBN 9781438476063 (pbk.) Further information is available at the Library of Congress.

10 9 8 7 6 5 4 3 2 1

for
my mother
SARASWATI DALMIA
née Srivastava of Lucknow
(1915–2010)
who so gracefully survived her share of struggles
and equipped us to survive most of ours

Contents

Preface ix

Introduction: North Indian Cities and the Hindi Novel 1

I. TOWARDS MODERNITY

1 Merchant Lives in Mughal Agra and British Delhi 55
2 Wife and Courtesan in Banaras 109
3 The Holy City as the Field of Action 150
4 Lahore, Delhi, and the Bitter Truth of Independence 203

II. MODERNIST CONUNDRUMS

5 City, Civilization, and Nature 255
6 Culture Wars and a Cult Novel 299
7 On the Rooftops of Agra 328
8 Culture, Claustrophobia, and the New Capital of the Nation 366

Epilogue 406
Index 429

Preface

OVER THE YEARS I TAUGHT at the University of Tuebingen in Germany, my scholarly work focused primarily on the genesis of Hindi and Hindi literature in the late nineteenth century. At the University of California, Berkeley, where S.H. Vatsyayan 'Agyeya' had established the Hindi programme and taught in the 1960s and 1970s, I began to teach the literature of twentieth-century Hindi in a more consolidated way. The project that led to this book was conceived in conversation with my colleagues and students there.

My Indonesianist friend Sylvia Tiwon introduced me to the work of Pramodeya Ananta Toer, whose *Buru Quartet* brought home to me the peculiar nature of British colonialism. George Hart, a Tamilist of international renown, made me aware once more of how young Hindi was in comparison with Tamil. He also made me aware of the very different caste and social structures that prevailed in the various parts of the subcontinent and how they were reflected in the literatures that evolved there. Munis Faruqui, scholar of Mughal India, and Alexander von Rospatt, Buddhologist and Nepal specialist who joined us later, made me realize more than ever the plurality of religious and literary traditions in South Asia and their intense interaction over the centuries. My most sustained conversations were with my friend Raka Ray, a sociologist whose special focus is on gender studies. Her work on the emergence of the middle classes in India and the culture of servitude in Bengal exposed me to new thought. It was thanks to her that I read Bourdieu again and evolved a deeper interest in social history. A wide circle of friends offered warmth, sustenance, and counsel, for which I thank them warmly: Usha and Santosh Jain, Karine Schomer, Ralph Shevelev, Barbara and Tom Metcalf.

In the University Press Book Store next to the 'Musical Offering', the charming classical music store and café where we often spent our lunch break, I picked up many books almost incidentally; so many of them later became key to my work, amongst them Niklas Luhman's *Love as Passion: The Codification of Intimacy*, which provides the backbone of my analysis of changing intimacies in the novels discussed within the present book.

I thank my graduate students at Berkeley, most of them professors now, whose questions and range of research projects widened my intellectual horizons: Anita Ananthram, Sujata Mody, Shobna Nijhawan, Snehal Shingavi, Preetha Mani, Rahul Parson, Nikhil Govind, Vasudha Paramasivan, Gregory Goulding, and Sonal Acharya.

Later, I encountered the work of the students of the Berkeley architectural historian Dell Upton; Will Glover's book on Lahore, Jyoti Hosagrahar's on Delhi, and Swati Chattopadhyaya's on Calcutta opened up new vistas on the history of the new and old cities of British India and the fraught relationship of the new to the old where the old existed, as in Lahore and Delhi. Preeti Chopra was to publish her work on Bombay later. Madhuri Desai's book on Banaras will appear in 2017. Visits with Madhuri in Banaras mediated another kind of relationship to this city, in its present layout primarily a nineteenth-century creation. These young scholars added yet other dimensions to the wonderful work of Veena Oldenburg and Narayani Gupta on Lucknow and Delhi.

I was able to visit all the North Indian cities I engage with in my book and get a sense of the exact location of the novels I discuss here, of neighbourhood atmosphere and house type. And with that, inadvertently, I got a better sense of my own family history, of life in the narrow rooms of the courtyard-centred eighteenth-century haveli in which my father was born, of the extended family house presided over by my grandfather in which my mother grew up, and the brave new world she encountered as part of the first generation of literate women in her family.

Many, many friends and colleagues supported my project. In Chicago, when I presented an early version of my paper on *Sara Akash* that also discussed many other novels (since dropped from my project), the late Carol Breckenridge was the first to point out the connection between private and public in my novels, a public that penetrated the most intimate spheres.

Of my Berkeley friends and visitors there I thank Harsha Ram of Slavic Studies for the subtlety of his thought developed through long evenings spent together; Amita Baviskar for a long conversation after she heard the first presentation of my paper on Mohan Rakesh in San Diego; Ramya Sreenivasan for encouragement at a particularly low moment; Richa Nagar for providing me with material on her grandfather Amritlal Nagar—which then also provided insights into the Agra of his time.

In Banaras I thank the late Anandkrishna for answering my many questions and for his memories of the city going back into the late 1930s, when Dal Mandi still functioned as the courtesans' quarter and when his family still lived in the heart of the city, not far from the house of their relative Bharatendu Harischandra; Shashank Singh of Ganges View on Assi Ghat where, on later visits to the city, I stayed so often and met so many interesting new people; Rakesh Kumar Singh of Harmony Book Shop for his hospitality and the stimulation provided by his wonderful collection of books; Inger Agger for the evening walk on Assi Ghat in Banaras in early December 2012, when she asked me to sum up my book in one sentence.

In Allahabad I thank Alok Rai for his hospitality, Arvind Krishna Mehrotra for taking Raka Ray and me around his city, and Manas Mukul Das for his presence. The conversation with all of them was a living reminder of the time when Allahabad was a centre of academic and intellectual life in North India.

In Lucknow a conversation with the late bookseller Ram Advani on the city's coffee house will long remain in my memory. Anurag Gupta, formerly a student in my Hindi seminars in Berkeley, now Professor in IIT Kanpur, took a day off from work and came to Lucknow to show me around the city he loved, from Chowk to Hazratganj to the gardens of the Old Residency.

For the relationship I was able to acquire with modern-day Agra, I particularly thank Rajendra Yadav. He granted me repeated interviews from his sickbed in Delhi, giving me insights into the Agra of the 1930s and 1940s, alive then with creativity and cultural-political debate, long since lost, but also introducing me to Jitendra Raghuvanshi of the IPTA, who spent a whole day taking me around the inner city of Agra and to the cluster of havelis in Raja Mandi, which also included Rajendra Yadav's own family haveli, where *Sara Akash* is actually set.

In Lahore I thank Madiha and Sheikh Ajaz, who took my brother and me around their wonderful city, driving us from one end to the other, from Anarkali to Model Town, when we spent some days there for the Lit Fest in 2014. I also thank Anand, Yashpal's son, who does not live in Lahore, much more in Montreal and Lucknow, but whom I nonetheless connect with the city, for providing me with so much information on his father and on the writing of *Jhutha Sach*.

Of the long-time friends I made in Tuebingen, I thank Srilata Raman, now professor in Toronto, for her moral and intellectual support; as also Eva Warth, now film professor in Bochum. I thank Barbara von Reibnitz, now in Basel, for introducing me to the work of W.G. Sebald, from whom I learnt the importance of city space in an utterly novel way; and Henry von Stietencron who never forgot to ask when my novels book would get done.

Back home in Delhi I thank Anuradha Kapur and Kumkum Sangari for the sustenance provided by their friendship, Sanjeev Kumar for constant supplies of information and contacts, and, as always, my family: my mother, who asked always how my book was doing, 'Agyeya' and my sister Ila for introducing me to Hindi literature in a new way, and my sisters Yashodhara and Sheela for their warmth as much as the inspiration they provided with their own work. Most of all I thank my children—Damini, Taru, and Samara for being pillars of strength all these years.

I have presented the material that has gone into this book at many venues over the years. I thank all those who gave me valuable feedback which helped shape my thoughts: the School of Oriental and African Studies in London, Halle University, Germany, Leiden University, Oxford, the annual conference of the Association of Asian Studies at San Diego, Chicago, Columbia, Hawaii University, Rutgers, the University of California at Los Angeles, the Centre for the Study of Social Sciences in Kolkata, Sarai in Delhi, the English Department at Delhi University, the University of Hyderabad for inviting me to give their Distinguished Lecture for 2012, the Premchand conference at Jamia Millia, and of course the Center of South Asia Studies, Berkeley.

Rashmi Sadana and Francesca Orsini, whose friendship transcends locations, have patiently read early drafts of many of the chapters and given such detailed feedback that I feel they have almost co-authored the book. Thanks don't suffice for what they have done. Nor for what Rukun Advani, long-time publisher of my work, has done for me. I thank him for agreeing to do this book on the basis of old trust, for his intense engagement with the mass of material I gave him, for getting me to fill the gaps in my argument, and for helping to finally shape the whole into a readable book.

A word on the translations of the many passages from the novels I discuss: to convey the essential substance and thrust of the original I have, in most cases, provided a literal translation; the functionality serves my purpose but does not always make for smooth readability.

Four of the essays in this book have been published in earlier versions:

Essay 1: 'Merchant Tales and the Emergence of the Novel in Hindi', in the *Economic and Political Weekly*, 23 August 2008.

Essay 2: 'The House of Service or the Chronicle of an Unholy City', Introduction in *Sevasadan* by Premchand, translated by Snehal Shingavi, Delhi: Oxford University Press, 2005.

Essay 3: 'Kashi as Gandhi's City: Personal and Public Lives in Premchand's *Karmabhumi*', in *Premchand in World Languages*, ed. M. Asaduddin, Delhi: Routledge India, 2016.

Essay 5: 'City, Civilization, and Nature: Agyeya's *Nadi ke Dvip*', in *Hindi Modernism: Rethinking Agyeya and His Times*, ed. Vasudha Dalmia, Berkeley: Center of South Asia Studies, 2012.

PHOTO CREDITS

The Alkazi Collection of Photography for:

Illus. 1: 'The City of Delhi before the Siege', Engraving, 16 January 1865, *The Illustrated London News*

Illus. 2: Kashmiri Gate, Delhi, Albumen Print, 1865, by Samuel Bourne

Illus. 3: 'The Mine in the Chutter Manzil, Exploded by the Enemy in the First Attack of General Havelock', Albumen Print, from *Lucknow and Delhi*, 1858–9, by Felice Beato

Illus. 4: 'The Chandni Chowk—Principal Street in Delhi', Albumen Print, by Samuel Bourne

Illus. 7: Portrait of a Courtesan, Gelatin Silver Print, *c.* 1890–1910, by an unknown photographer

Illus. 9: 'A Boycott procession in the market area', from *Collections of Photographs of Old Congress Party*, Gelatin Silver Print, *c.* 1930, possibly by K.L. Nursey

Illus. 11: 'Police arresting the women pickets at the Town Hall', from *Collections of Photographs of Old Congress Party*, Gelatin Silver Print, *c.* 1930, possibly by K.L. Nursey

PREFACE   xv

The Homai Vyarawalla Archive, Alkazi Collection of Photography, for:

Illus. 12: Congress Committee Voting for Partition, June 1947

Illus. 28: Connaught Place, New Delhi 1950s

Illus. 29: President Eisenhower at a public reception at the Ramlila Grounds, Delhi, 1959

Press Information Bureau, Ministry of Information and Broadcasting for:

Illus. 13: Refugee Camp, Ludhiana

Illus. 14: Rescued girl, from a Hindu family from Lyallpur

Illus. 15: Girl refugee, Jullundur Camp, 1948

Nehru Memorial Museum and Library for:

Illus. 24: Nehru addressing the nation, 15 August 1947

Victoria and Albert Museum for:

Illus. 8: Queen's College, Banaras, by Francis Frith

Gandhi Smriti and Darshan for:

Illus. 10: Gandhi spinning 1930s

Illus. 16: Gandhi's Delhi fast, January 1948

Illus. 17: Gandhi in death, 30 January 1948

Joerg Gengnagel for:

Illus. 6: Town Hall, Banaras

Anay Mann for:

Illus. 18: Kumaon Cottage

Devika Sethi for:

Illus. 20: Civil Lines Bungalow, Allahabad

Photos by the author:
Illus. 19: Lucknow Residency
Illus. 21: Allahabad University
Illus. 22: College Girls 1940s, from family album
Illus. 23: Anglo Indian Cottage, Allahabad
Illus. 25: Sangam, Allahabad
Illus. 27: Raja Mandi Lane, Agra

From the public domain:
Illus. 26: Sangh Drill

Disclaimer:
Efforts to trace the copyrightholder of Illus. 5: 'Courtesan 1870', have yielded no result at the time of going to press. If information is received from a proven copyrightholder, acknowledgement will be made before the next printing.

Introduction

North Indian Cities and the Hindi Novel

THIS BOOK TRACES THE changing configurations of urban lives as represented in eight Hindi novels set in six different North Indian cities: Agra, Allahabad, Banaras, Delhi, Lahore, and Lucknow. It begins with the emergence of a specific variety of middle-class speakers of a self-consciously Hindu Hindi in the second half of the nineteenth century, and ends in the last years of the Nehruvian era. The colonial and the post-colonial are thus viewed as integrally connected—culturally, socially, and politically. For, if the uprising of 1857 provides a cataclysmic end to one order and the beginning of another, Independence in 1947 would seem to provide another cataclysmic end and yet another beginning. However, to end the book in 1947 would mean accepting the nationalist myth that Independence really did achieve freedom, and that after it India began an entirely new era. Independence was won, as we know, at the price of Partition and the struggle of vast masses to find new locations, personally and professionally, making their lives look very much like the continuation of an older colonial story. The logical end of the book is for my purposes the early 1960s, when the illusion of Independence as a newly gilded age, and the idealism coupled with it, finally ceased to frame lives in North India.

It was in 1964 that Nehru, the chief remaining embodiment of Indian political hope, died, leaving in his wake a vacuum that his successors soon distilled into a political cynicism and larger moral decline that marked the real break from the nationalist idealism that had begun fifty years earlier, with Jallianwallabagh and Gandhi's arrival. And it was in 1968 that the 'three language formula', presaged by the foundation of linguistic states, was promulgated, making Hindi merely one of three languages taught in schools, putting paid to what had over the nationalist period been cast as a major objective of nationhood—Hindi as the sole national language of the country. There were furious anti-Hindi riots in 1966 across both North and South India, many of them bloody and destructive, the end result being the tacit acceptance and codification into a policy of the general preference for English in the upper echelons of society. It is for these reasons, then, that this book looks at the urban intellectual and cultural life of North India in the century or so that preceded the end of Nehruvian India.

Why urban North India and why the Hindi novel, when Hindi fiction is associated more with novels about peasants, particularly those of Premchand (1880–1936), now regarded as *the* classic Hindi author? For one, modernization took place at a greater and more discernible pace in cities than in the countryside. To focus on the city is to be able to look more clearly at the process of modernization. For another, the story of the rather more spectacular modernity of the Presidency towns—Bombay and Madras, and Calcutta in particular, the capital of British India from 1858 till 1911—has been told and retold. Generations of Bengali scholars have pioneered the study of colonial modernity and taught us to read it through *bhadralok* culture, particularly through the novels of Bankimchandra Chatterjee and Rabindranath Tagore. The North, west of Bengal, has generally been regarded as lagging, provincial, and late on the literary scene. Leaving others to judge whether this was really so, it seems possible to outline several reasons why its story seems worth telling.

Unlike Bengal, which had *the* great urban centre, Calcutta, founded by the British and developed as the capital of British India, the North had a number of scattered cities, all of them older and with distinct histories of their own. In these cities, there was already an identifiable elite culture in place, one that 1857 disrupted and shattered. The modernization that followed thereafter also had, then, other foundations than those to be found in Calcutta and the Presidency towns, and an important intellectual aspect of these was the Hindi literature that emerged within them. Modern Hindi was born in these cities of North India, where Urdu and Persian still prevailed, out of the need within an emergent Hindu middle class to find cultural and political expression. It was in these cities that this middle class faced the need to modernize, to accommodate and evolve social change, and where it received intellectual stimulation. This invigoration came from various encounters, through education in the new colleges in the cities, founded from the late nineteenth century on by the elite; from Western intellectual discourse as available through print—missionary tracts, newspapers, books; and through dealings with Western institutions of governance, the municipality and law court amongst others.

I start with a brief recapitulation of the novel as a genre, and its role in partly creating, partly anticipating the story of middle-class modernity and modernism. In the essays that follow, I do not necessarily circle back to the cities once I have located the novels concerned in their midst; much more, I use a description of their space and time to set the scene for the emergence of the characters in the story. I devote a fair amount of space to the narratives themselves, since they are largely unknown to English readers and likely to remain so until the availability of attractive translations, so that in some ways this book can also be regarded as a story of stories.

THE NOVEL AS A GENRE AND THE NOVEL IN HINDI

The novel's distinction as a genre is that it is capacious, and therefore best suited to show up the multiplicity of voices of a given era. Bakhtin defined it as

> a diversity of social speech types (sometimes even diversity of languages) and a diversity of individual voices, artistically organized. The internal stratification of any single national language into social dialects, characteristic group behaviour, professional jargons, generic languages, languages

of generations and age groups, tendentious languages, languages of the authorities, of various circles and of passing fashions, languages that serve the specific socio-political purpose of the day, even of the hour . . . this internal stratification present in every language at any given moment of its historical existence is the indispensable prerequisite for the novel as a genre.[1]

In the case of the Hindi novel, its tone and content changed radically every half decade or so, as we will see when we discuss the novels in the first section of this book, particularly the two novels by Premchand, written after a gap between them of several years. This articulation of the diversity of actual speech types is far more visible in the modern Hindi novel than in English, the latter being more the language of elites and which came later on the scene as a widely accepted literary language. Hindi was the language of resistance in North India, but also of assertion *vis-à-vis* the holders of power. The novels written in our timespan bear witness to the fact that the processes of modernization were best registered in Hindi, as well as to the fact that the most public and most intimate moments were expressed in Hindi—in short, the language most acutely encapsulating and articulating North India's processes of social, cultural, and political change. There is no equivalent of Premchand and Yashpal in the Indian English novels of the time, their representation of the diverse classes of people, of the conversations within the family and between spouses that were imagined and recorded in their pages.

Such was the cultural authority of the genre that the novel grew to become the site to which people resorted for information regarding matters of emotional life, and when needing help in, as much as naming, emotions. So, the adolescent Shekhar in the first part of Agyeya's novel *Shekhar: Ek Jivani* (Shekhar: A Life; 1941–4) turns to his novelistic knowledge (*aupanyasik gyan*) for recognition of his feeling when experiencing a deep oneness with his own state of being, which is in fact a state of non-being (*shunyatvamaya anubhuti*),

---

[1] Bakhtin 1981: 262.

an extrasensory feeling (*atinindriya*). It is with literary help from the realm of novels that he tentatively recognizes what he feels for Sharada—the young woman he meets in the southern mountainous region of the Nilgiris—as 'love'.[2] We are speaking of the late 1920s in an unusually progressive household. The possibility of falling in love, or even of finding one's own marital partner, is just beginning to glimmer on the horizon. Novels help, in the circumstances of this period, not only as tools to recognize particular emotions, but also to assess a person's character.

The uses to which the novel, and prose narratives in general, can be put are thus manifold. The Japanese novelist Kikuchi Kan, writing in 1926 in a country known for its adherence to decorum as much as for its own variant on the segregation of the sexes, says:

> Women don't know what kind of a man will make a good husband, and men don't know what to look for in a wife; and so they set themselves up for disappointment in life and disaster in marriage. But do they teach how to choose a mate in school? If a man wants to learn the truth of human life, he can't very well go out and conduct research on women; and women can't draw too close to men unless they want to invite trouble. But if it is through literature, one can come to know countless men and women, proper love, and all about married life. And it's all so very simple to do. Moreover, absolutely no danger is involved. Put another way, literature is life's laboratory—a completely risk-free guide to the facts of life.[3]

There are parallels with Europe, where, at least since the seventeenth century, as Luhmann has shown, novels had assumed 'the role of providing instruction and orientation in affairs of the heart . . .'[4] Luhmann sees the behaviour of characters in novels as animating rather than expanding the current social code, but there are also well-known examples in Europe of novels anticipating and setting a code. A spate of suicides followed the publication of Goethe's epistolary

[2] Agyeya 1966: 165.
[3] Ai 2014: 193. I am grateful to Francesca Orsini for bringing this work to my attention.
[4] Luhmann 1998: 11.

novel *The Sorrows of Young Werther*,[5] in which the protagonist, hopelessly in love, takes his own life. 'Literature acts upon cultural models which in turn act upon "real life" and transform it.'[6] Thus we have 'the mediation of literary model as form of experience, model of perception and elaboration of reality itself.'[7] Genre, in this case the novel, can be regarded as a generative matrix in more senses than one. 'What we should avoid is thinking of reality naturalistically, as though it were a simple datum,' Conte adds.[8] Thus, 'if the literary genre shares properties with something else, then it does so not with empirical reality but with the cultural model according to which it is perceived.'[9] Novels often portray changes in these very cultural models, with the generation of older folk often regarding them as threatening for the morals of the young and impressionable. In the world of Hindi, too, novels were often considered dangerous for the power they could exercise on the imagination of the young. As one commentator puts it, 'Reading is linked to desire, and there is a strident denunciation of the temptations reading induces.'[10]

True to the form, the novels considered in this book often go beyond the socially possible, anticipating behaviour that would become widely acceptable only several decades later. The early Hindi novels are sometimes roughly hewn, but, their formal unevenness notwithstanding, things that are not possible elsewhere in literature are anticipated and often made to come to fruition by imagining, by allowing for transgressions and giving them space, and by the sheer act of making possible in narrative form what is not yet socially permissible. As has been pointed out, 'the novel antedated—was indeed

[5] It appeared first in 1774.
[6] Conte 1986: 111.
[7] Ibid.: 112.
[8] Ibid.: 125.
[9] Ibid.: 110.
[10] Govind 2014: 98–9. The reference is to Jainendra Kumar's novel *Tyagpatra* (Letter of Resignation; 1937), in which the heroine Mrinal's characteristically narrow-minded husband has deemed her novel-reading evil.

necessarily antecedent to—the way of life it represented.'[11] The portrayal of such anticipations, whether realized in life or not, is not a phenomenon to be found elsewhere. Functioning, as Bakhtin says, in 'the zone of maximal contact with the present', the novel includes extra-literary forms, such as extracts from newspapers, as well as some of the genres named above, such as letters and diaries.[12] And the new subjectivity, visible in Hindi literature from the 1920s particularly in *chhayavadi* (the Romanticist) lyric,[13] also finds its voice in the novel of the period, which charts, if at times falteringly, the process of modernization as lived by young women and men, both in their relationship to each other as much as in their own lives.

The novels chosen for depiction and analysis in this book all have secure positions and enduring reputations in the Hindi literary canon, so I see this present project as no part of a struggle to reinsert them into literary history from putative margins. Nor am I trying, in selecting these particular eight novels, to construct a canon of fiction for modern Hindi; they do not together comprise a 'great tradition'.[14] I regret that I found none by women authors that fitted my categories, though many of those chosen are centred on powerful women figures. Three reasons determined the choosing of these specific works.

First, their urban location, which entailed reading the Hindi literary tradition against the grain, since the tradition has been known largely for the great peasant novels of the vast agricultural countryside which made up most of the North. Various urban locations began to interest me when I realized that over the past two centuries, from the time of the great uprising in 1857, no single urban location in the North could be identified as the epicentre of the region's cultural activity, or at least not such as that epitomised by Paris and London, and nearer home by Calcutta for Bengal, Bombay for Western India, and Madras for the South. The British chose to deliberately play down

---

[11] Armstrong 1987: 9.
[12] Bakhtin 1981: 11.
[13] See Schomer 1998 for the best survey of this age in English.
[14] In the style of F.R. Leavis' famous *The Great Tradition* (1948).

the importance of Delhi and Agra, seeing them as too powerfully connected to Mughal power and the authority radiated by the regime they were replacing, and so developed Lahore and Allahabad instead as regional administrative centres. However, the older cultural capitals refused to fade away. They became like some of the other cities of the North, with their own cultural and political histories, their older, often walled, cities cohabiting with newer residential areas—the military cantonments and the civil lines developed by the British.

When tracing the narrative of modernization in the North, then, my story shows a geographical topography and spread, with multiple urban centres and multiple beginnings within them. The novels are deeply rooted in these once-culturally vibrant cities of the northern hinterland, charting the path of the modernity on which the North embarked in the mid-nineteenth century, after the final overthrow of the Mughals.[15]

My second criterion of selection was the focus on young people, on those who were often in the later novels—at least from the 1930s on—university students, or characters striving to stabilize themselves in some social position, or in some suitable profession or the other, sometimes struggling in the process against what the older generation had laid out for them.[16] The university campus brought young people in touch with new ideas and new currents, throwing them together with other young people similarly moved. Their attitude to life, their ambitions, and their trajectories thereafter were determined by these new ideas, as was their romantic and marital life.

The third criterion for selection, which came about almost inadvertently but then became a determining factor, was the novel's depiction of the political climate of the era. The role played by

---

[15] I save discussion of the beginning of the novel in Hindi for this book's first chapter, which is centred on *Pariksha Guru* (1882), the earliest novel of note in Hindi.

[16] This became particularly clear to me in a conversation held on 14 October 2012, with the late Rajendra Yadav. I owe him thanks; sadly, he is no longer here to receive them.

politics in the lives of the protagonists in these novels was in fact all-pervasive, propelling them, affecting their identity and self-definition, and at times shaping their very existence. Private lives were touched and formed, and relationships forged, nurtured, or destroyed by the momentum these political moments generated. In some of the novels chosen here, nationalism is all-pervasive. It includes the social reforms of the early twentieth century that were seen as part of the nationalist agitation; the politics of municipalities and law courts, which were first set up and began to play a role in civic life in the colonial period; the Gandhian satyagraha against untouchability; World War II and its meaning for the Indian intelligentsia; Hindu and Muslim communalism, particularly at the time of the partition of the subcontinent; the moment of Independence in 1947 and the Nehruvian vision of progress; right-wing Hindutva; and, finally, the ruthless politics of the Cold War as it touched the lives of artists and performers, particularly in the national capital.

Nonetheless, to narrow the choice to just eight was difficult, given the variety and range of material available. As Gopal Ray has shown in his exhaustive history of the Hindi novel, the writing of prose narratives began in the early nineteenth century and has continued unabated to the present.[17] In order to locate the novels selected here in the larger frame that Gopal Ray offers, I will outline the very innovative periodization that he has set up.

The writing of novels in the vernacular happened at the behest of the British, who were eager to put together pedagogical material in Hindi for the initiation into Indian life of their administrators. Gopal Ray called this first period, which he saw as beginning in 1803 and lasting all the way till 1869, as a 'knocking on the door' (*darwaze par dastak*). He sees the next period, the second, with the time span stretching from 1870 to 1890, as a part of 'the new awakening in the North' (*nav jagaran aur Hindi upanyas*). Next, we have 1891 to 1917 as the third period, which he designates as belonging to

---

[17] Gopal Ray [2002] 2005.

romance, readership formation, and the novel (*romans, pathak aur upanyas*). Following this, the 1918–47 period, the fourth, is that of 'the new voices of realism' (*yatharth ke naye svar*), divisible into two sub-periods: the first, 1918–36, with 'the peasant as the focus', and the second, 1937–47, as 'a search for new directions'. Finally, Gopal Ray sees 1948 to 1980 as a fifth period, this one being of 'new horizons of discourse' (*vimarsh ke naye kshitij*).[18] I do not follow him beyond this point since my analysis does not go beyond the Nehruvian period ending in the mid 1960s.

My eight novels follow a rough chronology and fall naturally into two groups, the modern and the modernist. The periods delineated by Gopal Ray are represented in them, with two exceptions: the first period because the novels written in it seemed too slight, too incipient to bear extensive analysis; and the third period, which dwelt largely in the realm of the fantastic and produced no work to satisfy the criteria set up here.

The year of publication does not always determine where my novels are sequentially positioned or in relationship to each other. Their order has more to do with the periods they cover, their style and approach, and the general tone adopted within them. The modernist novel of the second section is more self-reflexive and self-doubting, and with unclear, open endings.

All such selections are necessarily subjective; it could be argued that other novels could as well have been included here. But their inclusion would conceivably have also been deemed insufficient and would, in any case, have required a longer and altogether different book.

The first novel discussed is *Pariksha Guru* (The Tutelage of Trial; 1882) by Lala Shrinivasdas (1850–87). Set in post-Mughal Delhi, it belongs squarely in Gopal Ray's second period, 'the new awakening'. It is a not altogether successful attempt to write in the new genre but

---

[18] Gopal Ray [2002] 2005: x–xi.

its very groping for form betrays its time of composition and interests. Didactic in the extreme, it also struggles to maintain an interesting storyline, while its uncritically nationalist tone reflects many of the concerns of the late nineteenth century. Similar didactic novels abound in the period, most of them much shorter, others destined to remain fragments, serialized in the countless short-lived journals that sprang up at the time and abandoned before they could be concluded.

It took a while for the novel to stabilize as a genre, and most of all to gain a serious readership. As Orsini has shown, it was the *tilismi* (fantastic) novel—foremost the voluminous and wildly popular *Chandrakanta* ([1887] 1891) and its sequels by Devakinandan Khatri (1861–1913), as also detective fiction,[19] primarily that of Gopalram Gahmari (1866–1946) that followed fast upon it—which made the novel a popular genre and Hindi itself widely accessible. People are said to have learnt the Nagari script in order to be able to read *Chandrakanta*. This is Gopal Ray's third period, which he sees as that of romance, readership, and the novel. I found no fiction of note in this period for my purposes.

It is thereafter with the advent of Premchand (1880–1936) that a realistic portrayal of middle- and lower-middle-class urban life enters the novel. In fact, Gopal Ray begins his period centred on 'new voices of realism' (*yatharth ke naye svar*) with the publication of the novel I deal with in my second essay, Premchand's *Sevasadan* (The House of Service; 1918). This was the novel that originally shot Premchand to fame. Set in the inner lanes of Banaras, it is centred on the life of the courtesan, and its great success considerably helped the process of creating a wider readership and enhancing social respectability for the novel. Successful courtesan novels, including Ruswa's famous *Umrao Jan Ada* (1899), had till then been written in Urdu; in Hindi they were a novelty. And even the ones in Urdu had been written

---

[19] Orsini 2009: particularly chapters 6 and 7. Chapter 7 deals with Khatri's detective fiction and its particularities *vis-à-vis* the Bengali (226–72).

not with a psychological focus on the life of a young woman, one who is unsuccessful as a wife but successful as a courtesan and who then abandons her profession for the nationalist cause. With its attention on the wider social fabric of the city and its concern with municipal debates on the removal of the courtesan quarter to the outskirts of the city—debates which became sharply polarized and communalized—*Sevasadan* is the outstanding novel of the second decade of the twentieth century. In its conclusion Premchand resorts to the idealistic realism (*adharshvadi yatharth*) that was his express purpose in writing his tales, deftly tying up all the loose ends of the narrative in order to achieve what became his hallmark: a morally satisfying conclusion.

Premchand's subsequent novels often turned with passionate intensity and intimate knowledge to the cause of the heavily taxed and exploited peasant, locating him on a wide social canvas and creating unforgettable characters in the process. This is especially true of his last and most famous novel, *Godan* (The Gift of a Cow; 1936), whose peasant protagonists, Hori and Dhania, initially prosperous and hard working, are caught in the Depression that sets in at the conclusion of the 1920s as much as in the vicious circle of exploitation by moneylenders and tax collectors. They die in poverty and pitiful anonymity but leave behind an indelible literary image of their life and struggles. On account of my focus on the urban, I have bypassed this and other agrarian novels.

Two other noteworthy novelists of the period who also wrote about the countryside and on occasion about the city, Jayshankar Prasad (1890–1937) and Suryakant Tripathi Nirala (1896–1961), were primarily poets.[20] Alongside Mahadevi Verma (1907–87) and Sumitranandan Pant (1900–77), they provided Hindi with new individualist, romantic lyrics that had no precedent in the language. Known as *chhayavad* (lit. shadowism), this movement in poetry evolved a language of subjectivity which could express an experiential

---

[20] For a short summary and assessment of their novels, see Gopal Ray [2002] 2005: 151–3.

intensity that also worked its way into the novel. The novels of Prasad and Nirala, particularly of Prasad, were well known and popular in their time, but none had the power, urgency, and ambition of Premchand's fiction.[21]

Nearly two decades after his first novel, Premchand wrote a second city novel, his penultimate, also set in Banaras. The action of *Karmabhumi* (Field of Action; 1932), the third novel I focus on, takes place primarily in the inner part of a modernizing Banaras, though it also moves between country and city. The politics of the time are formative not only for the two protagonists, a husband and wife, but also for their relationship with each other. They participate in a series of nationalist agitations—which serves to expand the narrative across a wide social and political spectrum—but are also involved in a power struggle with each other that is for them as existential as the political causes they espouse.

Jainendra (1905–88) was the most experimental and innovative novelist of the 1930s. His *Sunita* (1935) is known for its subtle depiction of a woman's interiority. Set in Delhi, it is also eminently political and deals with an underground revolutionary. Its urban setting provides no more than a frame for the plot, however, as does his second noteworthy novel of the period, *Tyagpatra* (Letter of Resignation; 1937). Considered a classic, the latter is set less in a specific urban site or specific political scenario and more within the inner self of a judge who chooses, ultimately, to resign from his position. This happens because he has been the helpless observer of a great social injustice to his young aunt who, having transgressed the moral strictures of her world, has fallen down the social ladder into oblivion and eventually to a poverty-stricken death.[22] This is symbolic of the general trend Gopal Ray calls 'seeking new directions'.

---

[21] The other popular novelist of note in this period who espoused nationalism and social causes but portrayed them with an often jarring directness was Pandey Bechan Sharma 'Ugra' (1900–67). See Orsini (1998).

[22] Nikhil Govind offers extensive analysis of Jainendra's work, as also of Yashpal's novel *Dada Kamared* (1941) about the socially daring and politically underground terrorist's life. See Govind 2014.

Jainendra's novels have both subtlety and depth but lack the 'diversity of social speech types and a diversity of individual voices, artistically organized' that Bakhtin spoke of when defining the novel, and which functioned as a criterion for my own selection.

I turn instead to a novel dealing with the 1940s, the epic *Jhutha Sach* (False Truth; 1958, 1960) by Yashpal (1903–76), serialized in the weekly *Dharmayug* and then published in two volumes. In his matter-of-fact tone and faithfulness to observed reality, Yashpal is closer to Premchand than to the novelists in the second section of the present book.[23] His adherence to history is such that he gives the exact dates of the political events which propel his characters, making his work seem akin to a chronicle. The first volume of *Jhutha Sach* is set in the inner city of pre-Partition Lahore, the second largely in the overcrowded old city but also in the Civil Lines of post-Independence Delhi. The three main protagonists are highly politicized, caught in the vicissitudes of Partition violence and the sundering of families, but also able to rebuild their lives and marital relationships—the period in which the novel is set allows such choices. Ironically, the political volatility ensuing from the creation of two nation-states also allows for social mobility of various kinds.

All these four novels have an omniscient narrator, though with each successive novel the narrator tends to recede and the focus is increasingly provided by the protagonists.

Novel writing sought new horizons from the late 1940s. Gopal Ray has, as noted, seen this as the period exploring new horizons of discourse (*vimarsh ke naye kshitij*). My second set of novels falls squarely within this period. The works I have picked are more modernist than modern, beginning with Agyeya's (1911–87) *Nadi ke Dvip* (Islands in the Stream; [1948] 1952), set in the early 1940s of

---

[23] Another novelist whose work I initially considered for inclusion was Upendranath Ashk (1910–96), who also explores lower-middle-class urban life in the Punjab of these years. His celebrated *Girti Diwarem* (Falling Walls; 1946) is also set in Lahore. However, the narrative is fragmented and inconclusive and I felt it would not repay closer analysis.

Delhi and Lucknow, and ending with World War II and the Japanese incursion into India.[24] Rekha and Bhuvan, the novel's two main characters, meet in the modernized section of the cities and find each other in the hills of Kumaon, outside city life with its compulsions and conventions. *Nadi ke Dvip* explores interiorities, intertwining poetry with a prose that is also lyrical and self-reflexive. Its lilting prose and the beauty of its speech rhythms surely owe something to the author's poetic sensibility. Agyeya was one of the leading voices in the *Nai Kavita* (New Poetry) movement, inaugurated in the early 1940s with the publication of *Tar Saptak* (Strings of a Septet; 1942), an anthology, the first of a series of three which he edited. The group of seven poets whose work was represented in these anthologies later split into two warring camps much affected by the Cold War: the *Prayogvadi* (Experimentalists), and the *Pragativadi* (Progressives) who were left oriented.[25] Agyeya himself was seen as belonging to the first group. The split also had a bearing on other novelists of the period, as we will see.

Lyricism also pervades the poet, novelist, and dramatist Dharamavir Bharati's (1926–97) *Gunahom ka Devata* (The God of Vice; 1949), which was to become a cult novel for several generations of youthful readers. Bharati belonged to the younger generation of the *Tar Saptak* poets. The novel was written as a rejoinder to the political split of the Hindi literary world into polarized camps in the wake of the Cold War. *Gunahom ka Devata* is Bharati's attempt to demonstrate that one can be progressive and left wing, yet speak of romantic love and even tend towards spirituality. The work is set largely in a Civil Lines bungalow in mid 1940s Allahabad. Written at a very young age by

---

[24] As far as the narrative is concerned, *Nadi ke Dvip* is less experimental than the author's *Shekhar: Ek Jivani* (Shekhar: A Life; 1941, 1944) referred to above, which moves through a series of sites, most of them non-urban, and therefore has not been considered here. Nikhil Govind (2014) offers a sensitive and insightful reading of the novel.

[25] This also had a bearing for other novelists of the period, as we will see.

Bharati as the love story of Sudha and Chander, it is a novel of youth, hope, and suffering. Though focalized through Chander, it revolves around the sorrow and distress of Sudha, his beloved, married to another man while grieving to be with him. Can sex, love, and marriage coalesce in a single union of two people is the question the novel asks and leaves largely unanswered. It ends with Independence for the country, Sudha's death, Chander's move to Delhi, and farewell to life in the bungalow.

For my last two novels I turn to two writers, Mohan Rakesh (1925–72) and Rajendra Yadav (1929–2013), who belong to yet another prominent movement in Hindi literature, namely *Nai Kahani* (New Short Story), which evolved in the 1950s and 1960s, and which they themselves, along with Kamaleshwar (1932–2007), inaugurated. The novel was not necessarily their forté, yet with their heightened literary sensibilities, attuned to catching the nuances of social change, particularly as these affected personal relationships, they aimed to capture reality in a new way. Both were determined not to yield to the idealistic frames set up by Premchand—whom they nonetheless acknowledged as their forebear—or those by Yashpal and Agyeya. Mohan Rakesh and Rajendra Yadav dealt largely with narratives in urban settings. They probed the interiorities of men and women, of professionals living in the increasingly nuclear family and accosting each other without the mediating instance of other family members.[26] As Preetha Mani notes, 'Uncertainty, disillusionment, self-doubt, skepticism, alienation, fragmentation, transitoriness—these were the compelling narrative tendencies that marked the quotidian lives of *nayi kahani* characters.'[27]

Several of the *Nai Kahani* writers' novels could have been consi-

---

[26] The fictional work with urban settings had a powerful counterpart, the so-called *amchalik* (regional) movement, which also used dialect-inflected Hindi. The best-known example of this trend was Phanishwarnath Renu's (1921–77) hauntingly beautiful novel *Maila Amchal* (Soiled Border; 1954).

[27] Mani 2016: 6.

dered for the kind of analysis attempted here, particularly those of Nirmal Verma (1929–2005), which were set in hill stations but also, very evocatively, in Delhi.[28] However, they did not have the diversity of speech that I was looking for and their publication dates fell outside my time span. This was also true of another major novel of the period, *Ap ka Banti* (1971) by Mannu Bhandari (1931–), which focused on the sensibility of a child of divorcing parents. I turned instead to the novels by Rajendra Yadav and Mohan Rakesh since they offered insights into two significant post-Independence cultural moments: first, the ultra-nationalist impulses which moved the Hindu Right; and second, Cold War politics as determining the direction of modernism, a movement which found at that time no sustained patronage from the Indian state.

With Rajendra Yadav's *Sara Akash* (The Entire Sky; [1951] 1960) we find ourselves in a haveli in the inner city of Agra in the early 1950s. The novel begins with the marriage of a young right-wing Hindu nationalist, Samar, his alienation, and eventual reunion with his educated wife Prabha. Their togetherness strains in the direction of a nuclear household and ends with Samar losing his bearings in increasingly hostile family and work environments.

Mohan Rakesh's *Amdhere Band Kamare* (Dark Closed Rooms; 1961) takes us back to Delhi, this time the Delhi of newly resettled refugee colonies, more specifically to the residential areas of New Delhi's Diplomatic Enclave and the residential areas of the city's South. The old city has been left behind, Mughal Delhi and the British are but a memory. The protagonists move and act within the political frame of the Cold War and the cultural insecurities of modern artists lacking clear-cut sources of patronage. Nilima and Harbans are a middle-class couple with ambitions in the arts and the narrator Madhusudan is a young reporter-narrator participating in their lives and struggles.

[28] Verma's *Ek Chithada Sukh* (A Ragged Happiness, 1979) and *Rat ka Reporter* (Night Reporter; 1989) are set in Delhi. Both fall outside the scope of the period delineated as Nehruvian.

NORTH INDIAN CITY SPACES AFTER 1857

Turning now to the cities themselves, let me outline city geography as it figures in this book. Transferred to literature, city geography can refer to a study of literature in space, and/or space in literature:

> In the first case, the dominant is a fictional one: Balzac's version of Paris, the Africa of colonial romances, Austen's redrawing of Britain. In the second case, it is real historical space: provincial libraries of Victorian Britain, or the European diffusion of *Don Quixote* and *Buddenbrooks*. The two spaces may occasionally (and interestingly) overlap, but they are essentially different and I will treat them as such: fictional space in the first two chapters of the book, and historical space in the third one.[29]

The present book is concerned with both. I begin by laying out historically the geography of the city space in question and the specific milieu represented by the author, which together produce a certain kind of sociality out of which grows a social person in the novel, to which he or she brings his or her individual traits and relationships. Thus in *Pariksha Guru* we have to do with Chandni Chowk, the city's main shopping centre, the merchant ethos within it, and two young men with two very different responses to it. In a later novel, the first part of *Jhutha Sach*, Tara and Jaydev Puri, two of the main characters, live and grow up in a lane (*gali*) of the historical city of Lahore, struggling against the lane's narrow mentality and the social bounds it places on them, aspiring for the freedom that other, more modern locations bring with them. The *gali* mentality determines the horizon and imagination of the older generation, which regards movement as transgression, while their youngers can imagine or at least dream of it. In *Sara Akash* the question is whether there can be a modern marriage in an old haveli in Agra. There is a vast gap between the old-fashioned expectations of Samar, which corresponds with that of his parents, and his wife Prabha's freer, more individualistic, modern vision. Thus, we shall have both to do with the actual history

---

[29] Moretti 1998: 3.

and geography of cities, and with their fictional representation. The fictional space within these novels grows out of actual city spaces and maps the fields of power contained therein, even as it draws out the social and personal tensions that produce and propel the narrative. The city thus provides the frame for the narrative, and each of the ensuing essays begins by laying out the where and the when. The history peculiar to North Indian cities, in brief, lays out the grounds for the story of modernity that I chart.

Towards the end of the long auctorial journey that he entitled his *Discovery of India*, Jawaharlal Nehru spoke evocatively of the region that lies at the heart of his book, and of which he himself was a product: 'The United Provinces (including Delhi) are a curious amalgam, and in some ways, an epitome of India. They are the seat of the old Hindu culture as well as of the Persian culture that came in with Afghan and Mughal times, and hence the mixture of the two is most in evidence there, intermingled with the cultures of the West.'[30] This Indo-Persian culture of which Nehru speaks was particularly marked in the prime cities of the region: in Delhi, the seat of government of ever larger tracts of the subcontinent from at least the twelfth century; in Agra, the alternative Mughal capital of the region from the late fifteenth century; in Lahore, patronized by Jahangir; in Allahabad, where Akbar built a fort; and in Lucknow, which emerged in the post-Mughal era as the capital of the nawabs of the region. Large parts of these cities would be practically wiped off the map over the reprisals that came in the wake of the 1857 uprising. It took a while before they became politically and culturally ready to 'intermingle', or negotiate in any substantive way with the language and idiom of the British.[31] Lahore came into the Hindi scenario

---

[30] Nehru 1946: 396.

[31] 'You can look at Sumit Sarkar, you can look at Bipan Chandra, you can look at the Cambridge School or the Subalterns and all schools of Indian history to know that modern Indian history begins after 1857.' Farooqui 2010: ix. The fact that modern Indian history begins after 1857, not with 1857, which determined the turn that North Indian history took thereafter,

later, after the British conquest of Punjab in 1849, when Urdu (or Hindustani) became the language of the province, to be partially overlaid by the Hindi brought to the region by the Arya Samaj in the late nineteenth century. Literary Hindi writing would emerge in Punjab, particularly Lahore, towards the tail end of the 1930s, to die out again after Partition. Our sixth city, Banaras, where two of the eight novels discussed are set, was culturally different from the other cities of the North. It had been the centre of Sanskrit learning for many centuries and naturally formed the core of modern literary Hindi as it took shape from the late nineteenth century.[32]

The havoc caused by the post-1857 retributions and the ruthless British revamping of civic and administrative life in Delhi, and of Lucknow in particular, can be seen as paradigmatic of most North Indian cities. It is worth recalling the major details of the urban changes that, so to speak, swept these cities clean. Meticulously documented by Narayani Gupta and Veena Oldenburg, amongst others, the changes set the stage for the nature and pace of the modernization that followed.[33] The old order was largely swept away, to be gradually replaced by interactions with the new power and mediated access to their culture.

Among the features of urban change in the Hindi belt worth thinking about are, first, the vastness of the destruction of property and lives after the uprising, this being something that none of the Presidency towns experienced; second, the new frame in which the population, particularly of the towns and cities, lived, as well as the hitherto unknown municipalities and law courts which now ruled their lives; third, access to higher education made possible by the colleges built at private expense in the cities, and the culture of informed critique

---

has of course to do with the complete wiping out of large tracts of the city, of which I trace some segments above, but also with the amnesia that followed, which was surely part necessary, given the sheer scale, brutality, and horror of Britain's vengeance.

[32] See Dalmia 1997 for a discussion of these developments.
[33] See Gupta [1981] 2002; Oldenburg [1984] 2001.

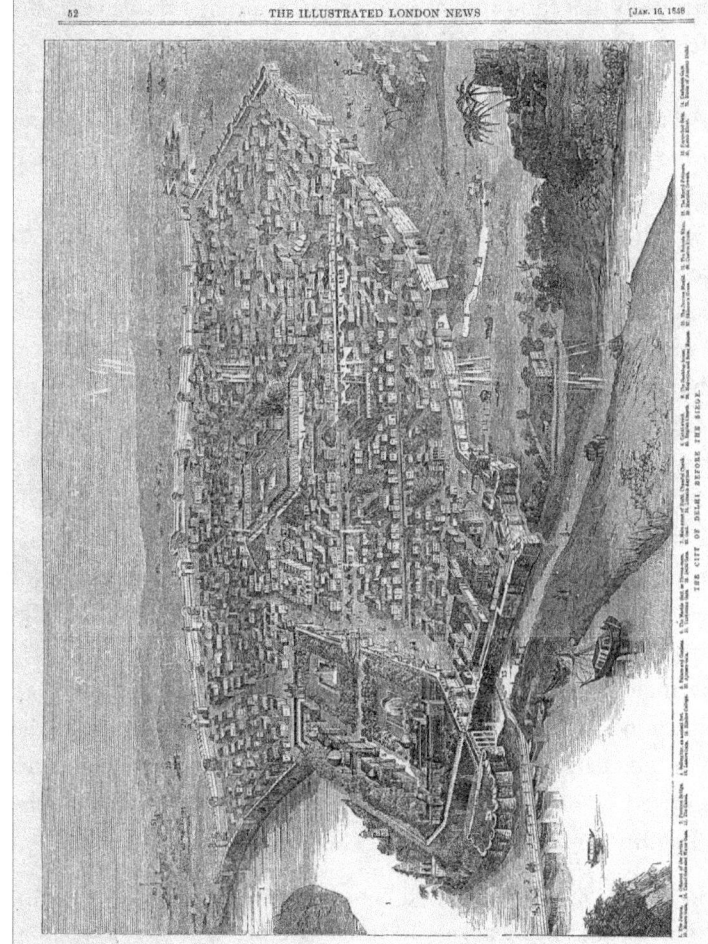

Illus. 1: 'The City of Delhi before the Siege', Engraving, 16 January 1865, *The Illustrated London News*

and insubordination that they eventually fostered; and fourth, the roads that the British cut through densely populated inner cities, symbolic of their attempts to cut through only a partially understood culture. Taken together, these amounted to the price paid for the modernization that followed, at its own pace and in a frame very different from that of the Presidencies.

Before 1857, Bahadur Shah 'Zafar', the last Mughal emperor, and Wajid Ali Shah, the last Nawab of Awadh (Oudh), though no more than titular heads of the regions over which they ostensibly ruled, had palaces in the heart of their cities, as well as a presence and symbolic power which the East India Company had initially been at pains to preserve.[34] Wajid Ali Shah was sent into exile in 1856 and Bahadur Shah banished to Rangoon after the uprising, but for a while their palaces remained intact. After 1857 these central symbolic sites were radically reconfigured, the Delhi palace being occupied by the army and thereafter being known as the fort. Many fine buildings within the fort were wiped away; as late as March 1859 the *Delhi Gazette* reported 'a good deal of blowing up.'[35] A space of five hundred yards around the palace was cleared of all structures, and many of the most beautiful establishments in the city blown out of existence.[36] Not many were left to complain of their extinction; the leading families of the city, many of them Muslim, had been driven out and the remaining male population indiscriminately slaughtered: gallows had been set up in Chandni Chowk, the broad shopping and residential avenue in the heart of Delhi. The violence of the random executions that followed was matched by the serial blasts that destroyed the ornate Begum (or Chandni) Sarai.[37] Set in an octagonal square at

---

[34] 'The cultural life of the city was dominated by the court, with Bahadur Shah acting as the presiding poet-scholar-archer-calligrapher-kite flyer-fount of all wisdom and grace.' Farooqui 2010: xxx.

[35] Gupta [1981] 2002: 27–8.

[36] They had evocative names: Kucha Bulaqui Begum, the haveli of the nawab wazir, the Akbarabadi Masjid, the palaces of the nawabs of Jhajjhar, Ballabgarh, Furrucknagar, and Bahadurgarh.

[37] Bholanath Chunder, describing the scene in Allahabad in the years after

the centre of the Chowk, and surrounded by double-storey shops, the Sarai had been built by Jahanara Begum, the daughter of Shah Jahan; the famous Nahr-e-Bihisht (Paradise Canal) formed a pool before it.[38] In the years following, these structures were replaced by staid Victorian architecture. A massive Town Hall was built over 1860–5 and adorned with a statue of Queen Victoria at its entrance. A Clock Tower now graced the centre of the square, a fountain would be added later; Begum Bagh, the garden at the back of the Sarai, was renamed Company Bagh.[39] The passing of the old order was being concretely marked and it would take some decades for the inhabitants of these cities to come to terms with the new architecture, the new administration, the new standards of behaviour.[40]

---

the uprising, says: 'The martial law was an outlandish demon—the like of which had not been dreamt of in Oriental demonology . . . It mattered little whom the redcoats killed—the innocent and the guilty, the loyal and the disloyal, the well-wisher and the traitor were confounded in one promiscuous vengeance. To "bag the nigger" had become a favourite phrase of the military sportsmen of that day.' He adds: 'One's blood still runs cold to remember the soul-harrowing and blood-freezing scenes that were witnessed in those days. There were those who had especial reasons to have been anxious to show their rare qualification in administering drumhead justice. Scouring through the towns and suburbs, they caught all on whom they could lay their hands—porter or pedlar, shopkeeper or artisan, and hurrying them on through a mock-trial, made them dangle on the nearest tree. Near six thousand beings had been thus summarily disposed of and launched into eternity. Their corpses hanging by twos and threes from branch and sign-post all over the town, speedily contributed to frighten the country into submission and tranquility.' Cited in Mehrotra 2007: 84, 85.

[38] Finbarr Flood, speaking of an earlier remodelling of the cities of North India after the Ghurid conquests, tells us of the effectiveness of the 'political utility of architectural iconoclasm . . . the shock of these events (unprecedented scale of destruction) must have resounded through all levels of society . . . The impact of the post-conquest arrangements on the population, their daily rituals, and experience of familiar cityscapes can hardly be doubted.' Flood 2009: 153, 156.

[39] Gupta [1981] 2002: 85/86; see also Hosargrahar 2005: 52.

[40] 'After 1857, the victorious British had the only game in town: they

Illus. 2: Kashmiri Gate, Delhi, Albumen Print, 1865, by Samuel Bourne

Land transactions pertaining to these actions in Delhi took up a good part of the 1860s. The houses of all Muslims who could not prove themselves innocent were confiscated and their owners shifted to other parts of the city. A large number of houses were demolished in order to build the cantonment and the railway line.[41] The East–West alignment of the railway line broke the concentric pattern of Shahjahanabad, cutting the city into two vertical slices and destroying a part of the city wall in the process. The hundred feet wide Queen's Road and Hamilton Road, driven through the town to facilitate troop movement over the densely populated regions of the city, displaced many hundreds. The new roads were consciously designed to symbolize an order forcibly established. Two-thirds of Mughal Shahjahanabad came to be remodelled, the inhabitants squeezed into two-thirds of the walled city and its poorer western suburbs.

It is in the narrow, densely built, but also constantly changing and modernizing environment of lanes in the inner cities that the chief characters of our pre-Independence—as also some of the post-Independence—novels live. One of the main women characters in Premchand's *Sevasadan* lives first in one of the many small, dark lanes branching off from Dal Mandi, the courtesan quarters in the heart of Banaras.[42] Tara in the Lahore volume of *Jhutha Sach* lives with

---

were "naturally" superior, and they made sure everyone realized it. Azad [Muhammad Husain, b. 1830] himself, in another context, described the result: "The important thing is that the glory of the winners' ascendant fortune gives everything of theirs—even their dress, their gait, their conversation—a radiance that makes them desirable. And people do not merely adopt them, but are proud to adopt them. Then they bring forth, by means of intellectual arguments, many benefits of this.'" Pritchett 1994: xv, xvi.

[41] Gupta ([1981] 2002: 23, 28–9, 30, 38, 56, 84, 86.

[42] I went to Dal Mandi on one of my visits to the city, both during the day when bazaar life was in full swing and vegetable vendors occupied large spaces of what today looks like a narrow street, and in the early morning when the ornate windows and balconies—lit up once from within in the evenings—became more visible. It was possible then to imagine how glamorous the street must have been once.

her family in the fictional Bhola Pandhe ki Gali in the walled city of Lahore. The main male protagonist Chander of *Gunahom ka Devata* lives in the older part of Allahabad.

Major demographic and cultural shifts were a natural corollary to these physical and architectural alterations. More Hindus were admitted back into the city than Muslims;[43] they began returning as early as January 1858 to Delhi. The Muslims, who began to be let in a year later, had to prove themselves innocent of any part in the uprising and be certified so. Those who derived the greatest profit from these transactions were the Hindu merchants who had remained loyal through 1857; the wealthiest of these bought up the biggest havelis in what had been the most exclusive parts of the city. Thus a Muslim-dominant Delhi changed character and became Hindu-merchant-dominant. Both Hindi–Hindu and Urdu–Muslim grew increasingly bifurcated. This became true of many of the major cities of the North. It was this Hindu culture of the cities of North India that modernized, and it is from the ranks of these Hindus that the protagonists of our novels emerge. The Hindi novels focus primarily on Hindus. There are, indeed, some Muslim characters in *Sevasadan*, and in *Jhutha Sach* the communist Muslim student leader Asad has an important role to play, but neither their internality nor their milieu is explored.

Once municipalities were set up in 1863, Hindus began to be nominated to the powerful municipal councils which ran the cities. They acquiesced easily in lopsided decisions, such as the one which in the 1860s allowed the Delhi municipality to expend 75 per cent of its

---

[43] 'The whole population had been driven out of the city on its capture, as has been noted. Dr Farquhar's report in December shows that they were still outside, chiefly in the neighbourhood of the Qutab and Nizam-ud-din, lacking shelter on the eve of the winter rains and the severest period of the cold weather. It was only in the New Year that the Hindus began to return and it was then reported that the city retained one quarter of its former population. The civil courts reopened in July 1858.

After the people came the buildings of the city. There was a cry that the whole city should be razed to the ground.' Spear [1951] 2002: 220.

revenue on maintaining the police, and a great portion of the rest in the upkeep of the Civil Lines—which now housed the British officials who had before 1857 lived within the city. The municipality would in fact radically alter, whether by commission or omission, all aspects of civic life. As we will see, the machinations of the municipality play a major role in the early Hindi novel.

Of the modernization that followed, early-nineteenth-century visitors remarked that the educated classes of Upper India had been barely touched in their mental make-up and lifestyle by the British. The polished urbanity of the Urdu culture that characterized Delhi before 1857 would regenerate somewhat, but the Anglo-Urdu intelligentsia which had emerged from the heady days of Delhi College in the 1840s would never quite recover lost ground.[44] Though the study of English had been introduced as early as 1827 in the Delhi College, Altaf Hussain Hali, one of its most renowned alumni, put it bluntly: 'We regarded the English section as a means for getting a job, not an education . . .'[45] After the transfer of the college to Lahore in 1877, there were periodic agitations, particularly over 1876–82, to restore the College to Delhi. But this was out of the question, the decision to remove the institution to Lahore being part and parcel of the much bigger move to politically reduce Delhi to size by shifting the administration of the city and its prestigious college out to the freshly conquered province of Punjab. Meanwhile, Kashmiri Gate, the hub of European social life, which never became as congested as the rest of the city, not even when the temporary capital was located in Civil Lines from 1911 to 1931, slowly began to set up new lifestyles. The area around Kashmiri Gate figures in *Nadi ke Dvip*.

The story of modern Lucknow, founded as the new capital of Awadh in 1775 by Asaf-ud-Daulah, follows much the same pattern of violent change as Delhi, and indeed of 'Agra, Meerut, Jhansi, Bareilly, Moradabad, and others, where rebellion converted the old

[44] Delhi College, founded in 1824, was the revival of the earlier Ghaziuddin's Madrasa. See Chapter One for more information on this college.

[45] Quoted in Gupta [1981] 2002: 7.

cities into battlefields.'⁴⁶ Kaisar Bagh, the large palace and garden complex where Wajid Ali's many wives had lived, was stripped and handed over by the British to loyal landowners. As Oldenburg tells us in her graphic account of the making of colonial Lucknow, after the vindictive repression of the uprising Colonel Robert Napier of the Royal Engineers set about mapping with surgical exactitude the demolitions that were to follow. The core of the city lay between the river Gomti and the central Chowk. Every building and garden enclosure not required by the army was razed; only a few palaces and the Imambara, useful for billeting troops and related strategic purposes, were allowed to stand and served for several decades after the rebellion as military posts. The debris was removed to create a 500-yard esplanade around the buildings that remained. The Jama Masjid would never again be a mosque. As in Delhi, through the dense core of Lucknow were constructed several broad roads connecting with new arteries to ensure swift troop movement. All that came in the way of the roads, house or mosque, was levelled to the ground.⁴⁷ Citizens dwelling in the midst of dust and debris tended to react in panic to the noise of dynamite charges but were warned that if they evacuated their houses too hastily their property was likely to be confiscated. Two-fifths of the city's material fabric was destroyed; the consequent radical demographic changes were again chiefly inimical to Muslims. The monument carefully preserved, and which stands to this day, was the ruin of the Old British Residency, a memorial to the famous siege of the city during the uprising. (There had been a Resident in Awadh from 1731 who had moved from Faizabad to Lucknow in 1775, when the capital shifted.) Before 1857, the modest complex of buildings on top of a hill was developed into one of the

---

[46] Oldenburg [1984] 2001: xxv.

[47] A memorandum of the Chief Commissioner of the city, 'Civil Organization of the City of Lucknow', dated 23 July 1858, describes demolition squads arriving in an area often proceeded without making sure that the houses to be erased were empty. '(T)he wonder,' he noted, 'is not that there is an exodus but that any people are left at all.' Oldenburg [1984] 2001: 35.

Illus. 3: 'The Mine in the Chutter Manzil, Exploded by the Enemy in the First Attack of General Havelock', Albumen Print, from *Lucknow and Delhi*, 1858–9, by Felice Beato

largest residencies in British India. By the early 1860s the ruins had been stabilized and most of the rubble removed, trees planted, a park laid out, and plaques set up. A key scene in *Nadi ke Dvip* is set in the Lucknow Residency.

In the eastern part of the city, the new Civil Lines and the Cantonment—meant chiefly for European use—with their bungalows surrounded by wide stretches of lawn, stood in sharp contrast to the dense weave of nawabi Lucknow. And corresponding with Delhi's Kashmiri Gate area, Lucknow's English middle-class shopping centre came up in Hazratganj, where scores of abandoned or destroyed shops were repaired and neatened, providing a sharp contrast to the city's bazaars. Another key scene in *Nadi ke Dvip* takes place in the Hazratganj Coffee House. Though Lakhnawis would begin to imitate

English middle-class lifestyles, allowing the Indo-Persian way of being to retreat ever more into the background, the process was slow. A modernizing English-educated middle class, consisting chiefly of lawyers and professionals and constituting an influential group, began to be a presence of sorts only by the early twentieth century. English education took hold late in the city. Canning College, which later formed the core of Lucknow University, was founded in 1864 by loyal *taluqdars* (large landowners) as a memorial to the late Earl Canning and supported by a perpetual endowment that they set up. Colvin Taluqdars College and Christian College were also founded in the early 1860s. It is worth noting that the famous colleges in most such cities were founded by private Indian initiative, though a few were founded by missionaries. Meanwhile, in 1877 Awadh was amalgamated with the North Western Provinces to form a single administrative unit. The capital was moved to Allahabad, reducing Lucknow to provincial status. It was Allahabad, then, that would gain in importance. *Gunahom ka Devata* is, as noted, set in Allahabad.

Agra, the Mughal city which served as capital of the North West Provinces from 1835 on, would suffer a similar eclipse with time. The retributive destruction of this old town was not as severe as of Delhi and Lucknow, but indiscriminate all the same. Lahore, similarly, suffered minor destruction as compared to Delhi and Lucknow, evolving into North India's premier metropolis. Here too, higher education in English began from the 1860s. The city's famous Government College, founded in the Old City in a haveli in 1864, was moved to the Civil Station in 1877. Other institutions set up were the Oriental College in 1863, the Punjab University in 1869, and the Dayanand Anglo-Vedic College—set up to counter the increasing Anglicization of the other colleges—in 1886. As elsewhere in North India, the English-educated class begins to make its presence felt only towards the end of the nineteenth and the beginning of the twentieth century. The first part of *Jhutha Sach* is set in this pre-Partition Lahore. It begins in the late 1930s, by which time Hindus, Sikhs, and Muslims were no longer living side by side, though they did coexist in the city. After Partition, as in the rest of West Punjab, the Hindu–Sikh culture of Lahore would be erased. The second part of *Jhutha Sach* then moves on to Delhi.

Apart from fluke occurrences, including the appearance of *Pariksha Guru* in Delhi, the Hindi novel as such emerged in Banaras in the late nineteenth century and found congenial quarters in Allahabad from the second quarter of the twentieth century. Banaras, we need to recall, was technically 'a native state', and a self-consciously Hindu one at that. Its figurehead dynasty remained ensconced in Ramnagar, on the opposite bank of the Ganga, all the way to 1947. The uprising of 1857 did not figure so greatly in city life, which was largely left intact after it. Modern Hindi found its literary base here before shifting gradually to Allahabad, with Lucknow—the other great Urdu centre—following as a Hindi literary site from the 1920s. Lahore, next, acquired a profile in Hindi letters from the late 1930s and early 1940s. Delhi, finally, began to figure as a significant site for Hindi literature and the novel only after Partition and Independence (and then very densely in certain parts of the city).

THE NORTH INDIAN MIDDLE CLASSES

The three Presidency towns of Calcutta, Madras, and Bombay held positions of pre-eminence. None of the subsequent inland capitals of British India became metropolitan in the way of these large port cities. The emergence and growth of the middle classes in the Hindi belt came to be associated with the emergence of the modern hinterland capitals of North India. In them, as also in some of the other larger towns of British India, there came into being large enclaves of Bengali bureaucrats and literati who set the patterns of life that others emulated. Though the plains of North India remained overwhelmingly rural and its urban society fragmented, it was in these towns that colonial authority ultimately confronted dissent, the sort that could not be beaten back by military action alone. We learn that, by the '1920s something like a north Indian middle class can be see emerging from a cluster of *rentier* service families and commercial notables.'[48] B.B. Misra, in his classic study of the middle classes, points out that as a result of the dependent economy of the country, social stratification first proceeded from legal, educational, and administrative changes, not as in Europe from economic diversification.[49] In the period before 1905 the Indian middle class took shape in two phases. In the first, under the rule of the East India Company, that is, till 1857, the middle class comprised private merchants and the Indian agents and employees of the Company who went on to build large fortunes and buy estates. They largely supplanted the old aristocracy and landed classes. A select few also educated themselves in the new way and played a leading role in commerce and education: we have only to think of Ram Mohan Roy and the Tagore family in Calcutta, and of the family of Bharatendu Harischandra in Banaras. The traditional gulf between learning and trade narrowed.[50] The second phase began with the gradual spread of English education among less well-to-do families, especially after 1870. The term 'educated middle class' came to signify those who acquired a Western higher education through the medium of English and joined one of the various professions, such as law, thrown up by the needs of the imperial government. It was from this period on that many of the best-known colleges of the North Indian cities were founded. Though the old literary castes were the first to benefit from this process, those who did so came to differ in their mental make-up, ethos, and lifestyle from those versed primarily in Sanskrit, Arabic, and Persian.[51] Thus, from the peculiar circumstances of their growth, the professional classes comprised those belonging to the higher castes.[52] And it is from these higher castes—Brahmin, Khattri, Kayasth, and Vaishya—that our novels largely draw their characters. The professions followed are often

[48] Bayly 1975: 17.
[49] Misra 1961: 343–4.
[50] Ibid.: 106.
[51] Ibid.: 147.
[52] Ibid.: 305.

legal, administrative, and sometimes professorial. Thus, for instance, Madan Mohan in *Pariksha Guru* is a Vaishya, though his particular subcaste is not specified; Suman in *Sevasadan* is a Brahmin girl; Amar in *Karmabhumi* is also a Vaishya; the Puris in *Jhutha Sach* are Khatris, and Puri's wife Kanak is a Brahmin.

The legal profession was the most significant of the new professions, emerging as it did from the constitution of British-style courts and legislative enactments after the introduction of the Cornwallis Code in 1793. Given that under the principle of contract recourse to a judicial decision became the only means to validate private property claims, the Code eventually gave a great boost to the legal profession.[53] Judicial practice also grew into a major industry in the various district headquarters. In Allahabad, for instance, there were by 1880 several courts above the *tehsil* level; honorary magistrates were recruited from local bankers and landlords, but of the fifty advocates at the High Court only three were Indian. The second grade of legal practitioner-pleader, or Vakil, consisted entirely of Indians; these were mostly Brahmins or Kayasths. As experts in land law, these vakils soon came to dominate the lucrative first appeal work of the High Court.[54] They also become the foremost element in the local national leadership.

In *Pariksha Guru* Madan Mohan's enlightened friend Brajkishor is a Vakil, as is the reformer Padam Singh in *Sevasadan*. Naiyar in *Jhutha Sach* is also a lawyer, who in the second part of the novel helps the two main couples to resolve the legal mess they are in.

The composition of the middle class would remain a matter of some perplexity for many in the North West Provinces. As an unsigned article in a Banaras journal, written as early as 1873 and entitled 'The

---

[53] Ibid.: 163, 168.

[54] For the greater part of the nineteenth century, and in practice also in the twentieth, 'natives' were not allowed to enter the covenanted services reserved for Europeans. Indians were to be educated for the express purpose of filling the lower ranks in the so-called uncovenanted services, in the ever-growing bureaucracies of the empire, in the engineering sections of the Public Works Departments, and in army and civil hospitals.

Present State of the Middle Class Men of the North West Provinces', put it, the 'term middle class is indeed comprehensive and one would be puzzled in the extreme to define it properly.' It comprised all four castes (*varnas*) which no longer followed their respective hereditary professions. These were matters of some concern. There was little doubt that by virtue of occupying the middle ground the middle class 'withstood with bold defiance the despotic injunctions of the high aristocratic class', while at the same time protecting 'serfs and the agriculturists from odious taxes and extortions of the opulent landholders and Zamindars.' Hence they could be said to represent the whole nation. 'In short, they interfere in every point that concerns the interest of the public.'[55]

This 'interference' was already being regarded as a matter of grave concern by the British administration. As they came to view it, the earlier policy of creating a middle class of educated Indians had been premature, for the class that had formed, as they saw it, was one whose 'knowledge is superficial, whose conceit is boundless, who are fluent and turgid in language, but who have no accurate conception of the words they use or the phrases they repeat.'[56] There was a slackening of growth and fall-off in educational aid to higher education in the first part of the twentieth century; primary education had never been seen as a priority by the colonial state, so teachers retained low salaries and low social status throughout our period. In the Hindi–Urdu belt, the Agra College (founded 1823) and the Bareilly College (founded 1837, raised to the status of a Government College in 1850), the foremost educational institutions of their areas, were largely left to fend for themselves. This may have slowed the process of politicization, but it did not successfully hold it back. Private institutions came up in the larger cities from Allahabad to Lahore, founded by wealthy landlords and merchants. It was here

[55] Written in English, in the predominantly Hindi journal *Harishchandra's Magazine*, 1/1, 15 October 1873.

[56] Lieutenant Governor Sir Auckland Colvin's speech to the Allahabad University Convocation, 12 January 1893, cited in Bayly 1975: 95.

that those aspiring to higher positions in government service but also greater political representation honed their leadership skills.[57] In Allahabad, for instance, the Kayasth Pathshala, where future Congress leaders were educated, was set up in 1873, followed by the Muir Central College in 1877, which came to be the kernel of Allahabad University a decade later, the intention in setting it up being to cut off the youth of the province from Calcutta University and the radicalism of Bengal.[58] The English-educated middle class, however, was becoming increasingly vocal in its discontent, many of those comprising it having been educated in these or similar colleges.

Given the different urban history of the major North Indian cultural locations from that of the Presidency towns, as also naturally of rural India, the fictional worlds and representations of the urban Hindi novel are identifiably distinctive. Its characters are drawn from this North Indian middle-class milieu which was self-consciously forming itself into a Hindu community seeking articulation in Hindi. Merchants figure prominently, as do the new class of lawyers, and those in government service. From our third novel, *Karmabhumi* (1932) onwards—that is, from the early 1930s—professors and college students begin making an appearance in the narratives. Most are, initially at least, male, but later also female, as for instance Tara and

---

[57] Cf. Bayly 1975: 94.

[58] The viceroy, Lord Curzon, considerably furthered the process of throttling higher education. He reduced the number of colleges and government's expenditure on higher education. He was forthright about the reasons in a speech given at an education conference held at Simla on 6 September 1901: 'There exists a powerful school of opinion which does not hide its conviction that the experiment [of English education] was a mistake, and that its result has been a disaster. When Erasmus was reproached with having laid the egg from which came forth the Reformation, "Yes", he replied; "but I laid a hen's egg, and Luther has hatched a fighting cock." This, I believe, is pretty much the view of a good many of the critics of English education in India. They think it has given birth to a tone of mind and to a type of character that is ill-regulated, averse from discipline, discontented, and in some cases actually disloyal.' Cited in Mishra 1961: 284–5.

her friends in the first part of *Jhutha Sach*, and Sudha in *Gunahom ka Devata*. Campus life appears as a key narrative space in these novels. Tara and Puri in *Jhutha Sach* are politicized primarily on campus; Tara forms her romantic attachment to Asad there. This book focuses therefore on selves that emerge from such educational and related institutions, on men and women who are educated or who educate themselves, on their romantic partnerships and marriage unions.

Though in the early novels the women characters are often courtesans—attractive, cultivated women who set the tone of city life for the elite, as in *Sevasadan*—so strong is the aura they radiate that we find them still hovering on the horizon in post-Independence fiction. Thus, for instance in *Andhere Band Kamare* (1961), the narrator Madhusudan thinks of Nilima's aspirations to be a dancer in connection with his memories of Amritsar's red light area and his father's book on courtesans. From the late 1920s, women figure in several professions, from being social and political activists in the Gandhian mould as in *Karmabhumi*, to governesses in elite families such as Rekha in *Nadi ke Dvip*. After Partition there is a major shift in women's roles as well as in family structures; women now also figure as high-standing government employees—for instance, Tara in *Jhutha Sach*.

MODERNITY, MODERNISM, NATION, AND THE SELF

As Benedict Anderson has shown, the two key forms of imagining the collectivity that ultimately became the nation in eighteenth-century Europe were the novel and the newspaper.[59] In the North Indian case the novels were written from the late nineteenth century on; the nation figured as a major point of reference from then, as we see in *Pariksha Guru*, *Sevasadan*, and *Karmabhumi*, and this lasted at least until Independence. In fact, as our close reading of these novels will show, the political life of North India at any given time—whether centred on nationalism, social reform, communalism, Partition, or the

---

[59] Anderson [1983] 1991.

Cold War—penetrates deep into private life. Contextual politics plays a large role in the formation of individual character, the goals set in life, sometimes even the initial choice of spouses and the eventual fate of marriages, the vision of life that informs character, these collectively then producing 'the kind of narratives in which we make sense of our lives . . .'[60] As Etienne Balibar puts it, '(e)very social community reproduced by the functioning of institutions is imaginary, that is to say, it is based on the projection of individual existence into the weft of a collective narrative, on the recognition of a common name and on traditions lived as the trace of an immemorial past (even when they have been fabricated and inculcated in the recent past) . . .'[61] This weft of a collective narrative influences individual behaviour, decisions, and directions. Chander in *Gunahom ka Devata* is an economist driven by an idealist mission who eventually figures in the nation's life as an economic planner. The flip side of this idealism is Samar in *Sara Akash*, another student whose dreams are nationalistic but whose reality is one of unemployment and misrecognition. In this context, what Lydia Liu has shown for the early Chinese novel is also relevant for the Indian. Though China was not colonized, nationalism played a major role in it. However, 'the violence of China's encounter with the West forces modern nationhood upon selfhood, and vice versa, under unique circumstances. Yet the modern self is never quite reducible to national identity. On the contrary it is the incongruities, tensions, and struggle between the two as well as their mutual implication and complicity that give full meaning to the lived experience of Chinese modernity.'[62] We will see these tensions in our novels. In the second, post-Independence volume of *Jhutha Sach*, once Tara starts working as a government officer there is much political discussion with socialist friends in the evenings. Tara goes along with the discussion but maintains a distance; she is a witness rather than a participant in the accompanying fervour, and with no

[60] Taylor 1989: 105.
[61] Balibar 1991: 93.
[62] Liu 1995: 82.

particular investment in the national. Bhuvan, the scientist in *Nadi ke Dvip*, has more universal concerns, and in *Andhere Band Kamare*, at the height of the Cold War, we obtain a very cynical picture of the nation.

Modernity and the idea of the nation go hand in hand. No straightforward formula applies to this modernity, neither the Western nor that of the Presidencies, particularly Bengal.[63] In order to chart the course of North Indian modernity in the post-1857 decades we need to take into consideration their specific cultural and historical contexts. As Dilip Gaonkar has noted, 'modernity always unfolds within a specific cultural or civilizational context and . . . different starting points for the transition to modernity lead to different outcomes. Under the impact of modernity, all societies will undergo changes in both outlook and institutional arrangements. Some of these may be similar, but that does not amount to convergence.'[64] What matters is how, given this particular past, this particular location, and these political moments, the individual is affected and the turns that the narrative takes as a consequence. As Sudipta Kaviraj puts it:

> What we call modernity in shorthand is a set of new practices in major spheres of social life: new practices of production, governance, scientific cognition, education, artistic and cultural creativity. These new practices can be new in two different senses. Some practices are so utterly new that these did not have any precursors or precedents in earlier history. In some cases, it might be possible to say that a practice central to modernity is simply without precedent; but in many, modern practices are really transformed ways of doing the same general thing.[65]

As we shall see in *Pariksha Guru*, new notions of merchant life, of acting in the national interest as much as for individual gain, lead ultimately to a self-critical assessment of behaviour and radical change. 'Reflexivity however cannot stop there, simply using

---

[63] This has been discussed at length in the spate of publications that followed the two *Daedalus* volumes, on early modernities and multiple modernities, in 1998 and 2000, respectively.

[64] Gaonkar 2001: 17.

[65] Kaviraj 2005: 20–1.

Western modernity as an exterior point of view that comprehensively undermines traditional cultures. The capacity for critical reflection extends to assessments of institutions and practices of Western modernity as well . . .'[66] If there is uncritical acceptance of colonial institutions in *Pariksha Guru*, in *Karmabhumi* the entry of the British law court, and in *Sevasadan* the central role played by the city municipality are viewed ironically.

The first four novels that I look at are, then, narratives of a nation coming into being and of a modernity that resists and attempts to reform what it regards as tradition, often with the certitude that change will be for the better. In the decade and a half immediately before Independence, that is, from the late 1930s on, as Fascism makes its appearance in Europe and new forms of repression become evident in India, the tone of the novels changes. New uncertainties emerge that allow of no simple moral resolutions. Two certitudes dissolve: the nation as harbinger of all that is good, and the marital union as a state of bliss. The social reform so closely intertwined with nationalism also loses its promise and is no longer seen as the resolution to intensely personal and interpersonal issues. Women begin to articulate their subjectivities and seek self-realization and happiness in a partnership; marriage is no longer a one-way street for men to find their desired partner and sexual and emotional fulfilment; the small step towards gender equality is a giant step towards irresolution and doubt.

As we shall see, the individual can remain deeply affected by nationalism, yet not fit entirely into the mould provided by it. Subsequently, with the impending arrival of the nation after World War II, nationalism tends to ebb, if not entirely disappear, from the novel's landscape. When it figures at all, it is as a problem, not something that shapes life but which may prevent the individual from developing fully. We see this in particular with Samar in *Sara Akash*, over his realization that nationalism can no longer fulfil the function it has in his life. Larger political issues appear on the horizon: socialism, the

---

[66] Ibid.: 27.

promise of science and progress after the disaster of the War and the atom bomb, Cold War polarizations, and the trauma of Partition. Its subsequent grand Five Year Plans notwithstanding, the nation enters on the scene in 1947 as the great promise unfulfilled.

It is necessary to distinguish between modernity and modernism. I see the second set of four novels as representing North Indian modernism, or a modernity no longer certain of either its potential as a guiding force for change or of the social and personal advantages it brings. Raymond Williams has this to say about modernism:

> The experience of visual and linguistic strangeness, the broken narrative of the journey and its inevitable accompaniment of transient encounters with characters whose self-representation was bafflingly unfamiliar, raised to the level of universal myth, this intense, singular narrative of unsettlement, homelessness, solitude and impoverished independence: the lonely writer gazing down on the unknowable city from his shabby apartment.[67]

I see the unsettlement, homelessness, solitude, and impoverished independence represented in, for instance, Rekha of *Nadi ke Dvip*. The novel consists in large stretches of interior monologue, its prose seeming no longer to serve as an adequate expressive medium, so that there are within it almost explosive bursts into lyric and song. In this variety of modernism we find the 'ego engaged in monologue and dialogue becoming the vehicle of the new narrative', with the novels throwing light on the 'hidden recesses within man and the individual', on the psychological undercurrents of events that are 'freighted with all the minute tremors of inner life', deploying the splitting of points of view that have their own dynamics, so that the author is often out of control.[68]

LOVE, MARRIAGE, AND THE FAMILY

The rapid pace of change over the century or so under consideration touched several aspects of material and affective life. The radical

---

[67] Williams 1989: 34.
[68] Kahler [1970] 1973: 143, 146, 151, 152, 153.

reconfigurations of urban space, as much as the family house, made for new kinds of movement in the city. New professions restructured the daily routine of individual family members. And affective relationships, so inextricably tied to economic, social, and political factors, also suffered change, 'for the family is not a mere unit of social structure but a cultural ideal and a focus of identity.'[69]

The very notion of what constitutes the extended family, the many mnemonic erasures regarding polygamy and slavery, the ongoing splitting into nuclear units for pragmatic reasons, the regional and class/caste differences brought about by region, class, and caste, all 'reveal that there has been no "family" in South Asian history that was not simultaneously a political, economic, social and juridical entity.'[70]

As the family changes, so do notions of love and romance. Basic semantic terms associated with affective relationships undergo radical change as words already in use take on different meanings, for 'we love and suffer according to cultural imperatives.'[71] Or, in an alternative formulation, 'Love may indeed be a universal feeling, but culture and language play a crucial role in defining it at every stage, from sexual arousal to codified sentiment, from norms of comportment to "significant stories".'[72] My effort is to trace the terms that Hindi novels use and how these change with time. It has been suggested that '(l)ife in older, locally denser social systems was characterized by complex networks of relationships which blocked both any self exclusion by individuals, but also a "private life" or any retreat into pair relationships. One was expected to share one's life within a framework easily understood by all that society's members.'[73] In this situation, 'while the stratified order and family remained intact, a semantics for love developed to accommodate extra-marital relationships, and was then transformed back into marriage itself . . .'[74]

[69] Uberoi 1993: 36.
[70] Chatterjee, ed. 2004: 35.
[71] Luhmann [1982] 1998: 4.
[72] Orsini 2006: 1.
[73] Luhmann [1982] 1998: 32.
[74] Ibid.: 5–6.

In North India '(t)he natural forum of cultural intercourse between men and women was the salon of the courtesan . . . The typical pair of lovers in a north Indian town was the nobleman and his concubine.'[75] But though '(t)he old difference of domestic reproduction and outside love affairs was not dispensed with',[76] it was transformed into the idea of passionate love for only one woman, mostly in the form of a monogamous union. We can follow the gradual decline of the cultural and emotional investment in courtesan culture, from the perspective of both courtesan and wife, in *Pariksha Guru* and *Sevasadan*. Nonetheless, there is no clear-cut linear development from extra-marital notions of love to marital love, for the narratives we deal with often circle back to the figure of the courtesan. There is, however, clear evidence of shifts in expectation. With time, monogamy, the companionate marriage, and the nuclear family become concepts to live by—we see this as we move from *Sevasadan* to *Karmabhumi*—and the companionate marriage bears the burden of fulfilling mutual expectations in potentially hostile family environments. The change, such as it is, is much more of increasing complexity in notions of self and of partnership than any sense of fulfilment because of romance-inspired marital unions, for those tended to bring their own complications. The changes in family life are reflected in the structure of the family house; the courtyard-centred home of extended family life gives way to the bungalow (in *Gunahom ka Devata*) and later to the apartment (in *Amdhere Band Kamare*) which houses the nuclear family.

To explore the changing notions of self and relationship in my chosen novels, I have often resorted to the expression 'structure of feeling' that has been in currency for more than half a century. Raymond Williams, who coined the phrase in *The Long Revolution* (1961), showed that structures of feeling are in part transmitted from one generation to the next and in part a response to the unique situation in which each new generation finds itself. Thus there are

---

[75] Rajat Kanta Ray 2001: 40.
[76] Luhmann [1982] 1998: 44.

continuities, but also new and creative responses. Williams was to explicate the term further in a series of interviews given to the *New Left Review* (1979), where he pointed out that, since the concept was developed in order to analyse literary works, it necessarily privileged the emotional world of certain sections of society. The concept needed to be used much more differentially between classes, the diversity itself being historically variable. And, of course, past structures of feeling were much easier to locate than the fluctuating present of which one was a part.

We see the difference in generational expectations in *Karmabhumi*, as also in *Jhutha Sach*, which is laid out on an epic scale: college life has introduced modern notions of love and marriage to Tara and Jaydev Puri, who are completely at odds with their lower-middle-class parents living in a narrow lane in the old city of Lahore. Yet more radical are the views of Rekha in *Nadi ke Dvip*. Her modernism is hard to accept, even for her scientist-lover Bhuvan.

We need to note that there were also historical experiences that did not find literary articulation. And then there is the vexed question of the accuracy of literary works as representations of social reality, an issue which in the case of love and marriage implies that novelistic depictions cannot lay claim to any straightforward reflection of social reality:

> Yet the pressure of the general argument was continually leading me to say, and I think correctly, that such works were the articulate record of something which was a much more general possession. This was the area of interaction between the official consciousness of an epoch—codified in its doctrines and legislation—and the whole process of actually living its consequences . . . a pattern of impulses, restraints, tones, for which the best evidence was often the actual conventions of literary or dramatic writing.[77]

The interplay of literary representation, social reality, and legislation is complex: sometimes novels anticipate change; at other times

---

[77] Williams 1979: 159.

they can even be cumulatively instrumental in bringing it about. Equally, they can reflect the subtle changes in behaviour that, for instance, legislation brings about. The legal codification of a trend that had already set in—monogamy for, instance, and its formulation into legislation—often followed the social change which was already taking place and which was registered early in fiction. Thus, the Hindu Marriage Law Act of 1955 was a major step towards monogamy for the Hindu male, which as a phenomenon exists in our novels from the 1930s on; the act also gave some rights to women. Not surprisingly, perhaps, it figures in three of our later novels, in *Sara Akash* as anticipation, and in *Jhutha Sach* and *Amdhere Band Kamare* as finally enacted. Over the time this legislation comes into being, the interaction between people changes, as does the tone in which they address each other. Bourdieu points out that

> The literary or artistic field is a field of forces, but it is also a field of struggles tending to transform or conserve this field of forces . . . It follows from this, for example, that a position-taking changes in the universe of options that are simultaneously offered for producers and consumers to choose from. The meaning of a work (artistic, literary, philosophical, etc.) changes automatically with each change in the field within which it is situated for the spectator or the reader.[78]

And as such, the form of the novel itself changes with time, tending to focus more on emotional transactions and the inner life. If the early novels work with an omniscient narrator, though they also use focalization,[79] the later works see the narrator recede as the narrative itself turns ever more inward.

HINDI PUBLISHING IN NORTH INDIA

Before turning to the novels themselves, let me briefly summarize the growth of Hindi publishing in the cities of North India, publishing

---

[78] Bourdieu 1993: 30.
[79] This is a term I shall use in many of my chapters. It is taken from Gérard Genette's *Narrative Discourse* and can be roughly defined as focus of narrative, or perspective represented. Genette [1972] 1980: 189.

activities being closely linked to the growth of literary sensibilities in urban spaces.

The earliest known printed books in Hindi were published at the very beginning of the nineteenth century at the instance of the Fort William College in Calcutta; they were meant for the use of students of the College and not intended for general circulation. Missionary and School Book Society publications followed, but it was the coming of lithographic printing which first provided the impetus for larger-scale book production by Indian presses. Whereas publishing in Lucknow was mainly confined to Persian and most of all Urdu, it was Banaras that gained importance in non-educational Sanskrit and Hindi publishing, producing, apart from the perennial runner that was Tulsidas' *Ramcharitmanas*, popular forms of chapbook literature, including religious tracts, tales, folk dramas, and almanacs.[80] These ventures prepared the ground for the activity that followed in the second half of the nineteenth century. As Stark has shown in her study of the publishing empire of Naval Kishore Press in Lucknow—founded by Munshi Naval Kishore (1836–95) in 1858, just as the city was beginning to recover from the devastations of the 1857 uprising—Hindi publishing in North India took off only after the 1860s.[81]

From the late 1860s the Naval Kishore Press, at the time the largest publishing house in the subcontinent, became also the most important source of cheap, mass-produced Hindi books.[82] The stature of the language gained substantially from official recognition. Hindi was awarded official language status in the Central Provinces in 1872, and the Nagari and Kaithi scripts were used by government order in large parts of Bihar. Though Hindi and the Nagari script would only be awarded official status in the North West Provinces and Oudh in 1900, in this case, official recognition came later than the cultural activity that preceded it.

[80] Stark 2007: 64.
[81] Ibid.: 33.
[82] The information that follows has been gleaned from chapter 7: 'Hindi Publishing in a Stronghold of Urdu', in Stark 2007: 385–444.

Initially, it was at the behest of the colonial authorities that Naval Kishore took up Hindi publishing, printing official matter and textbooks from the early 1860s. But the changing cultural climate of the Hindi belt also made for a much wider interest in literary Hindi. From the mid 1860s the Naval Kishore Press began to engage in Hindi publishing of its own account, bringing out in their large print runs the most popular devotional texts, such as those of Tulsidas and Surdas, various versions of the *Bhagavata Purana* narrativizing the life of Krishna, hagiographies of the Vallabha and Ramrasik sects, as also a cross-section of the verse of the heterodox *sant* tradition. The press also launched a series of editions with commentaries of these devotional texts, reaching out to both a scholarly and lay public. From the mid 1870s the Brajbhasha court poetry of the sixteenth to the eighteenth centuries, foremost that of Matiram, Bhushan, and Keshavdas, began to be produced on a large scale. Various popular plays appeared, in addition to important literary anthologies, but also, interestingly, the press turned to a new female readership with an array of instructional works. Non-literary territory was also covered: the press published medical works, compendia in Brajbhasha with Sanskrit commentary and Hindi translation, in addition to astrological manuals and almanacs. By and large, however, in this period the press focused more on known literary works rather than on providing an avenue for contemporary writing.

By the late nineteenth century, numerous other private presses had begun to mushroom in the North West Provinces. The number of printed books in Urdu and Hindi multiplied dramatically over 1868–95, that of Urdu nearly fourfold, and of Hindi nearly threefold.[83]

The other major publishing activity associated with Hindi was of the Khadgavilas Press, founded in 1880 in Bankipur near Patna. This played a valuable role in printing works which were beginning to form the Hindi literary canon, including that of Bharatendu Harischandra. The historian of this press, Dhirendranath Singh, has also provided

---

[83] Stark 2007: 70.

data on the important presses of Banaras, a city which by the second half of the nineteenth century shows a dense net of small and large Hindi publishers. The Medical Hall Press of the city was established as early as 1858 and the Banaras Light Press in 1860. The latter published not only a series of older poets but also contemporary Banaras poets. The Varanasi Sanskrit Yantralaya (founded 1860) brought out Hindi works while the Lazarus Press concentrated on Hindi. The second half of the century also saw the establishment in Banaras of the important Bharat Jiwan Press, founded by Ramkrishna Varma (1859–70). This brought out a series consisting of the verse of the *sant* poets as well as poetry in popular genres. Translations into Hindi of Shakespeare, of Bengali novels, and Sanskrit story literature were among its titles, even as it offered an outlet to contemporary poets such as Pratap Narayan Mishra, Jagmohan Singh, and Raghunath Kavi. The plays of Bharatendu Harischandra appeared from this press as well.[84]

Hindi publishing acquired significane in Banaras, Allahabad, Lucknow, Aligarh, and Agra, with Banaras showing a higher increase in publishing volume than the others and becoming by the early twentieth century the largest publishing location for Hindi books.[85] The year 1893 saw the founding of the most important institution for Hindi in the region, the Nagari Pracharini Sabha (Association for the Propagation of the Nagari Script), begun in the city by three enterprising students, Shyam Sundar Das, Ram Narayan Mishra, and Shiv Kumar Singh. The Sabha famously launched a search for Hindi manuscripts which led to the publication of the first standard editions of the classics of Hindi. Out of its work grew the Hindi Sahitya Sammelan (Association of Hindi Literature), established in Allahabad in 1910 and signalling a change in the strategy for propagating Hindi.[86] Whereas the Sabha had functioned within the framework of the colonial state, the Sammelan linked its work to that of the Indian National Congress, which was looking for political

---

[84] Dhirendranath Singh 1986: 69–81; Orsini 2009: 229–34.
[85] King 1994: 142.
[86] Orsini 2002: 137.

support for Hindi as the projected national language of the country. The Sammelan's publications, and a series of Hindi exams it instituted, did much to propagate this claim.

By the 1920s Hindi publishing can be said to have come into its own. A significant area of mass expansion in Hindi print was that of religious publishing. The Belvedere Press in Allahabad, in existence even today, was founded by Baleshwar Prasad as early as 1903. It focused not only on Kabir—whose work was also much published by other presses—but also, in its attractively printed series titled Santbani Pustakmala, on the less-known *sants* of a variety of other lineages.[87] More spectacular were the publications of the Gita Press in Gorakhpur.[88] Established by the enterprising Marwaris Jaydayal Goendka (1885–1965) and Hanuman Prasad Poddar (1892–1971) in 1923, the Gita Press published a large array of devotional works in Sanskrit and Hindi. The monthly journal *Kalyan*—still on its feet and running, with 200,000 subscribers—appeared first in August 1926; the English *Kalyan-Kalpataru*, started in 1934, still has 100,000 subscribers. Tulsidas' *Ramcharitmanas*, the *Bhagavadgita*, and the *Mahabharata*—the last two in Sanskrit with Hindi translation and made available in a wide range of formats—have sold in their millions.

In spite of its mass base, Hindi publishing only reached Delhi in a significant way after Partition. Given that it was widely expected to acquire national language status after Independence, Hindi publishing soon centred itself in Delhi's Daryaganj area, at the intersection of the old city and New Delhi. Of the many Hindi publishers based here, I mention only two as representative of many others: Rajkamal Prakashan, one of the best-known literary publishers in the subcontinent, was established in 1947 by Om Prakash, who came originally from Amritsar.[89] And Vani Prakashan, which was established

---

[87] See Orsini 2015, which contains invaluable information on Hindi publishing in Allahabad.

[88] As documented in Mukul 2015.

[89] Sadana 2012: 78.

by Premchand Mahesh in 1955. Both produce literary classics as well as new writing in Hindi, in a range of genres. Delhi also sees a wide variety of official publications in Hindi, amongst other Indian languages; both the Sahitya Akademi (the national academy of letters, established in 1954) and the National Book Trust, founded in 1957, are located in the capital.

REFERENCES

Agyeya, Sachidanand Hiranand Vatsyayan. [1941] 1966. *Shekhar: Ek Jivani: Pahla Bhag, Utthan*. Allahabad, Varanasi, Lucknow, Delhi: Saraswati Press.

Ai, Maeda. 2014. *Text and the City: Essays on Japanese Modernity*. Edited and with an Introduction by James A. Fujii. Durham and London: Duke University Press.

Anderson, Benedict. [1983] 1991. *Imagined Communities: Reflections on the Origin and Spread of Nationalism*. London: Verso.

Armstrong, Nancy. 1987. *Desire and Domestic Fiction: A Political History of the Novel*. New York: Oxford University Press.

Bakhtin, M.M. 1981. *The Dialogic Imagination: Four Essays*. Ed. Michael Holquist, transl. Caryl Emerson and Michael Holquist. Austin: University of Texas Press.

Balibar, Etienne and Immanuel Wallerstein. 1991. *Race, Nation, Class: Ambiguous Identities*. Transl. of Etienne Balibar by Chris Turner. London, New York: Verso.

Bayly, C.A. 1975. *The Local Roots of Indian Politics: Allahabad, 1880–1920*. Oxford: Clarendon Press.

Berman, Marshall. [1982] 1988. *All That is Solid Melts into Air: The Experience of Modernity*. New York: Penguin Books.

Bholanauth Chunder. 1869. From *The Travels of a Hindoo to Various Parts of Bengal and Upper India*, in Mehrotra 2007, *vide infra*.

Bourdieu, Pierre. 1993. *The Field of Cultural Production: Essays on Art and Literature*. Edited and Introduced by Randal Johnson. New York: Columbia University Press.

Chatterjee, Indrani. Ed. 2004. *Unfamiliar Relations: Family and History in South Asia*. Delhi and Ranikhet: Permanent Black.

Conte, Gian Biagio. 1986. *Genres and Readers: Lucretius, Love Elegy, Pliny's Encyclopedia*. Transl. by Glenn W. Most. Baltimore and London: The Johns Hopkins University Press.

Daedalus. 1998. *Early Modernities*. Special Issue. Summer, 127/3.

———. 2000. *Multiple Modernities*. Special Issue. Winter, 129/1.

Farooqui, Mahmood. 2010. *Besieged: Voices from Delhi 1857*. Compiled and transl. by Mahmood Farooqui. With notes on the Mutiny Papers and Governance by the translator. Delhi: Penguin Viking.

Flood, Finbarr B. 2009. *Objects of Translation: Material Culture and Medieval 'Hindu–Muslim' Encounter*. Princeton: Princeton University Press, and Ranikhet: Permanent Black.

Gaonkar, Dilip Parameshwar. Ed. 2001. *Alternative Modernities*. Durham and London: Duke University Press.

Genette, Gérard. (1972) 1980. *Narrative Discourse: An Essay in Method*. Transl. by Jane K. Lewin. Ithaca, NY: Cornell University Press.

Glover, William J. 2008. *Making Lahore Modern: Constructing and Imagining a Colonial City*. Minneapolis and London: University of Minnesota Press.

Govind, Nikhil. 2014. *Between Freedom and Love: The Revolutionary in the Hindi Novel*. London, New York, New Delhi: Routledge.

Guha, Sumit. 1998. 'Household Size and Household Structure in Western India *c.*1700–1950: Beginning an Exploration', *Indian Economic and Social History Review*, 35: 23–33.

Gupta, Narayani. [1981] 2002. *Delhi Between Two Empires 1803–1931: Society, Government and Urban Growth*. Delhi: Oxford University Press.

Hosargrahar, Jyoti. 2005. *Indigenous Modernities: Negotiating Achitectue and Urbanism*. London, New York: Routledge.

Kaviraj, Sudipta. 2005. 'An Outline of a Revisionist Theory of Modernity', *European Journal of Sociology*, XLVI, 497–526.

Kahler, Erich. 1973. *The Inward Turn of Narrative*. Translated from the German by Richard and Clara Winston. Princeton: Princeton University Press.

King, Christopher R. 1994. *One Language, Two Scripts: The Hindi Movement in Nineteenth Century North India*. Bombay: Oxford University Press.

Liu, Lydia H. 1995. *Translingual Practice: Literature, National Culture, and Translated Modernity—China, 1900–1937*. Stanford: Stanford University Press.

Llewellyn-Jones, Rosie. 2004. 'The Residency and the River', in *Lucknow, City of Illusion*, ed. Rosie Llewellyn-Jones. The Alkazi Collection of Photography. Munich: Prestel, 193–9.

Luhmann, Niklas. [1982] 1998. *Love as Passion: The Codification of Intimacy*. Translated from the German by Jeremy Gaines and Doris L. Jones. Stanford: Stanford University Press.

Mani, Preetha. 2016. 'What was so New about the New Story? Modernist-Realism in the Hindi Nayi Kahani'. Unpublished manuscript.

Mehrotra, Arvind Krishna. 2007. *The Last Bungalow: Writings on Allahabad*. Delhi: Penguin Books India.

Misra, B.B. 1961. *The Indian Middle Classes: Their Growth in Modern Times*. London: Oxford University Press.

Moretti, Franco. 1998. *Atlas of the European Novel 1800–1900*. London, New York: Verso.

Mukul, Akshaya. 2015. *Gita Press and the Making of the Hindu World*. Delhi: HarperCollins.

Nehru, Jawaharlal. 1946. *The Discovery of India*. Calcutta: The Signet Press.

Neville, H.R. 1921. *Agra: A Gazetteer*, Volume 8 of the *District Gazetteers of the United Provinces of Agra and Oudh*. Allahabad: Government Press, United Provinces.

Oldenburg, Veena Talwar. [1984] 2001. *The Making of Colonial Lucknow 1856–1877*. Princeton, N.J.: Princeton University Press.

Orsini, Francesca. 1998. 'Reading a Social Romance: *Cand Hasinom ke Khutut*', in *Narrative Strategies: Essays on South Asian Literature and Film*, ed. Vasudha Dalmia and Theo Damsteegt. Leiden: CNWS Publications. Delhi: Oxford University Press 1999.

———. 2002. *The Hindi Public Sphere, 1920–1940: Language and Literature in the Age of Nationalism*. Delhi: Oxford University Press.

———. Ed. 2006. *Love in South Asia: A Cultural History*. Cambridge: Cambridge University Press.

———. 2009. *Print and Pleasure: Popular Literature and Entertaining Fictions in Colonial North India*. Ranikhet: Permanent Black.

———. 2015. 'Booklets and *Sants*: Religious Publics and Literary History', *South Asia, Journal of South Asian Studies*, 1–15.

Pritchett, Frances W. 1994. *Nets of Awareness: Urdu Poets and its Criticism*. Berkeley: University of California Press.

Ray, Gopal. [2002] 2005. *Hindi Upanyas ka Itihas*. Delhi: Rajkamal Prakashan.

Ray, Rajat Kanta. 2001. *Exploring Emotional History: Gender, Mentality, and Literature in the Indian Awakening*. Delhi: Oxford University Press.

Raychaudhuri, Tapan. 1999. 'Love in a Colonial Climate', in *Perceptions, Emotions, Sensibilities*. Delhi: Oxford University Press.

Sadana, Rashmi. 2012. *English Heart, Hindi Heartland: The Political Life of Literature in India*. Ranikhet: Permanent Black.

Schomer, Karine. [1993] 1998. *Mahadevi Varma and the Chhayavad Age of Modern Hindi Poetry*. Delhi: Oxford University Press.

Singh, Dhirendra Nath. 1986. *Adhunik Hindi ke vikas mem Khadgavilas Press ki bhumika*. Patna: Rashtrabhasha Parishad.

Spear, Percival. [1951] 2002 *Twilight of the Mughals: Studies in Late Mughal Delhi*.

Stark, Ulrike. 2007. *An Empire of Books: The Naval Kishore Press and the Diffusion of the Printed Word in Colonial India*. Ranikhet: Permanent Black.

Taylor, Charles. 1989. *Sources of the Self: The Making of Modern Identity*. Cambridge, Massachusetts: Harvard University Press.

Uberoi, Patricia. 1993. *Family, Kinship and Marriage in India*. Delhi: Oxford University Press.

Williams, Raymond. [1973] 1985. *The Country and the City*. London: The Hogarth Press.

———. 1979. *Politics and Letters, Interviews with New Left Review*. London: New Left Review.

I

TOWARDS MODERNITY

1

Merchant Lives in Mughal Agra and British Delhi

THE NOVEL IN HINDI has a symbiotic relationship with its own modernity.[1] From the late nineteenth century individual Hindi novels imagined, anticipated, and documented vast cultural and social changes in North Indian society era of which the beginning can be dated to the years after the great uprising of 1857—though there is also a strange amnesia: 1857 is nowhere mentioned in our novels. Did the literary production that began from the 1870s in opposition to the newly reinforced colonial presence signify a rupture with past traditions? Must the emergence of the novel be seen as a radical break with the literary modes preceding it? Lately, there has been a greater appreciation of the enduring influence of older literary modes, and it is the continuities that have been emphasized.[2] The novel did indeed mesh, merge, and emerge from interaction with the narrative modes already current in the literary languages of the region—and here both the plurality of languages and the regional

[1] This essay has greatly profited from responses at the Centre for the Study of Social Sciences, Kolkata; Centre of South Asia Studies, UCLA; and Halle University, Germany. For their questions and suggestions I would like in particular to thank Anjali Arondekar, Gautam Bhadra, Stuart Blackburn, Rosinka Chaudhuri, Supriya Chaudhuri, Tapati Guha-Thakurta, Aamir Mufti, and Rajat Kanta Ray. Most of all, I am indebted to Francesca Orsini and Rashmi Sadana for their detailed and careful critiques.

[2] As for instance in my own essay on *Pariksha Guru* in Dalmia 1998.

specificity need to be emphasized—in order to produce various 'successful' hybrids peculiar to their regional contexts. However, the novel also sought to do something new. Here I trace both notions—the continuity, i.e. the embeddedness of the Hindi novel in the multilingual Indo-Persianate literary culture that characterized North India, as also the rupture, brought about by the radical changes in social and cultural sensibilities after 1857.[3] My focus here is Shrinivasdas' *Pariksha Guru* (The Tutelage of Trial, 1882), the first novel of note in Hindi, which emerged from the merchant milieu of Delhi and its environs.[4]

Merchant tales had their forebears in more recent history, as we will see, though late-nineteenth-century Hindi writers themselves tended to classicize and cite the seventh-century Sanskrit prose

---

[3] Literary histories of the novel in Hindi tend to move between two poles: the emergence of the genre in Hindi alone, as in Ray 2002, which, comprehensive and erudite, builds upon his earlier works on the novel, particularly the comprehensive *Hindi Upanyas Kosh* (1968/1969); or as part of a larger, pan-Indian trajectory, such as Mukherjee's bold and brilliantly synoptic *Realism and Reality: The Novel and Society in India* (1985), which, while being aware of regional differences, attempts a holistic view of the novel in India as a genre. For detailed discussions of early novel writing in Hindi, see McGregor 1970 and Dalmia 1997: 291–300.

[4] Though after awarding the work this distinction, literary histories tend to dismiss its achievement in the summary manner of some of Shrinivasdas' contemporaries. Gopal Ray (2002: 53) cites Balkrishna Bhatt's scathing critique of the novel in the December 1882 issue of *Hindi pradip*, the journal he edited. Bhatt found none of the sweetness and elegance here of the prose of Bharatendu, the leading literary figure of the day. There was not even a glimpse, he complained, of the erotic and the comic *rasa*s that provided the primary aesthetic pleasures of the novel, or for that matter of the heroic and the sorrowful. Instead there was dry, discursive prose which had no place in the novel, not even if the Hindi novel as genre were seen as mere imitation of the English. More modern literary history has also reacted with some impatience: Shukla (1947: 473ff.) devotes all of ten lines to it. Of late, however, it has begun to receive the attention it deserves: see Trivedi 1993: 211ff. for some discussion of the work, and Kalsi 1992, which offers an in-depth analysis and evaluation.

narrative *Kadambari* as an important model for the novels they were attempting to write.⁵ In order to trace the links to the eras preceding the modern and explore both continuities and discontinuities in perspective and literary format I shall, instead of going back to the classical past, juxtapose *Pariksha Guru* with Banarasidas' *Ardhakathanak* (Half a Tale, 1641), an early-modern merchant life story set in Jaunpur and Agra. By juxtaposing the two works I hope to trace and re-establish the links not only between the early modern and the modern, but also to show the intimate role of the novel in the unfurling of the modern.⁶

The first two sections of the four that follow engage the cultural matrix from which the modern novel in Hindi emerged. The first focuses on the language of the Delhi–Agra region and the modern Hindi literary idiom that sought to crystallize itself from within it; the second on the changes in the social structure of late-nineteenth-century Agra and Delhi and concurrent shifts in the merchant ethos. The subsequent two sections look at *Ardhakathanak* and *Pariksha Guru*, respectively. My concern in these later two sections is threefold. First, I pay particular attention to the genre designations the works themselves employ, the expectations they arouse, and the literary models they invoke, since these models bring with them their own form of experience and elaboration of reality. Second, I try to ground

---

⁵ *Kadambari* was translated early on from the Bengali by Gadadhar Singh and serialized in *Harishchandra's Magazine* from its very first issue in 1873; it was published in book form in 1879 with the subtitle *Prachin sanskrit upanyas* (Ancient Sanskrit Novel).

⁶ *Ardhakathanak* seems to be an almost picture-book illustration of the early modern in South Asia as it has unfolded in the scholarly discussion, especially in the works of Rao, Shulman, and Subrahmanyam on literature and historiography in South India. I find particularly relevant their notion of the early modern as marked most of all by its new sense of time and of self, of events 'strongly and necessarily connected to the prior context of intelligible causes', of the peculiarity of individuals 'with complex motivations and an interior depth' operating in a world which is 'no longer idealized or predictable' (Rao, Shulman, Subrahmanyam 2003: 136–7).

the notions of self and sociality in the two works, particularly as they relate to the merchant ethos, present and past, 'taking them either as models or as foils.'[7] Finally, as both works make explicit reference to the political time frame within which the action is set, I trace the relationship of particular moments in the given life story to these political frames.

By juxtaposing the nineteenth-century novel with the mid-seventeenth-century work I draw attention to the vulnerability of the merchant community, in particular to social and political change as it pertained to modernity, suggesting that the literary format offered by the novel seemed best suited to register the modernizing impulse as this found expression in the fate of the individual, even as it became tied to larger social, historical, and political forces.

THE SPEECH OF DELHI AND AGRA

In the past few decades there have been intensive debates about the Hindi–Urdu divide and the matrix from which they have jointly—or indeed separately, as some would have it—emerged.[8] Revisiting this vexed terrain in relation to early prose narratives in Hindi, what most immediately strikes us is the remarkable consistency with which writers specify the Delhi–Agra region as the location from which they are drawing the standard of their speech. Lallujilal (*c.* 1747–1824) finds himself compelled to say a few words about his use of language in a brief Preface to his *Premsagar* (1810), a retelling of the tenth canto of the *Bhagavata Purana* which became a perennial favourite. A Gujarati Brahman originally from Agra, Lallujilal was employed by the Fort William College to produce instructional material for teaching Hindavi in the Nagari script. Of *Premsagar*, one of the first works written with this express intent, Lallujilal is at pains to point

---

[7] Taylor 1989: 103.

[8] See the essays in Orsini 2010 for a discussion of the linguistic and literary field in North India before the nineteenth century, and the clear bifurcation into Hindi and Urdu of a formerly shared linguistic terrain.

out that it has been written in Khari Boli, the 'upright' speech of Delhi and Agra, setting aside the language of the Yavanas (*yamini bhasha chor dilli agare ki khari boli mem*), marking thereby the moment in which the deliberate process of extracting a purer Hindi idiom from the speech of Delhi and Agra, cleansed of its Perso-Arabic elements, begins.[9]

The speech of the region is invoked again by Pandit Gauridatta (1836–1905) of Meerut in his *Devrani Jethani ki Kahani* (The Tale of the Elder and the Younger Sister-in-law; 1870), regarded as the first novel in Hindi. A short work of only forty-eight pages, in it once again it is the speech of the merchant milieu of the area around Delhi and Agra which provides the social grid. Pandit Gauridatta specifies in his Preface that the work is written in a new way—in the language of women as spoken in the families of Banias, the business folk of this region.[10] Similarly, in *Bhagyavati* (1877), the second novelistic work of any note in Hindi, the author, Shraddharam Phillauri (1837–81), himself from the Punjab, specifies that he has chosen to write his work not in the somewhat rough (*rukhi-si*) speech actually current in Banaras, where the narrative is set, but in Hindi as spoken by the Hindus around Delhi, Agra, Saharanpur, and Ambala (extending it westwards), so that it will be widely understood and thus also be within the grasp of the men and women of Punjab.[11] By specifying the speech of the Hindus of the region, he is setting it off from Urdu, also spoken in this region and which in fact in its spoken form exhibits no difference from Hindi. Once again, it is by the extraction of an idiom from this shared social net, reflecting the lived urban ethos of the twin Mughal capitals, through which the author sees fit to fashion his text. He is, clearly, seeking to shape and define it by delineating it thus.

[9] The very term Khari Boli, as Lallujilal pointed out in his *General Principles of Inflection and Conjugation in the Braj Bakha* (1811: iii), as cited by Vedalankar (1969: 63), was used by the Hindus of the region to distinguish it both from Brajbhasha and the Perso-Arabic inflected Rekhta or Urdu.

[10] I cite from Gopal Ray's edition of the work: Ray 1966: 1ff.

[11] Phillauri [1877] 1973: 6.

With that we come to *Pariksha Guru* (1882). Its author, Lala Shrinivasdas of Mathura and Delhi, has an easier task, for his narrative is set in Delhi. The Preface to his *Pariksha Guru* begins by proclaiming that though by now a great many good books have been written in Nagari (he speaks of the script rather than the language) and Urdu, there has been none of the kind that he is putting before readers. It will be in the everyday speech of the people of Delhi:

> In this book a picture of an imaginary rai's of Delhi has been drawn and in order to show it as it is (that is, in its actual form) instead of a language made up of difficult Sanskrit or Persian-Arabic words, care has been taken to use the everyday speech of the inhabitants of Delhi. However, it has become necessary to use stray words from Sanskrit etc. where some branch of knowledge is being addressed. But for the ease of those who could have some difficulty in understanding these matters, such sections have been marked with the sign of a cross, so that they can be omitted and the narrative sequence still remain coherent.[12]

Whatever the location of the writer, whether Lallujilal in Calcutta, Pandit Gauridatta in Meerut, Phillauri in Punjab, or Shrinivasdas in Delhi, it is the speech of the Hindus, and the Hindus alone, of Delhi and Agra and their immediate vicinity that is employed as the grid. This geographical designation is all the more notable given that modern Hindi literature was to go through its first intense period of creativity not in Delhi and Agra—the sites of Persian and Urdu literature in the eighteenth and nineteenth centuries—but in Banaras and later Allahabad, in the eastern part of the broad stretch of North India that is today seen as the Hindi belt. Banaras and Allahabad writers were to use a more Sanskritic idiom, perhaps influenced by the example of Bengal,[13] and facilitated by the fact that they were employing a language that was not spoken locally. We could then well

---

[12] Shrinivasdas 1964: 155.

[13] Bharatendu repeatedly resorted to literary models in Bengali, particularly in the matter of dramatic composition. In *Natak* (1884), the lengthy treatise on drama written in the last year of his life, he was to refer explicitly to Bengali as the *bari bahin* (older sister) of Hindi. For more on Bharatendu's language, see Dalmia 1997: 146–221.

ask why the emphasis on Delhi and Agra in this early writing. There are surely several reasons: the political and social prestige that had so long been associated with these two cities, the standardization of the language for which they could now provide the measure, and—given the dissemination of such speech in the rest of the subcontinent—the wide comprehensibility the authors could reckon on when using it.

The intimate link of this Hindi literary idiom to Urdu was a matter of geography, history, and culture. Even as the two were deliberately made to part ways, Urdu continued to have bearings on the literature of Hindi, the two remaining closely intertwined till well into the twentieth century.[14] We need only think of Hindi's best-known author Premchand (1885–1936), who for the greater part of his life wrote his novels first in Urdu and only then in Hindi.

AGRA, DELHI, AND NINETEENTH-CENTURY SHIFTS

The reputation of Agra has been so reduced to the image of the one monument that its rich political and cultural history has tended to recede in the public imagination. Here I briefly rehearse some well-known facts about Agra, recalling the moments of glory rather than intervals of decay, in order to call to mind the prestige it continued to enjoy till well into the twentieth century.[15] After its foundation in 1506 by Sikandar Lodi (1489–1517), who shifted the capital there

[14] As A.S. Kalsi pointed out: 'It may be further noted that sister languages like Urdu and Hindi, faced with new identical educational needs, responded by producing similar didactic fictional works aimed at the education of women. That this should have been so is to be expected, that it should have remained unrecognized across the critical boundaries that lie between Hindi and Urdu cannot be described as satisfactory. At a broader level, the Hindi fictional works discussed above probably provide the first instance of Hindi drawing strength from its elder sibling Urdu in the field of fiction, of which the second important example was to be seen in the last decade of the nineteenth century when Devakinandan Khatri (1861–1936) drew upon the Urdu dastans for his *tilismi* novels.' Kalsi 1990: 44.

[15] I draw the citation that follows from Shailaja Kathuria's Introduction to Thomas Smith's *Agra* (2007), rather than from the more extensive Agra

from Delhi, Agra, known for its spectacular architecture and layout, became one of the twin capitals of the Mughals. Babur had laid out the first of its great Mughal palace gardens on the left bank of the Yamuna, designed on the fourfold Persian pattern. Akbar built the massive Red Fort which spawned further building activity, a moment Abul Fazl was to mark in his *Akbarnama*: 'The City within a short time became an ornament of the seven climes . . . The soil is congenial to the growth of the trees and fruit of Khorasan and Irak . . . The river Jumn . . . flows in the midst of the city. On either side of it nobles and servants of the state have constructed edifices of such beauty and elegance that they surpass description.'[16]

The new impulses generated by the intellectual ferment of the seventeenth century, the prolific cultural activity at Akbar's court, and the religious literature—not to speak of the theological debates of the adjacent Braj region with its many devotional communities—could only have added to the glitter of the city and the court. With its location at the intersection of the busiest trade routes of the time (between Bengal and Gujarat) and as host to powerful merchant families, bankers, and traders with connections to the court, the city profited and grew to possess an array of central markets for cattle, horses, muslin, silks, grain, spices, and a range of specialized local crafts. Shah Jahan moved the capital to Delhi, but Agra remained a powerful cultural and financial base.

Ardhakathanak would be unimaginable without this intellectual and mercantile context. Even when the British took over the city from the Marathas in 1803, and the Agra Fort came to be occupied by the military governor, the character and prestige of the city were not entirely lost. The British remodelled and de-centred Agra by building their Civil Lines west of the old city, and in the process several monuments were desecrated. But it became the capital of the North

---

Gazetteers, since it is easy to access and recalls many forgotten details of nineteenth- and twentieth-century Agra unlikely to be found elsewhere.

[16] Smith 2007: xvii.

Western Provinces in 1835, with its own Sadr Board of Revenue, Sadr Court, and a government hospital. From the 1830s there was intense missionary activity, led by the American Presbyterian Mission and Church Missionary Society, with a number of local presses which also served the colonial administration. The Agra School Book Society, founded in 1835, printed a vast number of school textbooks. The many Indian presses which sprang up in response added to the mass of print emerging from the city, making Agra the centre of educational printing, a position it was to hold till well into the 1850s.[17]

The events of 1857 did not scar the city to the extent they did Delhi and Lucknow. The British retained the fort throughout and though the reprisals were brutal everywhere, they could be called mild by comparison with those in Delhi. For our purposes it is important to remember that Agra continued to radiate power and influence through a great part of the nineteenth century as the British capital of the region. It lost this designation only in 1858, when the regional capital was shifted to Allahabad.

Delhi of course has a much longer history as the seat of political power. It played a major political role from at least the time of the Rajput kingdoms in the tenth and eleventh centuries, thereafter as the capital of the Sultanate, and later of the Mughals. Even after 1857, when, as retaliation against its central symbolic and strategic role in the uprising it was reduced to provinciality by being appended to the newly conquered Punjab, its cultural and historical significance could never be entirely suppressed, as is evident from the comments of a none too sympathetic observer in the *Delhi Gazetteer* of 1883–4: 'The history of the Delhi District, previous to the British rule, is the history of the city of Delhi, which has from the time of its founding been the seat of the ruling dynasty, Rajput, Pathan, Mughal or Mahratta. To write it in full would be to recite the history of Northern India . . .'[18]

---

[17] See Stark 2007: 49–53 for more information on printing and publishing in Agra in the nineteenth century.
[18] *Delhi District Gazetteer 1883–1884*: 22.

The core of Delhi in the latter half of the nineteenth century was still constituted by the Mughal city of Shahjahanabad. Though it seemed poised on the verge of the modern, its social and cultural life continued to draw from the life modes of the late Mughal period, even if the nostalgia that came to be associated with its past glory was of late-nineteenth-century origin.[19] The most important component marking the physical and symbolic structure of the city was the wall that encircled it, defining it as a culturally contained unit. Even after the brutal suppression of the 1857 uprising and the demolition of a good third of Shahjahanabad, the wall remained intact all the way up to the formal ending of colonial rule; the only openings in it were made for the railway when, in 1863, the East India Railway was built to pass through Delhi.[20]

Chandni Chowk, the main thoroughfare of the city, stretched from the Lahori Gate of the fort to the Fatehpuri mosque; it experienced a revival as a shopping and promenade centre towards the end of the nineteenth century with the resumption of trade once Delhi acquired a railway connection. The European 'piece goods' for which the city was known proved lucrative. By 1872 Delhi could boast of possessing the largest share in the volume of Indian trade compared to towns in the Punjab.[21] Chandni Chowk had begun to see prosperous days once again:

> Ghalib had mourned the 'ending' of the life around the canal in the 1860s but, quite soon after, the canal and Chandni Chowk were again throbbing with life. Private trade, public business, public worship and politics were concentrated here. Its narrowing width (120 ft in 1890, 84 ft in 1919) testified to pressure of trade and business... The spacious 'Company Bagh' around the Town Hall was another outdoor club where the maulvis, hakims, bankers and teachers met, while the Hall itself was used as the municipal office and, till the end of the century, also housed the public

---

[19] See Naim 2003 for a discussion of the late origin of this nostalgia. I thank Francesca Orsini for drawing my attention to this essay.

[20] King 1976: 212–13.

[21] Cf. Gupta 1981: 42–3.

Illus. 4: 'The Chandni Chowk—Principal Street in Delhi', Albumen Print, by Samuel Bourne

library and the European club. Religious as well as secular activity was concentrated in Chandni Chowk—the massive Jain temple, built in the 1870s, the Sisganj Gurdwara, the Baptist Chapel, St Stephen's School, the Fatehpuri Masjid . . . Chandni Chowk symbolized solid prosperity but also the cosmopolitan spirit. It was much loved by the inhabitants, because it symbolized continuity . . .

Continuity could be seen in the fragrance of fresh flowers and of watered earth in the back lanes, in the five variations of Urdu spoken in the city which made it a cultural oasis in a rural desert, in the story spinning by the *dastan-go* on the steps of the Jama Masjid, in the wrestling matches, *patangbazi*, *kabutarbazi* and *satta* gambling, in the gatherings during the evening in the Urdu Bazaar, with its culinary and bibliophile attractions, in the free ministering of the poor by the hakims every morning, in the bathing at the Jamuna in the course of the morning, the gatherings in the evenings at the canal. Change clashed sometimes and coexisted often with continuity.[22]

If one end of Chandni Chowk was dominated by the massive Red Fort, towards the other end the newly built Victoria Clock Tower (1873) became 'a symbol of the metropolitan presence, a constant reminder of a new orientation to time.'[23] Though there had been major demographic shifts—Hindus outnumbered Muslims in the city after the 1857 reprisals—by all accounts they continued to exist in relative peace with each other, much as they had over the reigns of the last Mughal emperors.[24] The many Khatris and Kayasths living in the area continued with their evolved Indo-Persian lifestyles, even as they adapted to the new forms of cultivation brought in by the British.

The one great regret among the elite of the city was the relocation of the Delhi College to Lahore. Founded in the late seventeenth or

[22] Gupta 1981: 50–1.
[23] King 1976: 219. There are tall clock towers in other North Indian cites, in Lucknow—the tallest in India apparently—as well as in Allahabad in the Chowk. I am grateful to Francesca Orsini for drawing my attention to these parallel structures.
[24] Hasan 2005: 30–2.

early eighteenth century as the Madrasa of Ghazi-ud-Din Khan, it had in 1825 been resurrected by the British as the Delhi College. The activities of the College have been seen as ushering in a short-lived but brilliant 'Delhi Renaissance'. This was the location of the first intense contact of the flourishing Urdu culture of the city with the best in European knowledge. English was taught from 1828 on, and, in the brief span of fifteen years, as many as 130 works in a range of scholarly fields, including the sciences and mathematics, were translated from English into Urdu. The College had produced a remarkable number of outstanding students, Muslim and Hindu, but the events of 1857 warranted in the British view the removal of this intellectually vibrant institution from the city, and subsequently its merger in 1877 with the Lahore Government College.[25] Even so, there were efforts to enrich the cultural life of the city. In 1865 Commissioner Hamilton inaugurated the Delhi Society for 'the advancement of knowledge and general welfare'; it had seventeen Englishmen and seventy-six Indians as members. Several 'of the Hindu alumni of Delhi College, who happened to be mostly Kayasths, were happy to be members of the Delhi Society, just as in former days, they had integrated into the cross-communal *musha'ara* culture.'[26]

Nazir Ahmad's *Mirat ul Urus* (The Bride's Mirror; 1869), the first novel of note in Urdu, emerged from this cultural milieu. An alumnus of Delhi College at the height of its intellectual activity in the 1840s,[27] Nazir Ahmad set his award-winning novel—about an ideal daughter-in-law who helps her family find its feet in the post-Mughal

[25] See the Introduction and the essays by Pernau in her edited volume on the Delhi College (Pernau 2006) for detailed studies of the architecture and students of the College.

[26] For more information on the activities of the Delhi Society, see Gupta 1981: 97ff., in addition to the quotation cited here.

[27] Nazir Ahmad (1831–1912) had learnt Persian and Arabic at the Aurangabadi Mosque in the city but had gone on to study in the Delhi College. He joined the British colonial administration thereafter to become Deputy Inspector of Schools. He acquired sufficient knowledge of English to translate the Income Tax Law in 1859–60, followed by a translation of the

city—in the vicinity of Chandni Chowk. Written in a colourful and racy style, it brims with details of social life in the *mohallas* of the city, from Chandni Chowk to Kabuli Gate, with its easy access to Sabzi Mandi, while also noting the poorer sections around Turkoman Gate. Most of all, it documents the transition from the old system of patronage by the Mughal nobility to the new by the British sahibs, who offered lucrative employment in the municipal offices that now ruled the city, and in the *kachahari* (law courts):

> Mukhtars, vakils, and pleaders of 'lower' and 'upper' grades were admitted to practice before specified jurisdictions, after passing relevant examinations. Often they were former government officials who now saw ways to use their knowledge of *kacahri* law and procedure to develop some private mine of good will and promising circumstance. Some legal practice, especially when it involved protracted litigation over zamindari holdings, could be extremely profitable. As permanent residents, legal practitioners had the benefit of connections and information denied to the frequently transferred government officials.[28]

Moral authority rested now with the law courts, and social prestige came in the form of honorary membership of municipal boards, the Indian members of which could only be nominated by the British. Nazir Ahmad set his novel in this world of transition, providing the model for later novelistic ventures, more obviously for Gauridatta, but also less directly for Lala Shrinivasdas.

Merchants and credit markets also became increasingly subject to the new legal institutions, whose rules required traders to alter their modes of operation. Traditionally secretive about its transactions and reluctant to reveal details of accounts in the law courts, the community experienced this change as a loss not only of financial credit in the bazaar but also of family honour. To be asked to produce account books in court could only be regarded as a matter of great shame:

Indian Penal Code in 1861. His interest in education led to a close association with Sir Syed Ahmad Khan and his Aligarh College.

[28] Lelyveld 1978: 62–3.

Merchant society worked on secret, inward lines of communication and trust, though government continued to provide employment and even honour. But some changes were perceptible. As in other spheres, the British tended to create a single customary law out of many different local customs. Practices like the 'plunder' by his peers of a bankrupt merchant were gradually replaced by recognised forms of arbitration of 'respectable mahajans' initiated through the law courts.[29]

These changes did not however mean that the twin models of traditional merchanthood, that of the frugal merchant and the great *sahu* (banker), so skilfully delineated by Bayly, ceased to operate.[30] The model frugal merchant led an austere and modest life, avoiding all show of excess. He observed the religious festivities of his community and performed acts of charity in order to consider his wealth engaged in a good cause. Religion and religious acts, however, did not necessarily represent only a public face; they also often reflected an inner piety which could be manifest as a personal imperative powerful enough to tip the carefully maintained balance between the spiritual and the commercial.[31] It was this balance that inspired trust in the community and its reputation in the bazaar, as well as in matters relating to women. In an age that did not require much domesticity or indeed even marital fidelity of men, the answer

[29] Bayly 1983: 372. Further: 'Merchant arbitrations and caste councils continued to operate but their judgements were increasingly challenged in civil courts; "respectable merchants" might then be asked to submit written evidence on custom, etc.' Ibid.

[30] For an extensive discussion of the merchant family ethos, see ibid.: 370–93.

[31] Cf. Dundas: 'One of the main concerns of Indian merchants, Jain and Hindu alike, in the early modern period was the gaining of *abru*, a Persian word signifying "prestige" or "reputation" (the equivalent Sanskrit term *pratishtha* was also used). It was *abru* which was the test of whether a merchant was creditworthy and competent and such respectability, when confirmed, served to generate further *abru* and still more credit and concomitant financial success. Reputation was based on publicly observable behaviour, itself regarded as an index of inner piety, which had to take the form of the organisation of one's life, and those of one's immediate relatives in accordance

seemed to lie once again in avoiding excess rather than having no relationship outside the home. The great *sahu* lived on a precipice if he was believed to lavish his wealth on wine, women, and song. He could lead a life rivalling that of kings and the great nobility, with whom he could also associate on a more familiar footing than his frugal brothers, thus inspiring admiration and envy. But a life of excess was also perceived as morally perilous, with a corollary of such perception being the strong likelihood of acquiring a reputation for financial unreliability. Excessive and injudicious spending could lead to the destruction of mercantile credit. 'From the perspective of the merchants themselves, the basis of mercantile society was the family "firm", its credit (*sakh*) and the totality of its relations with gods and men, creditors and debtors . . . Without "credit", a family could not trade or call on merchant arbitration at all.'[32] Subjective notions of respectability thus intruded into *hundi* (promissory note) transactions. If a merchant had social and commercial *sakh*, his *hundis* would be honoured without further ado in the bazaar, where word of mouth carried great weight and reputations could be made or unmade with great speed. News of this kind travelled fast, and modern means of communication such as the telegraph and the railway only intensified the process. The newspapers broadcast deeds, making for a public morality that superimposed itself onto that of the bazaar; and the law courts were then in a position to prise open the closed circuits of the bazaar.

Such was the life and moral grid of merchants. How would the ways of knowing and judging individuals change from the seventeenth century to the nineteenth century?

---

with certain essentially conservative principles. These would include lack of ostentation or scandal in the conduct of private and commercial affairs, strict vegetarianism and temperance, avoidance of overt involvement in political matters, carefully regulated marriage alliances and a cautious approach to business enterprises in which financial credit was generally advanced only on the basis of short-term returns, and active support of the religious sect to which one belonged.' Dundas 1992: 169.

[32] Bayly 1983: 375.

SEVENTEENTH-CENTURY AGRA: LOVE, LEARNING, AND THE UPRIGHT MERCHANT

Ardhakathanak (1641) is the story of a merchant based in Agra in the heyday of Mughal glory and power. A poignant and powerful tale, pragmatic and poetic in turns, it has attracted much scholarly attention since its publication in 1943.[33] The author, Banarasidas, belonged to the Shrimal clan of jewellers and bankers that included flourishing communities in the major towns, supported by a wide kinship network all over North India. Banarasidas was born and brought up in Jaunpur but based in Agra for long stretches and settled there towards the end of his life. He was a pleasure-loving youth, much addicted to the pursuit of women, but also dedicated to learning and with strong spiritual leanings. In the latter realm he was gullible and seemed to be especially drawn to holy men of various hues, Shaivas and Vaishnavas alike, irrespective of the credibility of their claims. He would come to abandon these holy men and in his years in Agra become a part of, and later play a leading role in, a rising protestant movement within Jainism: the Adhyatmi or 'contemplative' branch of the Terapanth sect, which at the time comprised both Shvetambars and Digambars.[34] Nevertheless, while providing one of its frames, his spiritual growth and the lessons to be drawn from it never seem to become the sole purpose of his narrative. Banarasidas tells the tale because it so pleases him (*man mem ai*) and he relates it for the benefit of his circle of friends; he exhorts them to listen to it attentive-

---

[33] The discussion was given a further boost with Mukund Lath's brilliant translation of the work into English, accompanied by an extensive introduction and detailed historical annotations (Lath 1981). The citations from the work are in Lath's translation, which I have occasionally modified to read more literally. Premi (1943) has a detailed discussion of Banarasidas' language, from which I draw here. Snell (2005) has discussions of the language and meter and analysis of several key passages, including the scene with his wife, to which I will refer later.

[34] See Lath 1981: xxxiv–lxiv for an extensive discussion of the Adhyatma sect.

ly (*sunahu kan dhari mere mitra*).[35] The tale is not only a spiritual biography; it unfolds as a reflection on Banarasi's own character, on his life experiences, and on the passage of time. Depicting the 'ripening of the hero's subjectivity, released in action', it marks an early-modern sense of biography as entwined with history.[36] And it is this self-reflexive mode that makes its juxtaposition with the novel in its late-nineteenth-century form of particular interest.

Language and Genre

Banarasi was acutely conscious of the many languages and literary cultures of the time, and his work seems to emerge from an amalgam of these. His grandfather, Muldas, had been in the service of a Mughal official of high rank in Malwa, in the capacity of a *modi* (financier), and had studied 'Hindugi' and Farsi. He informs us towards the end of the work that he himself has knowledge of Sanskrit and Prakrit, and diverse regional languages (*vividh desh bhasha*). He has made a special study of Sanskrit grammar and of Jain scriptural texts. He does not mention Persian, but given his close contact with the officials of the Mughal empire it is likely that he had at least a smattering of it. And, like his grandfather before him, he is equally likely to have known Hindugi, predecessor of modern Urdu and Hindi, and presumably the spoken idiom of a certain section of society in and around Agra. Certainly, he would also have known Avadhi, the language of Sufi poetry emanating from his native Jaunpur. When times were tough, he earned a meagre livelihood in Agra by reciting the Avadhi Sufi *masnavis*, the extended didactic-romantic narrative poems popular in Jaunpur at the time. He mentions the *Mrigavati* (1503) written by Qutuban at the court of Sultan Husain Shah Sharqi of Jaunpur, and *Madhumalati* (1545), also by a Jaunpur poet, Mir Sayyid Manjhan

---

[35] Ibid.: 7.

[36] As Rao, Shulman, and Subrahmanyam have shown for slightly later narratives from the South: Rao, Shulman, and Subrahmanyam 2003: 166–70.

Rajgiri.[37] Banarasidas calls the language that he uses as being that of the middle region or country (*madhyadesha ki boli*),[38] and writes in an idiom which was surely close to the one spoken in Agra in his time: Brajbhasha mixed with Khari Boli as we know it today. An early instance then, of the very '*Agre ki boli*' which would later be invoked by modern writers of Hindi prose. It is noteworthy that Banarasi makes no mention of the many Vaishnava communities in the adjoining Braj region, the rich literature spawned by their saint-poets, and the specific literary tropes they employed.

Banarasidas seems to be following the format of the Sufi *masnavis*, quatrains (*chaupai*) capped by a two-liner (*doha*), in his own biography. The *masnavi* is clearly a translingual genre not confined to a single linguistic tradition. The Jaunpur *masnavis* are in the language of that region, today known as Avadhi. Yet Banarasi chooses to write his tale not in his native Avadhi but in the language current in and around Agra. He writes without poetic flourish and displays no self-consciousness about his frequent use of Perso-Arabic words. The two genres he explicitly invokes to denote his work are elastic terms, used as self-denotation by a wide range of writing.[39] *Bat* (or *varta* in its purer Sanskrit form), used for verse and prose narratives composed for a variety of purposes, he speaks of as pure entertainment, for chronicling historical events and for hagiography, the most famous examples of which are the Vaishnava hagiographies of the Vallabha community stemming from the Braj area. The second expression he uses is *charita* or *charitra*. *Charitra* in Sanskrit denotes 'character', while *charita* denotes the deeds and exploits of a figure, meaning action or movement in life which can be either an imagined (*Dashakumaracharita*) or actual historical

---

[37] He makes no mention of *Padmavat* (1540), today the best-known Sufi masnavi from the region.

[38] On the shifting geographical boundaries of *madhyadesh* (middle country), used for centuries to denote the area covered by the Indo-Gangetic plains, see Lath 1981: 103–4.

[39] *Ardhakathanak* is its modern name.

event (*Harshacarita*). *Charita* is one mode amongst many of *kavya* (lit. poetry), in the broader sense of literature, and can be written as prose or verse. It is then not a genre as such but a mode articulated in different literary formats, though in specific historical-cultural contexts it can become generically stable. In Hindi usage *charitra* and *charita* have been collapsed to mean the same thing: a life story.[40] Tulsidas' famous *Ramcharitmanas*,[41] and *Banarasicharita* or- *charitra* are both then life stories, albeit of very different casts; the one has a clear theological frame, the other is biographical-spiritual-historical. The language and the literary format of the work are both part of a vast canvas spanning Persian, Avadhi, and the spoken idiom of Agra (*vividh desh bhasha*), and drawing from the cultural repertoire of Sufis, Shaivas, and Jains. Banarasidas departs from known models in that he addresses his listeners and readers initially in the first person, then shifts to the third person to refer to himself, making for an unusual blend of intimacy and objectivity.[42]

Merchant Ethos and Excess

In considering *Ardhakathanak* here I focus on what it conveys of the norms, normative instances, and transgressions of merchant life and the resolutions that Banarasidas eventually finds for his own idiosyncratic needs and excesses. *Ardhakathanak* reflects faithfully the merchant ethos discussed above: valorization of the frugal and censure

---

[40] I thank Professor R.K. Sharma for clarifying the use of these terms to me.

[41] According to Lath, the work was composed four years after the *Ramcharitmanas*, which served as a model for it. However, it seems unlikely that Banarasidas knew the work; he shows little awareness of its Sanskritic mould. He nowhere mentions it, nor does the omission seem deliberate, for he is eager to display what he does know, so manifest is his reverence for learning and literature. According to Snell, the *Ardhakathanak* was actually written a dozen years earlier than *Ramcharitmanas*.

[42] For reasons he explicates in his long introduction, Mukund Lath chooses to retain the first person in his translation.

of the extravagant. As becomes quickly clear at the beginning of the story, a merchant is both protected and ruled by the elders of the clan and its council of elders (*panchayat*), who keep a close watch on his moral and financial credit and creditability. Kharagsen, Banarasi's father, had risen from penury to wealth with the help of his kin. He managed the wealth of his former patron and partner when he died, and saw to the marriage of the patron's daughter. 'Kharagsen found a suitable groom for her and had her married with great pomp and ceremony. He presented her with a large dowry in gold and precious things and called a council of five elders to decide how much of the joint wealth he had shared with her father rightfully belonged to her. He gave her all that was judged to be her father's share, keeping nothing that was legitimately hers for himself.'[43] The *panchayat* of elders is then closely involved in decisions pertaining to wealth, shared property, and its distribution.

Banarasidas' indulgences manifest themselves early on. He is brought up in comfort and sent at the appropriate age to school to learn reading, writing, and accounts. But he becomes unduly absorbed in the pursuit of knowledge (*vidya mem rame*) and continues to study till well into his fourteenth year, far beyond the needs of a merchant. He then acquires another absorbing passion that keeps him from any thought of earning money: he falls in love with a courtesan in the wild and ecstatic manner of a dervish (*asikhbaj*). Forgetting all thought of family propriety and honour (*taji kul kan lok ki laj*), he devotes himself wholly to the worship of his beloved, even stealing money and jewels from his father in order to buy her choice presents. But a spiritual restlessness also drives him. He seeks out holy men, displaying excessive gullibility and falling time and again into the trap set for him by charlatans and rogues.

Banarasidas does go to Khairabad to bring his wife home after their marriage, suffering a severe illness in the process, but returns soon

[43] Lath 1981: 10–11. Cf. Bayly 1983: 376, n.16: 'Panchayats for the arbitration of separations in joint families took into account matters such as the imminence of a daughter's marriage.'

to his former pursuits (*pahali chal*). In Jaunpur the elders (*gurujan*) of the clan (*kul kutumb*) accost him gravely: 'Pay attention, son, to what the old and experienced have to say. Give up your ways of love, since love is for the darvesh, not for you. Give up your foolish pursuit of learning, since learning is only for brahmans and bards (*bambhan aru bhat*). A merchant's son (*banikputra*) should tend shop. Do not forget that a man who is too studious has to beg for food.'[44] The authority that stems from the elders of the clan is cited and forms a moral backdrop to the story, though it has no immediate impact on Banarasi. It is something that he nonetheless internalizes, making both for his own self-censure in retrospect, and for reform when a political crisis throws his life into disarray.

The Erotic and the Domestic

In the meantime, Banarasi remains unimpressed by the advice of the elders and continues in his dissolute ways, with gay disregard for the way of frugal and upright merchanthood. Love, learning, and spirituality continue to rule his days. Even as he studies Jain works with the newly arrived monks in town to satisfy his spiritual cravings, he writes erotic verse for his beloved. We get little sense of his love object; not surprisingly, she remains a 'type'. Later in life, when he begins to settle down, we get a rare glimpse of domesticity.

For a variety of reasons, Banarasi's business ventures remain unsuccessful. Having exhausted his means in a particular venture, he chooses not to go back home to his father empty-handed, but goes instead to his second wife, the sister of his first wife. It is clear that she sees him rarely. But on this occasion they talk through the night and he tells her of the fate that has befallen him in Agra. She spontaneously offers him the twenty rupees she has saved. 'Do not despair, my husband,' she says, 'for if a man lives he can yet achieve everything.'[45] She later corners her mother and tells her that her husband needs

[44] Lath 1981: 33.
[45] Ibid.: 53.

help but that his sorry state is to be kept a secret. She is quite explicit that she fears losing him: '"O mother," she beseeched her, "as I am your daughter, help me in my need. My very honour is at stake. If you cannot do something within a few days, my husband is sure to leave us. Though he does not utter a word, he is tormented with shame and humiliation."'[46] In a rush of emotion, Banarasi proposes that they both go to Jaunpur. 'But she dissuaded me, Jaunpur is in a state of turmoil, afflicted with a hundred troubles. Why not go once again to Agra? That is the right place for you.'[47]

Banarasi's wives (he has three in succession) share his troubled life in one way or the other, but they never enter the forefront of the story. The wifely type presented in the only domestic scene of the book, mistreated yet faithful, is a kind of constant, the other half, so to speak, of the classic pairing: courtesan as object of love and faithful wife as a resource to be drawn upon in the hour of need. We will meet her again in the nineteenth century, though tinged with a Victorian hue, over a similar scene in *Pariksha Guru*, when the wife will come to the rescue of her financially strapped husband by offering to clear his debts with her bag of jewels.

The Way of the Righteous

Banarasi is acutely aware of the state of his own mind and the desires and impulses that drive him. He is as conscious of the passing of time as he is of the ups and downs of public life, whether in Jaunpur or in Agra. In fact, the crucial moments in his life are often tied to political events, and he refers explicitly to them, thus marking time not only astronomically but also by critical junctures in polity. One such event turns out to be a turning point in his own life, setting off a series of chain reactions in him, and finally bringing about the change that his *gurujan* had so long sought. Till now he has spent the greater part of his life careening from one obsession to the next: erotic love,

[46] Ibid.
[47] Ibid.: 54.

book learning, holy men. In 1605, Akbar dies and people are filled with terror at the thought of the impending chaos that this event will bring: 'I was sitting up a flight of stairs in my house, when I heard the dreadful news, which came as a sudden and sharp blow. It made me shake with violent, uncontrollable agitation. I reeled, and losing my balance, fell down the stairs in a faint.'[48] When Shiva does not come to his rescue, he realizes that the holy man to whom he had been devoted was as fake in his claims as the one before him. One day, as he is crossing a bridge over the Gomati with some friends, he flings his erotic poems into the river. He comes to the realization that he has been leading an untruthful life, and so makes a radical break with his past ways: 'From this day on Banarasi began to truly desire righteousness (*karai dharam ki chah*), he gave up his licentious ways (*taji asikhi phasikhi*) and became an upright family man (*pakari kul ki rah*).'[49] Of note is the coupling of righteousness (*dharam ki chah*) with repute and financial trustworthiness in the world of merchants (*ab jas bhayo vikhyat*). Banarasi is now considered ready to shoulder the burden of supporting the family and becoming the breadwinner (*ab grahbhar kandh tum lehu, ab kutumb kaum roti dehu*).[50] His father entrusts him with merchandise and sends him off to trade in Agra.

Towards the end of the narrative Banarasi finds a new friend who initiates him into Adhyatma, 'a new religious movement devoted to the mystic doctrine of the Spirit.'[51] Though greatly drawn to it, Banarasi goes through a period of disorientation. The Adhyatma movement dispenses with all ritual, but Banarasi takes this to mean freedom from all social convention. He is unable to unravel its true nature. This gives him and his companions licence to indulge in behaviour that others find outrageous, such as dancing naked and hitting

---

[48] Ibid.: 38. A reasonably detailed discussion of Banarasidas in the context of the end of the Akbari dispensation can be found in Alam and Subrahmanyam 2011: 127–8.
[49] Lath 1981: 41.
[50] Ibid.: 43.
[51] Ibid.: 86.

each other on the head with shoes. His reputation in the community is once again tarnished.

Banarasi continues to mark the correspondences between historical, astronomical, and biographical time. Shah Jahan ascends the throne in 1627, and Banarasi's first son from his third wife dies soon after birth. The children born thereafter are fated to die in infancy. Domestic unhappiness compounds his alienation from those around him. His release from this condition comes in 1635 when a wise Jain teacher, Rupchand Pande, comes to Agra to stay at the house of Tihuna Sahu.[52] It is he who finally explains the doctrine that has so long eluded Banarasi. 'All my doubts and questionings were put to rest and I became a new man. I had, at last, gained true and profound insight into the Jain doctrine of relativism.'[53] With the resolution to his long-standing spiritual quest, we come to the conclusion of Banarasi's tale.

However, it is not to share his newly found wisdom alone that Banarasi seems to have penned his tale. Two years after the death of his third and last son, he tells us, he is still beset with sorrow. He takes melancholy stock of his life: 'A full nine children lived and died: bereft the parents twain, /as trees at leaf fall, stumps remain.'[54] This melancholy marks the last sections of the story.

---

[52] Ibid.: 90.
[53] Ibid.: 91.
[54] Verse 643 in Snell's translation: Snell 2005: 91. See Natalie Zemon Davis for similar strains of melancholy in Jewish merchant biographies of the seventeenth century: 'The autobiographical/biographical texts being used here have certain common sources, even while their authors had divergent learning. Glikl began to write her Yiddish memoirs in 1689 to help her fight the "melancholy thoughts" that followed the sudden loss of her first husband and then added to them during her years of widowhood and remarriage in Metz. Though her experience keeping business accounts may have encouraged her skills of self-observation, her autobiography was not a spin off from a ledger or a *livre de raison*, as was often the case in Christian Italy and France. Rather, Jewish life history was fostered by the centuries-old "ethical will", an exposition of moral lessons and personal wisdom passed on to one's children

The concluding verses contain the sum of his observations, of himself and of people at large. He says there are three kinds of people. The best are those who praise others and speak only of their own faults. The worst are those who praise themselves and find fault in others. In the middle are those who do a bit of both, and this is where he belongs. He details his good and bad features in five quatrains (*chaupais*). Never entirely the sober merchant, he describes his own personality as perpetually fun-loving, citing his love of dancing and fooling around, even as he proclaims his firm grounding in the Jain faith. Banarasi ends his story with psychological and moral reflections on his own personality, condensing the kind of philosophical observations that lie scattered throughout the work.

A man's life is supposed to reach its full span at a hundred and ten. Having reached the halfway point, with the future being something of which God alone (*bhagvant*) has knowledge, Banarasi tells us he can look back on his life in ways that others might find of benefit. The last couplet (*doha*) proclaims: 'The story of the last fifty-five years of my life covers half of Banarasi's deeds in life (*charit*). Wicked men will laugh at this tale, but friends will surely give it glad and attentive ear and recite it to each other. This work contains 675 dohas and *chaupais*. All those who hear, recite, and read it will benefit from it.'[55]

It is this frame, of the knowledge and wisdom derived from a whole lifespan, which makes his deeds (*charita*) worth narrating. It is a remarkable if not a model life, one that may well claim the designation '*charita*' in its title. It contains the spiritual dimensions of the Sufi *masnavis*, even if the plot follows its own course. And it can certainly fit into the large body of work that called itself *bat* or

---

along with instructions for one's burial and the disposition of one's goods. This connection helps us understand the moral tension in Glikl's text, a tension heightened by her insertion of folktales at several junctures to illustrate or comment on the story of her life.' Davis 1997: 65–6.

[55] Ibid.: 96–7. Lath's translation of verses 674 and 675, slightly emended.

varta, since it is a story well told, though it expands in new directions, becoming the life story of an individual who does not fit into the contours of merchant life. Even as he registers the moral authority of the elders of his clan and community (*kul kutumb*), and the spiritual guidance provided by the Jain laity as well as by monks,[56] Banarasi at no point suggests that his life is anything other than self-propelled rather than driven by material needs or, indeed, spirituality.[57] His self-reflexivity about having to function within the ethos of the merchant community as well as within a wider political frame, and his sense of historical time make his life story an early modern work of exceptional clarity and insight.

NINETEENTH-CENTURY DELHI: 'TRUE' MERCHANTHOOD AND THE WELFARE OF THE NATION

The traits of the merchant community depicted by Shrinivasdas (1851–88) in *Pariksha Guru* considerably resemble those shown by Banarasidas two hundred years earlier.[58] The cohesion and exclusiveness of merchant communities continued to be supported by caste *panchayats* which took care to resolve disputes wisely.

---

[56] Cf. Dundas: 'Banarasidas is the best documented early example of a trend within Jainism, albeit not a dominant one, which authorises lay people to take charge of their own spiritual affairs without reference to ascetic influence. He does not depict himself, even in his pre-Adhyatma period, the bulk of his life, in fact, in which he followed a relatively conventional lay's path, as having had any serious dealings with ascetics, although admittedly he did study briefly with a Shvetambara monk when young. This should alert us to a basic fact of lay experience in Jainism, namely that, contrary to lay ideology, the lay person does not gain identity solely through interaction with ascetics and that a satisfactory and fully Jain religious life may be constructed around events and practices in which ascetics play a minimal or non-existent path.' Dundas 1992: 167–8.

[57] Cf. Rao, Shulman, and Subrahmanyam 2003: 166.

[58] The section on *Pariksha Guru* is partly based on my earlier essay, Dalmia 1998.

Reputations and credit in the bazaar were still linked to lifestyles deemed either frugal or excessive, and the connection to temples and charitable works still determined status and standing in the community. In fact, as a consequence of modern modes of communication, news of fluctuations in repute travelled faster and further along long-distance networks better maintained than ever before.[59] All the same, the ways of the merchant world were changing. The civic life of the city and the new frame provided by the municipality and the law courts, not to mention the lifestyle of the new power-holders, all made for a shifting world. These changes seem to have inspired the first extensive narrative venture in the Hindi that emerged from the speech of Delhi and Agra (*dilli agare ki boli*). Many of the themes in merchant life that had preoccupied Banarasidas reappear in Shrinivasdas: excess, and the means for coming to terms with it. But Shrinivasdas also wrote from a noticeably nineteenth-century perspective. He did not try to privilege traditional ways in the face of change. Instead, he anticipated those changes in the new institutions and ways of learning being imported from the West, seeking to temper the traditional with these. The 'new climate of social and moral experience' asked for a new kind of morality tale for the merchants of the city.[60]

Shrinivasdas belonged to an affluent and influential merchant family of Delhi and Mathura.[61] The second of three sons, he was educated at home in Hindi and Urdu. He had some Persian and Sanskrit, and was widely read in English. He succeeded his father

---

[59] See Rajat Kanta Ray 1984: 244, 248, 250–2.

[60] Thus, Ian Watt on Defoe, Richardson, and Fielding, whose work he saw as being affected not only by the changes in the reading public of their time but 'surely more profoundly conditioned by the new climate of social and moral experience.' Watt [1957] 1987: 7.

[61] His father, Shri Mangilal, had been manager of the enormously wealthy estate of the Mathura Seths, Radhakrishnadas and Gobinddas, recent converts from Jainism to Vaishnavism under the influence of Swami Rangacharya, whom, as Growse tells us in his Mathura Gazetteer, they placed at the head of the great temple of Shri Rangji in Vrindavan. See Growse [1882] 1979: 14–16 for information on the family, and for more on the temple, ibid.: 260–2.

Mangilal as the agent of the Mathura Seths in Delhi, while his brother took over the management of a temple in Vrindavan. Shrinivasdas was a public figure of some note, the Punjab Government having asked him to occupy the posts of both Municipal Commissioner and Honorary Magistrate of Delhi. By all accounts he was urbane, courteous, and successful, devoting the time he could spare from business to literary pursuits. He wrote articles, four plays of varying quality, and the novel that drew from his own professional experience in the city. He edited the journal *Sadadarsh* from 1875 to 1876, when it was assimilated into *Kavivachansudha*, the journal edited by his close friend and literary mentor Bharatendu Harishchandra. Though he himself was linked through his family to an important new temple in nearby Mathura, there is in his novelistic work no mention of any religious or spiritual institution, or indeed of spirituality as providing any frame of reference for merchant life. Neither does he invest moral authority in caste *panchayats,* which are conspicuous by their absence in his novel. The sense of community is reduced to bazaar talk, a mode of information sharing which continues to make or break reputation, and where credit (*sakh*) is still relevant. But there are now also new institutions of moral and political authority; newspapers control local reputation, and matters of debt are resolved in law courts by British judges.

The span of Shrinivasdas' novel is not a lifetime, as in Banarasidas' tale, but five event-filled days in the life of a wealthy young merchant, Madanmohan.[62] He lives in the extravagant style of the 'great *sahu*' near Chandni Chowk, the residential and business centre of Shahjahanabad. Madanmohan wavers uncertainly between the ways of the older Mughal *rais* of the city and a shallow imitation of fashions from the West.

Set up as a model against this extravagance are the new middle-

---

[62] Gopal Ray cites Jnanchandra Jain as noting that the action plays itself out in five days, possibly replicating the five-act scheme of the well-made play. Gopal Ray 2002: 50.

class values represented by Brajkishor, the lawyer (*vakil*). He is the new professional man who continues to revere the good in the older lifestyle, but with some modifications. He is critical of Western influence, even as he allows select aspects of it to permeate his own life. What becomes apparent is that from this point on there are two competing value systems with which the merchant community must come to terms: the old, dominated by bazaar reputations, and the new, controlled also by law court and newspaper.

Reshaping a Tradition

There are also two literary traditions that are major reference points for the new writers of this period: the older Indian and the newer Western. The need to operate within both is reflected in the terminology Shrinivasdas uses in presenting his book to readers. As in Banarasidas' tale, this book moves between different genres, in its self-description as also in the narrative techniques that it adopts. In the Hindi title, Shrinivasdas denotes the work as a worldly tale; the subtitle of the work in its first edition is *anubhav dvara upadesh milne ki samsari varta* (the worldly tale of acquiring instruction by means of experience). Setting out the wide-ranging generic tradition of the *bat* or *varta*, it is the worldly-secular vein that is now foregrounded.[63] The modern novel is entering that secular space where personal and social issues are resolved without reference to religion or spirituality—spheres now seen as inhabiting an altogether separate realm. In the English dedication, it is the novelty of the venture that Shrinivasdas emphasizes, describing it as 'my humble attempt at novel writing'. This dedication is addressed to Lala Shri Ram, one of the first students from Delhi to have secured an MA and a most energetic member of the Delhi Municipal Council.[64] Shrinivasdas eulogizes him for his deep interest in 'everything connected with the weal of the People

---

[63] The author is well aware of the novelty of his enterprise in writing this in Hindi. On the back cover of the first edition of the work is the announcement that an Urdu translation will be appearing soon.

[64] For more information on Lala Shri Ram, see Gupta 1981: 60, 75, 99, 195.

of India by showing them by your own example the best means of Civilizing the Country.' He clearly does not see the need to explain the novel as a form to his English readers, but in the longer Hindi dedication he takes upon himself the task of explaining it to his readership. The work is written in an entirely new style. The narrative will no longer be sequentially ordered (*silsilevar*), and there will be no formal introductions of the characters at the beginning of the text. Instead, it will contain the portrait (*chitra*) of an imaginary gentleman (*kalpit rais*) of Delhi.[65] In order to make the portrayal more natural (*svabhavik*), special attention will be paid to everyday speech (*sadharan bolchal*). The author will not make explicit who is speaking, he will do so only when the need arises. With the introduction of paragraphs and syntactical marks (inverted commas, commas, colons, semicolons, interrogations, exclamation marks, parentheses, and full stops) the reader will learn how to read the work in the new way.

The business of novel writing in modern Hindi was framed as a response to changing perceptions of the self and society rather than as mere imitation of a prestigious European literary form. The new form was thus voicing and fulfilling what were perceived to be the new demands of the times. Nonetheless, in considering the formal aspirations of *Pariksha Guru*, we should keep in mind that the new reader was also the old reader. Shrinivasdas drew upon the literary cultures of the Indo-Persianate world familiar to his readers, alongside the newly opened Anglo-European one. He invoked as his model works as various as the *Mahabharata*, *Stribodh* (Instructions for Women, one of the many manuals for women in circulation at this time), *Gulistan*, the works of Oliver Goldsmith, the essays of Lord Bacon, and those in the *Spectator* (a moralizing eighteenth-century English weekly). Another important model was *Hitopadesha*, a collection of didactic tales (*niti-katha*) which was not explicitly invoked but frequently cited as moral authority.[66] The *niti-kathas* compiled in the *Hitopadesha* and *Panchatantra*, with their pragmatic

---

[65] Interestingly, he does not invoke *charita* or *charitra*.

[66] A wide range of Sanskrit works is cited, including the *Mahabharata*, *Harivamsha*, Valmiki's *Ramayana*, *Manusmriti*, *Vishnupurana*, Kalidasa's

this-worldly morality, gelled with the kind of moral observation, social realism, and idealized character portrayal—the perfect friend, the ideal wife—in the essays of the moralizing weekly and the writings of Goldsmith, particularly his *Vicar of Wakefield* (1766).

In spite of the fact that the forty-one chapters of *Pariksha Guru* are offered within a single narrative frame, they read more like weekly instalments. The chapters are kept short, an average of seven printed pages, as befits a weekly column. Every once in a while the narrator begs to be excused on account of a certain topic not being sufficiently dwelt on for lack of space. They have headings reminiscent of the aphoristic verses of *niti* tales, but also of the moral essay, such as *sangati ka phal* (the fruits of company), *mitra milap* (the meeting of friends), *savadhani* (caution), *sajjanata* (goodliness), *mitra pariksha* (the trial of friends), *sachchi priti* (true affection), and so on.[67] Apart from these moral reflections, there are scenes that read more like those in a drama, a trait inherited from traditional narrative genres meant for oral delivery such as the *dastan* and *varta*. The language is bright and colloquial. Even when the moralizing verges on the excessive, myriad tales are interspersed to illustrate a point and profuse citations from motley sources marshalled to support it. It is here that the chapters tend to assume the character of a moral essay, and when this happens the language becomes more Sanskritized, that is to say, it moves beyond colloquial speech to a more self-consciously elevated language.

Through the traditions invoked—the idealism of Goldsmith and the moral essay for one, and the stark pragmatism of *niti* tales for

---

Raghuvamsha, and *Vidurapajagara*; there are also several Persian citations from Saadi; the Quran is cited once. There is a profusion of citations and references to English authors: Chesterfield, William Cowper, Alexander Pope, Byron, and to two plays of Shakespeare—*Othello* and *The Merchant of Venice*—and an equally wide selection from the works of Hindi Avadhi and Brajbhasha poets: Kabir, Tulsi (*Ramcharitmanas* and *Vinaypatrika*), Gang, Vrinda (who seems to be a favourite), and Girdhardas.

[67] On the significance of the moral essay in this period, see Dalmia 1997: 260–7.

another—the primacy of worldly success and happiness is postulated as paramount. The *niti* tales took a dark view of human nature and tended to see human action as largely motivated by greed, lust, and pride. All goals, good or bad, can be reached; success depends on *upaya* (ruse). Whatever the final outcome, the kernel of the tales always concerned itself with relationships, that is, reflections on the reliability and constancy of friends and dependants. Nothing was to be taken at face value; the *svabhava* (nature) of each person was to be tested. One of the key concepts in the *Hitopadesha*, *pariksha* (trial) forms not only a part of the title of the novel,[68] it is repeatedly invoked in the work itself. Only *pariksha* can test the true nature of an object, only *pariksha* can lay bare the true *svabhava* of a person, and finally only severe *pariksha* can teach a much needed lesson and make a person see the error of his ways.

The primary difference between the novel and the much shorter episodic *niti* tales lies, however, not only in the idealistic resolutions found at the end but also in the sustained narrative that operates within a social world with clear geographical and historical bounds and within a clearly defined socio-political framework. The protagonists are seen as at least partly created by their education and environment, as being propelled by inner *and* outer forces, making them seekers not only of their own destiny but that of a larger collective, the nation. As Brajkishor says, the situations (*hal*) in which a man lives from birth till the present affect him subconsciously.[69] This corresponds well with the pragmatic call to take note of the mental composition of men and their needs.

---

[68] On the importance of the *niti katha* in the early literature of modern Marathi, see Raeside 1970. Blackburn has noted the importance of tales from the *Panchatantra* in early Tamil literature. The *Hitopadesha* itself was one of the earliest Sanskrit works to be published in translation by the Fort William College. Translated by Lallujilal into Brajbhasha, it appeared in 1860 under the telling title *Rajniti or Tales Exhibiting the Civil and Military Policy of the Hindus*. It was to see several reprints. For bibliographical details, see Krishnacharya 1966: 5f.

[69] Shrinivasdas 1964: 272.

How does one recognize good and evil? There are no hard and fast rules to determine these questions. Described in a chapter aptly entitled *bhale bure ki pahchan* (the detection of good and evil), the teaching is put in the authoritative words of Brajkishor. The dispositions (*vritti*) explicated at some length here take both social concerns and the psychology of the individual into consideration. In a given situation, all kinds of factors can be at play, and so the question is really a matter of asking what is allowed to take precedence. Righteous dispositions (*dharma pravritti*) often have to be weighed against more lowly materialist inclinations (*nikrshta pravritti*). Righteous considerations have equally to be tempered with more material ones. Only then can justice be done to God's creation (*ishvar ki rachana*), which would otherwise become meaningless (*nirarthak*), because no work of God, righteous or material, can be without meaning. The dialogue which explicates this begins with Brajkishor's statement, 'Without trial, not one person can be pronounced to be a true friend' (*pariksha hue bina kisi ko sachcha mitra bhi nahim kah sakta*).[70] The mental dispositions of men are to be critically assessed. And as almost a corollary to this there are sporadic glimpses of an interiority that is as self-reflective as it is self-critical.

Urban Modernity and the New Merchant Ethos

Banarasidas is acutely conscious of time and place throughout his work, noting all dates of arrival and departure from towns, of occurrences in the family and their coincidence with the crowning or death of monarchs. But he provides a set description of the city of Jaunpur and gives little sense of the topography of the urban landscapes through which he has moved, whether Agra, Delhi, Banaras, or indeed, Khairabad. The *niti* tales were of course entirely free-floating as regards time and place. But Shrinivasdas' narrative is set in an actual physical environment.[71] And it is this environment,

---

[70] Ibid.: 186.
[71] Ian Watt cites Defoe as 'the first of our writers who visualised the whole of his narrative as though it occurred in an actual physical environment.' Watt [1957] 1987: 26.

MERCHANT LIVES IN MUGHAL AGRA

in its peculiar mixture of old and new, that we are presented with as we learn the details of Madanmohan's lifestyle.

Madanmohan lives in grand style, with extensive arrangements in place for pleasure and entertainment. He maintains an elaborately laid-out garden, Dilpasand Bagh, on the outskirts of the city, and Shrinivasdas lavishes some care on its description:

> This garden was located a little further than Sabzimandi on the banks of the canal. On both sides of the path were rows of flowers. Flowers of all colours in their beds, carpets of green grass at places, the dense shade of trees or artificial waterfalls at yet other places, creepers of all kinds winding around trees or trellises, birds of all varieties calling out from the aviary, and on yet another side fish and water creatures of all hues in a marble pond, and at the centre of the garden an airy room with a marble verandah around it and around that, water fountains. When these fountains played, peacocks mistook *jaith*, *vaisakh*, the summer months for *savan-bhadom*, the months of the monsoon. A silk carpet lay spread in the middle room and a golden couch upholstered in the best satin, chairs placed at convenient spots, and above the side tables hung eight great mirrors. Chandeliers of great value swung down from the ceilings, bouquets of flowers arranged on round, oval, and square tables, and choice toys and objects of ivory, sandal, ebony, porcelain, and mother-of-pearl, and in decorative silver bowls cardamom and betel nut. A clock which told the time, date and month, a harmonium, a billiard table, a photo-album, binoculars, a sitar, a chess board and other things to while away the time were kept at appropriate places, the walls had floral mosaics to which the luster of mica added a silvery glitter. Material worth thousands of rupees was bought each month for this house.[72]

The very interior of his establishment reflects the change in lifestyle. Though modelled on the garden houses of the Mughals,[73]

---

[72] Shrinivasdas 1964: 177–8.

[73] Cf.: 'Mughal gardens were rectangular, surrounded by high walls broken by gateways, and topped with towers. The principal design, from which the most intricate and elaborate variations developed, featured a central pool containing a small open structure called a *barahdari* (summer house). Four wide canals led from the pool to the surrounding walls. Smaller canals branched off from the major waterways and subdivided the large rectangles.

Madanmohan has collected a variety of new-fangled articles of furniture: chairs and tables, and new 'toys' such as clocks, binoculars, and Western musical instruments. English furnishings also feature prominently in his house in the city, where he keeps a variety of new carriages for his conveyance and a stall full of the highest breed of horses.[74]

But what has his English learning brought him? False imitation (*jhuthi naqal*) of the English. He subscribes to a number of journals but reads them only for the advertisements of novelties from the West. He is a public figure of sorts since he is mentioned in the

---

Colored flowers, cypress trees (symbols of death and eternity), almond, plum, and mango trees (symbols of life and hope), plumed birds, and fish of different sizes and colors filled the duly appointed garden.

'Members of imperial and noble families built gardens on the banks of the Jamuna and in tree-shaded groves near the city gates. While the city was being built, Shahjahan laid out a garden called Khizrabad on the banks of the Jamuna about five miles south of the Akbarabadi gate of the city . . . Outside the Kabul gate of the city Shahjahan constructed a garden filled with neem trees called Tis Hazari Bagh (Garden of Three Thousand) . . . In 1650 Raushan Ara Begum constructed a large garden in Sabzimandi.' Blake 1991: 62.

[74] Udaya Kumar notes the fascination that English objects exercised on the novelists of this period: 'It is not accidental that many of the early novels in Malayalam display a fascination with collections of objects—these can be seen as located at an intersection of co-ordinates representing coherence and value. *Indulekha* presents two kinds of collections. The first is Suri's collection of valuable objects, all gold and silver, which he prepares to carry with him on his visit to Indulekha's house . . . In contrast to this, there is a collection of "English sorts of objects beautifully arranged in Indulekha's rooms." This second collection of objects is laid out in a certain style in order to constitute a new domestic space—that of modern cultivation and style—in the early novel. This can be seen especially in the description of the rooms of the Nair men in Malabar and Madras. Round tables, reclining chairs, painted mirrors, embroidered covers, glass lamps, carpets and, sometimes in the centre, glass cupboards of books in English and in Sanskrit, beautifully bound and embossed with golden lettering—these objects conjure up a new world of coherence, the universe of a new civility and new values.' Kumar in Mukherjee 2002: 164.

newspapers; he has some ambition to become an honorary member of the Municipal Committee for he has made some effort to keep up with the times and even indulged in some showy acts of patriotism. Gullible, innocent, constantly swayed to and fro, foolhardy but not evil in intent, he is surrounded by a host of hangers-on and sycophants, all of whom schemed and plotted for his favour in the best style of the *niti* tales.

Madanmohan leads a dissolute life, filled with wine, women, and song. He moves through the wide avenues of Chandni Chowk in his carriage. He halts at the Company Bagh, where the air is pleasant, the flowers and the greens attractive, and the breeze blowing in from the canal so refreshing that he is tempted by his good friend Brajkishor to stay for a while. But his wily manager Chunnilal lures him away from the good company of Brajkishor. Chunnilal wears a watch whose precision, he says, is guaranteed by the cannon shots issuing at regular intervals from the fort. This newly mechanized sense of time makes life more amenable to control. Chunnilal can put his watch forward, hurry Madanmohan along, and thus allow him no time to engage in

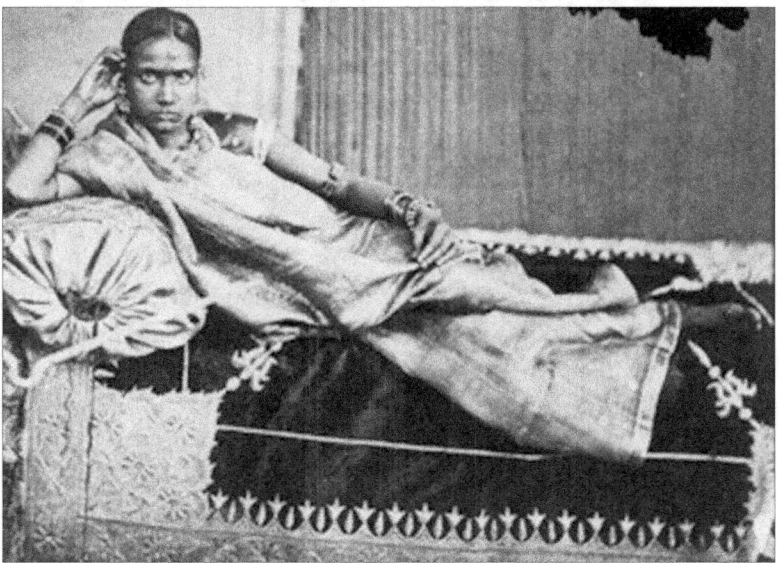

Illus. 5: 'Courtesan 1870'

conversation with Brajkishor. The new times, and the new sense of time, bring with them their own pitfalls and disorientation for the grand *sahu* of the new age.

It is noteworthy, however, that the old ways (*purani chal*), best represented by Madanmohan's father, are not merely glorified. A merchant of the old school—simple, thrifty, quick on the uptake—he was a self-made man. He lived frugally, without pomp and show, and with only a few trustworthy retainers. Most importantly, his credit in the merchant community was as good as gold (*Sahukare mem uski bari sakh thi*). Madanmohan, however, was educated by a father who was alternately indulgent and stern; he grew up to be indolent, and after his father's death a law only unto himself. The alternative to the old ways (*purani chal*) was then to be seen not in the new ways (*nayi chal*), but only in true and sound merchanthood (*sachchi sahukari*). In this new context the nature (*svabhava*) of men has to be probed and undergo trial (*pariksha*). Thus it is not only Madanmohan but whole new ways of life, the old as well as the hastily adopted new, that have to coalesce in the contemporary moment. The conflict can be said to be between the falsely new and the genuinely new.

Brajkishor, the young lawyer and one of the frequent visitors to Madanmohan's house, represents this newness. He is trying to revive the Delhi College with the help of some friends. But, most importantly, Brajkishor has access to the new method of dispensing and maintaining moral order: the law court (*kachahari*). And he knows how to make use of the new institutions. As a successful mediator between the old and the new, he represents the new ideal of the professional man who views progress as a matter of both personal and national responsibility. As he points out, all the conditions and materials required for the progress of the country are available in Hindustan, but *hath hilaye bina apane ap gras mukh mem nahim jata* (the morsel of food does not reach the mouth unless the hand is made to move).[75] That is to say:

[75] Shrinivasdas 1964: 199.

Those who study do so in order to join (government) service; they abandon the professional occupations of their forefathers. The aims of those who talk about the progress of the country are quite fake; they just make a lot of noise about nothing. They don't pay the attention they ought to to the progress of learning, the propagation of machines, new ways to increase the produce of the land and profit in commerce so that the losses in the country can be made good.[76]

In the catastrophic denouement of the novel, when Madanmohan's sins catch up with him and he is considered insolvent by his many creditors, the question that Brajkishor poses is not a psychological one but a larger social and political one: 'If Indians today have become addicted to imitating the English, why don't they, instead of imitating meaningless things like eating habits and so on, emulate their genuinely good qualities? Why don't they adopt their views on the welfare of the country, craftsmanship, and commerce?'[77] The fate of the individual has come to be tied up with larger issues. It is this widened perspective, this awareness of the individual placed in the larger context—social, historical, political—of past, present, and a collective future to be collectively shaped, that makes for the necessity of the single narrative framework provided by the novel and for the new spaces that this new literary form opens up.

Moral Authority: Bazaar, Akhbar, and Adalat

We enter the tale directly, without preamble. The novel opens at an English merchant's shop that offers fancy fripperies at exorbitant prices. The two English shopkeepers are depicted as self-seeking and exploitative, aware of the advantages they enjoy in the British Raj. At first we see the main characters in the novel presented in dramatic sequences, and only later, in chapters showcasing their arguments and counter-arguments on moral and social issues, do we become privy to their inner thoughts. Brajkishor presents 'the enlightened

[76] Ibid.: 201.
[77] Ibid.: 330.

view'; he propagates a cautious modernity where the new ways are modified and practised in moderation. Madanmohan and his friends champion new fashions and crave instant satisfaction. It is their *kathametat* ('how is this'), in the style of the *Hitopadesha,* which prompts Brajkishor to go on and on at times. It is only once we have come to know these friends that we are offered lively character sketches which integrate with elegant irony the speech and perspective of the character himself. In chapter 9, *Sabhasad* (Courtiers), we are offered a view of this gallery of rogues, colourful and unscrupulous in the best style of the *niti* tales, though here, in the novel, they are described in more psychological and idiosyncratic detail.[78] It is their vivacious commentary and conversation that makes for the vibrant realism of the novel. They are the scum that is formed by mixing the new with the old. They are clerks, middlemen, the newly forming lower middle class, half-educated and needy, with a smattering of knowledge about the new ways but with slim chances of rising in their own profession. An almost inadvertent gaiety characterizes their operations and counter-operations, with Madanmohan fluttering between them, torn between his own caprices and the interests of his courtiers.

But things can hardly remain suspended in this state of eternal pleasure-seeking. Amongst all these hangers-on there is also one, Harkishor, the clash of whose character with the rest brings about the catastrophic denouement. Harkishor's offer to procure goods is twice rejected by Madanmohan. Deeply offended, Harkishor asks for the money owed him for past services. The money does not materialize and Madanmohan's hangers-on manage to throw Harkishor out of the house. Harkishor promptly declares that the penurious state this

[78] Bharatendu Harishchandra had written a short autobiographical piece that could have grown into a novel, *Kuch apbiti, kuch jagbiti* (A story part experienced by the self, part by the world) in 1877, which described just this experience, of a young man of twenty-three, wealthy and inexperienced, surrounded by rogues of all kinds: pimps, and moneylenders and well wishers of motley hue who praise his beauty, learning, talent, dress, taste, his women, horses, and his very pigeons. For a detailed discussion of this piece, see Dalmia 1997: 297–9.

brings about makes for the loss of his *sakh* in the bazaar.⁷⁹ He duly sets out to take revenge, spreading a rumour about Madanmohan's impending insolvency in order to destroy Madanmohan's *sakh*. The narrator devotes a lively chapter or two to Harkishor's rumour-mongering. Various friends under various pretexts refuse to give Madanmohan the loan he now needs to satisfy the demands of his nervous creditors. The narrator dwells on the behaviour of these friends at some length. Some show regard for him initially, others simply avoid him. His *sakh* in the bazaar is ruined, and because of the modern modes of communication this news travels fast.⁸⁰

Meanwhile, Brajkishor devises a plan to send Madanmohan's faithful wife back to her natal home in Meerut. Left alone, Madanmohan's fortunes rapidly decline, and his household collapses in disarray and confusion. His servants steal shamelessly. In the face of domestic unrest, Brajkishor threatens to charge all servants under the Indian Criminal Code Article 408: 'You are tigers in your own lanes. You can do what you like here, but your roar will impress no one in the court.'⁸¹ The court is now being invoked to deal with

---

⁷⁹ Shrinivasdas 1964: 233.

⁸⁰ One of Madanmohan's most galling encounters, which also documents the role that the new modes of communication play in accelerating the pace of events, is described thus: 'In the meantime, a registered letter from a friend in Meerut arrived. It carried a *darshani hundi* or bill of exchange guaranteeing instant payment, for ten thousand rupees, with a note, which said, "you can ask for as many more rupees as you need; consider my house your own." Lala Madanmohan sprang up with happiness and launched into praise of his friends. He sent off the bill of exchange to be cashed immediately but the banker to whom it was addressed refused to cash it, saying that the very friend who had sent it in the first place had sent him a telegram asking him not to honour it. So the matter had come to light. What really took place is as follows. When the friend first received Madanmohan's letter, he had had no inkling about matters going awry for his friend, so to demonstrate his true affection for him he had sent off the bill of exchange. But when he heard about this from other people he panicked and sent off a telegram to block it.' Ibid.: 364.

⁸¹ Ibid.: 235.

domestic crises; soon its influence will permeate other spheres of Madanmohan's life.

In the next scene, Madanmohan sitting glumly in his reception chamber (*divankhana*), happens to glance at a newspaper. An article catches his eye, 'The Outcome of a Cultivated Life':

> Observing the initial ascent of a young, well-educated *rais* in our city, we not only nurtured the hope but even gave it expression that we would in a while surely see him act in a way that would have an immediate impact on the welfare of the country. This hope, we are sorry to say, has now been entirely crushed. In fact, all signs to the contrary are becoming manifest. In a matter of days, three of four lakhs have been entirely wiped out. There was a young man named Durmody (?) in the West who had such a sharp mind that at the age of nine he could be found teaching his fellow pupils Greek and Latin. But his ways thereafter did not bode well and the end result was very different from what one had been led by the start to expect. Indian reformers just appear to be reformers; they make no real effort to improve their nature or their thinking. Even if they display such tendencies when young, no trace of it remains once they leave the madrasa. The poor grow anxious about food and clothing and the rich have no leisure from the relentless pursuit of their own pleasure and enjoyment. Who has time to think about the progress of the country? Who will start discussions about Art and Learning? When we see the impoverished state of the country and the affairs of a wealthy man gone awry, we are filled with regret. But for the sake of the country, we only wish that those who make a show of working for the welfare of the nation, who create darkness under the light of the lamp, be immediately exposed. So that the eyes of the people are opened and they don't take the jackal in lion's clothing for the lion himself.[82]

His lost *sakh* and his conduct are now being broadcast, and hence judged in a forum that goes beyond the bazaar. The nationalist press administers this new morality, calling for a new sense of collective responsibility, not only for the community but for the nation at large.

[82] Ibid.: 383–4.

In his hour of need Madanmohan's only real friend, it turns out, is Brajkishor. Though temporarily alienated by Madanmohan, he has kept watch over the affairs of his friend. Brajkishor has not been entirely idealized, in the manner of Mr Burchell in Goldsmith's *Vicar of Wakefield*, nor is he quite so omnipresent. At one stage he admits ruefully that his legal profession has made him worthy and self-righteous. He knows he can be unduly verbose, often not knowing when to stop, even though it bores people.[83]

We are taken inside the courthouse to witness the finesse with which Brajkishor handles the debtors who are clamouring for quick repayment of the loans they had so freely given Madanmohan. Chapter 32 is entitled *Adalat* (Court of Law):

> The court is in session and the judge is sitting on his chair. The clerks are seated in their places. Nihalchand Modi's lawsuit is being handled. Latif Hussein is the lawyer on his side. Lala Brajkishor is putting the questions from Madanmohan's side. Brajkishor had learnt to read Hindi at Madanmohan's place in his childhood.[84] This is why he knew very well how bankers' records were kept and so he had paid a nominal fee and looked through his accounts thoroughly. No legal arguments were needed in this case, it was purely a question of taking and giving loans.[85]

The language of this chapter—as well as of passages connected with the law and lawyers—is full of the Persianate vocabulary that characterized this dimension of public life in the period, and the narrator does nothing to expurgate these expressions as alien. As Brajkishor's cross-examination quickly reveals, the loans had been agreed upon verbally through Madanmohan's servants; the details were not to be found in the account books. Why? Apparently Lala Madanmohan ordered that the sums he required be handed over instantly. What proof was there that this was so? There was no proof.

---

[83] Ibid.: 344.

[84] Possibly he has been educated in Urdu and Persian alone. By learning to read Hindi, he means accounts kept in Nagari numerals.

[85] Shrinivasdas 1964: 357–8.

Nihalchand, the banker who had advanced the loan, was reluctant to show his account books in their entirety because they would reveal the commissions he had given to Madanmohan's servants. Since this was illegal, both Nihalchand and the servants could be charged with crimes. The judge, who is shown to be kindly and considerate, says: 'Look here, if any kind of fraud is proved here, I am going to hand over the matter to the criminal courts.'[86] But Brajkishor just wants to scare the debtors into submission, not get them into serious legal trouble. While Brajkishor is thus busy in court, Harikishor manages to get a warrant for Madanmohan's arrest. Madanmohan suddenly finds himself thrown into a debtor's prison.

The Erotic and the Domestic

The transformation of Madanmohan's character begins in earnest as he faces his final test (*pariksha*). In prison for a night, he experiences extreme distress, causing a change of heart that leads to a restoration with his wife. We need to recall that Madanmohan leads a life typical of his kind. The many courtesans with whom he relates remain faceless, but we are told that they take up much of his time and money. His hangers-on speak temptingly of Amirjan, a famous courtesan of Lucknow who was visiting Delhi, as well as of a male dancer from there. They fix performances of well-known singers from the Gwalior gharana,[87] and plan a trip to the Qutub accompanied by

---

[86] Ibid.: 360. This idealized view of the court presided over by an English judge, who duly dispenses justice, was satirized just a little later by Fakir Mohan Senapati (1843–1918) in his Oriya novel *Six Acres and a Third*, serialized in 1897–9 and published as a book in 1902. Consider, for instance, the following scene from the closing pages of the work: 'While heated debate between two sides is going on lasting two and a half hours, the judge Sahib (H.R. Jackson, Esq.) managed to finish a four foot long newspaper and his midday meal. Had he not ordered them to stop, the lawyers would have talked on and on.' Senapati [1902] 2005: 179.

[87] The Gwalior gharana was considered the oldest and most prestigious gharana in North India: 'The City of Gwalior itself remains historically

a troupe of singers and dancers. Madanmohan's wife remains equally nameless and faceless. However, she is idealized in a way Banarasidas could not even have begun to suggest. Without the presence of the new kind of wife, the new way of life would be incomplete; it would only tell half a story. In this respect, Madanmohan's wife has stepped straight out of *Stribodh*—a manual for women, as it were—for she has all the Victorian virtues of a good and thrifty housewife and of a loving and caring mother who carefully supervises the education of her children:

> With such little expense has she made such excellent domestic arrangements that Madanmohan is spared all labour at home. When she has leisure, she does not sit idly gossiping about other people and chattering about jewels and jewellery, she practices reading and writing, embroidery and drawing pictures, etc. . . . The children are very little but while playing she teaches them the basic moral principles and, though unaware, by increasing their knowledge of things she stimulates their natural capacity for knowledge. But she does not burden their minds; there is no hindrance to their innocent play and laughter.[88]

The new merchant and the professional man both need the other half for efficient management of their domestic sphere. And it is this preoccupation with the role of the good wife in the domestic economy, the projection of a male nationalist fantasy that will become so vital to the evolving structure of the modern Hindi novel.[89] We need to note, however, that with her many virtues, Madanmohan's

---

important for all musicians because it is where Tansen is now buried. The Rajas of Gwalior had a long tradition of generously patronizing musicians.' Newman 1980: 148. For further information of the various Gwalior lineages, see ibid.: 152, 183.

[88] Shrinivasdas 1964: 293–4. The translation of these passages about Madanmohan's wife reflects the stilted quality of the original, which does not flow naturally from the narrative. It seems rather to have been transposed verbatim from a conduct book for women.

[89] The expression stems from Indrani Chatterjee in the very valuable Introduction to her edited volume: Chatterjee 2003.

spouse also embodies the model of the good wife (*pativrata*) that we know from *Ardhakathanak* and a myriad other tales:

> In relation to her husband, Madanmohan's wife was truly affectionate, well-wishing, a companion in pleasure as well as in pain, and obedient. Early on, Madanmohan held her in great affection. But when he began to keep the company of friends such as Chunnilal and Shimbhudayal, the addiction of dance and music entrapped him into raptures over the false airs and graces of the courtesans ... His poor, simple, able wife began to seem rustic to him. For a while things were kept secret, but how can there be pleasure in the flower of love after the worm has entered it?[90]

It will take a while for Madanmohan to revive the flower of love. The prison scene is remarkable for its focus on Madanmohan's interiority and its new valorization of family life. Once he is left alone in his narrow, pitch-dark dungeon of a cell, and the courthouse has been emptied with not a single person in sight, we are afforded a glimpse of a new sense of the inner self that Madanmohan experiences. He thinks of his past life and of his many friends who, failing his justifiable expectations, deserted him in his hour of need:

> At this stage, it is extremely difficult to reveal (*prakat karna*) the reflections of Lala Madanmohan. When he thinks of the luxury from his childhood to now, the darkness fills his eyes. The chatter of Lala Hardayal and other pleasure-loving friends, the false affection of Chunnilal, Shimbhudayal, and others, song and dance functions till the early hours of the morning, being surrounded by sycophants all hours of the day, saying yes to every wish of his, the praise lavished at every occasion, and at all stages their readiness to sacrifice even their lives: when he compares all this to his situation now and thinks of their ingratitude, his heart is steeped in sorrow.[91]

He wonders what will become of him at sixty if this is how he feels at thirty. He thinks of death and is immediately filled with the fear of ghosts. His imagination begins to play tricks on him. He

[90] Shrinivasdas 1964: 291–2.
[91] Ibid.: 403.

sees all kinds of monstrous shapes, hears deafening sounds, and feels physically burdened by the enormous weight of these apparitions. He thinks of his god and pleads for help, and in the end, overcome by fear and emotion, he faints. This could be a moment for spiritual revelation. Instead, when he comes to he finds his head cradled in a woman's lap. Could it be his wife? Is she also an apparition? Her hot tears wet his face. He shuts his eyes, refusing to believe it is a real person. Brajkishor has sneaked her into the prison, and shortly after she leaves he himself will appear. But in the meantime she offers her love and devotion. At first he keeps quiet out of fear. But when the woman tries to give him strength and courage he can no longer hold back his feelings: 'Of all the mistakes I have made till now, I have made the most mistakes with regard to you. I mistook a diamond for a mere pebble, and cast you far away from me, mistaking a valuable necklace for a serpent.'[92] The affections to be reserved for the wife, the domesticity that now includes small children—who make a brief babbling appearance—are served up with a sentimentality entirely novel in a tale of merchant life. We have only to think of the nine children Banarasidas lost, not one of whom he described, to see how the idea of the family, emerging as it does in the resolution of this novel, has become extremely significant.

Madanmohan's crisis in the prison cell does, however, bear some resemblance to Banarasidas' moment of illumination in *Ardhakathanak*. In that tale, the plunge into despair at the news of Akbar's death had set Banarasi thinking about his way of life. After his climactic fall from the stairs leading to his house, he gave up his literary and erotic pursuits, abandoned his licentious ways, and finally gained credit as a merchant in the eyes of his father and the community. But he had not thought to repair his relationship with his wife, nor indeed to view it as skewed to begin with. However, in the new climate of social change that we find in *Pariksha Guru*, where the banker is in an environment determined increasingly by Victorian norms, the

[92] Ibid.: 407.

conjugal family has become 'a metaphor for society and thereby a focal point for refashioning social reality . . . As father figure, the banker operated on the premise that social stability depended on domestic stability in individual families. In this scenario, bank failure [in our case, *sakh*] focused attention on the breakdown of the links connecting domestic and social relations.'[93] It is these links between the domestic and the social that need to be set right before the tale can come to a fitting conclusion.

Brajkishor manages to free Madanmohan from the clutches of his debtors; he clears his name and helps him recover his former position of power, even if as a wiser and sadder man. It needs to be noted here that, for all the narrator's love of virtue, it is characteristic of the pleasure that he himself takes in his roguish figures, and perhaps a mark of his particular brand of realism, that they are allowed to slip away unpunished. Characteristic of the social reform agenda of the novel and its documentary tone, once the error of his ways is apparent to its protagonist, Madanmohan wants his tale written and published so that others can benefit from it:

> The suffering that ought to have befallen me on account of my folly has now done falling upon me. I can see no advantage in sparing myself falsely now. 'For the sake of all these people I would like the whole account to be printed and made public,' Lala Madanmohan said.
>
> 'Is there need of it? Those who want to learn will find the world full of moral treatises,' said Lala Brajkishor, thinking over the matter with regard to his own person. 'There's no need to be ashamed of things which are true. I want with all my heart that once my faults become public, people have their eyes opened by seeing their [ill] consequences. I'll tell you all about the people I talked to and the things I said to them so that you can put them down in your account,' said Lala Madanmohan enthusiastically.[94]

[93] Alborn 1995: 203, 204. George Rae, author of the popular trade manual *The Country Banker*, claimed in the pages of the *Banker's Magazine* that the model manager should be a married man: 'and the reason is this, that a married man has in his own experience a knowledge far beyond that of an individual who remains single all his days . . .' Ibid.: 211.

[94] Ibid.: 422.

The primacy of social concern and corrections, as Ramvilas Sharma has pointed out, directly sired the didactic-realistic tradition to be found in the early novels of Premchand.[95]

Madanmohan's *samsari varta* or the *kalpit chitra* of a *rais*, which is at the same 'a humble attempt at novel writing', ends thus on a note very similar to *Banarasi charit* or *Ardhakathanak*. But the differences between the two works are also vast. If there are lessons to be drawn from the respective life-stories, in the one case these will be restricted to a circle of friends and fellows in the community of Adhyatma, in the second a wider, and more anonymous reading public. If we see 'the mediation of literary model as form of experience, model of perception and elaboration of reality itself', and genre as 'a model of reality which mediates the empirical world',[96] that which distinguishes the two works is also thrown into stark relief if we juxtapose the temporal frames within which they operate. Banarasidas' sense of historical time is acute, but it consists in registering with some consternation the coming and going of emperors, the corresponding births and deaths in the family, and the changing seasonal and ritual calendar. The narrator in Lala Shrinivasdas' novel operates with a sense of secular time divided into a past, present, and unknown future. He sets as the goal of his story the remaking of the self, of helping others to remake themselves, thereby creating a collective future—that of the nation. The novel is a part of this enterprise to create a modern sense of progress, and it is this vista that Lala Shrinivasdas opens up:

> For that project was intertwined with a new experience of historical time, and thus with a new conception of historicity—historical time divided into three great periods (Antiquity, the Middle Ages, and Modernity), accelerating forward into an open future . . . It was in Europe's eighteenth century that the older, Christian attitudes towards historical time (salvational expectation) were combined with the newer, secular practices (rational prediction) to give us our modern sense of progress. A new

[95] Sharma 1975: 93–9.
[96] Conte 1986: 112.

philosophy of agency was also developed, allowing individual actions to be related to collective tendencies ... one assumption has been constant: to make history, the agent must *create the future*, remake herself, and help others to do so, where the criteria of successful remaking are seen to be universal.[97]

These dimensions do not exist for Banarasidas, and nor does any notion of political change that lies outside his sphere of influence. It is in this respect, as a modern tale of change, that *Pariksha Guru* becomes remarkable, marking the point of emergence of the novel from the vast range of life-stories grouped formerly under *charita* or *bat*. Yet it remains a freak experiment in novel writing in Hindi: uneven in language and style, unsettled in its orthography, couched in the as-yet-unstandardized spoken idiom of Delhi and Agra. Such speech is most apparent in its lively dialogues, but it changes registers frequently, from essayistic Sanskrit-ridden passages for its homilies to a Persianate legal vocabulary for its court scenes. Nevertheless, it marks an important moment, for it is with merchants—given their vulnerability to political change and their need to stay in tune with it—that the early ventures in novel writing begin, made apparent as much by *Devrani–Jethani* with its small-time merchant milieu, and the more experimental *Pariksha Guru*, registering the impact of new moral instances and new interiorities.

With this the first potential also exhausts itself. It re-emerges elsewhere. A few decades later Premchand will take up similar themes in and around Banaras to explore them further, initially in Urdu but then also in Hindi.

REFERENCES

Ahmad, Maulvi Nazir. [1869] 2001. *The Bride's Mirror: Mirat ul-Arus. A Tale of Life in Delhi a Hundred Years Ago.* Translated from the Urdu by G.E. Ward (1903). With an Afterword by Frances W. Pritchett. Delhi: Permanent Black.

[97] Asad 1983: 18–19.

Alam, Muzaffar, and Sanjay Subrahmanyam. 2011. *Writing the Mughal World: Studies in Political Culture*. Ranikhet: Permanent Black.

Alborn, Timothy. 1995. 'The Moral of the Failed Bank: Professional Plots in the Victorian Money Market'. In *Victorian Studies*, 38/2. Winter.

Asad, Talal. 1993. *Genealogies of Religion: Discipline and Reasons of Power in Christianity and Islam*. Baltimore and London: The Johns Hopkins University Press.

Banarasidas. 1943. *Ardhakathanak*, ed. Nathuram Premi. Bombay: Hindi Granth Ratnakar.

———1981. *Half a Tale. A Study in the Interrelationship between Autobiography and History*. The *Ardhakathanaka* translated, introduced, and annotated by Mukund Lath. Jaipur: Rajasthan Prakrit Bharati Sansthan.

Bayly, C.A. 1983. *Rulers, Townsmen and Bazaars: North Indian Society in the Age of British Expansion, 1770–1870*. Cambridge: Cambridge University Press.

Blake, Stephen P. 1991. *Shahjahanabad: The Sovereign City in Mughal India, 1639–1739*. Cambridge: Cambridge University Press.

Brajratnadas. 1950. *Bharatendu-mandal*. Banaras: Shri Kamalmani-grantha-mala-karyalay.

Chatterjee, Indrani. ed. 2004. *Unfamiliar Relations: Family and History in South Asia*. Delhi: Permanent Black.

Conte, Gian Biagio. 1986. *Genres and Readers: Lucretius Love Elegy, Pliny's Encyclopedia*. Translated by Glenn W. Most. Baltimore and London: The Johns Hopkins University Press.

Dalmia, Vasudha. 1997. *The Nationalization of Hindu Traditions: Bharatendu Harischandra and Nineteenth Century Banaras*. Delhi: Oxford University Press. Reprinted Ranikhet: Permanent Black, 2010.

———. 1998. 'A Novel Moment in Hindi'. In Vasudha Dalmia and Theo Damsteegt, eds, *Narrative Strategies: Essays on South Asian Literature and Film*. Leiden: CNWS Publications Research School. Reprinted Delhi: Oxford University Press, 1999.

Davis, Natalie Zemon. 1997. 'Religion and Capitalism Once Again? Jewish Merchant Culture in the Seventeenth Century'. In *Representations*, 59.

Delhi District Gazetteer 1883–1884. Compiled and published under the authority of the Punjab Government. Reprint. Gazetteers Organisation, Revenue Department, Haryana, Chandigarh, 1999.

Dundas, Paul. 1992. *The Jains*. London and New York: Routledge.

Gauridatta [1870] 1966. *Devrani Jethani ki Kahani*. Patna: Granth Niketan.

Goldsmith, Oliver. 1966. *The Vicar of Wakefield*. In *Collected Works of Oliver Goldsmith*, ed. A Friedman. Vol. IV. Oxford: Clarendon Press.

Growse, F.S. [1882] 1979. *Mathura: A District Memoir*. Reprinted Delhi: Asian Educational Service.

Gupta, Narayani. 1981. *Delhi Between Two Empires 1803–1931: Society, Government and Urban Growth*. Delhi: Oxford University Press.

Hasan, Mushirul. 2005. *A Moral Reckoning: Muslim Intellectuals in Nineteenth Century Delhi*. Delhi: Oxford University Press.

Hitopadesha. 1949. Bombay: Nirnayasagar Mudranalay.

Kalsi, A.S. 1990. 'The Influence of Nazir Ahmad's *Mirat al-Arus* (1869) on the Development of Hindi Fiction'. *Annual of Urdu Studies*, 7.

——1992. '*Pariksha Guru* (1882): The First Hindi Novel and the Hindu Elite'. *Modern Asian Studies*, 26/4.

Kadambari: Prachin Sanskrit Upanyas. 1879. Translated from the Bengali by Gadadhar Singh. Allahabad: Indian Press.

King, Anthony D. 1976. *Colonial Urban Development: Culture, Social Power and Environment*. London: Routledge and Kegan Paul.

Krishnacharya. 1966. *Hindi ke Adimudrit Granth*. Banaras: Bharatiya Jnanpith.

Kumar, Udaya. 2002. 'Seeing and Reading: The Early Malayalam Novel and Some Questions of Visibility'. In Mukherjee 2002, *vide infra*.

Lallujilal. [1810] 1870. *Premsagar*. Revised edition. Calcutta: Ramsahat Pandit.

Lelyveld, David. 1978. *Aligarh's First Generation: Muslim Solidarity in British India*. Princeton: Princeton University Press.

McGregor, R.S. 1970. 'The Rise of Standard Hindi, and Early Hindi Prose Fiction'. In *The Novel in India, Its Birth and Development*, ed. T.W. Clark. London: George Allen and Unwin.

McKeon, Michael. [1983] 2003. *The Origins of the English Novel, 1600–1740*. Baltimore and London: The Johns Hopkins Press.

Mukherjee, Meenakshi. 1985. *Realism and Reality: The Novel and Society in India*. Delhi: Oxford University Press.

——, ed. 2002. *Early Novels in India*. Delhi: Sahitya Akademi. In Udaya Kumar, *vide supra*.

Naim, C.M. 1984. 'Prize Winning *Adab*: A Study of Five Urdu Books Written in Response to the Allahabad Government Gazette Notification'.

In Barbara D. Metcalf, ed., *Moral Conduct and Authority: The Place of Adab in South Asian Islam*. Berkeley: University of California Press.

———. 2003. 'Ghalib's Delhi: A Shamelessly Revisionist Look at Two Popular Metaphors'. *Annual of Urdu Studies* 18/1, 3–24.

Newman, Daniel M. 1980. *The Life of Music in North India: The Organization of an Artistic Tradition*. Detroit: Wayne State University Press.

Orsini, Francesca, ed. 2010. *Before the Divide: Hindi and Urdu Literary Culture*. Delhi: Orient Blackswan.

Pernau, Margrit. 2006. *The Delhi College: Traditional Elites, the Colonial State, and Education before 1857*. Delhi: Oxford University Press.

Phillauri, Shraddharam. [1877] 1973. *Bhagyavati*. Delhi: Sharada Prakashan.

Raeside, I.M.P. 1970. 'Early Prose Fiction in Marathi'. In T.W. Clark, ed., *The Novel in India: Its Birth and Development*. London: George Allen and Unwin.

Ray, Gopal. 1968. *Hindi Upanyas Kosh. Khand Ek*. Patna: Granth Niketan.

———. 1969. *Hindi Upanyas Kosh, Khand Do*. Patna: Granth Niketan.

———. 2002. *Hindi Upanyas ka Itihas*. Delhi, Patna: Rajkamal Prakashan.

Ray, Rajat Kanta. 1984. 'The Bazar: Indigenous Structure of the Indian Economy'. In Dwijendra Tripathi, ed., *Business Communities of India: A Historical Perspective*. Delhi: Manohar.

Rao, Velcheru, David Shulman, and Sanjay Subrahmanyam. 2003. *Textures of Time: Writing History in South India 1600–1800*. New York: Other Press.

Sharma, Ramvilas. 1975. *Bharatendu-yug aur Hindi Bhasha ki Vikas-Parampara*. Rev. ed. Delhi: Rajkamal Prakashan.

Senapati, Fakir Mohan. [1902] 2005. *Six Acres and a Third: The Classic Nineteenth Century Novel about Colonial India*. Translated from the Oriya by Rabi Shankar Mishra, Satya P. Mohanty, Jatindra K. Nayak, and Paul St Pierre. Berkeley: University of California Press.

Shrinivasdas. 1882. *Parikshaguruh arthat anubhav dvara upadesh milnem ki ek samsari varta*. Delhi: Sadadarsh Press.

———. 1964. *Shrinivas Granthavali*, ed. Shrikrishnalal. Banaras: Nagaripracharini Sabha.

Shukla, Ramchandra. [1930] 1947. *Hindi Sahitya ka Itihas*. Rev. ed. Banaras: Nagaripracharini Sabha.

Smith, Thomas. 2007. *Agra; Rambles and Recollections of Thomas Smith*. Edited with an Introduction by Shailaja Kathuria. Delhi: Chronicle Books.

Snell, Rupert. 2005. 'Confessions of a 17th Century Jain Merchant: The *Ardhakathanak* of Banarasidas'. *South Asia Research*, 25/1, May.

Stark, Ulrike. 2007. *An Empire of Books: The Naval Kishore Press and the Diffusion of the Printed Word in Colonial India*. Delhi: Permanent Black.

Taylor, Charles. 1989. *Sources of the Self: The Making of the Modern Identity*. Cambridge, Mass.: Harvard University Press.

Trivedi, Harish. 1993. *Colonial Transactions: English Literature and India*. Calcutta: Papyrus.

Vedalankar, Sharada. 1969. *The Development of Hindi Prose Literature in the Early Nineteenth Century*. Allahabad: Lokbharti Prakashan.

Vijayshree, C. 2002. 'Telugu Novel in the Nineteenth Century'. In Mukherjee 2002, *vide supra*.

Watt, Ian. [1957] 1987. *The Rise of the Novel: Studies in Defoe, Richardson and Fielding*. London: The Hogarth Press.

2

Wife and Courtesan in Banaras

As possibly the best-known Hindi–Urdu author of our time, Premchand (1880–1936) has found so secure, but also so dusty, a niche in the halls of fame as the author of rural North India, that it takes some refocusing of our lens to register the fact that when, with the publication of *Sevasadan*, he first rose to fame, it was as a sensitive and perceptive cartographer of a city. This city was none other than Varanasi,[1] the holiest of all North Indian cities, in the throes of modernizing and refashioning its image, even as it made a bid to drive away its once famed courtesans from the vicinity of Chauk, the central square at its heart, from which ran arteries into its nethermost nooks.[2]

There is much hidden cultural history in the publication trajectory of *Sevasadan*.[3] It was written first in Urdu in 1917 under the titillating title *Bazar-e-Husn* (Bazaar of Beauty), though, given the exigencies of the market and the whimsy of the publisher, it had to wait till 1924

---

[1] I refer to the city as 'Kashi' when speaking of it as a pilgrimage site with all the mythical connotations that this conjures up. Otherwise, in order to remain near Premchand's usage, I call the city 'Banaras', though the name of the city is now officially 'Varanasi', an older Sanskritic name for the city.

[2] The Urdu term for courtesans is *tawai'f*, the one more current in Hindi now is *bai*. For the sake of uniformity, I have used the term 'courtesan'.

[3] The text used for the translation of the novel is from the twenty-volume edition of Premchand's Collected Works, *Premchand Rachanavali*, published by Janavani Prakashan in Delhi in 2006; *Sevasadan* is in the second volume. All translations from the Hindi are mine.

to be published in its Urdu form. However, it shot to almost instant fame when it was recast in Hindi and published in 1918 under the sober and uninspiring title *Sevasadan* (The House of Service), a reference to the educational institution which was erected to house the daughters of former courtesans. *Seva* and *sadan* however also carried other meanings. *Seva* (service) could also be of the kind which the courtesans of the city supplied to their clientele, and *sadan* (abode) is also the name of one of the central male protagonists of the novel, an errant and largely unfulfilled young man. Sadan had been in love initially with the beautiful and enticing Suman, whom he had first met in the Bazaar of Beauty. But eventually he married her sister, the more pacific Shanta, to whom he had been betrothed all along and who had suffered the misery of her lot with virtuous resignation. Though the various connotations of the title must also have existed for contemporary readers, it was surely its most apparent meaning, with its obvious allusion to social reform, the puritanical rather than that which suggested the lurid, which accounted for the initial appeal of the novel. It was the era of high nationalism, Hindi was seeking to set up its own respectable literary canon, and if nation, woman, social reform, and the reordering of the city landscape could be brought together thus educatively, the novel could do none other than win massive public approval. But the novel's enduring popularity may have had more to do with the interplay of the various meanings, and of voices other than the calm and analytic auctorial, which make possible more than one reading of how *seva* and *sadan* came variously to be conjoined but also queried.

My effort here is to trace and recover this interplay of meaning in order to gain some understanding of the enduring power and popularity of the novel, as also of the central character of the novel, who is without doubt Suman. Her vision of herself changes a couple of times, as also—driven by events—does her understanding of the relationship to her spouse.

In addition to its vividly dramatic dialogues and its deep psychological insight into persons and processes, the novel's narrative is girded at all times by a keen sense of social history. It registers crucial social transitions even as they take place, from known patterns of life to new, untried ones. One such transition is from the country to the city; many of the central characters undertake or undergo this traumatic passage. After her marriage, Suman is transported from her well-to-do home in a rural district to the stench of the narrow lanes in the inner city and the claustrophobia of the small dark rooms in which she abides with her elderly husband. Sadan in running away from his landowning village home finds himself filled with fear and foreboding as he dashes across field and wood to catch his night train to Banaras. Two miles outside the village is a pipal tree, its dense foliage filled with ghosts which appear in all shapes and forms to hinder the wary traveller. Sadan freezes into inaction and can cross its dark presence only when he hits upon the idea of singing verses from Tulsidas' *Ramayana* at the top of his lungs to fend off the lurking evil spirits.

The city itself is changing rapidly. In the second decade of the new century, it continues to be dominated by the old time *rais* (gentry), the great landowners of the district residing in their town houses, and the equally powerful merchant aristocracy with its widely spread kinship networks. But alongside the gentry, the colonial government has allotted some public space to the new professionals, whom it also nominates to the municipal board, which has newly been granted some autonomy in civic government. This colonial modernity, both in personnel and administration, impacts the city as much as the rhetoric of social reform—as yet thinly represented by these new professionals—which is beginning to gain ground and provide unexpected twists to matters considered long settled. But even social reform is a two-edged weapon which can be used to further various ends, especially when it focuses on women. At the centre of the novel, as also of Banaras, is yet another crucial transition: the courtesans of the city are no longer to practise their art publicly, for the social reformers have taken up the cause of fallen women. This touches the heart of the relationship of Suman and Sadan. Suman's private problems become linked to the city's problems and its changing face. Private and public are thus inextricably intertwined.

THE COURTESANS OF THE CITY AND THE NEW NOVEL IN HINDI

The courtesans of the city had long occupied a central space in public life. Their reputation went back many centuries; there are references to them in Jataka tales and in Sanskrit works of various genres and periods.[4] As legend had it, the gentry had ever flocked to the best known amongst them, in search not only of the more obvious pleasures but also to enjoy the best in the arts: music, dance, poetry, and to luxuriate in an atmosphere radiating refinement in matters of aesthetic taste and judgement. Once a courtesan had acquired a reputation for beauty and mastery of the arts, she could attain high social standing. She would be asked to appear at the court of the Banaras maharajas, in the mansions of the rich and the powerful, but also in the most prominent temples and on the banks of the holy river on important religious occasions. The number of such women was small, though their power was often staggering, as the sober voice of James Prinsep, the first British census taker of the city, informs us in the second quarter of the nineteenth century:

> If, however, beauty and high vocal skill are comparatively rare, the witching influence of the arts and graces of these women is as much acknowledged and as powerful as ever. Examples are not wanting of large accumulations of wealth from the successful exercise of the skill and accomplishment of the profession: some of the best houses and the handsomest temples of the city have been erected by ladies of dancing notoriety.
>
> According to the census taken in 1827, there were 264 Hindooee and 500 Mosulmanee professional *Nach* girls in the town, not a very large proportion to the population. There were, however, four times the number of *khanehgee-kusbees*, who do not profess the accomplishments of singing and dancing.[5]

---

[4] See Motichandra [1962] 1985: 46, 89, 145.
[5] Prinsep [1831–3] 1996: 33.

Prinsep spoke prudishly of 'dancing notoriety', dancing fame would have been the more appropriate expression. The city was proud of the beauty of its leading courtesans and of their mastery of the arts.

Bharatendu Harishchandra (1850–1885), acknowledged father of modern Hindi literature, old-style merchant aristocrat and modern-style publicist, who seldom spent a night at home, had confessed that he went to these women in order to acquire cultivation and knowledge of the arts.[6] He was to note their all-pervasive presence in Kashi and the power they exercised on men, and to eulogize them in one of his short plays, *Prem Jogini* (The Yogini of Love; 1874–5), which provided vignettes of the city at its most pious but also at its most raucous.[7] He captioned the scenes, when they were published in book form, as *Kashi ke chayachitra ya do bhale bure fotograf* (reflections of Kashi, or a couple of good and bad photographs). In choosing the word 'photograph' he indicated both the modern character of his undertaking—he was considered a good amateur photographer—as well as the reality of the individual in social situations that the photograph as a medium sought to capture and hold fast. In seeking to ground the reality of city life, he placed the value of these public women at the top of the social spiral and thus of Kashi's claims to fame.

The city as a whole clearly had two sides, the exalted and the seamy. In fact, with the exception of Babu Ramchandra, the central protagonist and his *musahib* (agent) Sudhakar, the characters in the play consisted almost in their entirety of the rogues and charlatans of the city. At least half of the city, as the rogues and charlatans saw it, was overrun by prostitutes of all hues and classes:

[6] Harishchandra is reported to have told a friend, when he was moved to write a poem after the visit to a courtesan: 'It is for this that I cultivate intercourse with them. Tell me, how else could this true motif have been obtained?' For further details, see Dalmia 1997: 128.

[7] The play was published, *Premyogini*, subsequently as *Premjogini,* in three instalments in *Harishchandrachandrika*, the literary journal Harishchandra edited, between August 1874 and April 1875. The text is also accessible in the first volume of his Complete Works, *Granthavali* I (195–230), whence the following quotations.

> *Adhi kashi bhat bhanderia bahman aur sanyasi*
> *adhi kashi randi mundi rand khangi khasi.*[8]
>
> Half of Kashi is run over by bards and bhanderias, brahmins and ascetics.
> The other half with whores, widows with shorn heads, and very special harlots.

But even on the grander map, which offered the more representational face of the city, and which Sudhakar was to go on to offer as the corrective to the seamier version, the courtesans were placed at the pinnacle of the social order. Sudhakar's depiction of the city was mythical and modern at the same time. He waxed eloquent on the beauties of the riverside landscape, the well-laid-out ghats and the high mansions, five to seven storeyed, towering on one side of the river, interspersed with the temples of Gopallal and Bindu Madhav, of Vishwanath and Annapurna. It was a city graced by the presence of other godly beings as well. He eulogized the various rungs of the city's hierarchical order, beginning with the maharaja, who was the religious and cultural head of the city, backed by the civic and military authority of the British commissioner, the collector, and the magistrates. There were many wealthy merchants, there were scholars, the learned in Sanskrit and the servants of Hindi, there were able craftsmen. There were educational institutes and a number of public libraries and monuments. There were the famous ancient ruins of Sarnath. There were people from all parts of the country, and ascetics of the most diverse orders, who in their diversity encapsulated and encompassed all parts of the incipient nation. There was wealth, trade, textiles, handicrafts. The city blossomed and glowed. And finally, as a climax almost:

> The youthful *barabilasini*, courtesans, exotically dressed and ornamented, with fragrant betel leaves in their mouths, sauntering on the royal paths on the flimsiest pretext, whether it is going to the temples, to sing or to roam in parks, in order to dupe and ensnare men, poor, dim-witted men.

[8] *Granthavali*: 209.

What more can I say? Kashi is Kashi. There is not another city like Kashi in the three worlds. You'll believe it when you see it. It is useless to say more.[9]

Kashi was the pinnacle of subcontinental cities, wherein all regions and crafts were represented, and atop this pinnacle were perched the courtesans of the city. This exalted reputation of the women of the city was to continue unabated into the first half of the twentieth century.

When E.B. Havell (1864–1937), the great apologist for the high aesthetic value of Indian fine arts, came to write his two travelogues to highlight the tradition of art and religion in the subcontinent, he not only naturally turned to Banaras, but when doing so could not refrain from mentioning the central role of the courtesans in the culture of the city.[10] He compared the musicians and dancing girls, whom he saw as 'an indispensable institution' in the Hindu social and religious system, to 'the Gandharvas, the mythical musicians of Indra's heaven, who attend the feasts of the gods, and the Apsarases, the voluptuous charmers.' Passing lightly over the matter of the social origin of the dancing girls—he saw them as the unmarried daughters of the Kathaks—he went on to describe their mode of habitation and reputation in the city:

> They live in the quarter known as Dal-ki-mandi, a long street with houses of several storeys, some of them resplendent with silver furniture and crystal chandeliers. Unlike the dancing girls of southern India, they are not attached to any particular temple, or 'married with the god', but at special festivals and religious ceremonies they are engaged to chant the praises of Rama, or to sing Sita's love, in the classic songs of Tulsi Das,

[9] Prinsep [1831–3] 1996: 33.
[10] See Guha-Thakurta 1992: 149–59 and 175–87 for an account of the vast influence exercised by E.B. Havell (Superintendent of the Madras School of Arts in 1884 and later of the Calcutta School of Art), along with Ananda Coomaraswamy, in turning the tide of public opinion in Britain in the cause of Indian 'fine arts'. Havell published *Banaras, the Sacred City: Sketches of Hindu Life and Religion* in 1905.

or the more voluptuous odes which tell of Krishna and his amours. Of secular songs for pleasure parties they have an extensive repertoire, both old and modern. They are often very generous with the wealth they acquire, and in old age, when virtue has become a necessity, spend it freely in works of charity and religion.

Banaras from very ancient times has been famed for these sirens, whose amorous glances, alluring mimic, and pretty shuffling feet have troubled many a Hindu sage.[11]

The best-known courtesans exercised great social power; they played a significant role in most public occasions, as even the most puritanical retrospective accounts are constrained to admit:

Nevertheless, there is no doubt these women musicians and dancers made a substantial contribution to the music centre of Varanasi. Furthermore, on certain occasions, such as the worship of the Ganga, the songs of these women formed an essential part of the rituals.

Fees were taken by tawaifs for performing, excepting in certain religious places and on certain occasions that were attended by commoners. They sang free in the *akhada* of Sadhu Kinaram, in the Vagishwari Temple on the occasion of Saraswati Puja, in front of the Shitala Temple in the month of Chaitra, near Panchaganga Ghat in the month of Kartik, in the *akhada* of Naga Baba near Gai Ghat, near Panchaganga Ghat, near the Kali Temple on the Dashashamedh Ghat; and also on the various Ghats of the Ganga during worship of the river.[12]

When the well-known Hindi writer Amritlal Nagar set out to document the power and presence of the courtesans of North Indian cities after their profession was banned by law in independent India, Ramchandra Varma, one of the many *rasika*s (connoisseurs) he interviewed in Banaras spoke once more of their musical talent and of the importance of their role in the ritual life of the city: 'The assembly that takes place on the Lolark sixth of Kartik is quite famous here. At Baba Kinaram's place, the entire city's courtesans would perform. "Adi Vishveshvar" the older Vishwanath, was visited by

[11] Havell 1905: 86–7.
[12] Medhasananda 2001: 668.

courtesans every Monday. Each year, they held a *mela* there on the day of Gopashtami. That's why the trendy youth of the day called Adi Visheshvar "randhibaz Mahadev" (whore-mongering Shiva).'[13]

New poetic compositions gained wide circulation if they were taken up and performed by courtesans. A vital nerve thus connected the performing arts with literary composition and its informed appreciation and circulation. The connection would continue to be operative well beyond the era of late-nineteenth-century moderns such as Bharatendu. It is explicitly evoked in Premchand's novel by Kunwar Aniruddh Singh, a powerful Hindu zamindar involved in the controversy surrounding the eviction of the courtesans from their quarters in the centre of the city. Aniruddh Singh sees the paucity of literary works in modern Hindi as being directly linked to the decline of Indian musical culture. *Navin* (new) Hindi Literature could at most lay claim to a couple of plays by Harishchandra and to the popular novel *Chandrakanta*;[14] for the rest, there were translations from the English—made not even directly but via Bengali and Marathi. There was a great dearth of novels. This meagre production was the direct result of the decline of the musical tradition and of the artistic sensibility which was coupled with it:

> Yes, it's true, I like our own sitar. I start feeling nauseous when I hear the harmonium or the piano. These English instruments have destroyed our music, which is barely discussed today. And if there were something left to be destroyed, theatre has come forward to complete the task. Anyone you chance to meet goes on and on about the *ghazal* and *quawali*. In a bit, our music will disappear altogether, like archery. Music is what generates pure thoughts. With music gone, we are devoid of such thinking, and the worst impact of this loss is on literature. How sad it is for a country in which a work as invaluable as the *Ramayana* was created, where a work

---

[13] Nagar 1994: 154.

[14] Written by Devakinandan Khatri (1861–1913), the novel (1888), a modified version of the Urdu *tilasm* (thriller), proved an all-time bestseller, inspiring Khatri to write several follow-ups, amongst them the eleven-part *Chandrakanta Santiti* (The Progeny of Chandrakanta).

as delightful as the *Sursagar* was created, to take recourse to translation even for the simplest novels . . .[15]

But the indigenous music which was now being invoked as essential to the survival of the arts, performative as well as literary, had begun to change its contours and context. Aniruddh Singh speaks of Tulsidas' Avadhi *Ramayana* and the Brajbhasha devotional verse of Surdas in connection with the musical tradition he wished to see regenerated. Clearly, in being projected as national heritage, music was being entirely severed from its original performers in the bazaar of beauty. It was Hindu, middle class, and respectable, as indeed was the new novel in Hindi, and it was as such that it was sought to be situated within the city, which was also losing some of its mythical status. The new voices in the city were seeking to create an image of Kashi far removed from the one which was socially and ritually centred around the courtesans. In the public disputes about the location of the courtesans, the city's ill repute was seen as reflected in the sad fate of the nation, of its music, and of the Hindu woman. For, provocatively enough, Premchand had chosen to cast Suman as a Brahmin woman who had deserted her husband, rather than as a Muslim, and at least nominally single. Suman's move to the bazaar of beauty challenged the status of Hindu marriage as an inviolate social institution, and in portraying the psychological motivation of her move with more than a measure of sympathy the author seemed, at the very least, to be also questioning its claims to self-evident sanctity.

WIFE AND COURTESAN IN THE MODERNIZING CITY

Suman's father had been a district Sub-Inspector of Police who had brought up his two daughters to expect the best in life. He had indulged them by buying them all manner of beautiful clothes and expensive baubles and arranged for them to receive some education from a Christian lady who tutored them at home. But he had laid

[15] Premchand 2006: 135.

no money aside for the considerable sum he would be expected to expend as their dowry, and various disasters overtook the family when it came to finding a suitable match for them. Suman's mother was finally able to marry her off with little expenditure to an elderly bridegroom, relatively poor but with high standing within her own caste group.

Confined within the narrow walls of her new home in the city and initially humoured and pampered by her husband Gajadhar, Suman managed to lead an exemplary life as a dutiful housewife for the first two years of her marriage. But she was bored and frustrated at the same time and just opposite her lived the plump Bholi, luxuriating in the comfort of her well-lit and well-aired home and visited nightly by the town gentry. Bholi would beckon to her to come over, though Gajadhar reacted with disapproval and censure when she finally succumbed to the temptation to go over to her house. Money did not make the men who visited Bholi great by any estimation, he explained. In the arrogance of their being, the rich chose to ignore religion but Bholi was not purified by their coming, and he quickly forbade Suman to visit her. Suman then tried to become pious in her ways. She bathed daily in the holy river; she recited the Tulsi *Ramayana* to the women of the neighbourhood. If this did not bring peace to her soul, it gave her the satisfaction of being morally more elevated than the likes of Bholi. On the occasion of Ramnavami, the celebration of the birthday of Rama, Suman visited a great temple in the company of her friends. The temple was beautifully decorated; it glittered with electric lighting and so crowded was it that there was no space in its overflowing courtyard even for the proverbially tiny sesame seed to be accommodated in it. The sound of sweet music wafted in the air and her neighbour Bholi sat at the centre of all this festivity, each gesture she made observed eagerly by the most prominent citizens of the city, the rich, the learned, and the pious, many of whom she had seen at the riverfront. Suman stood there as if struck by a thunderbolt, her pride shattered to bits. Not only did wealth bow at Bholi's feet, even religion sought her favour: 'The very prostitute whom I wanted to humble with my pious ways is the recipient of esteem and honour in this assembly of great men, in this pure abode of the lord, while I find not even standing space.'[16]

Suman abandons religion thereafter. Gajadhar's earnest arguments regarding the ultimate worthlessness of the men who crowd around Bholi fail to convince her. The city's public spaces are reserved for public women, not for poorly dressed creatures like her—a second incident brings this home to her with painful clarity. She has accompanied her friends to Beni Bagh, which houses a small zoo and an aviary. Her peace is rudely shattered when she attempts to sit for a moment on a bench. The park watchman immediately unseats her. Just then, two finely dressed women arrive, one of them her neighbour Bholi. The watchman not only seats them on the bench, he offers them a hastily plucked bouquet of flowers. Once they depart, Suman upbraids him for his unseemly behaviour. His words sting her to the quick: 'Do you aspire to be their equal?'[17] He manhandles her when she tries to sit on the bench again. She is rescued by a well-to-do couple passing by in their carriage. The home of her benefactors, the lawyer Pandit Padam Singh and Subhadra, his cultivated wife, becomes a refuge for her.

But not for long. Padam Singh is elected a member of the powerful Municipal Board of the city and to celebrate the event he allows himself, one evening, to be persuaded to hold a *mujra* (song and dance performance). It is here that the next key event in Suman's city life takes place. The focalization of the scene is entirely through Suman. From behind the curtain, she and Subhadra watch Bholi Bai perform. Bholi is neither as pretty as Suman, nor does she sing particularly well. Suman has a good ear and a quick memory. She would not need more than a month to learn to sing better than Bholi. She can also cast sidelong glances and knows how to smile demurely:

> Suman sat there for a long time, trying to disentangle cause from effect. Finally she came to a conclusion: Bholi is independent while I'm shackled.

[16] Premchand 1996: 27.
[17] Ibid.: 30.

Her warehouse (*dukan*) is open and sees a rush of clients, mine is shut, so no one stands and waits. She isn't bothered by barking dogs; I'm scared of social censure. She isn't in purdah, while I am. She chirps freely as she hops from branch to branch, I cling to just one. It is shame, the fear of ridicule, which makes me the servant of another.[18]

Suman's deeply reflexive and dry conclusions, her estimation of marriage as a form of prostitution with a single client, can be regarded as no other than revolutionary for her times. Wives are easily acquired and easily disregarded. Social esteem is reserved for the very public women each married man would be quick to condemn at home. Men are fickle, easily swayed, and when it comes to taking quick, bold action to retrieve a situation, are usually found to be missing. If they come to the rescue at all, it is usually after the event.

Suman is beautiful and talented; she aspires to be free, to be admired and respected, to live in luxury, to be rid of her tyrant. The *mujra* at Padam Singh's house gets over very late. By the time she reaches home it is well past midnight. Gajadhar refuses to let her in, he tells her she has been afflicted by the water of the city (*shahar ka pani*). His insane jealousy, her own extreme dissatisfaction and her pride lead to a violent exchange between the two which results in her being barred further entry into her own house. Like Nora in Ibsen's *The Doll's House*, Suman picks up her suitcase and departs into an unknown and uncertain future. Is this a feature of the modern woman, her independence, in spite of the fear of it?

Initially, she seeks refuge with Padam Singh and his wife but her stay at their house is painfully brief. Padam Singh fears for his reputation once word about her putative relationship with him begins to spread in the bazaar. Only Bholi welcomes her warmly and takes her in. Bathed with perfumed soap, expensively clad, Suman views herself in the mirror and is struck by the radiance and beauty of her own person. It does not take her long to learn how to sing, for, as Bholi tells her, there is no need to labour at *dhrupads* and *tillanas* any more, nowadays a few catchy ghazals, some *thumris*, and a couple of

[18] Ibid.: 34–5.

popular theatre tunes can do the trick. Suman is an instant hit. Word of her beauty and talent spreads quickly, for Dal Mandi, the bazaar of beauty, thrives on scandal and sensation. Sadan Singh, young nephew of none other than Padam Singh, seduced by the wares of Dal Mandi, is just one of the many ardent suitors who linger at her door. And Suman cannot help being gratified by his wooing.

But the winds of change, of modernity, are also blowing in the holy city: theosophy, Arya Samaj, new education, and public lectures have all made an impact. If the narrative sets out to explicitly affirm the need for social reform, it also makes clear that at times it has a very blunt edge—when it is not in fact a double-edged sword. For, once again, the author works with a dual perspective. We are introduced to Vitthaldas, intrepid social reformer and zealous missionary in the cause of the public weal. Vitthaldas' endeavours are viewed with some scepticism and not a little irony by the author. We find, as so often in Premchand's work, that the speech surrounding the characters creates 'highly particularized character zones. These zones are formed from the fragments of character speech, from various forms for hidden transmission of someone else's word, from scattered sayings belonging to someone else's speech, from those invasions into authorial speech of others' expressive indicators (ellipses, questions, exclamations). Such a character zone is the field of action for a character's voice, encroaching in one way or another upon the author's voice.'[19] We find reflected in the author's words of introduction not only Vitthaldas' own estimation of his worth, but also a suggestion of the response of his sorely tried wife and the gratitude almost forced out of the recipients of his relentless service:

> Babu Vitthaldas was the life and soul of most civic-minded institutions in the city. Nothing could ever get done without him being in the middle of it. This personification of manly vigour (*purushartha*) bore his heavy burden with fortitude, never losing heart. He had no time for meals, found no leisure time to sit at home, his wife complained of his lack of

---

[19] Bakhtin 1981: 316.

affection. In his obsession to serve the nation (*jati*), Vitthaldas had forgotten to look out for his own happiness and self-interest. He wandered about with single-minded intent, raising funds for orphanages, arranging tuition fees for poor students. Each time a calamity befell the nation, he brimmed over with love of the country. In times of famine he was to be found going from village to village carrying a load of flour on his head. People were bewildered by the extent of his selflessness during cholera and plague epidemics. Despite the Ganga being in spate recently, he did not look to his house for days on end: he had donated his entire wealth to the nation, yet showed not a trace of pride in having done so. He had not had much of an education, his oratory was not above ordinary, his thinking lacked maturity and far sight. He was neither particularly skilled as a manoeuvrer, nor clever, nor wise. His patriotism was his great virtue; it won him respect among all and sundry in the city.[20]

Vitthaldas inspires grudging respect, for he rushes in where angels fear to tread. He finds simple remedies, he eradicates social ills, even if the people he set out to help could themselves be eradicated in the process. He is not one to wallow in doubt. He makes up his mind to rescue Suman, though it is he who had spread word in the bazaar about Padam Singh's putative relationship with her in the brief period she stayed at his house. He knocks at her door and takes her to task immediately. The dialogue which ensues is a classic case of two people talking well past each other, the one hell-bent on social reform, the other equally relentless in her dry and caustic analysis of the social processes of which she herself has been the victim:

> Vitthaldas: Now that our greatly revered Brahman ladies are treading the primrose path of dalliance, there can be no stopping our decline. Suman, you're responsible for the Hindu *jati* having to lower its head.
>
> Suman answered earnestly: *You* may think so, no one else does. A few gentlemen have just left after listening to the *mujra*. They were all Hindus, none of them seemed to have lowered heads. They seemed glad that I'm here. Besides, I'm not the only Brahmani in the Mandi; I could name a couple of others of very high families straight off whose kinfolk

[20] Premchand 1996: 62.

were unwilling to take care of them; they came here from a sense of helplessness. If the Hindu *jati* isn't in the least ashamed of itself, how long are frail women like us going to continue protecting it?[21]

Vitthaldas responds by admitting that the Hindu *jati* has indeed fallen very low. But its moral repute (*maryada*) had always been held aloft by Hindu women. It was their truth and stainless reputation which saved it from further decline. It was to protect Hindus that lakhs of women burnt themselves to ashes in crackling flames. They chose to bear pain themselves in order to protect others. And if ordinary women did not shrink from doing so, the expectations from Brahmin women were higher still. It was only the lower-caste woman who refused to bear up to suffering of any kind, who ran to her natal home if she took offence at her husband's behaviour. And if she did not get along even there, she ran off to a brothel. He ends in ringing tones: 'Suman, you have lowered the head not only of the Brahman *jati* but of the entire Hindu *jati*.'[22] Suman has to correct him repeatedly when he insists that people don't respect her. The highest in the city bow at her feet. There is not one in the city who does not go wild with delight when she deigns to cast a gracious look at him. But Suman is also on the defensive, Vitthaldas' words have stung her to the quick. She had resolved, she tells him, that she will dance and sing but have no sexual contact with the men who surround her.[23] Vitthaldas, never at a loss for remedies, recommends work at home,

---

[21] Ibid.

[22] Ibid.: 63.

[23] Premchand thus finds a route to preserve a measure of respectability for Suman; she is the courtesan who manages to remain physically unscathed by the profession she practices. This is the escape route also taken by Bhagvaticharan Verma (born 1913) in his ever-green novel *Chitralekha* (1934), which is set in the Gupta period and also focuses on a Brahmin woman, this time a young widow, who rises to fame as a dancer in the city of Pataliputra.

This sexual abstinence allows for a reading of Suman's character as an 'angelic victim' and makes for a peculiar kind of relationship to the society which has victimized her. Alok Rai has spoken of 'the cult of the angelic victim. This fecund genre, particularly in writings dealing with the question

cottage industry, to her. But even he can respond only evasively to Suman's query: 'Does a single lover of the Hindu *jati* exist anywhere willing to spend fifty rupees a month on my upkeep?'[24]

Vitthaldas shows little understanding of the predicament in which Suman finds herself; he is more occupied with her position as a symbol of respectable Hindu womanhood. As a once-married Brahmin woman she has to be extracted from the moral filth in which she finds herself mired. When he offers to find a place for her in a home for widows, she is extremely sceptical about the welcome she will receive there. She asks: is she expected to give up her life of relative security and comfort only to be regarded as a barely tolerated object of charity in a pleasureless abode? But Vitthaldas has yet larger goals in mind. He wants to remove prostitution from public places and do away with *mujra* entirely, abolish the social custom of song and dance on festive occasions.

In focalizing primarily through Suman, on the one hand, and Sadan Singh and Padam Singh on the other, the author seems to be propelling the reader to view the action through at least three perspectives which seem diametrically opposed to one another and often at odds with the professed auctorial stance. Sadan seeks to situate himself in the city as a man of some affluence and influence. He needs financial resources in order to woo Suman and manoeuvres to come by them. Later he goes through a spell of enthusiasm for social reform, and we share his reflections. But he finds short cuts and takes

---

of women, may be considered a sub-set of the cult of the ennobled poor. Here also the game consists of representing the woman-victim as being simultaneously damaged and undamaged, wronged but essentially unharmed, both needing salvation and deserving of it. The fact that such representations are necessarily ambiguous in the fashion just indicated, interacts curiously with the confusion regarding the proper relation between wrongs and rights. The consequence is a muddled valorization of victimhood which, curiously, works to soften and make manageable the critique of victimizing societies and institutions.' Alok Rai in Premchand [1927] 1999: 201.

[24] Premchand 1996: 65.

morally dubious decisions, finding a measure of stability only at the end. Padam Singh sees through the falsity of many social situations but seldom finds the courage to act boldly when directly challenged to do so. Once again we are privy to his thought processes. His marriage, troubled as it is, comes nearest to representing marital bliss, and his social reform endeavour comes nearest to being well reasoned and reflected upon. But we see him falter in his actions and seek shelter behind self-justification. If the author approves of marriage as a social institution, if he expressly supports social reform, in the action of its proponents we see these aims questioned if not contradicted. Of the three, the most empathetically portrayed character is that of Suman, and it is her speech that is psychologically more persuasive as also more convincing in its analysis of social ills, and of the resolutions she herself is compelled to seek. Suman's reasoned reflection, her spirited exchange with Gajadhar and her decision to accept Bholi's offer rather than seek reconciliation with her husband through the mediation of Subhadra, seem entirely comprehensible, given her particular situation. It is then the speech which surrounds Suman which most consistently refracts professed authorial intention.[25]

Suman's reflections bring home to the reader that marriage is a commercial transaction, particularly when negotiated on the basis of dowry. It is not unlike prostitution, which deals more blatantly with the financial exchange involved in buying sexual and other services. Society officially sanctions marriage while virtually imprisoning the woman within what it largely entails—a cheerless domestic servitude.

---

[25] As Bakhtin has shown: 'The language used by characters in the novel, how they speak, is verbally and semantically autonomous; each character's speech possesses it own belief system, since each is the speech of another in another's language; thus it may also refract authorial intentions and consequently may to a certain degree constitute a second language for the author. Moreover the character speech almost always influences authorial character speech (and sometimes powerfully so), sprinkling it with another's words (that is, the speech of a character perceived as the concealed speech of another) and in this way introducing into it stratification and speech diversity.' Bakhtin 1981: 3–4.

It does not explicitly sanction prostitution yet elevates the woman who is sufficiently adept, if she possesses the required talent and beauty, to a position of glamour and relative autonomy, celebrating her charms in lavish public displays. Suman makes a radical statement when speaking of both arrangements, the ones in which she and Bholi, respectively, find themselves, in terms of a *dukan* (shop; warehouse). In what ways is the one institution morally more elevated than the other? The social conduct of the men who patronize the warehouse contradicts their public stand on the issue.

Then there is the vexed issue of social reform which sets out to change the older social order, elitist and decadent, while attempting to put in its place a more middle-class morality, itself often flawed and feelingless. Those who advocate social reform, in self-promotion or bouts of self-remorse, seem more concerned with their own public and private ends than with the fate of individuals such as Suman, who are caught in these winds of change and buffeted about, compelled to believe in a public cause rather than in their own hard-won comfort and sense of well-being. The Hindu *jati* Vitthaldas speaks of seems to be a caricature of its own projected image and the social reform being called for no more than just another measure of social hypocrisy. Out and out social reformers such as Vitthaldas are often callous and unfeeling; those such as Padam Singh are narcissistic and noble in turn. The author seems to regard them with some aversion and suspicion, though his ostensible sympathies are with the cause they represent.

The rhetoric of social reform, as the author proceeds to show us, seems particularly amenable to misuse for communal purposes. Though Suman is Hindu, many of the courtesans are Muslim and the leading members of Hindu society are not slow to attribute the moral responsibility for the evils of this profession on Muslim culture. The clientele is mixed, but most shops around the Chauk are Hindu-owned, and it is the Hindu merchants who stand to suffer the greatest financial loss if the women are made to shift to another part of town. Could this be a ploy of the Muslim faction in the Municipal

Board to use this opportunity to deal a blow to the Hindus? The communalization of the debate seems inevitable.

DAL MANDI, SOCIAL REFORM, AND THE COMMUNALIZATION OF THE MUNICIPALITY

As discussed in the Introduction, most North Indian cities underwent radical structural transformation in the years after the 1857 Uprising. Not only was there a major reshuffling of social hierarchies, space itself was differently allocated and distributed. At the centre of most cities of any size or splendour was the Chauk—the town square—and somewhere near it if not located right there, were the courtesans of the city, the *tawaifs* or *bais*. In the cleansing operations which followed in cities such as Lucknow and Delhi, whole *mohallas* were uprooted, though in spite of widespread damage and destruction the famous Chowk in Lucknow was saved, and with it its equally renowned courtesans, who survived the loss of their old clientele.[26] In most cities, they were driven out finally only after 1956.[27]

The civic administration of the city also underwent rapid change after 1857. The Acts of the preceding decades regarding city government had called upon the inhabitants to take the initiative to restore civic order and administer it, for the system of *mohalla* or neighbourhood control and administration had begun to dissolve in the early decades of the nineteenth century. But these pre-1857 measures to put a civic government in place had been desultory and half-hearted. However, once the Army Sanitary Commission (1861) painted a dismal picture of the hygiene observed in Indian towns, further directives were issued to look after water supply, lighting, and sanitation under a more comprehensive policy laid down by the

---

[26] See Oldenburg 1984 for an account of the changes in the city landscape of Lucknow, following the violence perpetrated by the British in the wake of the 1857 Uprising, particularly the havoc wrought in the lives of the courtesans.

[27] Amritlal Nagar has recorded the reactions of the courtesans of Lucknow to this final ousting from the city and their profession: Nagar 1994.

Government of India. Over 1864–8 three further acts were passed, for Lucknow in 1864, Punjab in 1867, and the North West Provinces in 1868. The municipal administrative body was no longer to be voluntary, it was henceforth to be a nominated body, though still expected to cater primarily to the needs and interests of the British. If the nominated members consisted largely of prominent citizens such as bankers, merchants, and members of the aristocracy who had remained loyal in 1857—willy-nilly it also ended up including the new professionals.[28] The North West Provinces Act IV of 1868 provided municipal committees with one-third 'official' or nominated members and two-thirds elected members. According to this Act, the District Magistrate was to be president of the municipality. Members of the Council were to be appointed on the recommendation of the District Magistrate. Clearly, there was little effort made to extend the system of popular election. Municipal committees were thus highly centralized and bureaucratic. Powerful administrators, such as Sir Charles Wood and Sir Henry Maine, continued to advocate nomination rather than election of non-official members. According to them, respectable Indians did not wish to have to choose those who were to rule over them; they preferred to avoid contest. However, Lord Ripon's government issued a resolution in 1882 advocating election, but the number of official members was not to exceed one-third of the total. The North West Provinces and Oudh Municipalities Act of 1883 further provided that official members be restricted to one-fourth of the total membership. Boards were empowered to elect their chairman and vice-chairman, but the Commissioner or the District Magistrate continued to be invested with the power of control over the municipal body as a whole. Under the Acts of 1883 and a further Act of 1900, the legislative and executive functions were vested in the Board which was now entirely responsible for the administration

[28] See the pioneering study by Narayani Gupta (1981) for the changes brought about by the British in the imperial city of Delhi, once they took charge. On the politics of the municipal boards they created, see ibid.: 115–22 and 213–16.

of the city, though still under the control of the Commissioner or District Magistrate, as before. The United Provinces Municipalities Act No. 11 was passed to give effect to the reforms recommended by the Royal Commission on Decentralisation (1909) and the Resolution of Government of India (1915). Accordingly, the number of non-official members was increased and a non-official chairman appointed in every council. The details of the administration were delegated to a number of sub-committees. In larger municipalities, a new post of Executive Officer was created; he was appointed by the Board, subject to the prior approval of the state government. However, the state government and the district magistrate continued to control, dissolve, or supersede a municipal board. A power tussle was almost pre-programmed. 'The attraction for chairmanship to the intelligentsia was its executive power and the bureaucracy was unwilling to be divested of the influence of the board chairmanship.'[29] It is necessary to recall this long history of power constitution within the city and the tussles it involved in order to get some idea of the privilege it was to be nominated or elected a Board member. The stakes could not but be high.

Once the Municipalities Act of 1916 came into force, the non-official members jostled for power amongst themselves. As the *East India Progress and Condition of India During 1917–1918* report put it:

> A review of the whole subject of local self-government in India at the present moment would seem to indicate that in the immediate future important developments may be expected. Hitherto the control which government exercised over municipalities and district boards, while unquestionably preventing the commission of serious errors arising from inexperience, has done much to prevent the growth of a real feeling of civic responsibility.[30]

---

[29] This account of the evolution of municipal government of cities is based on the first chapter, 'Historical Perspective of Urban Local Government in India', in Nanda 1998. The citation is from p. 15. This Municipalities Act of 1916 continues to govern Uttar Pradesh even today.

[30] *East India Progress* 1918: 185.

But this 'real feeling of civic responsibility' was a euphemism for power long withheld and now allocated and distributed to factions which were known to be oppositional. The Report chided the municipal boards for the prevalence of fissures, though they had almost certainly also been fostered by the imperial government. It complained of the 'spirit of faction' which prevailed in several boards, and admitted—surely not without a smirk—that the 'maintenance of a double record of proceedings was not unknown.'

Banaras in the second decade of the twentieth century was also undergoing these changes, which in turn was restructuring the very social fabric of the city. Hindus and Muslims saw themselves as having to band together in their religion-based groups in order to defend what they saw as their common interest. But the views held by the individual members of the respective groups within each faction were anything but uniform. The merchants differed from the landed gentry in the interests they represented, while the new professionals, who came into more contact with modernizing trends, were likely to be those most earnest about social reform. However, even they could ill afford to ignore group loyalties and were thus automatically sucked

Illus. 6: Town Hall, Banaras

into the respective Hindu and Muslim factions. What kind of changes did the different social strata desire and with what rationale? As Alok Rai puts it, '(t)he early 1900s were a time of considerable ideological ferment in India. A sort of damaged modernity seemed available under colonial aegis, a modernity at once embryonic and addled.'[31]

Premchand followed these developments with much interest. In a remarkable fictional representation of these debates and the vested interests which sought to control city spaces for financial and social ends, he showed in precise detail how, in the matter of the displacement of the courtesans, communalism itself was a construct, a public face which masked commercial and political agendas and sought validation through it.[32] The professed concern for the welfare of the courtesans was an issue which was bandied about in a power battle between the communalized Hindu and Muslim factions in the Municipal Board in a manner which made the courtesans seem more like the victims of social reform than its beneficiaries.

If Vitthaldas' indefatigable efforts did not galvanize people into action, once Padam Singh took up the challenge, the movement to save the courtesans while banishing them from the city centre gathered unexpected momentum. Padam Singh was the son of a landowning family and a lawyer of repute; he was part of the old gentry, but also one of the new professionals, liberal in his views in spite of the *mujra* he had permitted to be held in his house. Propelled ever forward by his guilty conscience, he realized that he had allowed Suman to be cast out of his house too hastily and brought the matter of the courtesans to the attention of the Municipal Board.

---

[31] Alok Rai in Premchand [1927] 1999: 197.

[32] The move to oust the courtesans from the centre of the city was apparently a real consideration at the time, though it was never effected. Premchand's is therefore a fictional account, which Professor Anand Krishna attributes to his Arya Samaj indoctrination (personal interview, 7 January 2003). The famous courtesans of Banaras continued to operate in Dal Mandi till well into the early 1950s. According to Professor Anand Krishna, assembly (*majlis*) used to be held in Girija Bai's *kotha*, which was situated just opposite Chitra cinema hall near the Chauk.

Illus. 7: Portrait of a Courtesan, Gelatin Silver Print, *c.* 1890–1910, by an unknown photographer

The municipality officials had hesitated all along to bring up the matter, for they knew that they would be stirring a hornet's nest:

> They had long thought, Who knows what tumult will ensue in the city by even just raising the issue. There was no dearth of *ra'is*, government officials, and merchants with a connection to this love-market (*mandi*). One was a client, another a connoisseur (of the arts), who'd take the risk of antagonizing them? The municipality officials were puppets in their hands.[33]

[33] Premchand 2006: 99.

Premchand records the Municipal Board debates on the issue of the courtesans and the cleansing of the city centre with some earnestness and some outright satire. Once again, the individual members of the Board, introduced individually within their own factions, the Hindu and the Muslim, enter the stage under the spotlight of slanted speech which forms veritable character zones, integrating the speech of the characters themselves in invisible quotation marks, as also the public appraisal of them. The Board has eighteen members, eight Muslims and ten Hindus, the majority well educated. Within each camp there are social reform enthusiasts but also dissidents who take shelter behind communal verbiage, for entirely different ends, as we shall see.

The interest groups represented in the Muslim and Hindu camps are merchants and shopkeepers, religious leaders, landowners (zamindars), retired civil servants, and the new professionals. By and large, both Hindu and Muslim members are equally unwilling to lose the income the courtesans generate for them, and at any rate do not wish to seal off their own source of pleasure and enjoyment. However, they choose their words carefully, for the new professionals give the tone, and all subscribe to it publicly.

The deliberations of the Muslim camp are presented first. Haji Hashim Sahib exercises a great deal of influence on the populace and is generally considered the leader of the Muslims. He is against the removal of the prostitutes. Maulana Teg Ali is the Vali of the Imam Bara. Munshi Abulwafa is the owner of a perfume and oil factory. He owns a chain of oil and perfume stores in several big cities across North India. Munshi Abdul Latif is a big landowner, an absentee landlord who resides in the city. He loves poetry and is considered a good poet himself. Shakir Beg and Sharif Hasan are lawyers. They have very progressive social views. Saiyyid Shafakat Ali is a pensioned Deputy Collector and Khan Sahib Shohrat Khan is a famous hakim. These last two stay away from meetings and assemblies, but they do not lack for generosity and deep reflection. Both are religiously inclined. They command great respect in society.

Haji Hashim speaks of the matter as a communal challenge. He asks: Are you aware of this new ruse employed by our brothers of the same native land?[34] And Abulwafa, the oil- and perfume-factory owner, pointing out that ninety per cent of the *tawaifs* are Muslim, proclaims that this is an attempt by Hindus to reduce the number of Muslims in the city. The Hindus are out to claim as large a number of the populace as they can, including the Doms.

The two gentlemen who generally stay away from meetings are the most sweeping in their condemnation. Saiyyid Shafakat Ali, the pensioned Deputy Collector, wants the prostitutes to be removed altogether from the city. They are contagious; they spread immorality around them. Hakim Shohrat Khan goes a step further and wants to remove them altogether from Hindustan. They are black serpents with poison in their eyes. He views it as a matter of great misfortune that most *tawaifs* call themselves Muslims.

The new professionals are more charitable. Sharif Hasan, the lawyer, says he sees no harm in the fact that they call themselves Muslims. The problem is that no one tries to help them rectify their ways. Once a woman falls, Islam becomes indifferent to her. Surely these women also repent of their ways, but they have to continue in their profession because they know no better and because they have to consider the future of their children. If grooms could be found for their daughters, the situation would improve considerably. He does not want to reject the suggestion on a political basis, that is, merely because it comes from the Hindus. When Teg Ali, the Vali of the Imam Bara, taunts him, Shakir Beg, the other lawyer, asks people to calm down and offers instead a more moderate suggestion. The *tawaifs* should be removed from the centre to some corner of the city.

[34] As Harish Trivedi points out in his review of the English translation of the Urdu version of the novel (2004), Haji Hashim uses the term *biradaran-e-vatan* (brothers of the same native land) when speaking of the Hindus, and the more intimate *biradaran-e-millat* (brothers in religious faith) when addressing his Muslim compatriots.

The landowning gentry are not unlike the merchants in their aversion to this change, though their reasons are very different. Thus Abdul Latif, a zamindar, does not want to let go of the pleasure of the courtesans' cultivated company. His views are echoed by his Hindu counterpart. He speaks in jest but means it seriously: there are all kinds of shops in the Chauk—for soaps, leather, oil, textiles, pots and pans—so why not the warehouse of beauty? This kind of levity provokes sharp responses. Haji Hashim persists in regarding it as a Hindu–Muslim matter and has no hesitation in proclaiming that he will resist it precisely because it comes from the Hindus. Abulwafa, a factory owner, agrees, for the merchants on both sides are in any case against the move. But they present their arguments in communal terms.

Saiyyid Shafakat Ali, the pensioned Deputy Collector, is a genuine social reformer. He says that if the Hindus are doing something that will be of advantage to all, he has no hesitation joining them. He is against opposition for opposition's sake. There is no conclusive agreement on the matter and the assembly disperses.

Though Hindus and Muslims regard themselves and each other as homogeneous groups, they are actually split into different interest groups with coinciding demands that undercut the religious division. The Hindu camp in its agreements and disagreements presents thus almost a mirror image of its Muslim counterpart. The financially and socially most powerful are against the move. The financial losses the Hindu merchants incur will be regarded as a political victory for the Muslim group. Seth Balbhadra Das, a wealthy merchant, is Chairman of the Board. Lala Chimanlal and Dinanath Tiwari are also important leaders of the merchant community, while Lala Bhagat Ram is a contractor. Seth Balbhadra Das and Chimanlal own most of the stores in the Chauk, Dinanath most of the real estate in Dal Mandi. Lala Bhagat Ram's transactions are almost entirely dependent on Dinanath. These four men are decidedly against the removal of the courtesans from the centre of the city.

Only the four professionals are clearly for the removal of the prostitutes from Dal Mandi: the two lawyers, Pandit Padam Singh and

Rustam Bhai; and two others in new professions: Ramesh Datt, college professor and theosophist; and Prabhakar Rao, editor of the daily *Jagat*. Vitthaldas is not a member of the Municipal Board.

The vice chairman of the Board is Dr Shyamacharan, a medical practitioner, and ostensibly the most Anglicized of the group. He fears official disapproval. He wavers in his decision, preferring to shift responsibility to the larger Municipal Council. And finally, there is Kunwar Aniruddha Bahadur Singh, the biggest zamindar in the district. He is liberal in his views, he knows the best of both cultures, Surdas and Mozart, but is reluctant to give up the old-style pleasures of the cultivated. Both sides hope to win over Dr Shyamacharan and Kunwar Sahib, for victory or defeat seems to depend on them.

Since Padam Singh, the prime mover in the game, is still away at the wedding of Shanta and Sadan Singh (which will not take place once it is discovered that Shanta is Suman's sister), Seth Balbhadra Das calls a meeting to his *susajjit baradari* (ornamental reception rooms). Prabhakar Rao is known to be a fanatic opponent of the Muslims, so Balbhadra Das hopes to win him over by giving the debate a communal twist.

Dinanath Tiwari, owner of most of the real estate in Dal Mandi, begins the debate in words similar to Haji Hashim's: 'Our Muslim brothers have shown great generosity in this matter. They are operating on the principle of killing two birds with one stone. On the one hand they hope to acquire a good reputation through social reform, on the other they have found a pretext to damage Hindus. How can they lose such a good opportunity to gain a good name?'

Chimanlal, who owns most of the stores in Chauk, says with a straight face:

> I have no dealings with politics, nor do I go anywhere near it. But I have not the least hesitation in saying that our Muslim brothers have our necks in a vice-like grip. Most of the real estate in Dalmandi and the Chauk belongs to Hindus. If the Municipal Board accepts this, the Hindus will be wiped out. If one wants to learn how to hurt on the sly, one need only look at the Muslims . . . Sadly, some of our Hindu brothers have become

puppets in their hands. They seem to have no idea of the harm they will do their own *jati* with this ill-founded enthusiasm.[35]

Prabhakar Rao knows he is being trapped by this logic.

He looked helplessly towards Rustam Bhai, asking to be saved. Rustam Bhai was a fearless and clear-speaking man. He stood up to answer Chiman Lal. 'It grieves me to see you people twist a social matter to give it the appearance of a Hindu–Muslim conflict . . . It can bring profit to some Hindu merchants to riddle it with conflict, but it is difficult to estimate the harm it does to the cause of the community. There is little doubt that if the proposal is accepted, Hindu merchants will suffer the greater loss, but surely there will be repercussions on the Muslims too. There is no shortage of Muslim shops in Chauk and Dalmandi. We should not, moved by the spirit of dispute and opposition, suspect the integrity of our Muslim brothers. They are acting in the common interest; it is another matter if this is causing Hindus even greater losses thereby. If you ask me, even were Muslims to suffer the greater loss, they would decide similarly. If you agree truly that the proposal has been made with a view to the reform of an evil social custom, there should be no hesitation accepting it, whatever the financial loss. Money should play no part when it comes to social conduct.[36]

Prabhakar Rao is much reassured by this clear analysis of the matter. It transcends the communal. The issue is to be decided on moral and social grounds. One takes losses in one's stride, if one is to act for the welfare of the populace at large. He gives the example of the loss the government agreed to face in view of the moral rectitude of giving up the opium trade with China. This seems to be explicit social satire. Kunwar Aniruddha Singh, the leading zamindar of the region, points out dryly: 'Sir, you remain engrossed in the editorial work of your journal. When do you find the time for the pleasures of life? But we, who are free of such anxieties, need some amusement . . . Today, you bring this proposal for ousting the prostitutes of the city, tomorrow

---

[35] Premchand 2006: 117.
[36] Ibid.

you will say no one within the municipal district should dance, sing, perform *mujra* without permission: it will become impossible for us to live.'[37] When Prabhakar Rao suggests that he take up reading as a pastime, Kunwar Sahib answers with obvious pleasure: 'We are forbidden to read.' He knows the dance steps of France and Spain; he can play so well on the piano that he might put Mozart himself to shame, he has full knowledge of English social custom. He knows when to don a sola hat and when the turban. He also reads books, he has cupboards full of them but sees no need to remain glued to them. He also seeks other refined pleasures of the senses. 'We will be wiped out if this proposal of yours comes through.' Dr Shyamacharan, the other undecided member, remains evasive in his response. He first wants to put these questions in the Legislative Council.

Now follows the delicious social comedy. Seth Balbhadra Das is convinced of victory, he expects the proposal to be rejected.

> Now he could afford to remain impartial, which was the prerogative of the Chairman. He analysed the proposal in a weighty speech. He said: 'I do not believe in social upheaval. It is my belief that a society which needs change takes care of it (naturally, in the course of things). Foreign travel, caste difference, the useless restrictions on commensality, all bow their heads when faced with the changes wrought by time. I want to let society operate freely in such matters. Once there is complete consensus that people do not want to see prostitutes in the Chauk, what power in the world can remain deaf to it?'[38]

In conclusion, Sethji speaks in very moving tones:

> We are very proud of our music. Even those acquainted with the music of France and Italy acknowledge the *bhava*, *rasa* and blissful peace of Indian song. But such is the wheel of time that the very institution which our reformers are straining to rip out by its roots holds the proprietorship of this divine store of riches. Do you really want to destroy this institution and cruelly turn into dust this priceless gift of our ancestors? Did you

[37] Ibid.: 118.
[38] Ibid.: 118–19.

know that all the national and religious feelings that remain with us are due entirely to our music, no one now would know the names of Rama, Krishna and Shiva without it? . . . Ill custom is never eradicated by neglect or cruelty, it can only be destroyed with education, knowledge, and compassion. There is no direct path to heaven. We will have to cross the Vaitarani. Those who think they can spring directly into heaven by the good graces of some Mahatma are no stupider than those who think that banishing prostitution will make the poverty and sorrow of India vanish and cause a new sun to rise in the East.[39]

In order to appreciate the irony of these words, we need to recall that in the second decade of the twentieth century Indian music had come increasingly to be projected as Hindu music with an ancient Sanskritic past; its Muslim component, in production and performance, had been almost entirely sidelined. This classicizing process had been set in motion in the last decades of the nineteenth century on both sides of the subcontinent. In Calcutta, Sourindra Mohan Tagore had begun to write treatises on Hindu music, while in the Bombay Presidency the Parsis, followed by like-minded citizens in Pune, had begun to found musical societies which made this heritage available to middle-class boys and eventually also to girls. The dissemination of this music through the towering figures of Vishnu Narayan Bhatkhande (1860–1936) and Pandit Vishnu Digambar Paluskar (1872–1931) completed the process in the following decades. Bhatkhande wrote its history, set up a standard notational system, and codified the vast storehouse of ragas and raginis for teaching use. Paluskar evolved new modes of music pedagogy and set up a chain of schools, the hugely successful Gandharva Mahavidyalayas. A series of national conferences, convened severally by both men, further spread the word about the ancient genealogy of Hindu music, as also its contemporary respectability.[40] However, public singing by females continued to be the domain of courtesans till well into the 1920s. It was only in 1924, and thanks entirely to the efforts

---

[39] Ibid.: 119.
[40] See Bakhle 2005 on the nationalization of North Indian music, whence also the above information.

of Paluskar, that it became possible for a female performer to *sit* on stage while performing. 'Till then, female performers, who were mostly prostitutes, were supposed to stand on the stage when they sang. It is significant that Paluskar's school was the first to break this custom.'[41]

Seth Balbhadra Das, to serve his own ends, uses precisely this newly won status of music as national heritage to eulogize the courtesans and the monopoly of music that they still hold. In order to save the national heritage, as he pleads so eloquently, these women must be allowed to practise their art publicly till a future time when others can come forward to relieve them of their burden. To be effective, social change has to be gradual. It cannot be brought about by putting ill-conceived notions of social reform into operation.

'UNFORTUNATE SUMAN'

However, in the final run, it is the social reformers who prevail. Padam Singh returns to the scene and the matter is taken up again with renewed energy. The Municipal Board meets, all its members are present on the occasion, and Padam Singh presents the proposition. It has three sections: (1) the prostitutes should be removed from the central part of the city to some settlement far from it; (2) they should be forbidden to move about in the central spots and parks of the city; (3) those who arrange for their performances should be heavily taxed and all such festivities should be banned from public places. Kunwar Aniruddha Bahadur Singh has feared just this.

After some debate, whereby the same kinds of opinions are aired once again, Seth Balbhadra Das calls for a vote. The first section of the proposition is passed with the provision that those who marry within nine months or learn some craft to earn their livelihood be allowed to remain where they are. When Padam Singh accepts the provision, the reformist members who have thus far supported him desert him. Nine members vote for it, eight against it. Thus it is passed with the majority of one vote, that of Seth Balbhadra Das.

[41] Bhagwat 1987: 112.

The social reformers, in spite of actually being in a minority, and in spite of their last-minute split, win a narrow victory by virtue of their moral stand, which not everyone feels free to oppose publicly.[42] There is much acrimony after this is brought to pass, for most are unhappy with the outcome and Prabhakar Rao blocks all further activity. Once the dust settles, the other two sections are also passed. The prostitutes leave to be resettled on the outskirts of the town, repenting, almost all of them, of their lives. They now find themselves in Alaipur, the first station after Banaras Cantonment on the Choti (narrow) gauge railway line. Have all social problems connected to prostitution been resolved? One need only recall Seth Balbhadra Das' passionate words appealing for keeping the women in the city centre: 'Those who think they can spring directly into heaven by the good graces of some Mahatma are not more laughable than those who think that by banishing prostitution all the poverty and sorrow of India will be eradicated and a new sun will rise in the East.'

Meanwhile, pushed by events in the public sphere, matters have also moved on in the private sphere. When Suman and Shanta were cast out of the widows' home where they had initially found refuge, Sadan had happened to meet the two sisters. Through a series of coincidences and chance encounters it becomes possible for Shanta and Sadan Singh to be united as a married couple, as once planned. A now pregnant Shanta is reminded incessantly of Sadan's former attachment to Suman and she watches each move Suman makes with suspicion and dislike. Engrossed in their vision of the future, Shanta and Sadan, now backed by his family, pay little positive heed to *abhagini* (unfortunate) Suman. She finds herself increasingly unwelcome in their house.

---

[42] The conflict and lines of fracture in the municipality become much clearer if we view them also from the angle suggested in Bayly 1975. Here he convincingly offers the possibility of understanding all power battles as struggles between the older *ra'is* and the newer professionals who communalize/nationalize issues in order to disarm and oust them. Thus lifestyles are attacked and the courtesan question communalized. Bayly 1975: 271–2.

On her way to drown herself in the river, Suman meets Gajanand Swami, who is none other than her husband Gajadhar, turned secular sadhu and social reformer. He is at the centre of a movement to found a house for the education of the daughters of former prostitutes and he invites her to head that ascetic institution, set up somewhere on the outskirts of the city. The little girls will learn how to perform domestic chores effectively, sew, tend the vegetable patch, and sing patriotic songs. Suman is a wan, wry figure at the end of the novel, an educator of prostitutes' daughters who have no future in respectable society as wives or mothers. Ironically it is this pious ending to the conclusion which made the novel not only respectable but also wildly popular.

A review by Kalidas Kapur in *Saraswati*, the leading Hindi literary journal of the era, proclaimed that *Sevasadan* filled a yawning gap in Hindi literature, which had until then been forced to make do with little other than translations from the English, often through the medium of Bengali and Marathi.

> The good and bad plants of the entire world are here at hand. If you glance this way, you'll see the grafts of Bankimchandra Chatterjee and Tagore. If you glance that way, you'll see the creeper of *Saraswatichandra* from Gujarat. At other places, there are efforts to implant grafts taken from the historical novels of Hugo and Dumas. At yet other places you'll see some gentlemen trying to adorn their flower garden with the garbage of English literature. Here and there, tucked away in some small corners, can be seen a tiny number of literature lovers sowing the seeds of true service to literature.[43]

Sevasadan was obviously one such. Could it compare with the classics of world literature? Each novel, the reviewer felt, was grounded in its own *desh kal* (place and time)—what Bakhtin would call chronotope. Novels were appreciated primarily in the place where they took birth. 'This is why it is so difficult to translate social novels, it is in

---

[43] Kapur 1920: 102–3. I am grateful to Sujata Mody for drawing my attention to the review.

any case a useless enterprise. This is why it is so difficult to compare them and also so inappropriate. Their good and bad qualities depend on the depiction of their own society.' According to the reviewer, this is what *Sevasadan* has achieved. It has depicted the vice rife at the time without sensationalism, and with an art which, while making us understand how it came about, does not prevent us seeing it as despicable.⁴⁴ What is more, the novel has managed to show the way to slip out of the grip of such vice: 'That is the chief aim of this novel.' The crowning achievement of the work, however, is the character of Suman:

> Do not think it hyperbolic if I say it is the depiction of Suman's character which makes for the grandeur of the novel. She is its life-breath. The novel would be pointless if her character were in any way slurred . . . What saves Suman's character is the fact that she is an Indian woman (*bharatiya nari*). She is faithful to her husband; she strays because she seeks social prestige (*gaurav*) and bodily comfort. She has in the meantime seen that society has little respect for faithful wives . . . In a second scene we see her in a room in Dalmandi . . . She is saved by the interventions of Vitthaldas. There are many ups and downs, many traps for the unwary, many temptations, but she remains unscathed . . . the author saves her from all sides and in the end even awards her the position of Director of Seva Sadan. Suman has saved not only herself from falling but also the novel.⁴⁵

⁴⁴ As the reviewer further explained: 'Take the instance of Dickens and Reynolds. The poor of England have earned the kindness of both, both have sketched a picture of their endless misery, both have tried to show with compassion the vice that their poverty generates. Both harbour hatred for the characters of the rich in their country. But their procedure/mode is different. It is said of Dickens that if anyone has helped to ameliorate their lot, it is he. This is why his novels count amongst the literary jewels of that country. The less said about how far Reynolds has profited his country, the better. (It is best to leave the matter alone: literal translation.) By God's grace we hope to remain deprived of Reynolds' kind help in this regard. It is a matter of great good fortune that *Seva Sadan* had not made it to this rank.' Kapur 1920: 104.

⁴⁵ Ibid.

The reviewer closes with the hope that there will be 'many more good novels from the author's pen. If God wills, there will soon come a time when we also will have the good fortune of being able to proclaim that Hindi literature does not lack a Thackeray, Dickens and Scott.'

In this puritanical period at the beginning of the twentieth century, here was a novel which dealt with vice without sinking into it. It made a prostitute who did not in the end prostitute herself into its central protagonist, thereby finding a way to legitimate its intent even as it captured the reader's attention with its sensational subject matter and deep psychological insight. This, in fact, was Premchand's great achievement as a novelist. He conveyed several messages at once.

On the one hand, beautiful, passionate, headstrong Suman is tamed, and this could be seen as the triumph of virtue. But on the other she is also a tragic figure, the victim of a social system that first fails to accord her the respect that is her due as a virtuous wife, then makes much of her as a beautiful courtesan, and then the moment she steps out of that role proceeds to regard her as little more than a social outcast who can only be accommodated as one dedicated to the care of her kind.

Premchand felt deeply about the tragic fate of prostitutes, denied all space and respect by the male society which used them. Amrit Rai, his son, devotes some pages to his father's deeply emotional response to the newly available English translation of Russian novelist Aleksandr Kurprin's novel about prostitution, *Yama: The Pit* (1909–15). Recalling perhaps his own past experience while talking to his friend and fellow author Jainendra Kumar (1905–1988) about the novel, he choked in mid sentence and broke into tears. Though Jainendra and perhaps Amrit Rai saw his treatment of prostitution as dry and filled with social reformist sentiment, as we have seen he awarded his heroine both depth of feeling and the capacity for intelligent reflection.[46]

---

[46] Amrit Rai [1962] 1998: 517–20.

In the final run, very few are left to support her in the virtuous role allotted to Suman. Padam Singh does not even descend from the carriage, out of a mixture of shame, embarrassment, and unwillingness to get involved, when in the last pages of the novel Subhadra, his wife, visits Suman at Sevasadan, the exemplary institution located somewhere on the outskirts of the town. The dialogue between the two women, with which the book closes, is provided without authorial intervention. It is by citing this conversation that I too should like to close this analysis of a remarkable novel. It is a dialogically particularly poignant moment, saying one thing while also indicating several others. As Bakhtin has said of the art of the novel:

> The novelist does not acknowledge any unitary, singular, naively (or conditionally) indisputable or sacrosanct language. Language is present to the novelist only as something stratified and heteroglot. Therefore, even when heteroglossia remains outside the novel, when the novelist comes forward with his own unitary and fully affirming language (without any distancing, refraction or qualifications) he knows that such language is not self-evident and is not incontestable.[47]

Premchand shows us that the usefulness of Sevasadan, the institution, is itself contestable, for it continues to be regarded as a house of ill repute. The little girls there have an uncertain future; it is unlikely that any man will come forward to marry them, as Suman tells Subhadra. For another, even its benefactors shun it. It is clear that Shanta does not consider visiting her sister there. Suman fears also that Padam Singh will not let his wife visit again, though Subhadra assures her that, in fact, she intends to drag Sharmaji along to visit with her next weekend. But Subhadra herself is suspicious. Does Sadan still visit Suman? Suman's denial and closing words of gratitude speak more of her loneliness and isolation, and her need to be connected to the world she once knew, than of any real satisfaction derived from being there.

[47] Bakhtin 1981: 332.

When Subhadra was leaving, Suman said in a piteous voice—I will be waiting for you this Sunday.

Subhadra: I shall definitely come.
Suman: Shanta is well, isn't she?
Subhadra: I just received a letter from them. Doesn't Sadan come here?
Suman: No, but he sends a two-rupee donation each month.
Subhadra: It's time for me to leave, but you don't need to see me off.
Suman: Your coming here fills me with content. Your devotion, your affection, your extraordinary efforts, which shall I praise first? You are a true jewel in the community of women. (With moist eyes) I consider myself your servant. As long as I live, I will remain grateful to you. You held firm to me and saved me from drowning. May you both receive God's grace, always.[48]

It is this level of realism, I suggest, which asks to be read against the grain that accounts for the novel's enduring fame. The story of Suman, of her decline, rise, and decline—the questions it raises about the social institutions fostered by the modernizing middle classes operating under the benign/malignant aegis of British imperial rule, about the moral claims of the self-cleansing undertaken by the city and of the marginalization thereby not only of the courtesan but also of the wife—has lost neither its poignancy nor its significance in today's India.

REFERENCES

Bakhle, Janaki. 2005. *Two Men and Music: Nationalism in the Making of an Indian Classical Tradition.* New York: Oxford University Press; Ranikhet: Permanent Black.

Bakhtin, M.M. 1981. *The Dialogic Imagination: Four Essays.* Austin: University of Texas Press.

Bayly, C.A. 1975. *The Local Roots of Indian Politics: Allahabad, 1880–1920.* Oxford: Clarendon Press.

Bhagwat, Neela. 1987. 'Vishnu Digambar Paluskar', *Journal of Arts and Ideas.* 14/15, July–December

[48] Premchand 2006: 223.

Bharatendu Harishchandra. 1975. *Bharatendu Granthavali. Pahla Khaand* (cited as *Granthavali* I), ed. Shivprasad Mishra 'Rudra' Kashikeya. 2nd rev. ed. Banaras: Nagaripracharini Sabha (first edited by Brajratnadas, 1950).

Dalmia, Vasudha. 1997. *The Nationalization of Hindu Traditions: Bharatendu Harischandra and Nineteenth Century Banaras.* Delhi: Oxford University Press. Reprinted Ranikhet: Permanent Black, 2010.

East India Progress and Condition of India During 1917–1918. 1919. London.

Guha-Thakurta, Tapati. 1992. *The Making of a New 'Indian' Art: Artists, Aesthetics and Nationalism in Bengal, c.1850–1920.* Cambridge: Cambridge University Press.

Gupta, Narayani. 1981. *Delhi Between Two Empires 1803–1931: Society, Government and Urban Growth.* Delhi: Oxford University Press.

Havell, E.B. 1905. *Banaras, the Sacred City: Sketches of Hindu Life and Religion.* London. Reprinted Varanasi: Vishwavidyalaya Prakashan, 1990.

Kapur, Kalidas. 1920. 'Sevasadan Samalochana'. *Sarasvati*, 21/2, February.

Medhasananda, Swami. 2001. *Varanasi at the Crossroads: A Panoramic View of Early Modern Varanasi and the Story of its Transition.* Kolkata: The Ramakrishna Mission Institute of Culture.

Motichandra. [1962] 1985. *Kashi ka Itihas.* Banaras: Vishvavidyalaya Prakashan.

Nagar, Amritlal. 1994. *Ye Kothevalian.* Allahabad: Lokbharati Prakashan.

Nanda, Debidas. 1998. *Municipal Administration in India.* Varanasi: Ganga Kaveri Publishing House.

Oldenburg, Veena Talwar. 1984. *The Making of Colonial Lucknow, 1856–1877.* Princeton: Princeton University Press.

Premchand. *Nirmala.* [1927] 1999. Translated with an Afterword by Alok Rai. Delhi: Oxford University Press.

———. [1918] 2005. *Sevasadan.* Translated by Snehal Shingavi. Delhi: Oxford University Press.

Premchand. 2006. *Premchand Rachanavali.* In 20 volumes. Volume 2: *Sevasadan, Premashram.* Delhi: Janavani Prakashan.

Prinsep, James [1831–3] 1996. *Banaras Illustrated. A Series of Drawings.* Third Series. Calcutta: Baptist Missionary Press; London: Smith, Elder and Company. Reprinted Varanasi: Vishwavidyalaya Prakashan, 1996.

Rai, Amrit. [1962] 1992. *Premchand: Qalam ka Sipahi*. Allahabad: Hans Prakashan.
Trivedi, Harish. 2004. 'The Power of Premchand', *The Hindu Literary Review*, 2 May.
Verma, Bhagvaticharan. [1934] 1993. *Chitralekha*. Delhi: Rajkamal Prakashan.

3

The Holy City as the Field of Action

Though Banaras and its streets may have seemed unchanging to the older pilgrim and tourist, by the early 1930s much had changed in the city. Despite the inherent conservatism signalled by the many temples, religious organizations, and rituals performed at the ghats, the inner life of the city was undergoing rapid transformation. In fact, the radical social and political protests of the day involved not only the new intelligentsia but had also reached the streets. There were several clubs and venues where the many communities of the city could meet; there were four theatres that doubled as cinema halls.[1]

By now Banaras also had a dense network of colleges which threw some of the youth of the province into a new proximity. Its prestigious Queen's College, regarded as the citadel of Western education and founded as early as 1791, now boasted a history going back more than a century. The Nagari Pracharini Sabha (Society of the Propagation of Nagari, i.e. Hindi), had grown from a small cell founded in 1893 by three enthusiastic students to an august institution with a library, an assembly hall, a scholarly journal, and its own publication series. Modern Hindi, the prime medium of new thought, had also found other venues of perpetuation and propagation in this city of its

---

[1] Balmukund Varma, *Kashi ya Banaras*. I am grateful to Shri Shashank Singh of Ganges View Hotel, Banaras, for drawing my attention to this work and providing me with a photocopy.

birth—newspapers, journals, and literary gatherings at the houses of patrons and poets. The circle of poets and connoisseurs around Jai Shankar Prasad (1889–1937), for instance, intersected with that of Rai Krishnadas (1892–1985), scion of a wealthy merchant house and founder of an important art and sculpture collection.² And ever new visitors from Europe, in search of Indian art, music, philosophy, such as Alice Boner (1889–1981) and Alain Daniélou (1907–94), settled on the banks of the river, bringing their own kind of cultural impetus to the city.³

Theosophy, with its hankering for ancient roots but shot through with progressive impulses, continued to flourish on its beautiful new campus at Kamaccha, which was equipped with a library, theatre, and

Illus. 8: Queen's College, Banaras, by Francis Frith

² Housed later at Bharat Kala Bhavan. I look forward to the long promised publication of *Prasad ki Yad*, a 400-page MS in possession of the late Professor Anand Krishna, of which he gave me the typescript of the first chapter.

³ An only partially told story of the 1930s cosmopolitanism of Kashi.

assembly hall. Annie Besant had founded the Central Hindu College as an institution in 1898 which could rival Queen's College, and the Central Hindu Girls School in 1905. The Banaras Hindu University, founded in 1915, had now been in existence for a decade and a half. Explicitly and self-consciously 'Indian–Hindu' in its architecture and residence halls,[4] which, radical for the time, observed neither status nor intra-caste difference, the 'idyllic rural' lifestyles fostered in the residence halls and the generous space devoted to mango orchards, fields, and forests attracted students from all parts of India, though particularly from the surrounding region. Gandhi's call for Civil Disobedience in March 1930 elicited an enthusiastic response from the students here, male and female. Though the Women's College could be distinguished from the rest of the campus by its high walls, they did not prove high enough to hold back the girls from participating in picketing.[5]

The national movement energized and brought into the public sphere new sections of the population—'untouchables' and artisans, students and professors from increasingly politicized campuses, and for the first time in public life women of all ages.[6] Perhaps the most significant feature of the Civil Disobedience movement of 1930 was the massive participation by women—many of them below the age of seventeen—at all levels of public action. Women not only fought alongside men, they often propelled them into action. The agitation for national freedom came thus to be inevitably and closely coupled with personal freedom for women. As a police report astutely

---

[4] Renold 2012: 180–9 notes the architectonic features that distinguished the BHU campus from the exclusive Indo-Saracenic style followed in colonial buildings and campuses (for example, Allahabad and Mayo College in Ajmer) up to that period. Frank Lishman, the architect of the central campus buildings, added to the Indo-Saracenic style conspicuously Hindu features and ornamentation, such as the horizontal layering of temples—*shikhara*, *mandapa*, and the bell gracing temple entrances.

[5] See Renold 2005 for a graphic account of the early life of the campus; for the details above, see in particular pp. 183, 153 and 206.

[6] See Chapter 4, 'Women and the Hindi Public Sphere', in Orsini 2002: 243–89.

observed: 'The Indian woman is struggling for domestic and national liberty at the same time and like a woman, she is utterly unreasonable and illogical in her demands and in her methods, but like a woman, she has enormous influence over the stronger sex . . .'[7] *Karmabhumi* (Field of Action; 1932), Premchand's penultimate novel, charted the personal and public lives of men and women, and of groups in and around Banaras, as these became implicated in protest actions (*karma*) that were led initially by the educated, but with people of humbler origin in the second line of command who were ready to take charge once their leaders were thrust into prison.[8]

For, in 1932, after a life of wandering, as teacher, school inspector, and author-cum-public intellectual who had gained renown as the lively and innovative editor of the prestigious Lucknow Hindi journal *Madhuri* (1927–31),[9] Premchand had come back to live in the city around which he had constantly circled in his fictional work. He

---

[7] Note from UP Police Inspector Dodd, 3 September 1930, cited in Sarkar 1987: 290. Many who participated in mass actions, including Gandhi's Salt March, from which he had first wanted to exclude them, were the second generation of politically active women, influenced by reformist mothers who had participated in political actions even before the Non-Cooperation Movement of the 1920s. But now there were two firsts: large participation by peasant women, and police violence against women as well, irrespective of class. Over 1930–1, 20,000 women satyagrahis were arrested and sentenced to imprisonment. Radha Kumar (1993) remains the most easily accessible and vivid source on this period, particularly Chapter 5 titled 'Constructing the Image of a Woman Activist'. For Banaras, in particular, Renold 2005: 206: 'The women students were shown to exhibit exceptional daring and ability. BHU quickly gained a reputation for being a major centre of sedition.'

[8] *Karmabhumi* was written first in Devanagari and published in November 1932 by the Saraswati Press in Banaras. Its Urdu version was published in Delhi in 1934. According to Premchand's biographer-son Amrit Rai, it was written from April 1931 to 5 September 1932. See Rai 1962: 656. There is some difference of opinion regarding the time of its composition. See Premchand 2006: vol. 1, 63–4, for details. The text cited here is from *Premchand Rachanavali*, vol. 5.

[9] Amrit Rai's poignant biography of his father *Qalam ka Sipahi* (Rai 1962).

had moved to a house in Benia Bagh from his rural home in nearby Lamhi.[10] He brought with him not only an India-wide reputation as a short story writer and novelist, but also as an independent publisher in Banaras: he was the founder-editor of *Haṃs* (1930) and *Jagaran* (1932), literary-political journals which he continued to bring out to the end of his days despite being dogged by heavy debts and plagued by draconian government censorship. Between 1930 and 1934 around 348 newspapers and journals had been forced to shut down, including *Aaj* in Banaras, and the distribution of works by Gorki, Marx, Engels, and Lenin was banned. Premchand's own *Haṃs* and *Jagaran* had punitive bail terms clamped on them.[11] Though he takes the precaution of never mentioning Gandhi explicitly in *Karmabhumi*, not even as the Mahatma, as a Gandhian of radical progressive hue—in his editorials and articles as much as in this novel—Premchand continued to take a clear stand on the social and political issues that suffused his fiction and propelled his characters, participating intensively in the burning issues of the day—the widespread peasant unrest in the United Provinces and Bihar and its violent suppression, the polarization of Hindus and Muslims fuelled by right wing organizations, and the artificially created Hindi–Urdu divide. He also followed local politics, commenting in minute detail on the misconduct of the city municipal council, sparing neither the city notables who constituted it nor the colonial state which kept the municipality miserably underfunded and actively fostered communal divisions.

Though he kept his distance from organized religion, Premchand recognized the importance of ritual and temple worship in the life

[10] Rai 1962: 499.
[11] Awasthi 2012: 24–37, citing Pattabhi Sitaramaiya, *Bharatiya Rashtriya Congress ka Itihas*, vol. 2 (Delhi: Sasta Sahitya Mandal), p. 197. Rai cites from a letter Premchand wrote to Jainendrakumar on 7 December 1932, when *Jagaran* and Saraswati Press were asked to pay the heavy amount of Rs 2000 as bail: 'I was very upset, ran to Lucknow, spoke to Chief Secretary (Mumford) to explain what motivated the story. And supplied proof of my loyalty. I hope that the bail will be revoked now. They put a knife to one's throat for the smallest things.' Rai 1962: 510.

of the people around him and sided resolutely with Gandhi on the issue of Dalit temple entry. The Mahatma had just then embarked on yet another fast unto death. Begun on 20 September 1932, the fast was directed against Ramsay MacDonald's 'Communal Award' providing for separate electorates for Muslims and Dalits. It also targeted Ambedkar, who had backed the award.[12] In an October 1932 editorial in *Jagaran*, Premchand came out in strong support of Gandhi's stand, chastising caste Hindus for paying only lip service to the idea of caste equality. Though in this charged climate even the pious in Banaras, the holiest of Hindu cities, were ready to agree that untouchables were also Hindus,

> [they] do not want to give them social rights, wishing to see them remain downtrodden and Dalit. So, only one way remains—Hindus who regard Mahatma Gandhi as the true protector of Hindus must take an oath against worshipping at temples that are not open to untouchables, to people who are as dear to the Mahatma as his life; that they will give no ritual offerings to priests who regard the Mahatma as a foe of religion, or as a non-Hindu . . . If the Vishwanath Temple refuses to let in untouchables, crores of Hindus will join their untouchable brothers to construct another temple right here in Kashi, and ritually instal Vishwanath in it. Vishwanath is not the god of specific castes, he is the father and lord of all mankind, and all have an equal claim on him. There is need for such agitation and it is bound to happen soon.[13]

In the fictional space of his novel, Premchand could bring about this miracle; a central scene depicts the dramatic opening of temple doors to all.

Linked to Gandhi were also his beliefs regarding the reforms required to improve the lot of women. The Mahatma had been

---

[12] See Omvedt 2004: 47–55 for Ambedkar's stand on the vexed issue of the British policy of providing separate electorates. The Mahatma broke his fast four days later after making the country watch with bated breath, and a much harassed Ambedkar reluctantly agreed to a compromise resulting in the famous-infamous Poona Pact.

[13] Editorial in *Jagaran*, 5 October 1932, titled 'Kashi's Blemish/Disgrace [*kalank*]'. Premchand 2006: vol. 8, 141.

strident in his views.[14] And we have to remember, in speaking of them as strident—a fact easily forgotten when looking back from our post-feminist vantage point—that before the early 1920s most upper-caste/class Hindu and Muslim women in North India observed purdah, which barred them not only from higher education but also from entering every other kind of public space in any meaningful way. In the service they could perform for the nation and society at large—and here Gandhi was clearly addressing these very upper castes and classes—women were to be regarded as honoured comrades in common service. In some public acts, such as picketing against liquor and foreign cloth shops, they were even to play the leading role. Here they would find the 'opportunity of actively identifying themselves with the masses and helping them both morally and materially.' Though he allowed the family hierarchies to remain unchallenged and regarded the male head of the household if not as the sole then surely as the primary breadwinner, Gandhi also spoke out, as early as 1928, for women's right to have the final say in the choice of a marriage partner—'the only honourable terms in marriage are mutual love and mutual consent.' He also argued for equal property rights for women.[15] Political rights for women had already been secured, at least on paper, from the early 1920s. Between 1921 and 1930 the Indian provincial legislatures had extended the franchise to women, conferring equal citizenship on men and women who possessed sufficient qualifications—literacy, property, age, payment of taxes, length of residence. In 1931, the Congress Party was to pass a resolution at its Karachi annual session committing itself to the political equality of women regardless of status.

For the most part, Premchand could be regarded as echoing the Mahatma's known views on the role of women in the household as well

---

[14] As Madhu Kishwar showed in her pioneering two-part article (Kishwar 1985). It is from her, and Chapters 4 and 5 of Forbes 1998, that I draw information in the account that follows.

[15] Gandhi in *Young India*, 31 April 1930, *CWMG*, vol. 43, pp. 220–1, and idem, vol. 72, p. 137, as cited in Kishwar 1985: 1693, 1696.

THE HOLY CITY AS THE FIELD OF ACTION   157

Illus. 9: 'A Boycott procession in the market area', from *Collections of Photographs of Old Congress Party*, Gelatin Silver Print, *c.* 1930, possibly by K.L. Nursey

as in the freedom struggle. His wife Shivrani Devi has given us a lively record of her own short prison term.[16] But Premchand pleaded for yet greater autonomy for women than Gandhi when, for instance, he spoke of women's right to divorce. The narrator of his novel provided space for Sukhada to voice radical views on the rights of women within marriage, views which no one else in the novel shares, and on which the narrator also withholds comment, thus, in a sense, allowing them to stand unchallenged. That Premchand shared them, and went even further than his chief female protagonist Sukhada could, is apparent in his journal columns. Indian women were once regarded as clan goddesses (*kuldevi*), he tells us in his February 1931 editorial in *Haṃs*. But when Indian men came to be politically subjugated, they put their women through subjections far more severe. This is how Premchand formulated his charter of rights for women:

[16] Shivrani Devi 1956 [1991]: 126–30.

> This last year's satyagraha campaign has proven that the women of India can still sacrifice themselves on the altar of dharma. If men still cherish their fantasy of ruling over them, they had better get rid of it at once, because, whether they want to or not, women will not rest until they have won their personal rights. They should have all rights that men do, and decisions on which rights they wish for their well-being must be left to them. To our way of thinking, women are unhappy with the concerns listed below, and their unhappiness will need to be resolved as they themselves see fit:
>
> Marriage to a single person should be equally the rule for man and woman. No man should be allowed to marry during his wife's lifetime.
>
> A wife should have full rights to her husband's wealth. She should be able to spend it or pledge it away as she likes.
>
> Daughters should have the same rights as sons to the father's property.
>
> A law enabling divorce should be promulgated and should apply equally to men and women.
>
> At divorce, the woman should get half the man's property and a portion of his ancestral wealth, if there be any.[17]

Little wonder that Premchand took care to emphasize the fictionality of both the city and its characters in his Preface to *Karmabhumi*; he was taking radical liberties with both:

> There are also people in the world who read novels as if they were history. Such readers are urged to regard the characters in this novel as fictional, just as fictional as its sites. It is quite likely that characters such as Lala Samarkant and Amarkant, Sukhada and Naina, Salim, and Sakina actually exist in the world, but there is surely a difference between fictional and real persons, the difference that ought to exist between god's creation and that of a mortal. The Kashi and Haridwar of the book are equally fictional, and it is very likely that you'll fail to find the action and the scenes depicted here in either site of pilgrimage in the United Provinces. Since we weren't able to invent characters and sites that could sound convincingly fictional, we thought: why not stay with Amarkant and Kashi?[18]

---

[17] Editorial in *Haṃs*, February 1931, entitled 'Nārī Jāti ke adhikār' (The Rights of Women), in Premchand 2006: vol. 8, 70.

[18] Ibid.: vol. 9, 453.

Given that both these cities were conservative down to their fingernails, it was discreet of the author to present them as fictive. However, though the Haridwar of the novel was projected as imaginary, the abandoned Munni's tragic spell in the town and her various encounters there sound all too real. So does the recognizably contemporaneous cityscape of Kashi, which provides a vivid frame for the novel. There is in Premchand's work of the period a new sense of the realities of middle- and lower-class life, of the significance of social spaces, of living in specific localities of the city, of the details of house interiors, their domestic use and furnishings.

The novel moves between the classrooms of the venerable Queen's College, the chamber of the Town Hall where the municipal council meets, and the Vaishnava temple, a *thakurdwara* which sounds suspiciously like Gopal Mandir in all its colour and corrupt practices.[19] There are vivid, if brief, descriptions of Lala Samarkant's shop-cum-residence in Bula Nala, of the small house of the poorer setting in Nichi Gali, to which a defiant Amarkant drags his family; and of Govardhan Sarai, with its poor Muslim population and rundown housing.

Populated by a vast cast of characters, *Karmabhumi* is held together by an omniscient narrator who, however, limits himself to providing the bare storyline, quick character sketches, and minimal auctorial comment in the earthy idiom Premchand's readers had become familiar with. The narrative moves at a rapid pace, its short and crisp sentences seem to leap forward, whether describing action or reverie. In keeping with the pace of the novel, the chapters are generally short; they have a single scene of action and a particular narrative focus.

The novel is symmetrically arranged, moving between city and country in its five sections. But the balance tips in favour of the city sections. Not only are the first, third, and final sections Banaras-centred, they are longer than the other two. The shorter second and fourth sections are set in a small mountain village near Haridwar and its surrounding countryside. The village is primarily populated by

---

[19] Some key scenes in his novel *Premashram* (1922) are set there.

Dalits; Chamars or Raidasis with small landholdings. Much of the area belongs to an opulent Hindu monastic establishment with its young, deceptively friendly, saffron-clad monastic head.

While the major political and social movements of the day undergird the narrative, it is conceived of as the field of action of its two prime protagonists, Amarkant and Sukhada, husband and wife, in quest as much of themselves, within and without marriage, as of their express social and political goals. The personal and the political thus become inextricably intertwined. Dharma is reinterpreted entirely as nationalistic rather than ritual-religious. The private constantly expands into the public, only to shrink into the private in moments of reverie. The *karmabhumi* or field of action in question is both that of political action as well as the almost militantly competitive terrain of the marriage between a womanly man and a manly woman.[20] There is a new sense, then, not only of interiors but of a new self-reflexive interiority.

There are four major public agitations that create battlefronts with the colonial state but also within the marriage in question. The first, to save from capital punishment a raped woman who kills in retribution those white men whom she sees as representing her rapist, takes place in Banaras. The second, to gain temple entry for Dalits, also takes place in the city. The third, to organize collective resistance by an overtaxed peasantry to comply with the revenue demands of the imperial state, moves to the country. The fourth, to obtain housing for the urban poor, retrieving city-owned land from avaricious municipal councillors, returns once more to Banaras.

There is wonderful symmetry even here. For Amarkant and Sukhada, soon estranged from each other, separately lead two of these agitations, spurring each other into ever more radical action. Their rivalry with each other, their struggles with customary structures of feeling, as much as with the power-holders, their battle with each

---

[20] I am grateful to Snehal Shingavi for drawing my attention to the *yuddha* (battle) images being used as much in marital relations as in the political field.

other and with the powers outside them, and their sense of moral as well as public victory or defeat in their private and public encounters provide the central narrative tension of the novel. It is largely focalized through them and moves with them to their respective scenes of action.

CUSTOM, EDUCATION, AND THE NATIONALIST CALL

At first haltingly, but then with increasing self-awareness, Amar and Sukhada reflect on what they seek in their relationship—support, confirmation, encouragement, a new yearning for self-realization and fulfilment, *atma* now being interpreted not in a metaphysical sense but as the psychological sense of selfhood, a major secularization of the kind of spiritual self-realization sought through the ages by saint and sinner. There is in *Karmabhumi* also a newer kind of reflexivity, of self-awareness and deliberated action that points to a major shift not only in the author's practice, but also to a more general structure of feeling. Marriage for the educated young no longer means timid acquiescence to what fate has ordained. At the very least, for the male partner it means a level of communication that allows for self-growth. Exceptionally sensitive and charismatic, the narrator informs us,

> Amarkant was a thin, delicate, dark-complexioned young man of small frame. He was about twenty years old, but had sprouted no whiskers yet. He looked like a boy of fourteen or fifteen. He usually wore an expression of hurt resolve on his face, which seemed to suggest that he had no-one in the world. At the same time, his face radiated such brilliance (*pratibha*) and such mental power (*manasvita*) that, having seen him once, it was impossible to forget him.[21]

Amarkant was a coddled and indulged child but his mother died when he was young; his stepmother also passed away, leaving behind

---

[21] *Karmabhumi*, in Premchand 2006: vol. 5, 236 (hereafter *Karmabhumi*).

a daughter, Naina, who resembled Amar and loved him deeply. But in her time the stepmother had driven a wedge between father and son, who were not able to bond again. Much of Amarkant's subsequent life was shaped by resistance to his father. 'No ties of affection remained between father and son . . . Amarkant's character was moulded to a large extent by the hostility he felt for his father.'[22]

But after squandering away his years in school, Amar's interest in education suddenly revives. Against his father's express wish, he insists that he should continue his studies; perhaps it is this that gives him a new drive. His sole support in his battle with his father is his college friend Salim. His wife Sukhada, independent and imperious in her ways, has come into the family as the only child of a wealthy and progressive Lucknow family. 'Consequently, this young woman with masculine qualities was wedded to a young man with feminine traits and lack of manly enterprise (*purushartha*). If the two were to exchange clothes, they could well take the place of the other. Femininity is nothing but repressed manly enterprise.'[23]

The statement that Amar was not manly enough and Sukhada not womanly enough would seem to suggest that seeing them both restored to their conventionally assigned roles was the moral thrust and hidden agenda of the narrative, whereas what we see unfold before us is the process by which both outgrow their initial reserve and resort to karma, or action, irrespective of gender, leading them to becoming bitter rivals, combatants in their relationship. And if one were to push this thesis further, then the bigger social causes that they and others espouse, and the nationalism that undergirds these causes—Dr Shanti Kumar would also belong here—would become mere byproducts of their rivalry and thirst for public recognition. For all its insistence on nationalism, then, the narrative presents those who pursue it as more or less flawed.

There seems little doubt that Sukhada's modern ways pose a threat to many in the city. As Salim's succinct description of Sukhada

[22] Ibid.: 238.
[23] Ibid.: 239.

suggests, the difference between men and women seems to be narrowing, a change not entirely welcome in early 1930s Banaras:

> Besides, your wife is a new woman, educated, of free thought, who likes to go out, watch films, read newspapers and novels. May god protect us from such women! We have Europe to thank for this. We're reduced to being grateful for what our women now forget to do. It used to be boys trying to outdo each other teasing women, but times have changed. Now it's as likely the woman's taken the initiative and approached the man.[24]

However, at this early stage both Sukhada and Amar are preoccupied with their immediate domestic surroundings, their power battles, and making social statements which mark their difference from the rest of the family. The bigger battles come later.

Amarkant's family, consisting of his father, sister, and wife, lives in a traditionally constructed three-storey house in Bula Nala.[25] The ground floor houses Lala Samarkant's shop, several large windowless storerooms—possibly on the other side of the traditional courtyard open at least partially to the sky—and the kitchen. The upper two

---

[24] Ibid.: 325–6.

[25] Writing about such houses in the context of Lahore, William Glover offers the following description, useful to readers today in understanding the conflicts that could arise if one member of the family insisted on exclusive individual use of a room and individual décor: 'Every level of the house flexibly performed some sort of domestic function, and each level of the upper floors made accommodation for what was usually more than one generation of a family living together in the same structure. Ground floor rooms were used as work spaces and were sometimes rented out, but were seldom used for living, since the lowest floor of the house was considered the least desirable space . . . The multi-purpose rooms of the upper storeys were sparingly furnished . . . Most household furniture was lightweight and mobile, allowing for use in different rooms according to the need, the time of day, the season, or who was present at any given time. Europeans, when afforded the rare glimpse of an interior, commented unfavourably on the lack of comfort and taste. All of this was to undergo change in the process of modernization as specialized functions came to be assigned to rooms, as "a vigorous discourse . . . on urban sanitation and public health" invaded private space.' See Glover 2008: 126–30.

floors consist of large airy rooms which repeat the pattern of the ground storey in their layout and are used for various domestic purposes. Amar has chosen a small dark room on the ground floor for his activities; he spins the *charkha* (spinning wheel) for two hours a day, to the immense annoyance of his father, who has little use for the Gandhian way of life, or nationalism for that matter.

As against this austere outfit, Sukhada's room in the house reflects her education, her leisure-time activities, and Western-style furniture to accord with her individualized modern taste.[26] It is anomalous enough to merit description:

Illus. 10: Gandhi spinning 1930s

[26] Shivrani Devi noted Premchand's own vexed relationship to Western-style seating arrangement, to tables and chairs, which she refers to as 'furniture' also in the Hindi original, in the account of their Lucknow days: 'I procured furniture worth Rs. 50. I decorated the room with it. But he [Premchand] would always sit on the floor. He would keep a desk there and another for a child. He would teach that child himself every morning. But yes, if someone came to the room, he would use that furniture. And he cleaned it himself

Of all the rooms in the house, this was the largest and best-furnished room. There was a carpet on the floor and several symmetrically arranged upholstered as well as plain chairs. In the middle was a small, round, engraved table. Bound volumes of books spilled out of glass cupboards. The alcoves showed different varieties of games. A harmonium had been placed on a corner table. Paintings by Dhurandhar, Ravi Varma, and other artists adorned the walls alongside older prints. The room reflected choice, taste, and wealth.[27]

Courtyard houses were centripetal in their orientation, whereas the bungalow or Western-style house with verandahs that looked outwards were centrifugal in their very structure.[28] Amar is still functioning in the older style, adapting a ground-floor room to his particular need of the day, not furnishing it in any particular style. Sukhada has introduced a defiantly centrifugal move in a structure not meant to contain it. Amar's and Sukhada's lifestyles are thus as much at loggerheads as their temperaments. And ultimately, for both are modern in their individual ways, they find themselves pulled to and fro between two cultural poles—the customary or traditional,

---

daily.' When she tried to dissuade him from doing so, he declined always, saying he did not want to enslave her. Shivrani Devi 1956: 92–3.

[27] *Karmabhumi*, 243.

[28] 'The bungalow was invariably situated in a large compound, an area of marked territory which, in turn, was located at a distance from other buildings or places of settlement. The compound . . . was an enclosed space either leased, bought or appropriated by representatives of an incoming, "invading" society from the indigenous inhabitants of the land . . . In fact, the compound was simply an extension of the bungalow's internal space, an outdoor room, fulfilling a variety of social, political, cultural and psychological needs. Thus the bungalow was in direct contrast to the courtyard house in the "native city"; here a "central courtyard allowed the penetration of light and air; as the houses were three or four storeys high and there were closely clustered, cellular-structured buildings all around, the lower rooms were dark and cool. Activity in this courtyard house was centripetal: movement was inwards, towards the courtyard. In the bungalow, it was centrifugal, outward, on to the verandah, and further into the compound.' King 1984: 34–5.

as represented by Lala Samarkant, Amar's father, and the educated or modern as embodied by Dr Shanti Kumar.

Lala Samarkant, a self-made man, began life with a small-time agency for turmeric, to which he added molasses and rice. He was soon able to lend money on interest, and in a relatively short time amassed a handsome fortune. He had regular habits, took regular physical exercise, led a ritually correct life, and maintained a pious front. His was then a customary life, a cause for surprise to no-one. We have only to think of the two types of merchants we spoke of earlier—the frugal merchant and the great *sahu* (banker)—to locate the appropriate category for Lala Samarkant. The frugal merchant, we may recall, led an austere and modest life, avoiding all excessive show. He observed the religious festivities of the community to which he belonged and performed acts of charity. Education, beyond that which was absolutely necessary to negotiate periodic social change, had no place in this world. Banarasi's fellow merchants in seventeenth-century Jaunpur had admonished him to give up his foolish pursuit of learning; it was 'only for brahmans and bards. A merchant's son should tend shop. Do not forget that a man who is too studious has to beg for food.'[29] As in Banarasi's case, so too here the tension is not only between a frugal lifestyle—for Amar's is the life of an austere Gandhian—and an excessively opulent one; it is also between the customary and the educated:

> Most of us, before we get any kind of literary education, get to know and to value—also to feel the tensions of—a customary life. We see and learn from the ways our families live and get their living; a world of work and of place, and of beliefs so deeply dissolved into everyday actions that we don't at first even know they are beliefs, subject to change and challenge. Our education, quite often, gives us a way of looking at that life which can see other values beyond it . . . We know especially how much they are needed to understand change—change in the heart of the places where we have lived and worked and grown up . . . But it is more than a matter of picking up terms and tones. It is what happens to us, really happens to us, as we try to mediate those contrasted worlds . . . the

[29] Banarasidas [1641] 1981: 33.

making and failing of relationships, the crises of physical and mental personality . . .[30]

Amar's education in the era of high nationalism, coupled with the Gandhian call to social and political action, only serve to alienate him from the merchant existence of his father. College and university campuses had become precisely what Lord Curzon had tried to prevent earlier in the century—hotbeds of sedition. Even the most august educational institutions did not remain immune to the waves of nationalism sweeping through the country. The novels of the 1930s, peopled with students and professors, had begun to reflect this politicization. In *Karmabhumi*, it is Queen's College Professor Shanti Kumar, a middle-class professional, who serves as Gandhi's mouthpiece, forming the pole at the other end of the universe from that which anchors the lifestyle of Amar's father. Anglicized in his ideas and worldview, it is Shanti Kumar who brings social activism to the life of his students:

> Shanti Kumar was about thirty-five years old, very fair and handsome. His clothes and manners were English and, at first glance, he appeared to be English himself, his eyes blue and light-coloured hair. He had a doctorate from Oxford. He was a fanatic opponent of marriage, an enthusiastic nationalist devoted to social service. Of happy disposition, and warm-hearted, he never missed an opportunity to joke around. He was friendly with students. He took part in political movements, though covertly, disclosing it to no-one. But he could be relied upon to be thunderous when it came to social action.[31]

Here then we have the *Karmabhumi* of the novel's title. Professor Shanti Kumar's role as mentor will be key to Amar's later decision to abandon merchanthood altogether and embark on social reform and political action. Initially, it is just lifestyle choices, Gandhian self-help measures, and austerity that herald the split with his father. The Mahatma had placed high value on the process of producing handspun cloth, on the act of spinning, and on the spinning wheel

---

[30] Williams [1973] 1985: 198–9.
[31] *Karmabhumi*, 250.

as a symbol of freedom. Khadi had moral value for him and wearing it was a matter of dharma: 'Khadi and spinning were to become not only the unifying national cause in the peaceful struggle for freedom but also the basis of a new non-industrial, craft-based economic structure in independent India. As Gandhi himself admitted, khadi to him was something of an obsession: "Of all my foibles, of all my weaknesses and fanaticisms or whatever you like to call them, khadi is my pet one . . . This is sacred cloth."'[32] Khadi and the spinning wheel were not only seen as symbols of political, social, and economic protest, but as a weapon in family warfare in the house in Bula Nala, provoking a violent reaction from Lala Samarkant. For, maddeningly enough, Amar justifies the time spent at the spinning wheel as an act of self-purification: 'You regard a dip in the Ganga, puja, and reciting scripture as your prime dharma; I understand dharma as truthfulness, service and helping others.'[33] Dharma defined, then, not as the ritual-religious that Kashi is famous for, but as entirely Gandhian. And Amar undertakes the same kind of redefinition in relation to the *atma*. When Lala Samarkant threatens to disinherit him, Amar's reaction is contrary; severance from home will only open up new vistas for him: 'The day you undertake this virtuous act, the sun of my good fortune will rise. I'll be freed of this emotional bond and become independent. As long as I remain shackled to this, my self (*atma*) will remain undeveloped.'[34] When Amar speaks of the need to create space for his *atma* so that it can evolve to its fullest potential, he is surely adding new, almost Freudian, dimensions and connotations to the classic philosophical term, using it to mean the self of a modern individual. He sees, however, this quest for the self and its evolution as a lonely one, not necessarily coupled with the extension, or even reconfirmation, of the self in the partner, but as defined in action. His wife Sukhada belongs to the other side, so to speak. She sides with his father, reproaching Amar for his inactivity

[32] Tarlo 1996: 87, citation from *CWMG*, vol. 23, 106.
[33] *Karmabhumi*, 262.
[34] Ibid.: 264.

in business life. Only Salim, college friend and would-be poet, the son of another newly rich father, can be looked to for sympathy and understanding in this very modern quest.

MERCHANT SON AS POLITICAL AGITATOR

When Shanti Kumar leads a group of college students, including Amar and Salim, to a nearby village, it is the Gandhian programme of village uplift which drives the action. On the way back to the city, discussing the shocking poverty they have witnessed in the village, they come upon a sudden commotion: a group of villagers stand muttering under a tree, two white soldiers guard an *arhar* field, from within which comes the cry of a woman. The students rush towards the field, bamboo poles in hand, but they come too late to save the woman. She limps out of the field, trying to cover herself with the clothes torn off her body. 'Who could give back to her the precious thing of which she had been robbed?'[35] We learn later that she is Munni, a poor Rajput woman from the village. Her rapists are British soldiers.

The matter is hushed up and the soldiers quickly transferred. But the incident leaves a lasting impact on Amar. These two-penny white soldiers from the lowest social stratum in England dared do this because India was not independent. The rape of a Rajput woman symbolizes the rape of the nation. 'This terror would have to be removed. The chains of dependence would have to be broken.'[36] Amar glows with the prospect of becoming part of a larger cause, of the nationwide movement to free India from British oppression. Munni becomes the cause, the object around which protest can consolidate. She not only opens the field of action for him, offering him a legitimate avenue of escape from a profession to which he cannot subscribe, she provides him with a sure way of gaining the moral upper hand *vis-à-vis* Sukhada, whom he continues to find overbearing and impossibly self-willed, and with whom he finds himself locked in a

[35] Ibid.: 251.
[36] Ibid.: 252.

battle for power. But annoyingly enough, while others are busy organizing protest it is Sukhada who asks after the raped woman, offering to find shelter for her with her widowed mother Renuka Devi who has moved to Banaras: 'Why don't you go one of these days and find out how she is doing, or do you think you've done your duty by delivering speeches? . . . She's done nothing wrong, why should she be punished?'[37] The contest between husband and wife has now begun in earnest. Sukhada makes Amar feel inferior. Amar does not go to see the victim of the rape, but six months later Munni herself appears unexpectedly outside Lala Samarkant's shop, attacking and killing first one of the molesting white men who has just visited the shop, and then the other with a knife. She is not afraid of the noose, she tells the police superintendent who appears on the scene, she even prays for death. 'Now that I've been robbed of my honour, can I gain anything by living?'[38] Munni becomes a heroine for the populace. Two thousand people accompany her on her way to prison. But her triumph cannot be other than short-lived, as she knows best. She can never be integrated back into Hindu society, and, as the narrator shows with pitiless clarity, in the agitation that follows she finds herself being used by all those who set out to help her.

For three months there is immense excitement in town. Renuka, Sukhada's rich, widowed mother, also looking for a cause to throw herself into, has organized and funded the defence. She has become the queen of the city; Shanti Kumar and Amarkant are her right and left hands. On the final day of Munni's trial in the Sessions Court, presided over by an Indian judge with some years in the Indian National Congress to his credit, there is a voyeuristic thrill in the courtroom. Munni's person recedes even as she is being celebrated. The narrator is almost cynical in his report of what goes through our protagonists' heads: 'Amarkant was thinking the whites dared to do such a thing because they considered themselves kings of this country. Shanti Kumar had already composed a speech in his head, the

[37] Ibid.: 255.
[38] Ibid.: 271.

subject of which was men's tyranny of women. Sukhada was thinking, if she were to be released, she would keep her in her home and serve her. Renuka was taken with the thought of setting up a dispensary in her name.'[39] The judge is a Maharashtrian; a fallen Congressman who nonetheless cannot but be sensitive to the storm-wave of public sympathy. Munni is released. A procession all the way to the banks of the Ganga with Munni at its head is planned. A radiant Munni allows some of the fanfare to take place, but refuses to be further used by participating in the procession. 'You are making a show (*svang*) out of me.'[40] She is a fallen woman; as she tells Professor Shanti Kumar: 'This procession and this show do not become a woman as unfortunate as me. Please tell all these brothers and sisters to go back home. I lay in dust. You raised me to the skies, I don't have the ability to reach higher than that; it'll just make me dizzy. Please have me taken to the railway station. I fall at your feet and supplicate you most humbly (*pairom parti hum*).'[41] Shanti Kumar tells her about her husband, waiting with her son, ready now to accept her back. Refusing to see her waiting men, she leaves for the station and for a while ceases to exist as a person.

In the course that Amar's life now takes and the decisions he finds himself taking, the political and the personal become inextricably entwined. For one, Amar begins to claim Munni's release as his victory, for it is in these terms that he wages a veritable battle—against society, against his father, against his wife; he it was who had roped in his wealthy mother-in-law. He shoots into prominence in the city, he is elected Municipal Commissioner; he makes speeches and writes articles for the local newspapers. He participates in Dr Shanti Kumar's voluntary organization, *Sevashram* (Abode of Service), which Shanti Kumar runs alongside his activities as college professor. He is a winner in many ways but the avenues for further growth are hazy, as also the means to earn a living away from his father. Though

---

[39] Ibid.: 276.
[40] Ibid.: 287.
[41] Ibid.: 277.

he has begun to bask in the wealth and well-being around him and to fuss endlessly over his newly born son, the clashes with his father continue. When he declares he is ready to leave his father's house, to his immense annoyance Sukhada declares herself equally ready to leave with him. 'Sukhada was happy, she had won a big victory today (*vijay*).' Sukhada's battle at this stage is primarily a psychological one, with her husband. Her readiness to sacrifice the comfort of home, however, not only makes her a burden for Amar, who will have to organize a whole new household because of her, she relativizes his moral victory and somehow makes her own the greater victory. This moral triumph Amar chalks up against her. 'His ideals and his dharma had been put to the test today and he had become aware of his weak position. The camel had arrived at the foot of the mountain and taken stock of its heights.'[42] Amarkant and Sukhada view all their encounters with each other in battle terms, the narrator often describes them as *yuddha*s, their words as *shastra* (weapons) in their verbal skirmishes, and they themselves see the result of each effort made in the private—later also in public—domain either as victory or defeat (*jay-parajay*). All action, personal, social, subsumed in the nationalist, thus becomes part of their power battle against each other. As has been pointed out, companionate marriage enters as a problematic, even if desirable, notion in the novels from this period on. 'In truth, the problem of sexual and marital incompatibility was fully articulated by the 1930s.'[43] A climactic battle scene with Lala Samarkant leads to Amar moving out of his paternal home with wife, baby son, and sister Naina, to a much more modest dwelling in Nichi Bagh. He sells handspun cloth, earning little; but Sukhada outdoes him even here, for as a schoolteacher she earns considerably more than him. His struggle to define himself, to allow his *atma* to unfold, is met with a quick move on her side.

A lost and frustrated Amar has in the meantime met Sakina, a young Muslim woman who lives with her widowed mother, wife

---

[42] Ibid.: 268.
[43] Govind 2014: 23.

of a deceased employee of his father. Their extreme poverty, their small, dilapidated house in Govardhan Sarai, offer a novel insight into life in another part of the city. Amar is attracted to Sakina and, at a particularly desperate moment in his life, decides to fall in love with her. He contrasts her warmth and tenderness with Sukhada's marble-like beauty and domineering manner. He speaks of his newfound romance as love (*muhabbat*), invoking once more the need for the development of his self (*atma ka vikas*), with little care for what Sukhada or indeed Sakina might need or value. It is a significant moment nonetheless, a first articulation of the value attached to self-development as it is brought into direct connection with love. We need to note, however, that *muhabbat*—romantic love—is still located outside marriage; at no stage in the narrative is there any mention of romantic love within it. Married bliss at its optimal means sharing, veneration, and respect, however grudging, for each other.

Sakina's presence in the narrative and Amar's programmatic proclamations seem contrived, a way to highlight the possibility of intracommunal harmony and Hindu–Muslim amity. Amar goes as far as to declare that he is Hindu through sheer accident of birth, he is ready to convert to Islam and cast his defiant lot with her, though neither her mother nor an overwhelmed Sakina can take on the social burden this heroic act would impose on them. When a helpless Lala Samarkant turns up in Sakina's humble dwelling to dissuade his son from such folly, Amar uses the occasion to make further weighty statements. He is going to begin a new life in which women, instead of dragging a man down, bring happiness and light into life. Amar leaves Banaras without social moorings, not as a victor, which he has been for a brief spell, but a loser.

STREET ACTION AND A WOMAN AT THE FOREFRONT

Placed at the heart of the novel, in the third of its five sections, we have the story of Sukhada's meteoric rise to fame in the city, of her transformation from a spoilt rich girl to fearless leader championing the cause of the poor. Shanti Kumar is again the catalyst for the agitations that follow, as once more he and Lala Samarkant form the two poles representing extreme divergence of opinion regarding the immediate cause at hand, which now shifts to the issue of Dalit access to an important city temple. Initially siding with her father-in-law, once her passion for social justice has been roused Sukhada gravitates towards Shanti Kumar.

The unspecified Vaishnava temple, the *thakurdwara*, which becomes the centre of the agitation, enters the narrative as the location of Lala Samarkant's attempt, with his son gone, to regain public face as a pious Hindu. He doles out large sums of money for various religious occasions, and the temple congregation grows ever larger. The Naujawan Sabha, a youth organization, and Shanti Kumar's Sevashram boys, perform bhajans there regularly. But a number of Dalits have taken to cautiously edging their way into the assembly and it is not long before violence erupts in the temple. In the commotion that ensues, Shanti Kumar tells the godly to go ahead and feel free to hit Dalits, the government will not come to aid the downtrodden:

> And you religious rebels (*drohi*), remain seated, all of you, and take their kicks, as many as you can. Haven't you got the news that the god here is the god of merchants and bankers? . . . Your god must live in some hut or under some tree! This god wears jewels studded with precious stones. Eats sweet *mohanbhog* and cream. He doesn't like seeing the faces of people dressed in rags, or people who live off parched grain.[44]

Gandhian views seems inherent in the non-violent resistance that ensues thereafter; they colour Shanti Kumar's speech in the open field where the major part of the congregation follows him. Shanti Kumar tells no tales of gods and goddesses; there is no talk of the heroism of Kshatriyas or the power (*tejas*) of Brahmans. Instead, what unfolds is the character sketch (*charitra*) of a pure personality, the reference being clearly to the Mahatma, who remains unnamed,

[44] *Karmabhumi*, 369.

for whom purity of heart and action (*man, karma*) form the core of dharma: 'From this person emanated a vital message; upon hearing it, the audience felt released from the fetters binding the soul and the world became beautiful and pure.'[45] Dharma in this novel is devotion to the cause of the nation, to gain control of which calls equally for social reform at all levels. The people who have come to listen are the utterly destitute, many of them barely clad. Shanti Kumar then calls upon them to accompany him to the temple. They should not allow themselves to be cast out for fear of annihilation:

> *Dharma ki raksha sadaiv pranom se hui hai aur prano se hogi.*
>
> Dharma has always been defended by the sacrifice of life, and it will always be so.[46]

The narrator drily notes that Dalits have lived without the privilege of visiting temples for so long, it seems futile to them to sacrifice their lives for it. They march, but they are afraid. Amar's sister Naina, who weaves her way in and out of the narrative, follows the marchers. Lathi-armed priests are stationed at the temple doorway, along with Lala Samarkant. There is violence and the Dalits run. This is when Sukhada, standing in the doorway of their house, tells Naina, herself on the run, that Lala Samarkant has instigated the violence: 'I don't consider it right that untouchables enter the temple, but my blood begins to boil when I see bullets being fired. You can regard dharma as lost when it begins to need bullets to protect it. Look, look, that man has received a bullet wound. There is blood flowing from his chest.'[47] Sukhada thus finds herself in the midst of the redefinition of dharma. In saying that ritual life itself loses its value if it resorts to violence to protect itself, she is on her way to the Gandhian definition, which is also auctorial, which is Shanti Kumar's, and which will become that of the major protagonists. There is barely a moment to take note of this sudden turn in Sukhada's life as she jumps headlong into the fray:

---

[45] Ibid.: 370.
[46] Ibid.: 371.
[47] Ibid.: 375.

Sukhada didn't get into arguments. She was a self-willed woman. The pride that had made her luxuriate in comfort, that had kept her from contact with inferiors, that had prevented her submitting to anyone, now suddenly welled (*utsarg*) and spilled over. She leapt out of the house in a frenzy, put herself in front of the police, and admonished those who were running away: 'Brothers, why are you running off? This is not the time to escape, it's time to come out and bare your chests. Show them how you can sacrifice your life for dharma. Only those who fight for dharma get to god. Victory is never for those who run off.'[48]

Victory will be hers and won in the cause of the new dharma—nationalist and social reformist, Gandhian and austere—that she has adopted.

Courage is as contagious as cowardice, the narrator tells us. Within seconds, a human wall has formed with Sukhada at its centre. A bullet whizzes past her. Three or four men fall. There is more firing, more people are felled. Every man and woman present has now begun to understand that they are fighting for their dharma and their rights. So here we have the express equivalence of dharma as the claim of the Dalits to the same rights as the higher castes: '. . . and it was as glorious to sacrifice life for the moral code of untouchables (*achut niti*), as for the Brahmanical moral code (*dwij niti*).'[49] The narrator and Sukhada seem to have melted into one. Suddenly and unaccountably, there takes place the first of the change-of-heart scenes that will eventually resolve all social and political conflict in the novel. Lala Samarkant comes up and positions himself next to Sukhada as he shouts: 'The temple doors have been opened. Whoever wants to can receive *darshan*. There are no restrictions on anyone.' The wounded begin to be carried away on stretchers by the Sevashram students. The city merchants contribute what is needed for the death rituals. Custom and education, tradition and modernity, come together. That which real-life Banaras has resisted, the author realizes in the world of fiction.

[48] Ibid.
[49] Ibid.: 376.

The whole city is eager to celebrate the victors, and Sukhada becomes the goddess of victory as the pyres of the dead are lit on the banks of the Ganga. She comes to be regarded as the very personification of service and compassion (*seva aur daya ki murti bani hui hai*).[50] No surprise is expressed when she takes to the street and leads the action, no mention is made of the fact that she is an abandoned woman. Social and political service can now award such women a legitimate public role. And with this the poor and the destitute enter Sukhada's world for the first time. Rich and poor both begin to honour her. She begins to speak at public meetings. She may not be a particularly eloquent speaker, but her sincerity seeps through.

Sukhada's actions are accompanied by attempts at self-justification that bear closer analysis. She clearly finds it necessary to defend her defiant position *vis-à-vis* her absconding husband, to two persons in particular—the gentle and submissive Sakina, who could be regarded as portraying the ideal wife, and to Shanti Kumar, the modern middle-class professional who could be expected to understand her fiercely feminist stance. While visiting an ailing Sakina, and gently reproached for her lack of tenderness, Sukhada is driven to a passionate assertion of women's rights. A man can betray and then ask for understanding; can a woman do the same, she asks: 'He betrayed me. I can't pamper a guttersnipe. If I were to run off with another man, would he try and persuade me to go back to him? Maybe he'd come back to break my neck. I'm a woman and a woman's heart is never too hard, but I won't pamper him, to my dying day I won't.'[51]

Next comes a visit to Shanti Kumar, laid up at home since the violence in the field. Her warm words to him—she has received the fame that was his due, she has done little to deserve it—immediately mollify him, for he is feeling neglected and ignored, as the narrator, stepping in, tells us. Public servants are not immune to self-service—a topos that will be taken up again, later in the narrative.

---

[50] Ibid.: 377.
[51] Ibid.: 366.

Shanti Kumar notes drily that Sukhada has displaced Amar in the city, as he would find out were he to come back. Shanti Kumar himself could not even have dreamt of all that has happened the past year. But he responds conventionally enough when Sukhada begins to argue with him about who is to blame, man or woman, for the unhappy marriages that Shanti Kumar says have kept him from marrying. Man is not woman enough, he feels, not gentle, kind nurturing enough, there is some bestiality in his nature. If woman becomes a beast along with man, both end up unhappy. Echoes of Gandhi even here, for Gandhi regarded women as 'the best exemplars of moral force in society.'[52] Sukhada challenges him. So, a man wins either way? The fault always lies with the woman for being not woman enough to bear with suffering:

> I am neither generous nor thoughtful. But I do understand my dharma in relation to man. You're older than me and far more intelligent. I see you as an older brother. It brings me peace when I see your affection and goodness. I ask you shamelessly: What right has a man who does not fulfil his obligations towards a woman to expect a woman to fulfil hers? You are truthful, so I want to ask you this—were I to avenge myself tit for tat on account of his behaviour with me, would you ever forgive me?[53]

Dharma as a wife's rights *vis-à-vis* her husband? Here we have yet another modern definition of dharma, the moral conduct, the duty of a wife towards her husband, which Sukhada sees as mutual rather than one-sided. Shanti Kumar agrees that Amar's behaviour is inexcusable. Sukhada goes on to argue—and this is even more frank and to the point, she will comment on her own action later—saying she has never before spoken thus to anyone: men and women, once married, have to learn to make do with each other; the effort cannot be the woman's alone: 'I don't say that I am blameless. No woman can ever claim that, [but] nor can a man. I have had a meeting with Sakina. It's possible she has qualities that I don't. She is sweeter;

---

[52] Kishwar 1985: Part I, 1692.
[53] Ibid.: 382.

more tender. It's possible she can give more love. But if men and women set about comparing people to each other, how will the world fare? All we'll see is flowing rivers of blood and tears.'⁵⁴

Shanti Kumar is won over by Sukhada's sincerity; is the reader also being persuaded to share her point of view? Despite Sukhada's protest, a deeply impressed Shanti Kumar proceeds to write to Amar; he receives not a gratified but a troubled response. Amar's letter gives Shanti Kumar all credit for this awakening, but typically he sees Sukhada's gain as his loss, that is, he sees the whole matter once again in terms of a moral battle taking place within the marriage, of victory and defeat, of the gain by one as loss for the other. In this short time, a revolution has come about and Sukhada has become a figure of veneration for him; he feels ashamed that he did not appreciate her true worth.

> I weep when I think of how ignorant we are about those nearest to us . . . This ignorance dislocates me entirely . . . There is darkness before me . . . Nothing occurs to me . . . All my (new-found) self-confidence deserts me . . . Where I am, in what direction I am going, I know nothing. There is no future for me in this life, I have no faith in my future. All my aspirations turn out illusory, my fantasies false. To be honest, Sukhada is making me dance to her tune. I've become a puppet in her magical (*mayavini*) hands. First she shows herself to me in one sort of guise and cowers me down, and now that she's showing herself in another guise she defeats me. What is her real form? I have no idea.⁵⁵

Her rise is his fall. A defeated Amar is not yet ready, any more than is Sukhada in her victory, to think in terms of reconciliation.

Before embarking on yet another agitation, Sukhada once more visits the ill Sakina, as if to once again justify her action. Salim has become enamoured of Sakina in the meantime, thus a communally suitable match is in the offing. Sakina's house has been rebuilt; there is more prosperity all around. She has begun to take lessons from

---
⁵⁴ Ibid.: 383.
⁵⁵ Ibid.: 386.

a Christian lady who lives nearby. Sukhada speaks to her with an open, generous heart (*udar man*). She can see that there were occasions where Amar was likely to have registered her behaviour as unfeeling, indifferent. He should have told her what offended him: 'If he was hungry for love, so was I hungry for it. What he wanted of me, I also wanted of him. If I couldn't give what he wanted, why did he, in his turn, react rebelliously? Was it because he is a man, and if a man wants to, he can treat a woman like his shoe, but it's a woman's dharma to remain looped around his feet?'[56] A woman's dharma towards her husband is not unconditional, it requires mutual respect. Sukhada is asking for treatment as an equal from Amar. She is better informed now; she no longer just reads novels, she busies herself with historical and philosophical works; she lives a regulated and more austere life.

She teams up with Amar's mentor now. The second public agitation of which she becomes the leader is set in motion by Shanti Kumar. He has resigned from his post as professor in Queen's College and formed a trust with the financial help of Sukhada's mother Renuka. Sukhada supports Shanti Kumar's new plans for housing for the poor, to be located inside the city rather than in some outpost, so that the poor can find work in the city.

The housing project is, however, doomed to failure, given the vested interests in land and the presence of the very persons with vested interests on the municipal council. The land in question is to go to Seth Dhaniram, a prominent municipal counsellor and Naina's new father-in-law, for development. His son Maniram, sadistic and pleasure loving, has taunted Sukhada about her own abandoned state when she visits Naina. Even Shanti Kumar has retreated from his initial enthusiasm, he is cautious now that he has become head of the trust. It has taken him over, and he has begun to regard it as the end rather than the means to perform social service. Sukhada is appalled at this withdrawal and plunges out on her own

---

[56] Ibid.: 389.

to seek support in order to stage a full strike. Not surprisingly, the municipality has voted against the measure of housing for the poor. The temple, the *thakurdwara*, once again becomes the base for her operations. Initially, all the lower-caste representatives turn up there. There has been an awakening in the city; there is new knowledge of rights (*svatva ka gyan*) amongst Sukhada's followers, an excitement simmering everywhere—the dhobis are meeting somewhere, elsewhere the chamars, mehtars, barbers, and kahars. They have been waiting for months to get better housing.

The poor, largely Dalit, groups are now presented in sketch after sketch as stereotypes; individually and in group action, they come across almost as caricatures, a stylistic feature which to some extent we will also encounter in the village sections. A brief digression may be in order here. With the sole exception of Munni, with her quick intelligence and the ability to articulate her feelings and reflections, the presence of the poor and the rustic in the narrative often does little other than fulfil a social function; this can also happen in Premchand's best-known peasant novels. In their interaction with middle- or upper-class urban characters, and when seen from their perspective, they can often freeze into stereotypes. Their presence in the narrative does serve to enormously expand the social horizon both of the protagonists and of the probable reader, as Raymond Williams in his analysis of George Eliot's novels has pointed out,[57] '(b)ut as themselves they are still only socially present, and can emerge into personal consciousness only through externally formulated attitudes and ideas.'[58] The difficulty, Williams admits, is acute, of bringing together 'an analytically conscious observer of conduct with a developed analytic vocabulary, and of people represented as living and speaking in mainly customary ways; for it is not the precision of detailed observation but the inclusive, socially appealing, loose and

---

[57] Premchand was acutely aware of George Eliot's work. His translation of her *Silas Marner*, with the title *Sukhdas* (1920), is available in Premchand 2006, vol. 16.

[58] Williams [1973] 1985: 168.

repetitive manner that predominates.'[59] But however functional and ephemeral their presence, these marginalized sections of urban life do form the base of most of the action in the novel, and it is on their behalf and with their support that the social and political agitations can be, and are indeed, launched.

Sukhada's leadership role now means that she attempts to move the housing agitation forward at as rapid a pace as possible. There is no court of appeal now, she tells the straggling community of the dispossessed. The people are their own high court; they are the judges: 'We are not going to do battle or instigate a riot (*fasad*). We are just going on strike to show that we don't accept the Board's decision. And this strike won't last only a few days. It'll go on till the Board annuls its decision and gives us the land.'[60] Most back out; they stand to lose their livelihoods and jobs at the houses of the very people who run the city. Only the sweeper, Matai Jamadar, supports her. Sukhada remains unmoved, she cannot tolerate opposition. This is her first experience of defeat in public life. She introspects deeply (*gahara atma-chintan*) when alone that evening: 'If Maniram had not insulted her, would she have invested such energy in the strike?'[61] Her spirits surge again when she is arrested the next evening. She can respond as passionately as ever to her outraged father-in-law: 'After my arrest there may be a period of quiet because the clamour of people's destitution (*hahakar*) ceases to reach them, but the day is not far when these tears will turn into the sparks that will burn this injustice to ashes. And these ashes will be stoked and kindle a fire that will shake the very skies with the flames that come out of it.'[62] Fiery words and, once again, moral victory when she seemed to be on the verge of losing. The police officer is respectful; men and women line the streets.

How are victory and defeat to be negotiated with her husband? Unexpectedly, she seems to bow to him. For, once inside the car, a gratified Sukhada suddenly experiences an epiphany. She acknowledges

[59] Ibid., 169.
[60] *Karmabhumi*, 409.
[61] Ibid.: 414.
[62] Ibid.: 415.

THE HOLY CITY AS THE FIELD OF ACTION 183

Illus. 11: 'Police arresting the women pickets at the Town Hall', from *Collections of Photographs of Old Congress Party*, Gelatin Silver Print, *c.* 1930, possibly by K.L. Nursey.

her moral defeat (*parajay*). She is subscribing now to the very principles that had caused her separation from her husband—service and renunciation (*seva, tyag*). She has become her husband's follower. For the first time, she feels she can forgive him. But typically, she speaks of forgiveness, something which in principle is directed from a morally higher ground to a lower; she does not speak of submission. Though still partly expressed in traditional terms, worship and incense (*puha, dhup-dvip*), she sees the way forward as one of comradely co-operation. There is no sense of acceding to hierarchies already in place. This is an entirely new notion of marriage: 'There was no pity in this forgiveness; rather, there was sympathy, compassion, comradeship (*sahayogita*). They were both wayfarers on the same path, devotees of the same ideal . . . For the first time she felt an inner compatibility (*atmik samanjasya*) with her husband . . .'[63] Worded in

---

[63] Ibid.: 419–20.

apparently Gandhian terms, as a companionship in *seva*, Sukhada's notion of marital accord goes well beyond *seva*, to something that sounds remarkably like companionate marriage, of the married couple as partners. There is to be no subservience to one another. Sukhada speaks of *sahayogita* and of *samanjasya*, and of *atmik*, that is, 'inner' accord. The free choice of a marriage partner is as yet no part of the horizon of expectation of any character in the novel. And thus it is that, though she speaks of moral defeat, in speaking of forgiveness she comes once again to occupy higher moral ground. In her defeat is her victory. And it is such that Amar will receive the news of her imprisonment as yet another occasion when Sukhada steals the limelight, the lead from him, and is accorded public recognition. We seem to have come full circle. He had shot into fame in the city with the Munni episode, Sukhada for her widely acclaimed public service, for Dalit entry to the temple, and soon also with regard to housing for the poor.

POVERTY, TAXATION, AND A MAN OF THE PEOPLE

As in all Premchand novels, the city and the country are presented as deeply interconnected. The second and fourth sections transition effortlessly into the countryside, ruled and administered as it is by powers either based in the city or with strong links to it. Despite the myriad, rapidly sketched characters who people the small Dalit village in the eastern ills, where Amar lands after his wanderings, the two village sections are held short, with seven and eight brief chapters, respectively. Section 2 lays out the ground for action, as Amar is absorbed into his new village community, while Section 4 is constituted by the action. Amar's action is both exemplary and problem-ridden as far as his own motives unfold, to himself only to some extent, much more explicitly to the reader. This bifurcated narrative perspective, which seems to postulate the action itself as unquestionably noble, but the complex motivation propelling it as less than noble, is characteristic of the narrative as a whole. The village narrative follows a clear social reform agenda, as will become apparent in the reading that follows here; the psychological insights, the narrator's and Amar's own, seem less programmed, a part of the dynamic of the characters taking on a life of their own, one that the explicit agenda cannot entirely direct.

The village setting in the eastern UP hills has almost a textbook character, where social reform can find fertile soil. The chamars (leather workers) as the dominant caste in the village are not subject to the usual humiliations of the conventional caste hierarchies; they have a measure of autonomy in social matters. They call themselves Raidasis—after the fifteenth-century Dalit poet-singer-saint Ravidas—a Banarasi of the same caste, revered by many North Indian devotional communities—signposting that they have begun to claim more respectable status. There is no zamindar in this village and Gudar functions as the village head (*mukhia*), his foreyard is the meeting place for the village council. Three years earlier, Gudar's eldest son had fished out of the river and brought home as his bride-to-be the trouble-torn Munni, who had first taken refuge in Haridwar, only then to succumb to an accident himself. After his untimely death, Munni stays on as part of the family, becoming its female head, in the absence of a mother-in-law.

Gudar immediately recognizes the value of Amar's presence in the village; with his knowledge of English he can help with the upward mobility already apace. Saloni, the old woman who gives Amar shelter, provides temporary space for the little school that Amar soon sets up. Thus it comes about that a Dalit village provides refuge for two who seek shelter from the moral codes of respectable society that they have wittingly and unwittingly transgressed. Munni as a raped woman has no place in a society that regards her as tainted, and Amar has sought marriage with a poor Muslim woman.

It is in this setting that Munni comes into her own, to form the third of a triangle that will persist past the utopian closure of the novel. She is beautiful, vivacious, and intelligent. She and Amar soon strike up a flirtatious relationship. Amar's gentle demeanour, and a stance so soft that it seems almost womanly, propel Munni to take the initiative:

> Why didn't god make you a woman (*mehariya*), Lala? I've never seen a man with such a soft heart. It would've been good if you hadn't come over . . . You must be saying to yourself, what a shameless woman. But tell me, if a man becomes a woman, doesn't a woman have to become a man? I know you keep running away from me, keep trying to save your neck from me. But I won't let you go. I ask nothing else from you. I just want you to accept me as your own.[64]

Once again, as with Sukhada, we have an inverse gender relationship. The vivacious Munni takes the clearer and stronger position, a wooing one, *vis-à-vis* Amar. And as easily swayed as ever, Amar offers to go away with her and tell everyone she is his wife. But Munni vehemently rejects this offer. She does not want to become his mistress (*rakhail*). She tells him her story in due course, a long excursion that the narrative makes space for. She had gone to Haridwar, where abandoned Hindu women take refuge. But before a family she meets can deal with the problems that her presence creates, her husband tracks her down in Haridwar. She refuses to accept him, though tempted in every possible way to do so. She feels that she is unclean and will remain so, even if they were to find a way to make society, somewhere, somehow, accept the reunited family. She rejects him, not once but on a couple of occasions. For her own part, she tries to commit suicide by jumping into the Ganga; it is then that she is rescued by the Mukhia's son. Her husband loses his mind, he dies a most miserable death, and the child is lost. She is free, but scarred for life. Her lone state in the world, and her survival thereafter, make her the more vulnerable, now that someone from her world turns up in her life. Munni's devotion to him, and a lovelorn letter from Sakina fill Amar with pride.

[64] Ibid.: 339–40.

The Dalit social order with its flexible social mores has thus provided refuge to Munni, as also to the financially destitute Amar, and they repay their debt with village uplift work. Amar and Munni persuade Gudar and others in the village to give up alcohol, and then to give up eating meat, their hereditary right and custom. Amar's school prospers. He has been joined in his work by the radical Swami Atmanand, no Gandhian, who has left Shanti Kumar and the city, disillusioned by the compromises necessary to function in any organization there. Amar has connections; he has already visited Salim, newly posted to the district as a civil servant. He has noted the contrast in dress, way of life, social position, and power between himself as he lives now and the life Salim leads. 'Amar observed there was an upholstered couch in the room, brass flowerpots, carpet on the floor and a round marble table.'[65]

This is where the dynamics of character prevail over the narrative agenda of social reform. The meeting with Salim is an occasion for Amar to articulate his thoughts clearly to himself. Sukhada has joined him on his activist path; he worships her. Thus, like her, he also speaks of worship, an almost distancing emotion, rather than romantic love. But this does not lead to a power equation. There can be no reconciliation. He cannot write to her for two reasons:

> For one, it was shame, and the other, what he imagined was his defeat (*parajay*); her domineering mode (*bhav*) seemed to mock him. The thought that Sukhada could freely map out a path for herself, that she had not an iota of need for him—this thought put immense pressure on his affection for her. The most he could do now was to become her follower. She was not satisfied with anointing him with a saffron mark on his forehead (*tilak*) before he jumped into battle; she had jumped into the battleground before him. This hurt his self-esteem (*atma gaurav*).[66]

[65] Ibid.: 422.
[66] Ibid.: 423.

Military metaphors once more: battle, battleground, defeat, transferred also to his marriage as battlefield. With her moral victory, her sure head and hand, Sukhada poses a threat to Amar's sense of self, to his mode of action. She rushes into impulsive action where he hesitates. There never seems to be any question of subservience; it is he who must bend before her, the focalization is entirely through Amar, who now perceives 'service of the nation' in terms of 'power', 'arrogance', 'fame': 'Sukhada had managed to accomplish things he would not even have dreamt of; but whatever it was, it was [a sign of] the same arrogance (*amiri*), love of power, only in slightly transformed shape. The craving for fame, nothing else; but then he reprimanded himself. How do you know what goes on inside someone? Today, thousands are engrossed in the service of the nation. Who can say which one of them is egocentric and which a true servant?'[67] This is a key moment in his life as a nationalist and activist but also in the narrative as a whole. There is no question at this stage, however, of turning the searchlight on himself, no hint of self-critique. Amar's insights into Sukhada's character, her possible motivations, turn into a generalization about the thousands engrossed in service to the nation. What is the nature of the gratification they get when their actions are crowned with recognition, if not success? To what extent is their genuine concern for the deprived shot through with notions of self-gain? Which has the upper hand, and at what point in time? A brooding Amar withdraws from Munni as much as from Sakina, avoiding the usual banter, focusing only on his struggle with Sukhada, in which he sees her as surging much ahead of himself: 'Sukhada had reached the peak (*shikhar*), and he needed all his inner strength and concentration (*atmabal aur manoyog*) to get anywhere near her.'[68]

The Great Depression, that worldwide *mandi* which plunges the peasants into utter destitution, provides the occasion for action and leadership. As has been shown, the '(D)epression sharply enhanced

[67] Ibid.: 424.
[68] Ibid.: 432.

the burdens of revenue, rent and interest payments, and the people worst affected were the relatively better off or "middle" peasants with the surplus to sell (unlike the post-1918 inflation which had hurt the poorest sections of the population).'[69]

'The peasants of our village cannot meet the tax demands of the local Zamindar, a Mahant, who lives in luxury and taxes in the name of the temple deity.' Swami Atmanand's fiery words of collective action against the Mahant meet with much enthusiasm at the village meeting. Some speak of leaving farming altogether; Atmanand is the leader of the moment. Amar's words of caution find no resonance and send him post-haste to Munni, looking for solace.

Amar's encounter with the local authorities allows the reader a glimpse of the unrelenting imperial power structure in place. Both the landowning Mahant and the District Magistrate offer ready sympathy but look to safeguard their own interests. The Indianization of government service has only led to greater frustration on all fronts. Expectations have risen, but there is a limit to the power Indian civil servants enjoy or are indeed willing to exercise. Mahantji is a fair, strapping six-foot, thirty-five-year old. Corpulent and pleasure loving, he luxuriates in his opulent surroundings and the devotion offered him: an extravagant kitchen overflowing with the good things of life, an equally extravagant cowshed, horses, a stall of elephants each with its own name, trappings, and personal groom. But Amar finds a gracious man, inclined to leniency, who promises to get the tax reduced by half. District Magistrate Ghazanavi turns out to be a cultivated man, he has a literature degree from Oxford; he knows Shanti Kumar. He gets along famously with Salim and, still new to the service, sympathizes with the downtrodden and their nationalist aspirations though he is unwilling to exert or expose himself unduly. And thus he resorts to the usual slowing tactics. The trouble, Ghazanavi says, is that the Mahant is himself in arrears. He likes to keep his coffers filled. There will have to be an inquiry; he

---

[69] Sarkar 1983: 258.

appoints a reluctant Salim to carry out the investigation. There is hope in the village and even Atmanand comes around temporarily. All seems set for reconciliation and compromise.

At all the nodal points in the struggle with the authorities, the action is propelled not only by the need of the hour but also the power struggle between husband and wife. For when Amar hears from Naina that Sukhada is in prison, he is touched to the raw and throws caution to the winds. He needs to embark on yet more spectacular action. He sees Sukhada everywhere, in the firmament, in the mountains, and in the clouds. He does not know what he says at the meeting after that. 'Amar's inside brimmed over with gratitude. He felt that there was a protective hand extended over him, just as the moonlight that suffused the landscape. It seemed to him that something had been ordained for his life, a command, a sanction, a truth, and that he was to protect and preserve it at each step. For the first time in his life, he felt that he was in contact with a great aspiration, a great consciousness.'[70] He delivers a fiery speech and asks the peasants to withhold tax. He will realize later that his impulsive decision, prompted by the need to outdo Sukhada and provoking inevitable counter-violence, will not serve the peasants well. Violence will give the state the opportunity to act. Some will be killed; many will end in prison. District Magistrate Ghazanavi understands the plight of the peasants, he understands Amar's need to play the leader, he sees swaraj coming but more powerful is the immediate need to quell the fire. It is not as difficult to put a stop to open rebellion as to stop this kind of wind blowing (*khule fasad ko rokna itna mushkil nahim, jitna is hava ko*).[71] 'The most serious threat, alike to the British and to the policy of compromise now being sought to be followed by the Congress leadership, came from deepening rural discontent as prices touched a record low,' says the historian Sumit Sarkar. The situation in the United Provinces was explosive.

[70] *Karmabhumi*, 441.
[71] Ibid.: 443.

Amar's words to Munni and the villagers who try to stop the car carrying him away to the city, and into police custody, revert to his Gandhian non-violent stance: 'This is our *dharma-yuddha* and our victory depends on our ability to renounce (*tyag*), our readiness to sacrifice (*balidan*) and on our truthfulness (*satya*).'[72] Though Amar invokes 'satya', he does not speak of 'satyagraha', the politically more charged term. Once again, the author seems to be protecting himself and his work from censorship. However, the moral-militant *dharma-yuddha* is no less charged, a term the Mahatma had glossed as early as 1924 in his preface to *Satyagraha in South Africa*:

> That is the beauty of satyagraha. It comes up to oneself; one has not to go out in search of it. This is the virtue inherent in the principle itself. A *dharma-yuddha*, in which there are no secrets to be guarded, no scope for cunning and no place for untruth, comes unsought; and a man of religion is ever ready for it. A struggle which has to be previously planned is not a righteous struggle. In a righteous struggle God Himself plans campaigns and conducts battles. A *dharma-yuddha* can be waged only in the name of God, and it is only when the satyagrahi feels quite helpless, is apparently on his last legs and finds utter darkness all around him, that God comes to the rescue.[73]

Amar in his excitement has violated the terms of the agreement with the authorities. His battle is righteous; the ends were righteous but not the means. Amar will realize the extent of his folly in ignoring the means, in the self-introspection that will follow once he is in prison. Meanwhile, it is too late to stop the brutal police action which will strip the village of all it possesses; Amar's school will be gutted, the cattle auctioned and butchered, with Salim personally whipping a defiant old Saloni in an unsuccessful bid to reduce her to submission. Official violence is taking a new path, following a policy described as 'civil martial law', a rule 'empowering civil officials with

---

[72] Ibid.: 450.
[73] *CWMG*, vol. 29: 5.

sweeping, near-military powers, instead of directly calling the army as at Amritsar in 1919.'[74]

BONDING IN BONDAGE

The fifth and last section shifts from city to countryside and back again, bringing Sukhada and Amar together with the insights they have gained in their time apart, but with their heads still held high. As we have seen, Amar's two authority figures, his father and his mentor Dr Shanti Kumar, have almost come together. Lala Samarkant no longer offers opposition—he has been to the village and speaks of *dharma-yuddha*, much like Shanti Kumar—though he still harbours hard thoughts about his son, voiced now to his imprisoned daughter-in-law. Sukhada defends him: whatever Amar did, good or bad, there was always resistance at home. And Amar's two women also come together now. Sukhada meets Munni in prison, classed in an inferior prison category but as spirited as ever, resisting the prison matron's directions to assign her as Sukhada's personal attendant. A proud Sukhada decides to join Munni in her prison class.

In prison, Amar undergoes a similar transformation. The death of inmates, visions of the violence visited on old Saloni, darkness and despair all make him turn inwards, first to God and then away from him. Brooding over cause and effect, it hits him one day, like a flash of light. This new self-reflexivity is manifest through an inward turn of the narrative, as new in Premchand's oeuvre as in Amar's own development, brings him to a sudden realization of his own motives:

> That letter of Naina's and the news of Sukhada in prison. That's why he grew so frenzied (*avesh*) and abandoned the well-advised path of finding a compromise (*samjhauta*) and turned instead on that ill path. It was as if the knock had opened his eyes. He understood, in the guise of

[74] Sarkar 1983: 318. The phrase 'civil martial law' comes from Low 1977: chapter 5.

service, it was the play of personal rivalry (*vyaktigat spardha*), of desire for glory (*yash*). What else could be the outcome of such thoughtlessness and frenzy?[75]

Amarkant sees that he has had no goal, no ideal, no steadfast resolution (*vrata*) till now. He is driven to face the fact that he has been swimming in a wave of opportunism (*upayogavadita*).

> He had no steadiness, no discipline, no [real] aspiration. There was arrogance (*dambha*) in his service, intoxication (*pramad*), ill-will (*dvesha*). It was this arrogance that made him disregard Sukhada. Instead of attempting to get to the truth that dwelt in that woman of comfort, he rejected her. His outer eye covered the inner. With this arrogance he put up a show of love (*prem*) for Sakina. Was there even a trace of love (*prem*) in that madness? . . . now he could see nothing other than desire (*lipsa*) in that love. And not only desire, but a kind of lowliness. He had tried to still his desire by using the lowly social position of this simple woman. And then Munni came into his life, destroyed by disappointments and filled with desire. How dissembling his behaviour had been with that devi! True he had evinced no physical desire. It was how he explained it to himself, but examined now the truth was that in that enjoyment, in that attachment (*anurag*), there had indeed been an element of physical desire.[76]

He is filled with self-reproach. Why had he reacted so hastily? New for Premchand is this kind of extended self-analysis of past actions by the protagonist himself, in which he makes sense of his life, creating his own personal, historical narration and an awareness that will inflect his future action.[77] For all this new sense and articulation of interiority, however, it is worth noting that romantic love (*muhabbat, prem, anurag*) is still reserved for the relationship outside marriage. Within marriage, it is in terms of reverence and admiration that he will learn to regard his wife. Sukhada has been through a similar process, and now the same thing happens to Amar. There has been

---

[75] *Karmabhumi*, 467–8.
[76] Ibid.: 480.
[77] Taylor [1989] 1996: 251.

loss of life, women widowed, children orphaned in that denial of tax payment. Leaders were being cast into prison; the next lot of capable people taking over were being similarly transported into prison. The state was reacting with extreme brutality in the village, now in a condition of near ruin.

As readers, we witness unbelievable violence, which there is no effort to mitigate or make bearable. It is in this dark hour, when all seems set to wipe out every trace of resistance, that the narrative takes a deliberate turn. Premchand was intensely aware of what he was doing when he twisted the narrative thus, in order to become inspirational rather than plunge into yet lower depths. As early as January 1925, in an article for the journal *Samalochak*, he had reflected on the difference between the realist and the idealist novelist; he used the English terms, placing himself squarely in the latter category. The realist novelist shows things as they are, he wrote,

> because in this world the fruits of good deeds are not always good and of bad not always bad, in fact, its opposite—the good suffer blows, suffer atrocities, bear distress, are humiliated, the fruits of their good deeds are the obverse of good, and the bad prosper, gain fame, obtain glory, the fruits of their bad deeds are the obverse of bad. Strange are the laws of nature . . . The realist is bound by the shackles of experience, and because there is a preponderance of bad characters in the world . . . in truth realism makes pessimists of us, we cease to believe in human nature, we see only what is bad around us. There is no doubt that realism is well fitted to expose the corruption of society . . . When we tire of working in a dark room, we long to get out and breathe in the fresh air. Idealists fulfil this need. Idealism makes us acquainted with characters whose hearts are pure, who are devoid of selfishness and lust, who have good dispositions . . . [However] it is less difficult to imagine a divine being than to fill this being with life.

If they can fill the good characters with life, they achieve this difficult merger. Litterateurs (*sahityakar*) have a high status, they can show the way, awaken our humanity, fill us with good intentions, broaden our gaze. This is why, he says, those novels rank high in our esteem where realism and idealism blend with each other.[78] This novelistic idealism dovetails neatly with Gandhian notions of allowing for a change of heart in political opponents. 'The appeal of reason is more to the head, but the penetration of the heart comes from suffering. It opens up the inner understanding in man.'[79]

Thus it comes about that, one after another, the prime villains succumb to a change of heart, providing resolutions to one menacing political conflict after another. Lala Samarkant is able to bring around Salim, who now embarks on a real investigation of the situation of the peasants and cannot believe what he sees. His detailed report provokes both pity and impatience from Mr Ghazanavi. No new truths are revealed in this report, he tells him. Withhold it. But Salim sends it up, ignoring Ghazanavi's words of caution, with the result that he is removed from service within the week. The new civilian, a Bengali by the name of Ghosh, sent in his stead has no compunctions in carrying the brutality further. Salim becomes a peasant leader and joins Atmanand.

Meanwhile, in spite of Sukhada's absence, the action in Banaras is gathering pace. There are Gandhian speeches on the maidan by Lala Samarkant and others, each more eloquent than the next. Shanti Kumar, not to be held back any longer, gives a most Gandhian address. It is not clear whether the people will win or lose, but strike they must, bearing ill will (*bair*) towards none: 'Humanity cannot always be trampled upon. Equality is a truth of life. It's the only situation that makes for the stability of society . . . This is the age of enlightenment (*jagrti*). Enlightenment cannot tolerate injustice . . .'[80] His imprisonment propels Naina into action. She has held back thus far, out of consideration for her in-laws and because of her own shyness. She steps forward and speaks on a hillock of bricks in the golden light of the full moon. She confesses that it is her father-in-law who had bought the disputed land: 'You will have seen, there were

---

[78] Premchand 2006: vol. 7, 292–3.
[79] Gandhi [1931] 1999. As cited in Mantena 2012: 17.
[80] *Karmabhumi*, 488.

green and flourishing villages here. The Municipality constituted an Association for the Development of the City. The land of the peasants was snatched away for a throwaway price, and today that same land is being sold for gold coins, only so that bungalows for the rich can be constructed here.'[81] She predicts that the time is not far when the poor will grab power. She asks them to accompany her to the municipality and thousands follow her in disciplined formations. She sings, and they sing with her as she marches. Women from 'good' homes have entered the public sphere, they court arrest; they face violence.

The scene shifts to the Municipality Board meeting. If in *Sevasadan* this still new institution had played a central role in deciding the fate of Suman and her fellow courtesans and prostitutes, here it becomes the scene of climactic confrontation between regressive and progressive social forces. Not as the battleground for newly communalizing Hindu and Muslim formations, but the newly rich, both Hindu and Muslim, whose rapaciousness, in collusion with the colonial state, knows no bounds, with only a few professional men ready to speak in the voice of reason and justice. The Board members can only be glad that Shanti Kumar has been taken prisoner. But Mr Shafiq, university professor, who knows Shanti Kumar, steps up and warns of the terrible violence that will now ensue. Just then, the District Superintendent of Police (DSP) calls, he wants orders to fire on the procession being led by Naina Devi. The vote in the Municipality Board is twelve to ten in favour of firing. Seth Dhaniram, Naina's father-in-law, remains neutral. The phone rings again with the news that Manilal has shot his wife dead; he will be lynched by the crowd and it is her corpse which is being carried at the head of the procession now. Naina's death provides the resolution to the crisis in the city. Dhaniram is the first to come around, then Hafiz Halim, Salim's father. They step out to address the people and Hafiz Halim's is the last speech to the crowd. He speaks of the beginning of a new phase (*naya daur*). Naina's corpse is carried to the Ganga: 'The battle

---

[81] Ibid.: 490.

which had been initiated by a devi six months ago had been brought to a close by another devi by sacrificing her life.'[82] Not Amar, but his women win. And the narrator dwells lovingly on each moment of this idealized reality.

The congregation in prison undergoes similar reconciliations. It is Sukhada whom Amar has most wronged and he asks for forgiveness before everyone. But Sukhada does not let him off so easily. When alone, she accuses him of being filled with anger, anger from top to bottom (*upar se niche tak krodh krodh*). Had he made overtures, written to her, he might have moved her. The fault was not hers but of her upbringing. All could be laid to rest now, but both proceed to claim victory. Even at this moment of reconciliation, battle metaphors persist. Sukhada tries to clinch the argument by saying, 'You instigated rebellion and I quenched it by disciplined action.' They continue to squabble, and it is he who has the last word: 'You fulfilled what I had set out to do.'[83]

> As for Munni, she was standing apart, filled with a sense of detachment. A bird had come from somewhere to perch on the edge of the vacant field of her life. She had filled the flowing end of her sari with grain and, calling out to him, she had tiptoed towards him, to then take a leap and catch hold of him. She had spread the grain on the floor. The bird picked at the grain and looked at her with eyes full of trust, as if to ask, will you look after me with affection or will you also cast me adrift, without support, after you've amused yourself with me for a bit? But just as she reached out to catch him with her hand, it flew off and went to sit on a faraway branch. It seemed to be looking at her with eyes full of deceit (*kapat*) as if to say: I inhabit the skies, what have you in your cage for me save dry grain and water in a clay cup?[84]

But the very last word on the nature of their relationship will be saved for Munni. The committee set up by government to settle the issue between government and the peasants is to have two nominated

[82] Ibid.: 494.
[83] Ibid.: 500.
[84] Ibid.: 499.

members, Amar and Salim; the remaining three members are to be selected by these two. Amar says warmly, Whoever the other two may be, one will certainly be Munni. It is with her words that the novel ends: '"Do you see Bahuji? This is how he always teases me." She turned her head away as she said that. Her eyes had filled with tears.'[85]

Munni's predicament can be understood variously: that there are no socially accepted ways to fulfil the desires of a woman once she comes to be regarded as tainted by society at large. We have only to think of wistful Suman as we left her at the closing of *Sevasadan* and of the warm-hearted and tragic prostitute Zohra in Premchand's *Gaban* (1931), whom Ramanath, the male protagonist of the novel, newly reunited with his estranged wife Jalapa, remembers at the end of that novel: 'But Zohra's face still continues to hover before his eyes. The seedlings she had planted, the cat she had kept, the clothes she had sewn, her room, all these signs of her memory, when Rama seeks them out, Zohra's image comes and stands before him.'[86] Munni can stay on with Amar and Sukhada—but as one who continues to be tantalized by memories of the past and by her present situation. Yet her presence is also a constant reminder that Amar and Sukhada's union remains incomplete without her. It is she who does not resist Amar's need to play the leader; it is she who is also ready to submit to Sukhada's claims of superior status, morally, socially and within the marital union. Munni can be nicely accommodated in this union, regardless of what the arrangement may mean for her. It seems almost fated to remain triangular, as so often in Premchand's novels.

CONCLUSION

The narrative has negotiated its way through the tangle of relationships, through the new social parameters: dharma defined as social reform, nationalism, equality between women and men in marriage

[85] Ibid.: 504.
[86] Premchand 2006: vol. 5, 231.

that the strong-willed educated couple at its heart are setting themselves as they explore their potential in this period of political growth. But it has also exposed the limits of its growth, as Amar and Sukhada come up against the boundaries of the possible, both by way of self-fulfilment and fulfilment in their relationship. The 'deeper inwardness' and the 'radical autonomy',[87] coupled with each strong individuation, thwart the very togetherness that they have simultaneously sought and at the end partially achieved. Premchand is too much of a 'realist' after all, for fairytale harmony to be established at the end; the personal power struggle between the two cannot and does not allow that. For such are the challenges and contradictions of the twofold thrust of their endeavour, their quest for expansion of self *and* for fulfilment in partnership, that they need that third, Munni, who herself can only be left unfulfilled. Companionate marriage may be desirable, but it enters the North Indian middle class as a problematic proposition. The ambitions undergirding their *seva*, their thirst for public recognition, makes for precarious social and psychological balance for the protagonists. Thus it is that till the very end Amar and Sukhada, though realizing in their own way the Gandhian ideal of marriage as also service to the nation, remain locked in their power struggle and in a relationship defined in terms of victory and defeat, *jay-parajay*. The personal, political, and social remain at all times deeply implicated in each other.

The Gandhian frame, though dominant in the early 1930s, is neither all-encompassing nor unbroken. Amar seems more explicitly Gandhian than Sukhada—his spinning activities, his selling khadi, his work in the village, his move to help peasants, to actually reach across lines of religion and caste in his personal life. But he also vacillates; he resorts to a kind of armed resistance at the end, driven by his competitiveness with Sukhada and his personal ambition. However, Sukhada's politics move beyond the frame that Gandhi reserved for women. She is the dominant partner in a marriage where conventional

---

[87] Taylor [1989] 1996: 363.

hierarchies cannot be entirely restored. It is also possible that here the author is not able to exercise the kind of control that would make for a neat ending, just as with Munni, who eludes control, claiming a place at Amar's side, refusing to be banned entirely into social service.

And finally, the city. Premchand was perhaps right to claim that the Banaras of his novel was not the city of that name and that literature could not be read as history, for fiction had allowed him to turn dreams into reality—temple entry by Dalits in a central city temple, the reversal of the land scam action by the municipal council, the reconsideration of revenue demands by government, and the integration, however uneasy, of a raped woman in a respectable middle-class household. But the ideal could only be regarded as 'ideal' if it was juxtaposed with the 'real', with a bleak reality that could not be allowed to take its own course if it were also to be read as a lesson in morality. Premchand had spoken in the passage cited above of the need to create characters filled with life, but if they became part of events so unbearably bleak, so relentlessly credible in their almost documentary faithfulness to contemporary experience as to culminate not only with pessimism, some harmony had to be restored, some compromises made with the imperial state. The ideal gained its character by being coupled with the real at all times, and the city as it emerged at the end of the novel could only be portrayed as partly ideal because it was also real. The real could function without the ideal, but the ideal could only shine if it were coupled with the real.

REFERENCES

Awasthi, Rekha. 2012. 'Samgathan ki Rashtriya Anivaryata'. In *Naya Path*, January–June 2012, Special Issue on Seventy-five years of the Progressive Cultural Movement in India.

Balibar, Etienne and Immanuel Wallerstein. 1991. 'The Nation Form: History and Ideology'. In *Race, Nation, Class: Ambiguous Identities*. London, New York: Verso.

Banarasidas. [1641] 1981. *Ardhakathanak* (Half a Tale). Jaipur: Prakrit Bharati Sansthan.

Forbes, Geraldine. 1998. *Women in Modern India: The New Cambridge History of India*, 4/2. Cambridge: Cambridge University Press.

Gandhi, M.K. [1928] 1999. *Satyagraha in South Africa*. In *The Collected Works of Mahatma Gandhi* [*CWMG*], vol. 29 pp. 1–269. Delhi: Publications Division, Ministry of Information and Broadcasting, Government of India.

———. [1931] 1999. 'Speech at Birmingham Meeting'. In *The Collected Works of Mahatma Gandhi* (Electronic Edition), vol. 54, 43–48. New Delhi: Government of India.

Glover, William J. 2008. *Making Lahore Modern: Constructing and Imagining a Colonial City*. Minneapolis, London: University of Minnesota Press.

Govind, Nikhil. 2014. *Between Love and Freedom: The Revolutionary in the Hindi Novel*. Delhi: Routledge.

King, Anthony. 1984. *The Bungalow: The Production of a Global Culture*. London: Routledge and Kegan Paul.

Kishwar, Madhu. 1985. 'Gandhi on Women: Part I', in *Economic and Political Weekly*, vol. 20, no. 40, 5 October; Part II, *Economic and Political Weekly*, vol. 20, no. 41, 12 October.

Kumar, Radha. 1993. *The History of Doing: An Illustrated Account of Movements for Women's Rights and Feminism in India, 1800–1990*. Delhi: Kali for Women.

Low, D.A. 1977. *Congress and the Raj: Facets of the Indian Struggle, 1917–1947*. London: Heinemann.

Mantena, Karuna. 2012. 'Another Realism: The Politics of Gandhian Nonviolence'. *American Political Science Review*, vol. 106, issue 2, 455–70.

Omvedt, Gail. 2004. *Ambedkar: Towards an Enlightened India*. Delhi: Penguin-Viking.

Orsini, Francesca. 2002. *The Hindi Public Sphere, 1920–1940: Language and Literature in the Age of Nationalism*. Delhi: Oxford University Press.

Patel, Sujata. 1988. 'Construction and Reconstruction of Women in Gandhi', in *Economic and Political Weekly*, 20 February.

Premchand. 2006. *Premchand Rachanavali*. In 20 vols. Vols. 1, 5, 8, 9, and 16. Delhi: Janvani Prakashan.

Rai, Amrit. 1962. *Qalam ka Sipahi*. Allahabad: Hans Prakashan.

Renold, Leah. 2005. *A Hindu Education: Early Years of the Banaras Hindu University*. Delhi: Oxford.

———. 2012. 'A Hindu Temple of Learning: The Hybridization of Religion and Architecture'. In *Banaras: Urban Forms and Cultural Histories*, ed. Michael S. Dodson. London: Routledge, pp. 170–91.

Sarkar, Sumit. 1983. *Modern India, 1885–1947*. Madras, Bombay, Delhi: Macmillan.

Shivrani Devi. 1956 [1991]. *Premchand, Ghar Men*. Delhi: Atmaram and Sons.

Tarlo, Emma. 1996. *Clothing Matters: Dress and Identity in India*. London: Hurst and Co.

Taylor, Charles. [1989] 1996. *Sources of the Self: The Making of the Modern Identity.* Cambridge, Mass: Harvard University Press.

Varma, Balmukund. 1935. *Kashi ya Banaras*. Banaras: Self-published.

Williams, Raymond. [1973] 1985. *The Country and the City*. London: The Hogarth Press.

4

Lahore, Delhi, and the Bitter Truth of Independence

THE PARTITION OF PRE-INDEPENDENCE Panjab and the years after the cataclysm, as played out in the centuries old Lahore–Delhi nexus, form the backbone of the two volumes of *Jhutha Sach* (1958, 1960; False Truth), Yashpal's epic novel. The first volume focuses on communally torn Lahore in the year immediately before Partition and a little thereafter, the second largely on a post-Independence Delhi milling with refugees; together they add up to more than a thousand pages.[1] The matter-of-fact tone, short sentences, and dry reportage-style prose of the novel provide vivid detail without dwelling on description, inner turmoil, and emotional upsurge. And yet the novel manages to convey a milieu, a period, and an urban landscape with a rapidity and power quite unmatched in the Hindi novel. This is particularly true of the first volume; the second slackens in pace and intensity.

Yashpal (1903–76) grew up in the environment he writes about in this novel. His mother was an ardent Arya Samajist who sent him to the extremely puritanical Gurukul Kangri when he was seven or eight. He was later at the Dayanand Anglo-Vedic School in Lahore,

---

[1] Part One of the novel was serialized in the Hindi weekly *Dharmyug* in 1957 and published in book form in 1958. Part Two was begun in 1959 and published in 1960. Citations are to 'JS' and relate to the Lok Bharati Prakashan, Allahabad, edition.

and then at the National College in the same city. He came into contact with Bhagat Singh there and became part of the Hindustan Republican Association. He was in prison from 1932 to 1938, where he started writing in Hindi as part of a conscious decision. This and much other interesting information is available in *Simhavalokan* ([1951] 2005), his memoirs.

Yashpal's 'important note' at the beginning of his novel best describes his close weave of fact and fiction:

> An attempt has been made in both parts of *False Truth*—'Homeland and Nation' (*vatan aur desh*) and 'The Future of the Nation' (*desh ka bhavishya*)—to depict the contemporary (*samayik*) political atmosphere of the country in its historical reality (*yatharth*). In order to give shape to this historical reality and make it credible, the names of certain historical persons have cropped up, but they are not historical persons, just characters in a novel. There are certainly some historical events or occurrences in the novel but the narrative as a whole is based on imagination; it is not history . . .[2]

The political happenings in their 'historical reality' in fact colour the whole novel as much as they affect the course of the lives of its characters. Yashpal borrowed the files of a newspaper, possibly *The Tribune*, when writing the novel,[3] which is peppered not only with the precise dates of key political events but also of the personal events that often follow as a direct consequence of the day's headlines.[4] In a novel

---

[2] Yashpal's son Anand's translation of the novel into English, *This is Not that Dawn*, was published by Penguin India in 2010. The translations here are mine. Information regarding the circumstances of writing the novel stems from Anand.

[3] Nemichandra Jain, in his analysis of the novel, also links the two genres—newspaper and novel—very closely: 'The description of this life is so very "realistic" and "authentic" (*pramanik*) that the portrayal of a whole epoch becomes available, as if countless cuttings from newspapers had been arranged in a specific sequence with great caution and dexterity' ([1966] 2002: 71–2).

[4] 'He did travel extensively throughout Punjab before writing Part 1 (esp. Jalandhar and such cities), talking to those who had been through the

framed by history, when does event so dominate that the individual recedes, being reduced to the role of a witness as the chronicling takes over? Education and professional occupations bring together diverse people in a modernizing city, desires transgress the borders of class and religion. What scope is there for transgression before and after Partition, as the force of circumstance uproots people and places them in new spaces and contexts? What power do these spaces exercise not only in their imaginings of their lives but in the decisions they feel compelled to take? And finally, how do the mores of specific city spaces limit or open the choice of partnership and profession?

Jhutha Sach is very much a chronicle not only of the lives of its protagonists, but of Lahore before and immediately after Partition as well as of post-Partition Delhi. The location and description of the houses situated in a given locality in the city, which Yashpal almost always specifies, and the environment and life-style of its inhabitants provide some indication of the mental horizon of the people who live in the houses as much as of their differences with characters living in other localities.

There are myriad characters but the focalization on the action takes place largely through the perspective of three young people, the siblings Tara and Jaydev Puri (the last referred to as Puri throughout), and Kanak Datta, Puri's beloved. The story of the sibling pair is closely entwined in the first volume, not only with the chronicle but also with each other. For a good part of the volume it is Puri who is politically active, while Tara and Kanak are subsumed in his action. But it is Tara who undergoes the pain of Partition most intimately: in a certain way, it is her body that is pulled asunder when the subcontinent is pulled apart. It is on Tara's story, and partly on that of

---

ordeal. He consulted the archives of several newspapers. Borrowed bound files of the old issues of a newspaper published from Ambala (probably *The Tribune*) were with us until the middle 1960s when they were returned to the newspaper.' Email from Anand, 27 October 2009. In a sense then, the novel is based on oral history.

Puri—caught in the limitations, the 'customary',[5] of their particular family and their neighbourhood as they try to transcend it—that I will primarily focus.

All three, as we meet them at the start of the novel, have begun to try crossing social divisions because they desire socially unattainable partners. But gender, poverty, and affluence or the lack of it all inflect trajectories, hold back Tara, and to some extent Puri, but less so Kanak on account of her wealth and the power that it brings. Only the seismic violence of Partition, with its destruction of the once-shared Hindu–Muslim–Sikh landscape, and the tearing of the social fabric of Lahore, will break mental barriers, specially of the older generation, so that new social identities and newer kinds of unions can be forged.

The Lahore which the Puris and Dattas inhabit is a palimpsest of its layered history. In the attitudes and generational differences of the families we shall encounter the age-old as well as the most modern. At the northern edge of the walled city lies Akbar's palace and fort (1584), to which Aurangzeb later added the massive Jama Masjid. Akbar had strengthened and extended the city's wall to encompass a larger area, and provided it with the thirteen gates that exist at the same sites today.[6] The great Mughal emperors all made their

---

[5] For the conflict is precisely between the 'customary' and the 'educated', as used by Raymond Williams, and as cited in the previous essay. I cite the relevant passage from Williams once again for convenience of reference: 'Most of us, before we get any kind of literary education, get to know and to value—also to feel the tensions of—a customary life. We see and learn from the ways our families live and get their living; a world of work and of place, and of beliefs so deeply dissolved into everyday actions that we don't at first even know they are beliefs, subject to change and challenge. Our education, quite often, gives us a way of looking at that life which can see other values beyond it: . . . We know especially how much they are needed to understand change—change in the heart of the places where we have lived and worked and grown up . . . But it is more than a matter of picking up terms and tones. It is what happens to us, really happens to us, as we try to mediate those contrasted worlds . . .' Williams [1973] 1985: 199.

[6] Sara Suleri on the old city as it exists today: 'the Old City, as it is known, has luckily escaped a museum or a mausoleum atmosphere, and remains

presence felt in Lahore; the city is dotted with the monuments they built.[7] These later served the British when they conquered Panjab in 1849—they situated several key offices in retrofitted Mughal tombs. But the British also gradually added a number of new institutional buildings: 'factories, hospitals, prisons, lunatic asylums, clubs and racecourses, parks, arboretums, zoos, hotels, courthouses, museums, universities, cinema halls, gymnasiums and so forth.'[8] There were also the famous Lahore colleges—the Government College, the Forman Christian College, and the Dayanand Anglo-Vedic (or DAV) College, culminating in the establishment of the Panjab University in 1882.[9] As the intellectually most vibrant capital of the North, Mughal–British Lahore easily overshadowed Delhi which, denuded of British patronage after 1857, had become a provincial city on Panjab's south-eastern edge.

In his study of the bungalow Anthony King has offered a fine survey of Lahore's layout, which reflected the city's layered history:

> The 1935 map of Lahore shows four very distinct types of spatial pattern in the built up area of the city, which it is tempting to associate with different kinds of values, social relations and behaviour. The old walled city with its intricate, meandering network of streets and tightly packed houses, suggests a traditional society and culture; the 'civil lines' area to

---

a node of obsessive activity or pleasure. Whether its getting and spending involves wreaths and garlands, jewellery and garments, dancing and singing, piety and prostitution, the Old City of Lahore defies the monotony of centuries.' Suleri 2005: 164.

[7] Glover provides the most information on the history of the architecture and layout of the city, including this: 'Jahangir and Nur Jahan were buried in tombs outside the city. Shah Jahan (r. 1627–57) was born in Lahore. He remodeled his grandfather's palace and built the famous Shalimar Gardens a few miles east of the river (1634–42). Sikh rule in Panjab (1799–1849) left no remarkable architectural remains behind.' Glover 2008: 8f.

[8] Ibid.: xiii.

[9] 'In 1901 the literacy rate among the city's 200,000 citizens, literacy rate low, 5% though 5 liberal arts colleges, 3 professional colleges, 28 secondary schools, 112 primary schools and several religious institutions offering instruction.' It had scores of printing presses.' Ibid.: xii.

the south with its spacious bungalows, wide metalled roads and sparse development intimates the 'ruralised', middle class values and leisured lifestyles of the European governing elite; the rectangular grid system of the military cantonment implies the formal social organization of the army; the more relaxed, yet still geometrical, lay-out of Model Town suggests the social life of the retired official whom Tandon describes.[10]

We have primarily to do with the walled city, and with Gawal Mandi and Model Town at the other end of the town and the wide social spectrum provided by their inhabitants. This spatial separation both reflects and strengthens the social cleavages dramatized in the novel, though the segregation is not absolute and the characters in our novel break through the barriers in the course of their education. But by and large the Lahoris of the old city, more mired in the old than the new, remained socially separated from those in the new neighbourhoods. These in turn may have been more progressive and modern than those in the old city, but for them too older social codes lingered and carried weight. The very architecture of Model Town houses reflected the contradictions inherent in their pattern of existence:

> Each house was divided into two parts by a huge vestibule in the middle. On one side were dining and drawing-room and an office room: on the other side the bedrooms, with dressing rooms and bathrooms. The front verandah overlooked a lawn surrounded by flower-beds and cypresses. Here male visitors were received. On the other side was a verandah, where meals were served except on winter evenings, and an enclosed paved courtyard, the women's domain, with kitchen and storerooms . . . In its own way the house was like the British bungalows in front and granduncle's house at the back.[11]

Even more significant than the geographical and social division was the religious one. The divisive politics of the British Raj had made for

---

[10] King 1984: 57. The reference is to Prakash Tandon's classic account of his family as embedded in undivided Panjab, *Punjabi Century: 1857–1947*. Tandon [1961] 1968.

[11] Ibid.: 237–8.

the allocation of government positions according to the religion of the applicant. The world we see in this novel, of college, newspaper, law court, and publishing, was thus an increasingly communalized one. The resentments fostered and envy engendered by the privileged position of high-caste Hindus—whose dominance came to extend from the higher government service to the professions outside, such as medicine, law, and engineering,[12]—further emphasized social and religious difference.[13] Though a majority in India, Hindus remained a minority in late-nineteenth-century colonial Panjab. They had found themselves wedged, as Kenneth Jones put it, between two converting religions, Islam and Sikhism. For them the advent of Dayanand Saraswati, with his dynamic message of education not birth as determining social status, served as a catalyst for modernization, change, and identity formation as much as self-assertion.[14] The upper layers of society, most of all the commercial castes—Khatri, Arora, and Sood—responded eagerly to Dayanand's call for social reform, education at large, particularly girls' education, and widow remarriage.[15] The Dayanand Anglo-Vedic College (1886), founded after Dayanand's death, to which was attached the school in which Tara and Puri's father taught, was established in order to counter the Anglicization of students trained in the British colonial university system.[16] Intensely nationalist, it provided education in Hindi, Sanskrit, and English to its students: English for adjustment, Hindi for communication, Sanskrit and Arya Samaj literature for moral uplift, and science for material progress.[17] It was the Arya Samaj

[12] Jones [1976] 2006: 286 and 61–2.

[13] The seating arrangement in municipal corporations, for instance, reflected this: on the left sat the Muslims, the Hindus on the right. See Jones ([1976] 2006: 310.

[14] Cf. ibid.: 36. Dayanand remained in the Panjab for more than a year, from April 1877. During his tour, an Arya Samaj was founded in every province of Panjab. Ibid.: 40.

[15] Ibid.: 22.

[16] Glover 2008: 92ff.

[17] Jones [1976] 2006: 85.

that supported and propagated Hindi as the national language of the nation-to-be; which is how it came to the Panjab.[18] But even then it tended to remain gender-specific. While Tara is proficient in Hindi, Puri works for the Urdu newspaper *Pairokar*.[19]

THE TOPOGRAPHY OF THE NOVEL

The novel opens in the space below the constricted house of Master Ram Lubhaya in a neighbourhood inside Shah Alami, one of the thirteen gates of the walled city of Lahore, which housed a large population of Hindus.[20] Master Ram Lubhaya's mother has died and the *syapa* (funerary mourning) is under way.[21] An older, religiously

---

[18] In his memoir, *Simhavalokan*, Yashpal speaks of knowing the Panjabi Arya Samaj milieu intimately, his mother being an avid follower of the sect.

[19] 'Hindi, in the Devanagri script, arrived later and was confined at the beginning to the Brahmins and our women, the latter through the influence of the Arya Samaj. Literacy among our Hindu women thus began with Hindi, and this created some amusing situations, because in my mother's generation there were many women who could not communicate with their husbands when they were away from each other, as they could only write in Hindi and their husbands in Urdu or English.' English and Urdu were the languages of the men. The problem of communication within the family was resolved when middle-class girls learned English and became trilingual. They spoke in Panjabi, wrote in Hindi to their mothers, and in English or Urdu to their fathers. Tandon [1961] 1968: 67.

[20] 'Old Lahore's Shah Alam was inhabited mostly by Hindus. Named after the Mughal Emperor Shah Alam, this neighbourhood was akin to Delhi's walled city. Also known as "Shahalmi" in Punjabi, this locality suffered colossal rioting, plunder, and near annihilation during Partition as most of the houses and buildings were set ablaze.' Citation from the Pakistani journalist and author Raza Rumi 2013: 9.

[21] 'Yashpal was always fascinated by the city of Lahore. He spent many years there (National College, working, etc., and after he was declared an absconder). He was prohibited by the British Govt. to visit the city after his release in 1938, but made 2 or 3 short forays to Lahore incognito. The partition of Punjab must have sown the seed of a novel in his mind. In 1955

more tolerant Panjab, is also dying. Master Ram Lubhaya is a staunch believer in the Arya Samaj, but he succumbs to the pressure of the family and his neighbours in the *gali* (lane) to hold a traditional ceremony for his mother. He teaches in the city's famous DAV School attached to the College and is bringing up his five children—of whom Puri is the eldest, then comes Tara—in the beliefs within which he is so firmly entrenched. They live, crammed together, on the second floor of a house in the fictive Bhola Pandhe ki Gali, in a one-room apartment with a verandah; they have the use of a *barsati* (rooftop room created for shelter from the rain) adjoining a shared bathroom, and a tap in the courtyard below. The pattern is repeated in most houses. Not only is it impossible to keep a secret within the house, the *gali* houses, tightly fitted next to each other, also keep constant vigil on the neighbours.[22] And the voice of the lane's inhabitants, as well as their reactions to the shared newspaper headlines, ring out each

---

he and Prakashvati [his wife] visited Lahore on way to USSR by land via Peshawar and Kabul. Prakashvati remembered that *Jhootha Sach* began to take a firm shape in his mind at that time . . . For the *syapa* in the opening scene of Part 1, he consulted several ex-Lahore women: my mother's grandmother Laxmi Devi Kapur and the wife (Suhag Rani) of my eldest maternal uncle (mama) Radhakrishan. Both of these must have attended *syapa* similar to the one in Pt. 1.' Email from Anand, 27 October 2009.

[22] 'While houses came in many shapes and sizes, the most common form was a narrow, roughly rectangular building with its short dimension fronting the street . . .

Houses were built beginning at the street edge itself, with no space for a sidewalk or other passage separating buildings from streets. Not every house fronted onto a main street, however, and many were constructed within the interior of a block. The latter houses were accessed by narrow lanes or *gullees* that usually broadened out at the end into an open space (*katra*) shared by the residents of each building that opened onto it. In most cases the only space opened to the sky on an individual plot—besides the roof (which was invariably used for living space as well)—was a small open courtyard near the center of the house. A majority of houses in the eighteenth and early-nineteenth centuries drew water from a private well located in the courtyard.' Glover 2008: 103.

morning. Providing heteroglossia at its most vivid, this *gali* ethos is generally regressive, and 'customary' in the widest possible sense.

Kanak, the third major protagonist, is positioned at almost the other end of the social scale. She lives with her parents and a younger sister in a modern house in Gawal Mandi, a rich, recently built neighbourhood.[23] Her father Girdharilal is a wealthy Urdu publisher. Her older sister Kanta and her husband, the lawyer Mahendra Naiyar—referred to as Naiyar in the narrative—live in the posh Model Town, the brand new 'garden-city' settlement in the Civil Lines.[24] Naiyar functions as the older brother of the sisters, an upholder of the law alongside their father. Both he and Girdharilal reflect in their person the coexistence of the modern and traditional, patriarchal, aspects of their houses. Recalling Prakash Tandon's description, in spite of the modern front of their house the heart of it remains traditional. The patriarchy they embody is thus embedded in the very structure of the house. They allow Kanak to go thus far and no further.

The first chapters of the novel fill out the social and political context and provide a series of flashbacks to give us the early 1940s. Puri has been to Dyal Singh College with its progressive Brahmo ethos.[25] The

[23] Glover on Gawal Mandi and similar Lahore suburbs: 'In the early 1920s, Indian residents began building suburban settlements in Lahore's civil station with little oversight by government officials. In new developments like Kishan Nagar, Gowal Mandi, Ram Nagar and Farooq Gunj, Indian residents crafted a model of urban residence and commercial organization largely on their own terms.' Ibid.: 151.

[24] 'Model Town embodied many of the planning ideas developed by Ebenezer Howard in his book *Garden Cities of Tomorrow*: Diwan Khem Chand, a barrister who studied at the bar in England in 1909, was the guiding force behind Model Town's creation and an admirer of Howard's ideals. Howard's garden city was meant to combine the restorative elements of the countryside (gardens and open space) with institutions appropriate for a decentralized civic society (small industry, shops, professional services, schools and the like).' Ibid.: 152.

[25] In 1881, Dyal Singh Majithia, a Sikh aristocrat, philanthropist, and close friend of the Bengali Brahmos of Lahore, founded the *Tribune*, an English-language newspaper. The newspaper was staffed almost entirely by Bengali Brahmos. Jones [1976] 2006: 63.

professors there disliked communalism and socially regressive ideas, and in her first year of the BA Tara, who had also been a student there, participated in inter-communal dining organized by the College on an outing to Jahangir's mausoleum.[26] In 1943, when he was in his second year of the MA, Puri was awarded a two-year prison term for work in a nationalist secret society. This is the first and only incidence of a major character being propelled by nationalism. It is worth noting that it does not recur in this novel of nation-building. In fact, the closer we get to Independence, the more nationalism recedes and the more anomalous it seems.

But to return to the narrative: Puri was never to complete his degree: when released in May 1945—only because the Allies won the war, the country was no freer than it had been—he saw no point in studying further. He didn't want to join British service, and the financial needs of the family constrained him to seek work. He had a flair for writing and hoped to make a living by writing short stories. The academically brilliant Tara continued at Dyal Singh College without her brother. They had long crossed the narrow confines of the *gali* and the borders of the 'customary' and emerged into the world of the 'educated'—intellectually and to a large part also emotionally. If in Premchand's *Karmabhumi* the only students visible were male, from the late 1930s even lower-middle-class girls from white-collar families such as Tara's could aspire to education and a wider expectation of life than marriage. There was a great difference between the ethos of the *gali*, with its gender differentiation and segregation, and the easy mixing of the sexes on campus. For inner-city students the urban landscape had broadened into a world full of possibilities.[27] Puri and Tara imbibed similar progressive currents from their college environment; they shared a world that was intellectually stimulating, socially progressive, politically informed, and critically nationalistic. Education brought out their particular talents, enabling them to enter other city spaces—student associations, debating clubs, the world

---

[26] JS, 21.
[27] Ibid.: 22.

of newspaper reporters—and mix with like-minded people. After some professional meandering Puri, who had built a reputation as a writer, manages to get work as a reporter for the pro-Congress Urdu daily *Pairokar*. With her brother's moral and financial support, Tara is also set forward into heady campus life: 'If her life is becoming too heavy for you, I can carry my sister's burden', Puri has told his mother. 'There is no match between her first division and a boy who was caught copying something in his exams'[28]—this is how Tara, engaged to be married to an unsuitable boy despite first divisions in all her exams, manages to enter the B.A. programme.

THE SOCIAL AND RELIGIOUS DIVISION

We now find ourselves in March 1947. Their cultural capital allows both Puri and Tara entry into higher social worlds. Tara soon begins to tutor in the haveli of Dr Pran Nath, who has at a relatively young age established a towering reputation as an economist; educated at Oxford, he had accepted a professorship at Panjab University and become a war-time advisor to Governor Jenkins, retaining this position after the war. His views were often akin to those of the Communists, but he kept his distance from the party, which he found too doctrinaire. Pran Nath was especially beholden to Tara's father, who had in turn tutored him for several years in his youth. His haveli in the old walled city, with its four large courtyards, where Tara teaches his young nieces and nephews, speaks of his family's affluence. He is single and has taken a liking to Tara, a matter which makes for some tension within his larger family and eventually leads to her ouster.

Puri is asked to tutor Kanak for the Hindi 'Prabhakar' exam by her father who respects his writing talent. Girdharilal Datta is an old Congress worker who has once been in prison for his work. Here too, nationalism lies in the past; it is no longer an active force in the lives of the major protagonists. It is important for Puri to be treated as an

[28] Ibid.: 51.

equal by father and daughter; he works in an honorary capacity, and it is as such that he and Kanak are mutually attracted, physically as much as intellectually. They will soon confess their love and pledge themselves to each other. Tara quickly guesses the nature of Puri's relationship to Kanak.

In fact, both siblings are trying to cross the social—and in Tara's case also the religious—divide. She has been engaged against her will to Somraj, a boy from a rich Khatri family whom the brother-sister pair find utterly unsuitable for her. Somraj Sahni has no academic ambitions, no interests that coincide with Tara's. His family is against Tara studying further and, in their estimate, stealing a march on their son. Somraj had recently made headlines in the local newspapers—which gave the matter a communal twist—when he assaulted his Muslim teacher upon being caught cheating in his exams.

She is consoled by Puri's assurance that he will not let the marriage happen. But she can't tell him she has fallen in love with a Muslim co-student, Asad Ahmed, even as the communal situation in Lahore and Panjab worsens. Studying for his MA in the Forman Christian College, curly-haired Asad is not only active in the Students' Federation, he belongs to the Communist Party; he can explain the issues at hand in a few sentences, he has thought through his views, and best of all his humour is contained, not jarring like that of the other boys. As they discover their mutual attraction, Asad asks her: Can you leap over the gulf of sect, religion, and *biradari* that divides us? Tara assures him she can if he holds her hand the while.[29] We are not allowed insight into Asad's interiority. He is presented as Tara sees him. Asad also goes to Dr Nath's house to talk to him; he is often there when Tara comes to give her tuition. It doesn't take Nath long to understand the relationship. 'To be in love is a pleasant feeling,' he tells her in English.[30] This love is a novelty in the locality Tara comes from; we do not find it in the Banaras of Premchand's

---

[29] Ibid.: 85–6.
[30] Ibid.: 70.

Karmabhumi, where there is no question of basing marriage upon a romantic attachment. The attachment comes after marriage, if one is fortunate, not before.

Nath tells her the people in the house have become jealous of Tara, they think he likes her, they worry that perhaps he will marry her, so they have terminated her tuition. He seems to be feeling his way into the situation. 'You are nineteen, I am thirty. These women don't understand, why would a nineteen-year-old marry a middle-aged thirty-year-old man . . . These women can't imagine that I can like you without thought of sex.'[31] He explains his peculiar family situation; he is actually the son of his mother's union with one of his father's younger brothers. His father married again and had other sons, but as the official elder son he remains the family heir. He tells Tara, 'I like you.'[32] Their relationship will only be picked up in the second volume, much after Partition, in another location, in another social setting. Perhaps it is only then, denuded of their former positions, clad in their new office, that they can face each other as man and woman. He is now situated so far beyond her universe that Tara cannot even conceive of an attachment to him.

Her views on love and marriage find no echo at home. The *gali* ethos, with its caste consciousness and set views on how marriages are arranged, does not tolerate new-fangled love, and certainly not between people of different faiths. When Tara and her mother speak of the family idea of arranging a favourable match for Puri with a girl in their community whose family is apparently ready to 'show' the girl, Tara bursts out with, 'What kind of a meeting is that? No conversation of any kind. Nowadays, people meet each other several times before they get engaged, they continue to talk to each other.' Her mother scolds her (she is still talking in the terms we have seen in Premchand's novel): '. . . this is not engagement, this is illicit love (*ashnai*). This can happen in houses in Anarkali, Gawal Mandi, and

[31] Ibid.: 71.
[32] Ibid.: 73.

Mall Road. What'll people in the *gali* and neighbourhood say if they hear of this?'³³ She little realizes that not only does Tara aspire to just such a union, Puri's desires too are lodged in a house in Gawal Mandi. He is attracted as much to Kanak's person as to her open, easy-going life-style; she can meet whom she will and can, in contrast with his own sister, study as much as she pleases. But he is also drawn to the power exuded by her publisher-father and their affluence. He dreams of owning her father's publishing concern.

As Lahore is propelled into communal riots, the private becomes inextricably entwined with the public and the chronicle character of the narrative merges effortlessly with the fictional world of our protagonists.

COMMUNAL AND PERSONAL DISASTERS

History forms not only nations, it also shapes personal trajectories, specially in times such as these. The sequence of political events which now follows has an immediate impact on the lives of all three protagonists. In fact, the newspaper and the novel merge seamlessly into each other as genres, underlining the historical-political bent of the narrative. The urgency and the drama compensate for any dryness that could ensue. We see how the precise dates of political events, as they follow fast upon each other, are keyed into the lives of Puri, Kanak, and Tara. The headlines in *Pairokar* shout out the news. On the night of 2 March 1947, Sir Khizr Hayat Khan, leader of the loyalist landowners' Unionist Party, increasingly veering towards the Muslim League, resigns from the Panjab Legislature in spite of holding the majority in the house. Panjab comes under Governor's Rule. The Muslim League stakes its claim to form the government. The big question is: will the Congress support the League?

On 6 March Puri hears that there has been a disturbance near Mochi Gate, not far from Shah Alami, the largely Hindu neighbourhood where they live. The shops around Shah Alami have shut; the

---

³³ Ibid.: 88.

city is under curfew. In the disturbances that follow, the *gali*'s beloved Daulu Mama, a vendor who sold sweets to children, is stabbed. Puri is deeply moved by Daulu Mama's death. A subeditor asks Puri to write the editorial for the paper in his stead. Puri adds an op-ed entitled 'Daulu Mama' to it. The people of Bhola Pandhe ki Gali read Puri's emotional words:

> Daulu Uncle, you were Uncle to so many children in so many of Lahore's lanes. You left behind the many children to whom, all your life, you brought laughter. They weep bitter tears now, lamenting the tyrant who has snatched away their precious toy. Did Daulu Uncle have an enemy? Did he have any business with the Unionist Ministry or with the officeholders of the League? He was a human being, a gentle human being. His murder is the murder of humanity . . . Whose path to office and state rule had he impeded?[34]

Much more damning is his impulsive editorial on the question of the Muslim League forming the government in Panjab; it has been written in a burst of youthful enthusiasm:

> To the trustees of the Congress and the League! . . . The Congress and the League were both born as institutions to help free the nation from bondage . . . Today, both these institutions, the Congress and the League, bear responsibility for handing over the government of the Panjab to the Governor. Both these political parties are now the puppets of a hostile government, and friends to those who have always swindled them; they are now declaring the anti-imperialist forces who have supported them thus far as their enemies. The very toady who rained blows on their non-violent demonstrations has become the League's friend . . . The very Khizr who cast Congress Leaders into prison during the War, sacrificing them at the feet of imperialism, has today become an intimate (*apna*) of Congress leaders . . . If Muslims in eight provinces can believe in the Congress government, why won't Hindus tolerate a cabinet formed by the League?[35]

[34] Ibid.: 114.
[35] Ibid.: 114–15.

Of this there are few chances. Taking a dramatic stance against the proposition of the League forming the cabinet, the Akali leader Master Tara Singh pulls out the sword in front of the Assembly Hall, a provocation that causes an immediate uproar. He will not let Pakistan be created. League followers take out a procession through the streets of the walled city, spilling over into other parts; they demand the taking over of government by the League, enabling the creation of Pakistan. But the governor does not accept the League's offer and terrible riots break out, first in Rawalpindi and then in Lahore. It is as if the countdown to violence, to Partition, has already begun. The lovers are prevented from meeting each other. Puri's outspoken views are much admired in progressive circles; Tara's heart warms to him, though when he goes to seek approval from the house in Gawal Mandi, he finds Naiyar and his wife there with Kanak. Naiyar reads the *Tribune*, not Urdu or Hindi papers. When an offended Puri leaves, Naiyar tells the women drily that he, Puri, is socially 'out of place' and culturally ill at ease.[36] Later he speaks of him as a ticketless passenger.[37]

On 7 March 1947, Puri is thrown out of his job by his enraged pro-Congress editor. Puri's spontaneous reaction to a key political event has a direct bearing on his fate, and eventually also on Tara's, as we shall see, for Puri will lose his voice in the family and be both unwilling and unable to prevent her marriage. This is a key moment in the narrative, when the political sphere actively deflects the lives of the major protagonists in a direction they have not reckoned on.

Tara's final exams have been postponed; but the date of her marriage is fast approaching; though she still resists the match, she's been engaged for two years. Her uncle curses: Have you become English-Christians, like the people of Gawal Mandi and Model Town? Get her married, he tells Tara's parents. Puri remains jobless and frustrated, driven to doing hackwork. And very soon, Kanak's father has put

---

[36] Ibid.: 117.
[37] Ibid.: 242.

him in his place: 'All round situation . . . uh . . . status . . . class connections.'[38] He may no longer visit Kanak. If class difference remains the primary obstacle for Puri, in Tara's case the communal situation adds to the impossibility of her union with Asad. Their entry into taboo zones and the transgressions attempted—from Bhola Pandhe ki Gali into Gawal Mandi, where people can take such liberties—are tolerated until they reach a crisis point, after which they are bound to be rebuffed. The turmoil that ensues closely parallels the deepening political crisis in Lahore and the country at large.

Tara also faces losses on all sides. Asad simply backs out of accepting her when she tells him she has forsaken home and family and come to him. The Party does not allow marriages across religious borders, he tells her. It is careful about its public face, about the reputation of its members. When Tara offers to kill herself, so hopeless is her position in the family, his response is almost dogmatic: 'If death comes, let it be in a fight for justice, not in surrender to injustice.'[39] Puri also retreats into tradition: he backs out of any support for a cross-religious alliance when he spots Tara and Asad coming out of

Illus. 12: Congress Committee Voting for Partition, June 1947

[38] Ibid.: 178.
[39] Ibid.: 200.

a restaurant together. Feeling betrayed by her daring, humiliated by Kanak's family, and frustrated, he no longer backs Tara, who sees the direction things are taking—Puri has double standards, there is one measure for his relationship with Kanak, another for Tara and her Muslim beloved. Henceforth, their ways part entirely.[40]

From the last half of May, killings and incidents of arson rise dramatically in the city. Lahore is in flames. The city of old, where Hindu, Muslim, and Sikh lived side by side, is being destroyed in the process. There will be no way of retrieving that lost space. In the first week of the month, on 3 June to be precise, Partition is announced; the Muslim League accepts the Congress' offer that Pakistan be formed out of Muslim-majority areas in Panjab and Bengal. Lahore's fate remains uncertain. How will Tara and Puri be impacted? Where will they find themselves in the conflagration that follows? Partition and personal events are closely linked in the rest of the narrative in the first volume.

From the rooftops of Model Town, as yet safe from violence, the Naiyar family and Kanak can see the fire in the old city. Large flames leap out from the area around Shah Alami and lick the skies. The people in the walled city are the most vulnerable to the political violence that follows the turn of events in Panjab, whereas the privileged find quick refuge: the Naiyar family leaves for Nainital and Pandit Girdharilal finds safety in an abandoned haveli in Delhi. Naiyar has heard that Muslims from East Panjab have occupied Hindu houses in Gawal Mandi and Model Town, even as Hindus pour out of the city. Kanak's family may reject Puri, but she persists. He too will leave Lahore at the end of July, after Tara's wedding, before the great Hindu and Sikh exodus from Lahore and from West Panjab. Kanak has all the self-confidence of property, wealth, education; she defies her family by inviting Puri to Nainital. Puri will remain

---

[40] It is difficult to agree with Nemichandra Jain, who sees the vilification of Puri in the second volume as entirely manipulated for purposes of the plot. He finds no internal cohesion in the construction of his character (*antarik sangati nahim*). The self-centred and self-serving aspect of his character is prefigured in volume one, as we can see. Jain [1966] 2002: 78.

jobless till after Partition, but his attachment to Kanak will offer him some protection. All in all, the affluent take losses better, they can escape to safe havens; it is the poor and the white-collar lower middle class, where Tara belongs, which have less mobility and suffer the main brunt of Partition. As a woman of her class, Tara has virtually no space for action. She is more or less bludgeoned into marriage.

A WOMAN ALONE

Abandoned to her fate by Asad and her brother, Tara's marriage has taken place in a quiet ceremony on 28 July 1947. Her ordeal begins in earnest after that. The narrator does not deflect the violence away from her; on the contrary it is mercilessly visited on her person. Tara is initially received warmly into her new home on the night of her wedding. She sees signs of new money, but none of cultivation, of modernity. Her mother-in-law is kind; neighbours and relatives approve of the choice. The marriage atmosphere engenders hope and a resigned Tara, decked in all her finery, awaits Somraj with some expectation of happiness. But he taunts her for hiding her face; he has heard she did not want to marry him. How much shame did she show when she bared her face in demonstrations on Mall Road and Anarkali? With whom did she have a love relationship? Slept with whom? When Tara responds with grim rage, he throws her on the floor and, using his belt, lashes out at her, making an effort to take her violently. She rolls on the floor and tries to protect her face, not submitting to him. Just then, a terrible commotion breaks out in the lane below. It is as if the violence of his action is echoed by the violence in the old city. Somraj jumps up and thunders down the staircase. Tara cannot follow; flames leap up the stairs.

The narrator will restrict himself to dry detail, as always, moving rapidly through events, marking the unmitigated violence that is visited upon her person with a power that allows neither the characters involved nor the reader any respite. Nemichandra Jain has seen this scene as one of the most affective in the novel as a whole, as one with the most intense sense of interiority.

Tara escapes to the roof and springs to the next house, but there is a substantial difference in height between the two roofs and she limps as she descends into the next house. The Muslim family in the house throws her out unceremoniously: self-protection is their primary impulse. By and large, there is little intra-communal solidarity. The next morning her family will hear of the fire and the rioting and be told that Tara was killed in the conflagration.

Dead-alive Tara is now truly a woman on her own, fleeing through the narrow lanes of a city in flames, fleeing from Somraj as much as the fire.

This is the second time that history interferes in Tara's life. The fire has made possible her ejection out of the whole system of family ties and obligations. We have to remind ourselves that, theoretically, she could have returned to her husband's family, flames or no flames, but she runs. This is one resolution to being caught in the strangulating web of her marriage. These are the weeks immediately before the proclamation of Independence on the midnight of 14/15 August in newly created Pakistan and India. The services are divided along communal lines. There is no police or army protection to quell the arson, looting, bloodshed, rape. British authority has retreated, abandoning any pretence at control. The newly installed interim governments stand on shaky feet. Stripped of all protection, of any sense of individual identity, of community, family, partner, she will personally experience the atrocities Puri will later be a mere witness to.

The streets of the walled city teem with violence. It is not long before a man on the street lays his hands on Tara's shoulder and drags her off. She tries to protect herself, the man's wife's screams abuse at him, but Nabbu is rough and uncaring. He tears off her salwar, only the waistband hangs around her, she implores him to spare her. He throws her on the bed and then on the floor. She resists his violent efforts to take her. He ties her hands; mercifully, she slips into unconsciousness. She represents the countless women who become victims of rape, humiliation, mutilation, and murder in the months that follow Khizr's resignation and the subsequent announcement of

Partition and Independence. Much later, we learn that her abductor had raped her and that she had contracted some variety of venereal disease. This is the month of Ramzan and the rhythms of normal life continue unabated, lending deeper poignancy to the anomalous happenings of the time.

Next morning, Tara hears a Panjabi qawwali in Asavari raga to wake up the fasting before dawn. Naked, wounded, lying on the floor, she tries to kill herself. She wonders: What have I done wrong, what am I being punished for? For not wanting to marry Somraj? For going with Asad? Am I not even free to kill myself? It is as if the 'customary' surfaces in her too, in her hour of extreme suffering; the 'educated' deserts her.

Nabbu has left for the day's pieties, the neighbourhood women gather around Tara, sympathizing with her violated womanhood. Nabbu's wife says: 'Never mind a young woman, if he sees a cow, buffalo, or goat, he can't leave her alone.' Mehar, a neighbour, says: 'The bastards fight each other but they defile the bodies of women (*mitti kharab karna*).'[41] The only protection, if it can be called that, is this unexpected moral support from women who witness, indeed share, Tara's fate. In their voices, in their sympathy, Tara will find some sense of solidarity. Tajo Tayi, the Asavari singer, scolds Nabbu in front of the gathering of neighbourhood men and shuts him up. This is not jihad. 'This is debauchery in the name of religion. Your tongue will shrivel up and fall off.'[42] Nabbu's wife tells them he has sold Tara to a pimp for twenty-five rupees.[43]

---

[41] Ibid.: 341.

[42] Ibid.: 343.

[43] Butalia provides some figures for the havoc wreaked by Partition: 'Estimates of the dead vary from 200,000 (the contemporary British figure) to two million (a later Indian estimate) but that somewhere around a million people died is widely accepted. As always, there was widespread sexual savagery: about 75,000 women are thought to have been abducted and raped by men of religions different from their own (and indeed sometimes by men of their own religion). Thousands of families were divided, homes were destroyed, crops left to rot, villages abandoned.' Butalia 1998: 3.

Tara is saved from prostitution; neighbours take her to Hafiz Inayat Ali Sahib, who has been an officer in the Intelligence Department for thirty years and is now pensioned, suitably rewarded for his services by the British Government. He spends his time accounting for the creed of Islam in scientific terms and doing missionary work, making good Muslims out of bad Muslims. Hafizji is pious and kindly. He recognizes that Tara is from a good home; she is educated, intelligent, and good-looking. He tries to convert her, he would like to keep her in the house, marry her to his son, who is sub-inspector in Amritsar. But he also tells her that Hindu civilization is primal and barbaric, that they treat women as beasts of burden, as property. Tara has little belief in religious creed and communal sentiment but she doesn't take kindly to this critique of Hindu custom. She realizes that Hafizji and his family are good people, but strictly orthodox. She asks to be taken back to her family but hears that the Hindus of Macchihatta and Shah Alami have all gone east and the Muslims who've come from there have settled in their stead. She recalls Asad's words: Hindus have plural belief systems; they are free to choose from among them, though they have no choice in matters of social conduct. Islam does not tolerate such freedom of thought. It is a creed not of thought but of belief.[44] Tara thanks Hafizji for his care but tells him she cannot suppress her understanding and her mind. She will never forget the favour he has done her, but asks to be taken to the Hindu camp. In this typical lane-house, she completely bypasses Independence Day: here there is no happiness, no celebration, no awareness of any climactic political event. Her sole identity in the days that follow is that of a Hindu woman. Meanwhile, Amjad, Hafizji's sub-inspector son, is back in Lahore from Amritsar. Muslim members of the services are being discharged in India, asked to take off their uniforms, so he is bitter: '18 August. The last day of Ramzan. From the rooftop of the house, Tara sees the green flag of Pakistan fluttering on housetops across the city, marking Lahore and Panjab as foreign territory. The

[44] JS, 354.

flags proclaim she is a prisoner, far from her own people, imprisoned in an alien country.'[45]

Somraj and Nabbu trampled on her body, but Hafizji's family wants to destroy her by trampling on her mind.[46] There is no-one to escape to; nowhere she can go; there is no going back to her family; they would send her back to Somraj. A few days after Independence, there is no sense of freedom, only continuing bondage. The Hindus of Shah Alami have left the city. She has no sense yet of a safer place called 'India'. On 22 August Amjad tells them there is a new law; all Hindus need to be reported to the police and the Indian Liaison Officer informed. It is a problem to keep Tara now, unless she agrees to convert. Otherwise, she classifies as an abducted woman. In the next days, he agrees to take her to a Hindu refugee camp. She will be transported there in a jeep the next morning.

THE TRAIN RIDE

Puri is part of the Independence Day celebrations in the security of the New Club in Nainital. For a short period, even the high-up bureaucrats and their fashionable wives, who were no part of the freedom struggle, made common cause with those who were part of it. The drinking crowd gathers around the radio to hear Dr Rajendra Prasad, President of the Constituent Assembly, speak in Hindi, and Pandit Nehru make his famous English speech about the nation's tryst with destiny at midnight on 14 August 1947. Kanak and Puri press each other's hands in secret. For Puri as much as for Tara, Independence will signify false independence—*jhuthi azadi*—an expression used by a wide array of socialists at the time. Though the expression *jhutha sach* (false truth) is used later by Tara to describe her marriage with Somraj rather than for Independence, the sense of the shallowness of this newly won freedom persists. A day later, on 16 August, Puri's reaction as he wakes up can only be bitter: 'He

[45] Ibid.: 361–2.
[46] Ibid.: 363.

had wagered his life for his country's independence, asked for nothing for himself, but . . . the country's independence wants no responsibility for his livelihood. Isn't this his country's ingratitude? What irony!'[47]

What follows seems almost to be a novelistic device to give us a glimpse of the violence on *both* sides of the border and of the price that thousands pay for political freedom. As Puri has no news of his family, he decides to go back to Lahore to look for them. His epic train ride across Hindustan provides extensive views of the violence perpetrated by Hindus and Sikhs on Muslims—on men, but, as always, much more so on women. Puri plays a witness role; it is an effective literary stratagem at this stage to weave into a personal narrative some sense of the atrocities perpetrated on Muslims, of bestialities in the same unmindful, almost impersonal mode. Puri appears once again as a sensitive, caring, concerned young man, frantic about his family in Lahore, though his other traits—his growing indifference to the fate of Tara, his unreflecting self-interest—have also clearly begun to surface. The train rushes through the plains of Hindustan—Bareilly, Moradabad, Saharanpur—Muslims crowding in at each big station. A massive crowd at Ambala swarms onto the top of the train, the police force it to descend: they are left behind, sobbing. After Sirhind a mob with guns, spears, and swords attacks the train. They bring the train to a halt, hack down and slit the throats of older people, throw out the young towards further violence outside, and so half the train is emptied. They dash away when military jeeps come charging down. In Ludhiana the passengers are evacuated and sent to the Muslim Evacuee Camp.

Puri is nauseated. He tries another route, from Ludhiana to Lahore via Ferozepur. The train doesn't seem to want to move from Moga station. The violence goes on and on. Rural Jats with rural Muslim girls that they've caught, young and scantily clad, climb into the train joking coarsely. Puri is aghast at the violence: 'Has the world gone

---

[47] Ibid.: 382.

mad? How have people acquired this insane urge to kill and destroy? And Tara sacrificed to this . . . Have women no refuge but death to escape abuse and torment? . . . Is this bestiality natural? . . . Men too often oppose this bestiality and want justice, they'll even give their lives in the cause. And yet I could do nothing this time round . . . No-one seems to be able to do anything.'[48]

At Ferozepur there is a Sikh *langar*. Puri searches through refugee camps, finds destitution and hunger, takes the Ferozepur–Amritsar train, reaches Jalandhar at dawn. He sees young Muslim women weeping as they are auctioned off. Puri remembers how his blood boiled when he read in the papers of Hindu women being stripped and marched in a procession. 'People on one side show their bravery by being deaf to the pleas of women, so how can the other side accept being any less brutal? Why should they fall behind in the race to be more bestial?'[49]

Illus. 13: Refugee Camp, Ludhiana

[48] Ibid.: 392–3.
[49] Ibid.: 406.

LAHORE, DELHI, AND THE BITTER TRUTH

Puri's experience of Hindu violence is placed *before* the account of Tara's imprisonment and ordeal in Shekhupura at the hands of a Muslim, the last act of existential deprivation and humiliation before the first densely packed volume closes. Long before pioneering academic writings based on interviews with men and women who had suffered the brutality of Partition,[50] this novel documented the deterioration of humanity at such climactic moments, providing an ethnography of violence, apportioning equal moral responsibility to both sides for the brutalities. No-one is better, no-one worse.

COUNTRIES OF RELIGION

The last episode of Volume One is treated in graphic detail, without commentary, without mitigation of any kind, just sparse fact piled on sparse fact, interspersed with Tara's thoughts. It is as if the facts speak for themselves, all further embellishment is superfluous and the very act of speaking the unspeakable, of finding words for the inexplicable, makes for a hardly bearable intensity of experience, both for those exposed to the violence as well as for the reader. This is Yashpal at his best and in these last pages of his epic is encapsulated the plight of women, young and old, Hindu and Muslim, at this juncture of the subcontinent's history.

The flags, the soldiers, proclaim threat as well as protection. Tara is thrust into the jeep which is to take her to the Hindu camp, two men get in with her. Fake policemen, fake promises, as she will find out.[51] The jeep also carries captive hens in a basket, tied down, with helpless eyes. As they leave the city behind and cross the Ravi bridge even the familiar becomes unfamiliar; they pass Jahangir and Nur

---

[50] Butalia 1998; Bhasin and Menon 1998.

[51] As Kamla Patel, well-known social worker, said to Ritu Menon and Kamla Bhasin: 'If a woman found her way somehow to these camps then she would be sent to her own refugee camp, the one set up by her own country, But if she did not manage to reach this safe place and was picked up on the way, then either the man would keep her for himself or sell her off.' Menon and Bhasin 1998: 81.

Jehan's mausoleum, Shahdara. Tara resists, is roughed up, head thrust in a basket, like the hens. She realizes before she faints that Amjad has sold her. When her eyes open she sees a courtyard, as if in a fog; three women are fighting over her clothes. She realizes, when she can take stock of the situation, that one wears only a *kamiz*—this is Banti; the other just a salwar—Durga; and the third is entirely naked—Satwant. There is another who is also naked, Lakhi; she had first refused to eat, when she finally did she got such cramps and diarrhoea that she was always in pain. They are imprisoned; the door to the roof is locked. They bathe under the water pump in the courtyard; they excrete by squatting on the drain. Their unclad state, their complete ignorance of where they are being kept, and the shackles on the door make escape impossible. The only human being they regularly see is an old woman, a Kanjari, who traffics in women; she comes with *roti*s every day. It could be a Beckett landscape, so devoid is it of scenic props, of any comfort.

Banti befriends Tara; she offers her moral support, solidarity, and pulls her out of her state of intense self-pity and despair. Banti has her faith to support her.

> 'Are life and death in the hands of human beings, sister?' Banti said. 'Do you think you're the only one suffering such pain and trouble? There's no-one here who arrived better preserved than you. We're looking at you, we've also suffered; we've also seen others. It's human nature to make more of it the less one suffers. Look at the others. They just carried you here. There are some scratches on your face. They would have taken less care of their mothers and sisters. You don't know what the others have been through.'[52]

Durga, the bare-chested one, is beautiful, though her face is deeply pockmarked. They all have tales to relate. Banti tells her own story. They were small landowners and moneylenders in a village, their Muslim neighbours assured them protection, Muslims and Hindus were used to coexistence, but people from the outside, Maulvis

---

[52] JS, 413.

from the city, had incited them. Another familiar trope: the seeds of mistrust, aggression deliberately sown among people coexisting in relative peace. The times changed swiftly; the very people who had been their dependants turned against them. The men were driven off at spear-point, children snatched away from young women, her sister-in-law did not manage to jump into the village well, she was held back and then violated with sticks and poles and left dazed by the side of the well. Later, Banti was carried off by their captor, Gafur.

Tara tells them she is single. She has been stripped of all protection; in the very act of being stripped, in her moment of extreme degradation, she strips herself of the baggage she carries: no family, no tyrannical brother, no husband who violated her very sense of being. In her imprisonment she invents a new self, at first out of despair, later out of determination, the one that she will maintain not only through the present ordeal but also through her eventual emancipation from it. She has no family left. The women find out that Tara is educated, that she knows English, 'Shastri' (as they call Hindi), and perhaps Persian; they stand in awe of her. Once again, it is her education and progressive views, and her ability to communicate that award her a special position, that of being their spokesperson and leader, though this brings little comfort.

For then begins a reign of terror. The old woman decides to starve them. She doesn't appear for three days, the women are prey to intolerable hunger. Satwant and Durga are physically violent with each other. Banti has her faith to support her; she turns her face towards the wall and prays. When the old woman does come on the third day, she brings just eight *roti*s, blaming Gafur for not paying her. She comes late the next day and brings just five. Sure that she has brought the women to their knees, she asks Tara to go with her. Tara turns away in disgust.

One morning, Gafur brings in two very young girls who have been snatched from a convoy (*qafila*). Gafur comes to count them the next day and brings them twenty-five *roti*s. Some overeat; once again Lakhi gets very sick. The old woman brings eighteen the next day, and sweet words. They are being fattened for the sacrifice. The final humiliation and shock takes the shape of Gafur arriving with two rustics who will choose the woman they want. Durga is dragged off. Tara's education saves her; in her anger she speaks Hindustani, which alienates the men.

She knows that the imprisonment and hunger are making an animal of her. The women are starved of the most basic needs, completely isolated in a country which is no longer theirs and within it a locality they are ignorant of, with no sense of any protective institution or person to turn to. She thinks, if the old woman shows affection once more, she'll agree to go with her. It's an overcast day, still morning. The door shackles are rattled; can it be Gafur? The women run and hide in the one room with a door. An inspector, four policemen, some soldiers and an army officer enter. There are also two men in civilian suits and a white-khadi clad woman with no fear on her face. The

Illus. 14: Rescued girl, from a Hindu family from Lyallpur

woman is Kausalya Devi, a representative of the Indian Government who has come to rescue abducted Hindu women.[53] One of the two men in civilian clothes is Asad. It is quite natural that Tara speaks for all of them, once again a part of her reinvention as a leader. They get clothes, Lakhi a stretcher. They move in a fleet. Asad gives Tara some news of her family, that they have probably left Lahore, that Puri is in Nainital; that they had all thought her dead. Tara gives very little information about herself. They reach the DAV College camp; he asks her hesitantly if she would like to become Muslim and stay in Lahore with him. He is proposing. The force of events is too strong, even Asad retreats in her imagination. They notice only now that Lakhi on her stretcher is dead.[54]

Asad will come around five in the evening. The women are to be taken across the border immediately. There's no time for decisions. Tara can't wait for Asad. Packed into a bus, they become witness to scenes of desolation, destruction, and violence. The bus driver has seen a lot; he is the voice of the people. As he drives to and fro across the border, he sees what happens on either side. From his relatively safe perch in the bus he can see the plight of the Muslims, carrying their worldly goods on their shoulders, as much as of the Hindus: people reduced to being 'Hindu' or 'Muslim' and driven out of their homeland.

---

[53] 'Nearly 75,000 women . . . had been raped and abducted on both sides of the border at Partition. This figure would have been higher if Kashmir had been taken into account—perhaps close to 100,000.' Butalia 1998: 132. 'As early as September 1947 the Prime Ministers of India and Pakistan met at Lahore and took a decision on the question of the recovery of abducted women. It was at this meeting that they issued a joint declaration . . . This made it clear that the governments of the two countries and of East and West Panjab would make every effort to recover and restore to the families the girls and women thus abducted. This was sealed by the Inter-Dominion Treaty of 6 December 1947.' See ibid.: 138, 143. It is likely that the actions referred to took place some time after September 1947, since the author has so closely adhered to historical dates.

[54] JS, 431.

They cross the border to Wagah. A naked woman hangs upside down from a bamboo pole, her legs forced open. A couple of naked women are being pushed towards the Muslim *qafila*,[55] faces covered with their hands. 'Take them, take them. Take your mothers and daughters to Pakistan.'

Speaking of his uncle's fleeing family, Prakash Tandon recalls: 'They were put up at uncle's old DAV College, which had become a vast temporary camp. From here they moved on in smaller convoys, and uncle's party eventually arrived at the new frontier post of Wagah, a tiny hamlet which was now in the limelight as a scene of dramatic activity. As the truck passed the barrier into "India", they looked back at Pakistan, their homeland which did not want them.'[56]

Western Panjab has ejected its Hindus and Sikhs. Almost by default, for it claims to be secular, Hindustan has become the nation for people of these religions. Except for the opening pages of the narrative, *Jhutha Sach* is a novel remarkably devoid of nationalism. The violence of the nation's birth makes nationalism seem a travesty—'Partition is the unspeakable sadness at the heart of the idea of India: a *momento mori* that what made India possible also profoundly diminished the integral value of the idea.'[57] The rupture in landscape, social fabric, family, and personal life is absolute. There is also a literary break because of the loss of a culturally shared terrain, where Panjabi, Hindi, and Urdu existing side by side and feeding into each other. There will no longer be any Hindi in Lahore. The old city with its shared religious culture of Hindu, Sikh, and Muslim, its aspirations, its tales of personal strife and of work, labour, and education—a city still somewhat intact at the beginning of the first volume of the novel—has

---

[55] 'People travelled in buses, in cars, by train, but mostly on foot in great columns which could stretch for dozens of miles. The longest of them, said to comprise nearly 400,000 people, refugees travelling east to India from western Punjab, took as many as eight days to pass any given spot on its route.' Butalia 1998: 4.

[56] Tandon [1961] 1968: 247.

[57] Khilnani [1997] 1998: 201–2.

ceased to exist. Those who survive the mindless violence can begin again, but the cracks can only be papered over, never healed. Like many thousands, Tara is now an alien in her homeland, thrust into her nation, as a Hindu and a woman. India is her only option and she can be glad that she has it. In fact she has no choice, and Asad can be no part of her future. In the first volume of his novel, Yashpal merges fact and fiction, the political and the personal, Lahore and the nation, to produce one of the great Hindi novels of our time.

THE VIOLENCE IN THE AFTERMATH OF PARTITION

The young nations will go through yet more violence before they can settle into new lives. Volume Two is entitled *Desh ka Bhavishya* (The Future of the Nation). It covers ten years, from just after 1947 till the second general elections in 1957, following thus the history of the new nation, and as framed by it the history of the three main protagonists.

This second volume is longer than the first; it has almost 600 pages, and once again it introduces myriad new characters on its vast canvas. It covers a much longer period, a decade instead of the first volume's single year. It is more ambitious; in shifting to the capital, Delhi, it covers in greater detail the national in addition to the regional and the personal. No critical account can adequately cover the narrative that emerges, for it evolves several strands and sub-strands. The compactness which makes Volume One so powerful dissipates thus in the second and often enough the personal and the political narratives part ways.[58]

---

[58] This is what Anand has to say about the period in which Yashpal was writing Volume Two: 'I think Pt 2 is a bit loosely written and wobbly compared to Pt 1. Why? The time between 1958 and 1960 leading to the writing and the eventual publication of Pt 2 was full of happenings. Yashpal published a total of 10 books between 1956 and 1960. Some were works that he had done earlier (translations for other publishers, *Amita* the novel, etc.) but others were done simultaneously as he wrote the second part of *Jhootha*

Lives take new shapes, are given new twists in this new context. As Tara says later: 'A lot was destroyed during Partition, but the solid layers of earth with which society was smothered have been cracked, as if an earthquake has burst open the walls of a prison, freeing those inside—even if they have been injured in the process. Many perished, many never recovered from their injuries, but Panjabis are a vital lot, they seem to have fallen on their feet.'[59] The cracks will remain, as will the memories. Tara herself is left with an internal injury and venereal disease, yet finds her base in a profession, something inconceivable in her earlier life. Ultimately, she becomes a civil servant of the central government in Delhi; Puri becomes a Congress Member of the Legislative Assembly in Panjab, his base the market town of Jalandhar; Kanak becomes a journalist. In their separate ways, all three become actively involved in nation-formation, as builders of modern India.

The urban landscape changes abruptly, radically. Lahore has been left behind. The action now takes place partially in Jalandhar, partially in Lucknow, but largely in Delhi, still the segregated city

---

Sach. In 1958 he went to the Tashkent Writers' Congress. In 1959 my mother had begun to build a house in one of the new suburbs of Lucknow. She was dissatisfied with the existing dwelling for several reasons . . . About the same time my mother had succeeded in importing some printing machines from the USSR, which had arrived and [been] installed in 1960. For this she had to go all over (Delhi, Calcutta, etc.) which meant she could not give as much time to running the business and managing the house and family affairs as she normally did. All this, I am sure, had some effect on Yashpal's concentration and focus; he had far less diversions during the time he wrote Pt 1. For example, Yashpal took time off from writing Pt 2 to translate and publish the Hindi translation (*Zulaikhan*) of Askad Mukhtar's novel *Sisters* . . . This surely cut down the time and energy he could have devoted to writing the second part. Perhaps, most of all, since someone had to supervise the building of the house and my mother was often away arranging for the import of the printing machines, he often went to the building site to keep an eye on the workers and, at the same time, write. To supervise workers in India is a full time job.' Email from Anand, 23 October 2009.

[59] JS, 497.

of the British Raj with its 'native' inner areas and enclaves outside, the serene avenues of the older Civil Lines and Lutyens' New Delhi inhabited by the elite, no part of the city prepared for the onslaught of refugees. The character of the sedate capital changes as refugees occupy the areas vacated by Muslims and new violence erupts, this time directed at the Muslims who remain. We know that 'In 1947 Delhi lay mainly within the old city wall. Lutyens' New Delhi was outside it, southward at one extreme; and the old Secretariat complex and civil lines outside it, northward at the other. With Partition, some 47.5 lakhs (4.75 million) migrated to India. Of these 4,95,391 came to Delhi.'[60] That is, half a million refugees poured into the city, occupying every vacant space they could find. 'Of the total population in Delhi in 1951, refugees comprised 28.4 per cent.'[61] Of these, a sixth had belonged to Lahore.[62] Tara settles in Delhi, as does Kanak's family, a replay of the old Mughal Lahore–Delhi nexus, this time in a new guise, that of refugee transfer, which recreates Lahore in pockets of Delhi. For Tara in particular, it will become possible to overcome the limitations that the city, the neighbourhood, and the family had forced on her, achieving a transition impossible in her Lahore days; relocation then, as reclamation. In depicting this formative aspect of Partition, as much as the aftermath of destruction, the novel once again anticipates the insights of later studies. Many years after *Jhutha Sach* was written, a refugee, Bibi Inder Kaur, set about educating herself, transitioning through various positions as lecturer in a series of Delhi colleges to become principal of a newly opened college in Amritsar. When interviewed she said quite frankly: 'Partition provided me with the opportunity to get out of the four walls of my house. I had the will power, the intelligence . . . In Karachi

---

[60] Datta 1986: 442.

[61] Cf. ibid.: 443f. The new government set up a Ministry of Rehabilitation in September 1947. The ministry in turn set up three large refugee camps. The Kingsway Camp, located outside Kashmiri Gate, with its 30,000 refugees, was the largest. Ibid.: 445. Several smaller camps also dotted the landscape.

[62] Ibid.: 451.

I would have remained a housewife. Personally I feel Partition forced many people into taking the initiative and finding their own feet.'[63] This phenomenon raises, in a complementary study, many questions 'about the State's patriarchal, yet benevolent intervention into the lives of these women . . . [But] I tell this story merely to point to a lesser known fact of the trauma and upheaval of Partition, that in many ways, out of the tragedy, grew a sense of independence and opportunity for many people and particularly for women.'[64]

Long stretches of the novel treat of the differing rehabilitations of the sibling pair: Tara's in a Delhi office, Puri's in Jalandhar's Model Town as a corrupt Congress politician. (Ironically, he has the means to live in Model Town here, having been denied entry into the world of Model Town in Lahore.) Kanak marries Puri—it excites no comment after Partition—breaks up with him as his worst qualities surface, and evolves into a professional in her own right, and eventually remarries.

In this looser second volume, two incidents of violence stand out, each depicted with power and conviction, both typical in their own way for the course the tale takes. Both occur early in the narrative and involve Tara to a degree, but the relations of the chronicle to the personal, the factual to the fictional, and of history to biography are more tenuous, practically disappearing in the second incident. I focus also on the incident that concludes the novel, in which all the main characters are locked in a struggle with each other that is as much political as it is personal.

The first incident is particularly poignant for the depiction of violence visited upon abducted Hindu women subsequent to their retrieval.[65] Not all lives find new avenues of existence. Education, the

[63] Bhasin and Menon 1998: 215.
[64] Butalia 1998: 368.
[65] In spite of his critique that the novel focuses overly on women, Nemichandra Jain concedes that this scene in particular is practically explosive for its *tivrata aur bhav gahanata*, its intensity and its depth of emotion. Jain [1966] 2002: 79.

LAHORE, DELHI, AND THE BITTER TRUTH   239

determination to start afresh and leave the old behind, the ability to resituate ambitions, can help to carve out new spaces, as it does in Tara's case. Illiterate and rustic, Banti is less fortunate, more embedded in the customary. Her spirituality can no longer help her. In families that cannot think beyond customary lines, abducted women are irrevocably tainted.

Yashpal's depiction of life in refugee camps is probably unparalleled in Hindi literature, so little space has it found in contemporary or post-Partition literature. He shows Tara and Banti in a refugee camp in Delhi, located just outside Kashmiri Gate. The scenes that follow provide a vignette of life in these camps as the state struggles to provide amenities and people begin to take stock of their new situation. Tara tries to remain anonymous in the camp; she does not seek to be reunited with her family; it provides no refuge for her. The two women have formed a firm bond in captivity, and Tara accompanies Banti on a series of forays into the city to look for her husband and her young son.

Delhi is a city in chaos, but Banti has shown resilience before and searches relentlessly for her men. On one such excursion, the women are directed to a locality called Paharganj. Once inhabited by Muslims, the area has now been occupied entirely by refugees from West Panjab.[66] '*Chhota-mota shahar hi samajho*' (think of it as a small town), a Sardar tells them.[67] Banti chases down each of its many lanes, asking after her husband's family. It is getting to be late evening, Tara fears for their safety. Suddenly, Banti espies her little son, a waif sitting in the lap of an older woman, her mother-in-law, and she falls upon him with a shriek. Tara sweats in relief as Banti holds the boy tight, crying terribly; Tara tells the curious surrounding

---

[66] 'A European witness reported seeing "car loads and lorry loads of armed Sikhs freely going around" and the *Daily Mirror* of 9 September [1947] reported that the Paharganj area was "like a battle-field with blazing houses, hordes of refugees, dead cattle and horses and the rattle of automatic weapons."' Pandey 2001: 129.

[67] JS, 112.

them about their stay in the haveli in Shekhupura. The reaction is mixed: Who'll keep such women now? The mother-in-law snatches the child and goes in: *Tu ab ham logom ke kis kam ki?* (Of what use are you now to us?)[68] Tara speaks up: it is not Banti's fault, the family left her behind because they were afraid. She's been looking for them for nine days. Heteroglossia again: the crowd is divided in its opinion, the sympathy shifting from one to the other; a youth speaks up for them, 'That's right, if there is a fault, it is yours. Aren't you ashamed, leaving your woman behind like cowardly jackals? . . . Is the house the old woman's or the wife's . . .?'[69]

When Banti's husband and brother-in-law return from work, the verdict remains inflexible: Banti can't be taken back. The narrator's unemotional reportage style mirrors the sparse finality of absolute rejection. Tara watches in horror as Banti hits her head again and again on the threshold of the house. In death, safely out of the way, Banti has found solidarity, understanding, even some respect. A bier is made for Banti's corpse, she is wrapped in red cloth; four men carry her. Not recognized in life, in death she is to be cremated like a married woman.

Banti has not acquired sufficient shape, enough interiority, to become a character in her own right, and though she is a friend, Tara does not play more than a witness role in this scene; in this respect it has somewhat the same function as Puri's train ride back to Lahore. It is a powerful scene, but it does not affect the course of the main protagonists' lives.

Emotionally, Tara is deeply affected by the futility and ferocity of the climax of the search. Back in the camp, we see a resurfacing of the *gali* ethos. The voices in the tent she shares with other women are like those of Bhola Pandhe ki Gali in Lahore. They observe everything narrowly, comment on everything mercilessly. If anything, there is more frustration, more aggression in their words. A woman

---

[68] Ibid.: 116.
[69] Ibid.

alone, especially if destitute, is treated with suspicion, anger, and contempt; Tara has been away the whole night. There is no space to move unobserved by unsympathetic eyes. The co-inhabitants of her tent do not spare her: she is a 'loose woman'.

Dr Shyama is the camp's woman doctor; she does voluntary service there and moves in Delhi's high society. She comes to the emotionally battered Tara's rescue and gives her office work. She rises quickly in the camp hierarchy, out of reach of the women in her tent, most of whom continue to watch her mistrustfully. She wanders the streets of Delhi looking to teach in a girls' school, fruitlessly. But once again her education and her personality finally come to her rescue. Dr Shyama introduces her to Mrs Agarwala, a socialite and social worker, and she is engaged as a governess to her two small children. With her, Tara makes the great social and spatial leap in the city, the one that had not been possible in Lahore. She moves to elite quarters, to Lutyens' Delhi, learns the ways of the Delhi elite, witnessing, partly in Mrs Agarwala's company, partly through drawing room conversations, the historic events that follow in the weeks thereafter.

We move to the second scene of violence. It comes as the climax of Hindu communal violence and has to do with no less a personage than Mahatma Gandhi. It has such significance that the narrator allows it to stand by itself, without feeling the need to knit it into the lives of his protagonists, except in the most general way.

The communal bloodbath in the city continues. Scores of Muslims are killed in Karol Bagh, Sabzi Mandi, and Paharganj, thousands seek refuge in Jamia Millia, Purana Qila, and Humayun's Tomb. The city's monuments acquire another legacy, of granting refuge to the needy, a historical gesture from the past to the present. The bloodshed prompts the drama of the frail Mahatma's last satyagraha, the Delhi Fast, and his subsequent assassination, both enacted on the national stage, subsuming all else. On 12 January, Monday, the radio brings the news that Mahatma Gandhi has vowed to fast unto death unless the communal violence ceases, particularly in Delhi. Another kind of countdown has begun. The Mahatma has also demanded that India pay Pakistan Rs 550 million, its share of undivided India's sterling balance. The Indian cabinet has voted against this as there was no question of paying Pakistan during an armed conflict between the two countries in Kashmir.

The fast begins on 13 January. Delhi, the nation, Pakistan and the world anxiously watch the frail Mahatma and his indomitable will.[70]

Illus. 15: Girl refugee, Jullundur Camp, 1948

[70] Yashpal is no Gandhian, he belongs rather to the socialist Left. That he awards Gandhi so prominent a place in the first quarter of the second volume of his novel speaks for the respect he gives to the only political figure with the moral authority to curb the communal frenzy that breaks out in North India. The novel presupposes some knowledge of Gandhi's role in quelling communal riots at their worst. Simeon n.d. provides a moving account of

There are excited discussions in the Agarwala drawing room; many voice their disapproval of Gandhi's action.

A couple of days later, Mrs Agarwala, along with some other women, including Tara, figuring now as representative of refugee women at large, are sent as a women's delegation to the Mahatma, to assure him of Hindu women's support in his struggle. On the way they meet a procession of refugees shouting slogans against Gandhi; they want him to die. Nehru sweeps by in a car, the women witness his impulsive reaction: he jumps out and confronts the demonstrators. 'Gandhi is the soul of the nation, the spirit (*ruh*) of the country. With his death, you, I, the whole nation will perish. What will the world think of us?'[71] Tara's reflection at this juncture is that 'This great soul (*punyatma*) is giving up his life to stop the violence, he's doing penance for us all. He really is the soul of the nation.'[72] We are privy to her thoughts, she is deeply moved but can only be a mute witness, like so many others, though from closer quarters. The Mahatma is declining while the world holds its breath.[73]

Gandhi's last days, briefly recounting the Mahatma's vital role in quelling the massacre in Calcutta after Jinnah proclaimed Direct Action Day on 16 August 1946. Gandhi could successfully restore calm in the city with his fast. He managed the same in Noakhali, North Bengal, later in the year: 'From November 1946 till February 1947, he walked through the villages of Noakhali. This pilgrimage for harmony became legendary, as his prayer meetings healed the public psyche, encouraged Hindus to return to their villages and Muslims to discard their animus.' Of the Delhi Fast, Gandhi proclaimed at the prayer meeting: 'I shall terminate the fast only when peace has returned to Delhi. If peace is restored to Delhi it will have effect not only on the whole of India but also on Pakistan and when that happens, a Muslim can walk around in the city all by himself . . .'

[71] JS, 169.
[72] Ibid.: 170.
[73] 'Addressing a gathering of three hundred thousand people on January 17, Maulana Azad announced seven tests given him by Gandhi to be fulfilled and guaranteed by responsible people. They included freedom of worship to Muslims at the tomb of Khwaja Bakhtiar Chishti, non-interference with the

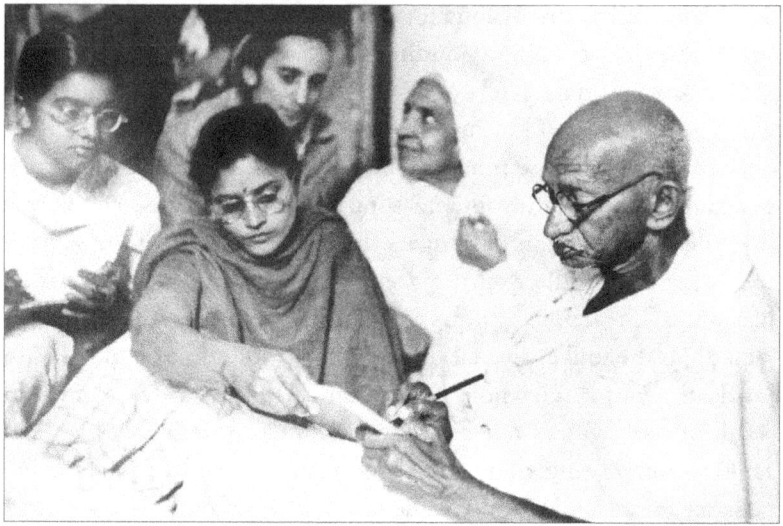

Illus.16: Gandhi's Delhi fast, January 1948

On 16 January the newspaper headlines declare India is ready to pay Pakistan what it owes. Everyone appeals for peace and by the evening two lakh Delhi citizens have signed a peace pledge undertaking to fulfil the Mahatma's demands. Two days later the Mahatma breaks his fast.[74] Once again, the drawing room in the Agarwala house fills

---

Urs festival due to be held there within a week; the voluntary evacuation by non-Muslims of all mosques in Delhi that were being used for residential purposes or which had been converted into temples; free movement of Muslims in areas where they used to stay; complete safety to Muslims while travelling by train; no economic boycott of Muslims; and freedom to Muslim evacuees to return to Delhi.' Simeon n.d.

[74] 'In his reply [to the pledge], Gandhi said: "I am happy to hear what you have told me, but if you have overlooked one point all this will be worth nothing. If this declaration means that you will safeguard Delhi and whatever happens outside Delhi will be no concern of yours, you will be committing a grave error and it will be sheer foolishness on my part to break my fast . . . The leaders from the whole of India have assembled here. Men had become beasts . . . We have to consider whether or not we can accomplish what we are going to promise. If you are not confident of fulfilling your pledge, do

with arguments on the pros and cons of the Mahatma's politics and Congress policies; the tone is critical, negative. Tara defends Gandhi's non-violent mode but the others think fasting as a political strategy is liable to misuse.

On 20 January there is news of a Panjabi youth throwing a bomb at the prayer meeting.[75] On the 30th comes the news of the Mahatma's assassination. Life comes to a halt. The cremation next day is a grandly military ceremony for which the Agarwalas go to Rajghat. Tara and the children witness the huge procession from a rooftop on Akbar Road. We hear the voices of people, represented by comments such as, 'The government of the rich has stolen the poor man's Gandhi from poor men . . . They'll build a memorial for him to rival the Taj Mahal and bury his principles under it . . . He'll follow the Buddha and Christ, someone not to follow but to worship.'[76]

The mass violence depicted in Volume Two is brought to an end with the Mahatma's death, a catharsis after which the tension can only abate. Intense as these scenes are, as part of a narrative that charts the course of fictive lives they are arguably too large and engulfing, they burst out of the novel's seams. Once again, though all are affected by the Mahatma's passing, his death has no immediate impact on the course of the major protagonists' lives.

---

not ask me to give up my fast. It is for you and the whole of India to translate it into reality. It may not be possible to realize it in a day. I do not possess the requisite strength for it. But I can assure you that till today our face was turned towards Satan, we have now resolved to turn towards God. If what I have told you fails to find an echo in your hearts or if you are convinced that it is beyond you, tell me so frankly . . . Taking into consideration all these implications, if you ask me to break my fast I shall abide by your wish. India will virtually become a prison if the present conditions continue. It may be better that you allow me to continue my fast and if God wills it He will call me."' Gandhi 1999: vol. 98, 254–7.

[75] 'One Madanlal Pahwa was arrested. Six other men escaped in a taxi. This was the fifth attempt on his life since 1934, and all of them were made by extreme Hindu nationalists.' Cf. Simeon n.d.

[76] JS, 194.

246 THE NOVEL AND THE CITY

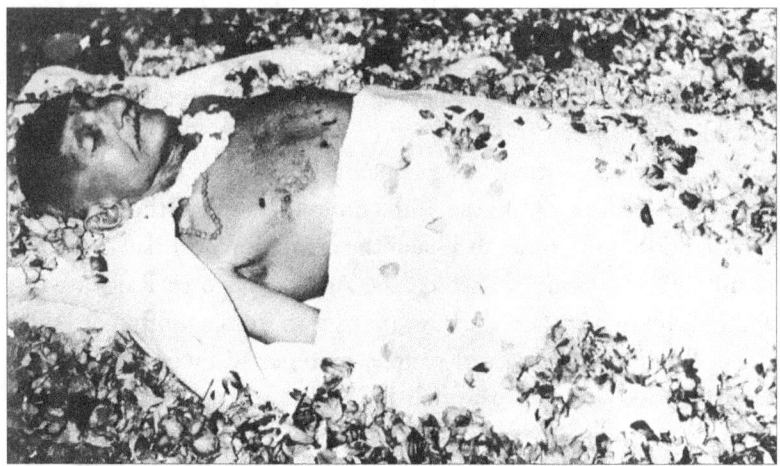

Illus. 17: Gandhi in death, 30 January 1948

If the characters are subordinated to the action on the national stage in this and sometimes other chapters of Volume Two, the last chapter manages to deftly entwine the results of the Second General Elections in Independent India with significance for the lives of the protagonists, with narrative twists which untangle the knots in their lives.

THE SECOND GENERAL ELECTIONS AND THE RIGHTING OF ALL WRONGS

Tara is working with the Ministry of Information. She now lives in an apartment in Panchkuian Road, one of the many refugee concentrates in West Delhi. The narrator takes some pains to describe how she hastily furnishes her living room in preparation for Dr Nath's initial visit, remembering his life-style in his Lahore haveli. She changes the curtains and cushion covers and the rearrangements she makes indicate her transition into the educated, affluent middle class. The social and spatial differences that were so marked in Lahore are being obliterated. Her efforts garner Dr Nath's praise.[77]

[77] Ibid.: 384.

Dr Nath is Advisor to the Planning Commission, with an office within the power circuits of Lutyens' Delhi. He works closely with a Dr Salis, perhaps modelled on the statistician-economist Mahalanobis, the brains behind India's Second Five Year Plan.[78] After her marriage to Dr Nath much later in the narrative, Tara moves to his spacious bungalow in the Civil Lines. Her park-like garden, trees, and greenery show how far she has come from Bhola Pandhe ki Gali in Lahore.

Vishwanath Sood, an unscrupulous Congress worthy from Panjab—Puri's patron but also Somraj Sahni's, Tara's former husband (to whom she is still formally married)—is standing for elections. Sood's supporters are industrialists and business people who oppose the socialism of the Second Five Year Plan. Sood has not pardoned Dr Salis and Nath for being its engineers; he is not one to forgive enemies. Puri is a link figure, connected to both Kanak and Tara, of whose existence he has long known, but whom he has refused to officially recognize. Sood's plan is to snare Nath with information about Tara's past life: Nath and Tara's wedding photos have appeared in the newspapers. Dr Prabhudayal, an old neighbour in Bhola Pandhe ki Gali, now on his way up socially and politically, remarks on this to Sood, whose doctor he is. Soon thereafter both Tara and Nath receive sealed envelopes. They have transcripts of the secret depositions to the Special Police by Puri, Somraj, and Dr Prabhudayal. How could a still-married Tara marry again? Nath sees this as a conspiracy against him. Sood, and Puri as his pawn, want to see him removed from the Planning Commission.

Kanak has now come together with Pritamsingh Gill; both are reporters. However, Puri is refusing to give Kanak a divorce. Gill advises Tara and Nath that they too consult Naiyar, a thoughtful

---

[78] 'The members were by no means all economists, but they were chosen by Nehru for their broad agreement with his political project: Committed to "socialistic" and reformist ideals, in the Indianized version of social democracy, and above all scepticism about the market and a belief that the state had to take responsibility for allocating resources in the economy.' Khilnani [1997] 1998: 85–6.

lawyer.[79] Naiyar has come to Delhi from Jalandhar in connection with the Kanak-Puri case. He regrets that Nath and Tara have not made use of the new law, for by 1957 the Hindu Marriage Law Act has come into force, which would have allowed Tara to file for divorce on grounds of desertion *before* she remarried. They will have to resort to law to resolve this knot.

Somraj should have claimed Tara as his wife: had they received notice from the court to this effect? Naiyar asks Tara formally whether it is true that she is Somraj's wife. She says it is *jhutha sach*, a false truth. They now have to prove the real truth. This is a noteworthy moment for the meaning of the novel's title, but it comes almost as an afterthought, at the tail end of the narrative, somehow losing its significance. The title seems much more to stand for the entire political situation, the promises and hopes associated with Independence and nation-building.

Kanak agrees to step forward as witness, to testify that Puri knew about Tara's survival all along, thus setting in motion a plan which will lead to the resolution of her own crisis. Meanwhile the Second General Elections are under way. Gill, Kanak, and their socialist friends, criticize the Indian National Congress for using Gandhi for election purposes while ignoring his ethics (*niti*). In the third week of January 1957, over the bitter cold of the North, Kanak rushes to Nath and Tara: she has received a divorce notice from Jalandhar. The Hindu Marriage Law has made it possible for Puri to file for divorce. They congratulate her, but Nath suspects it is a political move to put into question any testimony that she might bring against Puri.

In Jalandhar, Sood's votes are counted. There is much excitement. The Congress opponents have put up a joint front against the party, the first time they have done so, though the Congress still has the majority in the province. One of the journalists in Gill's office in Delhi says that the sentiment is against Sood's maladministration. News comes in, the Congress candidate has been defeated. Gill tries to phone Nath, then rushes out, buys sweets, and takes a taxi.

[79] Ibid.: 572–3.

Tara and Nath meet him, shining eyes, they've received a letter in the meantime. Nath tells Gill: 'We have been exonerated.'[80] Sood has been defeated by 17,000 votes. Nath speaks the closing lines of the novel; all has come right in the end, the threads of all their lives have been interwoven into this episode and can now be tied into a neat knot: 'You'll have to believe now that the "The future of the nation" is not in the fists of leaders and ministers, it is in the hands of the people.'[81]

CONCLUSION

What is remarkable in this second volume, concerned primarily with nation-making and the lives of those who have survived the violence of Partition (and into this second round of storytelling) is the absolute lack of enthusiasm for nationalism in the characters. Partition has tempered any joy that Independence might have brought. It has cut deep into the course that lives take, both the events that lead up to it in the weeks before Independence and then the violence of severing what had once belonged together into two nations. Partition ejects Tara out of the system into which she has been born, out of Bhola Pandhe ki Gali, out of her natal family, and out of marriage. It is the major happening of Volume One, which is tightly held together by it, the psychology of the characters interacting with the political events as they unfold to give the turns and twists to the narrative of their lives.

There is also a deal of psychological credibility in the turns that the lives of the siblings take in Volume Two. They do socially and financially well after their relocation, to Jalandhar and Delhi respectively, because life in the building of the new nation provides them with a fresh start and new opportunities that they are qualified to avail of. Puri does remain single at the end, at least for the time being, after Kanak leaves him and ultimately files for divorce, but he has his talents: we have seen that in Volume One, he now has political

---

[80] 'Exonerate' in the original English: JS, 581.
[81] Ibid.: 583.

clout and moves in powerful circles. He manages to cling to power, for, in spite of the small losses in the elections, the Congress Party retains control of the centre.

It is less the turns that lives take and more the structure of the second volume which exceeds the economy of the narrative in the first volume. It is looser, more straggling and there is the rather too perfect symmetry of its closure. By this time we are convinced that Tara and Nath, Kanak and Gill, and their friends have their hearts and values in the right places. In their pairing, the right people seem to have come together with the right people and the evildoers, at least for the time being, are vanquished.

At a yet wider level, there is the course that the country takes. The nation has corrupt rulers, and, it is repeatedly suggested, an ineffective prime minister. It affords the reader moral and emotional satisfaction to know that, in spite of this, much can come right at the local, regional level, that corrupt politicians such as Puri and Sood cannot always hoodwink voters. Nikhil Govind has spoken of the perhaps overly transparent 'moral clarity of Yashpal's imagination'.[82] This creates a credibility gap in the narrative, but perhaps it can be no other way with an author who writes to convey so clear a moral message. The struggle has to have been worth it and all has to come right at the end. Yashpal cannot be judged only by the patchiness and neat closure of the second volume. The general pace of the narrative, the intensity and vigour of the first volume, is matched by the author's interest in sheer storytelling in the second, and this does ensure, as we turn away from it, that our interest seldom flags.

REFERENCES

Bhasin, Kamla, and Ritu Menon. 1998. *Borders and Boundaries: Women in India's Partition*. Delhi: Kali for Women.

Butalia, Urvashi. 1998. *The Other Side of Silence: Voices from the Partition of India*. Delhi: Penguin India.

---

[82] Govind 2014: 26.

Datta, V.N. 1986. 'Punjabi Refugees and the Urban Development of Greater Delhi'. In *Delhi Through the Ages: Essays in Urban History, Culture and Society*, ed. R.E. Frykenberg. Delhi: Oxford University Press.

Gandhi, M.K., *Collected Works of Mahatma Gandhi Online*. http://www.gandhiserve.org/cwmg/cwmg.html.

Glover, William J. 2008. *Making Lahore Modern: Constructing and Imagining a Colonial City*. Minneapolis and London: University of Minnesota Press.

Govind, Nikhil. 2014. *Between Love and Freedom: The Revolutionary in the Hindi Novel*. London, New York, Delhi: Routledge.

Jain, Nemichandra. [1966] 2002. 'Bahya ka vistar: *Jhutha Sach*', in *Adhure Sakshatkar* ['Expansion of the External: *Jhutha Sach*', in *Incomplete Interviews*]. Delhi: Vani Prakashan.

Jones, Kenneth W. [1976] 2006. *Arya Dharm: Hindu Consciousness in Nineteenth Century Punjab*. Los Angeles, Berkeley: University of California Press, and Delhi: Manohar.

Khilnani, Sunil. [1997] 1998. *The Idea of India*. London: Penguin Books.

King, Anthony D. 1984. *The Bungalow: The Production of a Global Culture*. London: Routledge and Kegan Paul.

Mahajan, Karan. 2015. 'India's Forgotten Feminist Epic'. In *The New Yorker*, 27 March.

Pandey, Gyanendra. 2001. *Remembering Partition: Violence, Nationalism and History in India*. Cambridge: Cambridge University Press.

Raza Rumi. 2013. *Delhi by Heart: Impressions of a Pakistani Traveller*. Delhi: HarperCollins India.

Simeon, Dilip. n.d. 'The Legacy of Mahatma Gandhi'. Unpublished paper.

Suleri Goodyear, Sarah. 2005. 'Lahore Remembered', in *City of Sin and Splendour: Writings on Lahore*, ed. Bapsi Sidhwa. Delhi: Penguin Books.

Talbot, Ian. 1988. *Punjab and the Raj 1849–1947*. Riverdale, Maryland: The Riverdale Company.

Tandon, Prakash. [1961] 1968. *Punjabi Century: 1857–1947*. Berkeley, Los Angeles: University of California Press.

Williams, Raymond. [1975] 1985. *The Country and the City*. London: The Hogarth Press.

Yashpal. [1958] 2000. *Jhutha Sach*. Part One: *Vatan aur Desh*. Allahabad: Lok Bharati Prakashan.

———. [1960] 2003. *Jhutha Sach*. Part Two: *Desh ka Bhavishya*. Allahabad: Lok Bharati Prakashan.

———. [1951] 2005. *Simhavalokan* [Memoirs]. Allahabad: Lok Bharati Prakashan.

———. 2010. *This is not that Dawn. Jhutha Sach*. Translated into English by Anand. Delhi: Penguin Books.

II

MODERNIST CONUNDRUMS

5

City, Civilization, and Nature

AGYEYA'S SECOND NOVEL, *Nadī ke Dvīp* (1952; Islands in the Stream; hereafter ND), created as much sensation in its time as his first novel, *Shekhar, ek Jīvanī* (Shekhar, a Life) had done almost a decade earlier. ND made several departures from the novels of its day, some of which radically disturbed settled notions of propriety.[1] For one, there was a new gender equation. The protagonists, Rekha and Bhuvan, both middle-class professionals, meet each other as equals and love each other as equals. Yet more radically, neither of them sees marriage and domesticity as the express goals of their relationship. As several critics have pointed out, this was a first for Hindi novels of the time.[2] What has received less

---

[1] Sachidanand Hiranand Vatsyayan (1911–1987) wrote under the pen-name 'Ajneya', a Sanskrit term meaning 'unknowable'. Its modern Hindi pronunciation is reflected in the spelling most often used in English, 'Agyeya', the version I follow. There is some uncertainty regarding the date of first publication of *Nadī ke Dvīp*. In her fine essay on the novel, Archana Varma (2011) reports Rajendra Yadav recalling the original year of publication as 1948 or 1949, its publisher being the short-lived Pragati Prakashan of Delhi. The second edition, with which Varma worked, was published in 1951 by the Saraswati Press of Allahabad. The matter remains vexed. It is likely that Agyeya revised the novel a couple of times, since later editions, including the one I use, give 1952 as the copyright year.

[2] Rajendra Yadav, of the Progressive camp and ideologically expressly opposed to Agyeya's circle, in an article published in April 1987, in his journal *Haṃs*, a few months after Agyeya had passed away, reprinted in Yadav 1997: 93–4.

critical attention is the novel's near-absolute rejection of city life and its comforts, which Rekha equates with the ills of civilization. Instead, there is a new celebration of nature—uninhabited, untamed nature—providing for realms of experience beyond those expressed in the Hindi romanticist Chayavad poetry of the 1920s and early 1930s.

In so far as this goes, ND is surely one of the first, if not *the* first, modernist novel in Hindi. It breaks with all known social norms, setting up new frames of reference. The experience of the self as an island in the stream of life, and moments of intimacy made possible in, and perhaps even by, nature, is one of the powerful frames within which the narrative moves; it is articulated early on by Rekha in the form of a radical critique of urban middle-class civilization; a familiar trope in modernist works.[3] She sets her own existence as a counterpoint to this middle-class sedateness; she is homeless and solitary. Raymond Williams has spoken of the modernist work as a 'singular narrative of unsettlement, homelessness, solitude and impoverished independence . . .'[4] The other frame, presented by Bhuvan at various points in the narrative, while also participating in these perceptions, is provided by 'science' as an ethical and humanitarian enterprise, seen as civilization's highest achievement and capable thus of offsetting its excesses; a universalistic, cosmopolitan frame, another modernist feature.[5] Here I explore Rekha and Bhuvan's relationship with themselves and each other as they seek to create and find space within these frames.

The most powerful scenes in the novel take place in the mountains: in the wild beauty of Naukuchia, a tiny hill station in lake-dotted

---

[3] See Childs 2000: 30 for a discussion of the modernist critique of civilization.

[4] In his essay 'When was Modernism?'. Williams 1989: 34.

[5] In his Introduction, Pericles Lewis (2011: 6–7) lists this phenomenon as being characteristic of the European modernistic avant-garde. I have found the same qualities in Agyeya's work and Bharati's; the latter is discussed in the next essay.

Kumaon, and on the banks of Lake Tulian, high up in Kashmir. Bhuvan and Rekha spend their time in Naukuchia, in a dak bungalow, which takes care of basic needs, and in tents pitched on the banks of Tulian. The freedom and openness of these places is juxtaposed with the claustrophobia of North Indian cities of the 1930s. Delhi and Lucknow, as they appear in the novel, are cities of the period between 1932 and 1942, not the overcrowded, traffic-jammed, polluted cities they are today. What can be threatening about them and for whom? What kind of spaces, public and private, can middle-class people who don't fit into known patterns of life inhabit and occupy?

New Delhi has just been inaugurated. Connaught Place, the shopping centre of the new city, sees little activity yet and finds bare mention in the novel. Most of the action takes place on the borders of the old city, in the Kashmiri Gate area, near the wall encircling the city that the British rebuilt in 1835 as a structure with double gates. It now carries cannon shot marks of the 1857 uprising. The area around Kashmiri Gate had evolved as the main shopping centre of the European community; most of their social activities took place here. Rekha and Bhuvan find a measure of autonomy in this

Illus. 18: Kumaon Cottage

space, away from the constrictions of the inner city, to which there is no reference in the novel.⁶ This is a remarkable difference from the protagonists of the novels discussed thus far, all of whom live or originate in the lanes of the old city and are ruled by the norms of their traditional families. In ND, by contrast, the protagonists move in spaces frequented by Europeans, that is, in modern spaces, displaying a freedom of movement and thought hitherto unknown in Hindi fiction. There are no parents, no siblings, no families observing and restricting their movements. Rekha and Bhuvan walk in the picturesque ruins of the mid-eighteenth century, now laid out as a venue of leisure and recreation, the Qudsia Park; they visit the restaurant of the Carlton Hotel, just off Kashmiri Gate; Rekha stays in the YWCA, the sole hostel for working women, established at the turn of the century. The couple see each other in the waiting rooms of the newly built Delhi railway station, its red brick recalling the colour of the Red Fort and the Jama Masjid.

Yet, once again, it is a modern environment not entirely free of the old. An important scene in the new city is also set in an older monument, Jantar Mantar, the observatory built by Sawai Raja Jai Singh in 1724, now at the heart of the new city; and in Davico's, an English-owned restaurant in Connaught Place. Finally, there are the

---

⁶ As King (1976: 198) tells us: 'With the removal of troops to the extramural cantonment in 1828, more space had become available in the area of Kashmiri Gate. Here, between 1829 and 1836, was constructed the community's church. Standing in its own ten-acre grounds, the "church of St James" provided a locale for the performance of rituals and the expression of religious beliefs. It acted as a centre of social activity, serving to cement a sense of identity within the group. It provided for the interment and visual commemoration of the community's dead and, for indigenous and immigrant inhabitants, it was an important visual symbol, signaling the presence of the colonial elite. The church was to become the natural focus of the community, strengthening the claims of the Kashmiri Gate neighbourhood to be the principal European section of the city. Shops began to be established here and the area, with its arcades and wrought-iron, increasingly took on the character of a comparable metropolitan environment.'

still and sandy banks of the Yamuna. It is worth noting that it is in this Mughal-British city that Gaura lives, the young upper-middle-class woman, first presented as a child, who grows up and is educated under the guidance of Bhuvan, a family friend.

Reduced to a sub-provincial status from the second half of the nineteenth century, when the capital of the province was shifted to Allahabad, Nawabi Lucknow also has its monuments and the gardens laid around them. The ruins of the Old Residency, lovingly maintained by the British as a memorial to their final triumph in the 1857 uprising, are witness to a key encounter in the novel.

There is also Lucknow's Hazratganj. Very modern, very European in its shops, Hazratganj, like the Kashmiri Gate area in Delhi, has been developed as a European shopping centre;[7] once again,

Illus. 19: Lucknow Residency

[7] Oldenburg (2001: xi) notes the changes in the city after 1857: 'In Hazratganj, scores of shops that had been abandoned or destroyed during the siege were claimed as government property, repaired and neatened with uniform façades. This was developed as the fashionable centre of the

it affords Rekha and Bhuvan a measure of autonomy. The Coffee House, established in 1935/6, is a centre of informal gossip but also of intellectual interaction.[8] It is also visited by those women, of one profession or other, who feel confident enough to come together there for a cup of coffee. They are often Anglo-Indian. Later in the novel Rekha refers to its function for her. The Coffee House is haunted by Chandramadhav, a journalist who works for the *Pioneer*, which is still a very colonial paper. He also visits two cinema halls, Mayfair and Elphinstone, which show English-language films. As in Delhi, we get more glimpses of the modern part of the city than of the old. Apart from these public places, there is the Chowk, the old-style centre of the old city with old-style amusements. And once again, as a relief almost, Bhuvan and Rekha can meet, this time along with Chandramadhav, on the banks of the River Gomati.

The novel is structured around the meetings, musings, and conversations of the four main characters of the novel: Bhuvan, Rekha, Gaura, and Chandramadhav. Finely orchestrated, almost like a musical composition or a long poem with a refrain, it has eleven sections ranging from twenty-five to fifty pages. Of these eleven, two each are devoted to and named after one of the four characters, focusing on them or focalized through them. Two further sections, entitled *antarāl* (interludes), consist entirely of letters without date or place. The first interlude occurs after the third section, the second after another four sections. The novel ends with a section on Gaura, who ultimately

---

colonial city, as opposed to the specialty bazaars of the old city . . . The shops were leased mainly to European traders who offered a wide variety of foreign "novelties" and merchandise, including cloth, wines and liquors, tobacco products, cutlery, china, glassware, and Western furniture and furnishings for sale.'

[8] For information on the Coffee House and its atmosphere in the 1930s and 1940s, I thank the late Ram Advani (1920–2016), Lucknow's famous bookseller, whose shop was located in the Mayfair building, which once also housed the Mayfair Cinema, where the protagonists go to see English films.

becomes the meeting point for the other three characters. The novel concludes with a short final section, *upsaṃhār* (epilogue), consisting of an unsent letter, musings, and the echo of a poem.

The narrator has a minimal voice, moving largely in the 'character zone' of the characters in focus and often merging with them.[9] The intensely subjective tone of the novel, the exploration of interiorities, most of all of Bhuvan,[10] is reflected not only in its lyrical prose but also in the many genres and subgenres—notebook jottings, poems, letters—which interleaf the narrative.[11] The poems, most notably those of D.H. Lawrence and T.S. Eliot,[12] serve as climactic moments

[9] Bakhtin's notion of character zone has particular significance for this novel of subjectivities. Character zones 'are formed from the fragments of character speech, from various forms for hidden transmission of someone else's word, from scattered words and sayings belonging to someone else's speech, from those invasions into authorial speech of others' expressive indicators [ellipses, questions, exclamations]. Such character zone is the field of action for a character's voice, encroaching in one way or another upon the author's voice . . .' Bakhtin 1981: 315.

[10] This exploration of Bhuvan's interiority, as reflected in his relationship most of all with Rekha and to a lesser extent with Gaura and Chandramadhav, is well brought out in Henry James' (2011: 51) description of his own novelistic technique. In speaking of Isabel Archer in *A Portrait of a Lady* (1881–2), James says: 'Place the centre of the subject in the young woman's own consciousness,' I said to myself, 'and you get as interesting and as beautiful a difficulty as you could wish. Stick to *that*—for the centre; put the heaviest weight on *that* scale, which will be so largely the scale of her relations to herself. Make her only interested enough, at the same time, in the things that are not herself, and this relation needn't fear to be too limited. Place meanwhile in the other scale the lighter weight (which is usually the one that tips the balance of interest): press least hard, in short, on the consciousness of your heroine's satellites, especially the male; make it as interest contributive only to the greater ones . . .' In the case of our novel, things do get out of balance, as Rekha wins more weight than perhaps intended, sharing Bhuvan's space and sometimes overpowering it.

[11] Bakhtin (1981: 33) once again: 'Since it is constructed in a zone of contact with the incomplete events of a particular present, the novel often crosses the boundary of what we strictly call fictional literature . . .'

[12] The influential literary critic F.R. Leavis saw the early decades of the

and their echoes—a lyrical phrase, a whole line—provide internal cohesion to the narrative and even explicate it, given that so much is left unsaid.[13] But this intimacy is not a stable entity. Its very intensity makes for its unstableness.

This poetic work represents a novelty in Hindi, a 'first' that was never quite replicated. Tagore's *Shesher Kobita* (The Last Poem) had provided a model in Bengali for it. But whereas Tagore used his own poems, in ND we have citations from poets other than Agyeya.[14]

---

twentieth century as the 'age of D.H. Lawrence and T.S. Eliot'. Leavis ([1955] 1964: 317. No-one was better aware than Leavis of the differences, amounting to hostility, between the two writers, given Eliot's disdainful rejection of Lawrence, his person as well as his works. In *Scrutiny*, the journal (1932–53) he edited, and in his book on Lawrence, Leavis wrote at length in defence of the novelist. Both Lawrence and Eliot were to leave their mark on Agyeya, Lawrence through his subtle perception of and sensuous absorption in nature, as much as by his critique of industry and civilization; Eliot by his ruminations on time.

[13] In the Acknowledgements to the English translation of the novel (1980), Agyeya points out that 'the characters in this book frequently quote or allude to the works of Browning, Eliot, Heine, Lawrence (D.H. as well as T.E.), Jayshankar Prasad, Plomer, Rosetti (D.G. and Christina), Shelley, Swinburne, Tagore, Toller and others . . .' However, it is the Lawrence and Eliot poems which enter most deeply into the characters' own reflections about their actions and reactions.

[14] I am grateful to Anindita Mukhopadhyay for sending me her beautiful translation of Tagore's novel *Shesher Kobita* (The Last Poem; 1929), which uses both prose narrative and poetry 'to produce a distinctive lyrical prose.' Tagore [1929] 2006: 1. The female protagonist is very much like Rekha, a sophisticated working woman, and her relationship to Amit, the male protagonist, is too deep for ordinary conversation—thus the poems in which they communicate, which make for an intimacy beyond the conventional. As in *Nadi ke Dvip*, '*The Last Poem* is about a reaching out of conversational tentacles to feel the presence of the sexual Other, shorn of the weight of social conventions that only allow the parroting of meaningless phrases at the tea-table—where there is no true communication, where personalities simply hide behind the empty mask of manners.' Ibid.: 3. As Mukhopadhyay also points out, the relationship is too intense, too romantic for marriage, of

The verse heightens the lyricism of its most emotionally powerful moments. It is also a mode of communication between Rekha and Bhuvan, who respond instinctively to the quotation of a stray line by one of them, the rest of the poem becoming the unsaid between them.

ISLANDS AND BRIDGES

Rekha's image of human beings as islands afloat in the stream of life is one of the primary leitmotifs of the novel. As part of Rekha's character zone, this image appears in the speech of other characters and permeates Bhuvan's and possibly also Chandramadhav's perception of the world around them. Rekha communicates the idea and the image to Bhuvan at one of their first meetings in the Lucknow Coffee House: 'To me it seems that we can at most be little islands in that stream, surrounded by it yet distinct; rooted in the earth and stable, yet always helpless before the stream—for there is no knowing when a wave will carelessly wash an island away, leaving no trace of it, however beautiful the green of its cover may once have been!'[15] With varying connotations the islands are repeatedly invoked in the novel and are reflected in part by the verse by Shelley which prefaces it, where they are seen as providing brief moments of repose:

> Many a green isle needs must be
> In the deep wide sea of misery
> Or the Mariner, worn and wan
> Never thus could voyage on.[16]

---

which institution Tagore is openly critical: 'This tight emotional intellectual reciprocity where the lines of communication are like high voltage wires, is to be sustained in marriage, is it possible?' Ibid.: 6.

[15] ND, 22. All citations in English are from Agyeya's own translation of the novel (1980), sometimes slightly amended to reflect the lyricism of the original Hindi prose. In the notes, ND refers to this 1980 translation.

[16] Opening lines of Shelley's poem 'Lines Written Among the Euganean Hills'. Shelley 1954: 182–91.

Rekha introduces a second leitmotif, this one relating to 'time', which also connects with the first. She speaks of time as a kind of insulation, as one lived moment against another, securing the present against the future and against needs projected into the future: 'And that's why all journeys' ends become false and there are no roads. I really do not want to go anywhere—I don't even want to want. For me there isn't even a flow of time—there is no flow, only a succession of moments (*kṣaṇa*). Like humanity, the flow of time too is just a concept for me: the reality is the moment. The moment is absolute (*sanātana*).'[17] The island can expand or retreat into itself, but, resembling the singular moment, it remains unconnected to the next strip of land. The notion of a succession of moments, though nowhere philosophically explicated in the novel, echoes both existentialist ideas circulating at the time as well as Buddhist notions of 'momentariness'.[18] Rekha's ideas and belief about time, of the moment as the eternal present unconnected to the next, directionless and leading anywhere, are difficult to sustain, even for her. But these are not stray images, they are part of her perception and actions. Even at the risk of self-destruction, Rekha struggles to live by the notions her images embody.

Her notions about islands and the insularity of the moment will permeate Bhuvan's perception and his speech, but with a different inflection, allowing for the possibility of the islands becoming part of a collective. For Bhuvan's is the more expansive view of humanity,

[17] ND, 37.
[18] The idea that existence is but a flow of moments is Buddhist, and the use of the term *kṣaṇa* underlines this: informal conversation with Alexander von Rospatt, Buddhologist at Berkeley. The spin this passage puts on it, namely that only the present moment matters, may not be a direct borrowing from Buddhism, though there was a strong current within Buddhism taking a similar position. This resulted in the juxtaposition of instantaneists who seized upon the present moment in a vein similar to that of the passage, and gradualists who stressed the path of gradual development, albeit without abandoning the idea of existence as a flow of discrete, infinitesimal moments.

as connected to and forming a larger whole, with which it can become possible to identify: 'Perhaps you're right. It is perhaps too much to latch on to humanity: but when I spoke of life, I really meant an order of shared comprehensive living (*ek saṃyukta, vyāpak, samaṣṭigat jīvan*), larger than myself, with which I would like to identify myself. If that is a vast flow, I would still like to span it with my arms, or if that sounds too ambitious, to build a bridge over it, even if for a short while.'[19] Once again, there are in this the echoes of existentialist notions circulating at the time, in for example Sartre's famous speech of 1945, 'Existentialism is a Humanism' (published a year later), which make it possible to reconcile the extreme subjectivity in Rekha's notion of human beings as isolated islands with the human universality of which Bhuvan speaks. However, Rekha and Bhuvan draw their ideas from numerous sources other than existentialism.

Bhuvan does not clarify how the bridge spanning humanity is to be built; later he suggests that an ethically grounded science could play a role. He is echoing the later humanistic ideas of M.N. Roy which Roy had begun discussing with friends from the early 1940s. However, Roy's emphasis on the importance of the freedom of the individual is more to be found in Rekha, in her fierce independence, than in Bhuvan. As Roy put it, 'There can be only one measure of the degree of freedom enjoyed by any class or country, and that measure is the degree of actual freedom enjoyed by the individuals composing that country or that class.'[20] Yet the significance of the individual as a rational being, so emphasized by Roy as partaking in but

---

[19] Ibid.: 21.

[20] During a discussion of this essay at the University of Hyderabad (31 August 2012), Nandkishore Acharya pointed out that Agyeya was part of the circle around M.N. Roy (1887–1954) in the late 1940s and early 1950s. Bhuvan's notion of science as the possible anchor and saviour of mankind resonates with Roy's formulation of the place of scientific thought in a radical humanism. The quotation above is from a lecture delivered at Students Hall, Calcutta, on 30 January 1947, published later in Roy 1960, and republished in Roy 2004.

also driven by a new humanism—more radical than the old humanism because now based on a scientific knowledge of man and human nature—signposts Bhuvan's thought, something that Rekha accepts as redeeming him from the ills of civilization that falsify lives and the communication between most urban people.[21]

Bhuvan's relationship to Rekha is driven more by impulse, by an immediacy that finds expression in poetry rather than rational exposition. He does not express these ideas to Rekha; her intensity, emotionality, and intellectual wherewithal almost overwhelm him. However, his thoughts exhibit a certain consistency and he speaks of them more extensively in his letters to Gaura, expanding on his Utopian notions of human collectivity to include science as an ethical pursuit undertaken for the good of mankind.[22] It is, then, his relationship with Gaura, pedagogical and almost paternal, that allows and even asks for an explication of his notions. When war breaks out in September 1939, Bhuvan writes to Gaura of his fears of the

---

[21] 'This new humanism is an integral humanism, distinguished from older forms of humanism, which were more poetic and romantic, by being based on a scientific knowledge of man and human nature . . . Knowledge in our days has become departmentalized. But true scientific knowledge presupposes an understanding and coordination of all the departments of science. The function of philosophy is precisely that. It must supply a coherent picture of the various branches of knowledge acquired by human experience at a given time.' Ibid.: 145.

[22] Once again, we see echoes of Roy's thought here: 'Man did not appear on the earth out of nowhere; with his mind, intelligence, will, he is an integral part of the physical universe. The latter is a cosmos [Roy refers to this as 'nature' at times]—a law-governed system. Therefore, man's being and becoming, his emotions, will, ideas are also determined. Therefore, man is essentially rational. The reason in man is an echo of the harmony of the universe. Morality must be referred back to man's innate rationality. Only then can man be more moral, spontaneously and voluntarily. Reason is the only sanction of morality, which is an appeal to conscience, and conscience in the last analysis is nothing mystic or mysterious. It is a biological function of consciousness. The innate rationality of man is the only guarantee of a harmonious social order, which will also be a moral order because morality is a rational function.' Ibid.: 181. The extract draws from Roy [1952] 1955.

possibly bleak future of science. Scientists had once been 'deeply moral men if not ethical philosophers, and could be proud of their record of science.' He sees the war as 'a period of crisis for science as also a crisis of morals and a crisis of culture', and feels 'We have to win not just the war, and not just for peace; we have to win back culture, science, morality. We have to win back man's freedom and dignity. Will the lessons of this war give us a new kind of scientist who will free science not from morality but for morality? We cannot afford to lose hope . . .'[23] One study of Roy points out that 'This particular quality of mid-century humanism, with its concern for the cross-cultural category of "man", arose from experiences of devastation and vulnerability, not from the bravado of "grand theory narratives".' [24] Science is Bhuvan's vocation; this is what takes him to Lake Tulian—to measure cosmic rays at an elevation, and then to the high seas in the midst of war. Being a man of science allows for a freedom from the constrictions of middle-class life, a freedom that Rekha, in her turn, draws from her notion of islands and of time. Yet, though both belong to the middle class, their social situations differ. Bhuvan is a bachelor, an up-and-coming scientist who has just received his doctorate and become a lecturer in a small-town college. Rekha, a governess and tutor, hovers on the edge of respectable society.

A MIDDLE-CLASS WORKING WOMAN AND THE UPSIDE-DOWN TREE

Rekha is a single woman; she works for her living. These are facts she herself points out and dwells on. As she tells Bhuvan when he receives her at the railway station, she will be staying at the YWCA while at Delhi. 'Independent, that is to say, working women can stay there.'[25]

[23] ND, 85.
[24] Manjapra 2010: 160.
[25] ND, 107. She is aware of the class difference between herself and the second main woman character of the novel, Gaura, daughter of a high-standing bureaucrat. When Gaura hesitates to take the bangles she is offering her,

Rekha has grown up in Calcutta, where her family, though originally from Kashmir, had settled some generations earlier. She lost her only brother while young; soon thereafter she also lost her parents. She now works as a governess for the daughters of 'native' rulers. For recommendations to them she is often beholden to Chandramadhav, who as a journalist has a wide circle of acquaintances and can recommend her to the royals, many of them known for their pro-British stance. Particularly vulnerable at this nationalist moment in history, they are eager to oblige journalists.

Widely read, independent in her views, Rekha has a beautiful singing voice. Snippets of Tagore's songs spring from her when she is happy or moved, thus both music and lyrics are formative for her personality as much as for the novel. She is twenty-seven when her tale opens, has been married eight years, though separated from her husband after the first year or two. Her husband now works for a multinational rubber company in Malaya. He has same-sex inclinations, though there is a suggestion that he also consorts with 'loose' women. Moving from native state to native state wherever she can find a position, without permanent home or drawing room to stabilize her, always on the move—in trains, railway stations, waiting rooms, her meeting places with friends and acquaintances either a coffee house or park benches and river banks—Rekha radiates both strength and vulnerability. The modernist work has been described as part of a 'new literature that was rebellious, questioning, doubtful and introspective but confident and even aggressive in its aesthetic conviction.'[26] This is also an apt description of the tone that Rekha adopts when speaking of herself to Bhuvan, searching but also confidently self-assertive. As she tells him when they both head towards their separate journeys on a train that has just left Lucknow:

---

she says ruefully, 'You are thinking of the constraints of a working woman.' ND, 185.

[26] Childs [2000] 2008: 20.

'Then, I suppose, I am like the Tree of Knowledge—the Upside-Down-Tree—my roots adrift in the sky. But please don't think I am complaining.'

> The train had started. At the next station, Bhuvan had said again, 'If a person like you wanders around, it must be by choice—it's difficult to credit it being out of necessity. And wandering by choice is a reflection of inner strength.'
> Rekha laughed. 'The inner strength comes from the wandering, Dr Bhuvan! Because when there are no roots to hold the soil one has to draw sustenance from elsewhere to survive while drifting in the air. Wandering by choice? Yes, I suppose you might call it that; because one has chosen not to be crushed into the dust, not to be lost in the dark abyss—one has chosen to struggle for survival.'[27]

Being crushed, being lost in a dark abyss, are references to her married life, and the need to draw strength not from a socially secure position but from within. Her roots are ethereal rather than earthly, a reference to the evocative image from the *Chāndogya Upanishad* (6.11), which celebrates the Upside-Down Banyan Tree's vitality. With its roots in the sky and branches below, it draws its strength and wisdom from higher, unmanifest sources.[28]

Rekha's hard-won strength of mind, her beauty, and the fire within, for which both Chandramadhav and Bhuvan struggle to find expression, mark her as special, even in the utter ordinariness of her existence. Both men speak of her strength rather than of the vulnerability of her position:

---

[27] ND, 33.
[28] Cf. Zaehner 1969: 358–61, his commentary on verse 15.1 of the *Bhagavadgītā*, where the reference to *ūrdhva-mūlam adhaḥ-śākham aśvattha* has acquired negative connotations, taken over most likely from the Buddhist *Saṁyutta Nikāya* (iv.160, 161), asking, just as in the *Bhagavadgītā*, that the tree be cut down. The Upanishadic reference is joyful, positive, as is the yet earlier reference in the *Rigveda* (1.24.7). I am grateful to Srilata Raman for referring me to Zaehner.

Rekha is truly beautiful: hers is a beauty illuminated from within by a lively, radiant personality, even if it is a radiance encased in a crystal shell of reserve . . . Chandramadhav could almost think of a large opal, smooth on the surface, folding scattered rainbows within and having at the very heart a smouldering fire . . . Diamonds are judged by the 'water' within, an opal or a sapphire by the 'fire' . . . And this jewel has gone around for years waiting for a man of discrimination to cherish it.[29]

As Chandramadhav and Bhuvan joke with Rekha about the stuffy Carlton Hotel dining room in which they find themselves, suggesting that she could well be a heroine in a Peter Cheney thriller, Bhuvan muses about the literary prototypes for one such as her. Thomas Hardy, Sartre, Greek tragedy, Bhuvan searches for a way to classify her, grasp some essence which will help him understand her:

'No, certainly not for Peter Cheney.' But then for whom? For Hardy perhaps? Yes, even Fate would be fortunate to find a marionette such as Rekha. But Rekha is not innocent enough; there is a basic toughness about her which— Dostoevsky? But does she have that peculiar split consciousness—that superior human logic which is really a form of madness? . . . Perhaps the ancient Greek tragedies—One against the gods . . . But does Rekha have the kind of ego that would make the gods pick her out for their special attention? . . . Perhaps Sartre—the eternal moment, the moment of eternal suffering . . . Rekha did seem to have an endless capacity for endurance—some inner strength to bear endless joy . . . The ultimate of joy, the ultimate of suffering—yes, even the gods would choose her because the ultimates meet in her; man reaching out for the sky, man rooted to the earth—natural vehicles for tragedy—the wings of Icarus, the fire of Prometheus . . . Greek tragedy was not merely the tragedy of the ego, it was the tragedy of the potentialities of man . . .[30]

Pushed to take extreme measures at the height of her own daring ('endless joy'), an almost reckless reaching out for the sky, and plunged into pain that will threaten to destroy her ('endless suffering'), is she then a natural vehicle for tragedy? Rekha speaks of her own sense

[29] Ibid.: 55.
[30] Ibid.: 25.

of *hubris* when, at the end of the novel, she writes to Gaura, Bhuvan's pupil and ultimately his chosen partner: 'Gaura, happiness is not the be all (*sab-kuch*) of existence but it is a great thing; and happiness is not in material prosperity . . . It is an attitude of mind. I was too greedy; I wanted to hold a whole skyful of stars in my embrace. You have more patience. You will be able to reach out to the sky. The stars shall be your stepping stones . . .'[31]

CIVILIZATION AND CITY SKIES

As Rekha sees it, cities are for the 'civilized', for those who have settled for known patterns of life and into the moulds and behaviour they call for. Civilization is in fact coeval with the city and middle-class life. It is characterless, faceless, fraudulent, and hollow; a glittering veil, it covers up all that is natural and spontaneous, whether it be joy or suffering. Rekha moves in such a powerful 'character zone' that her speech, her ideas, the images she uses, saturate the vocabulary of the men she associates with, and even seemingly of the author.[32] It is her assessment of city life that permeates the novel.

Thus the narrator, speaking almost in Rekha's voice, points out that the summer sky of Delhi has 'its blue tarnished by the dust

---

[31] Ibid.: 345.

[32] Indeed Bhuvan speaks of *Rekhā kī chāp*, i.e. imprint (ND, 202), translated as the more neutral 'influence' by Agyeya (ibid.: 207), as he works in his laboratory in the days after Tulian. 'Had it been Rekha's imprint that he too had become an island in a slow, imperceptibly-moving river? Rekha . . . he rarely recalled her face or specific events or situations involving her: he did not even invoke a remembered touch or a caress. There was a total awareness of Rekha's existence which seemed to illuminate some deep area of his consciousness: the reflected light of this illumination suffuses his entire being with colour as the light falling on a mountain lake is reflected and lights up the valley around it . . . Sometimes in the evening he would pick up the Bible and sit down to read the *Song of Solomon*; he would get so absorbed in reading that he would begin to read aloud: then his voice would startle him with a stark awareness of Rekha, overwhelming him with a sense of her presence . . .' Ibid.: 207.

of civilization'.³³ Though the blazing heat of the afternoon sun in summer can burn through this dust to restore the sky to its original blue, so that the human heartbeat can almost become audible, the city sky submerges natural sight and sound; one can only make drawing room conversation as it arcs over civilization and the civilized.

> Rekha said again, 'Although one should see the sky only in the mountains or at the sea-side, in the country sometimes, especially at the end of the rains, the sky talks, it sings—and what melodies! The city sky—the city sun-set—it is like a living room conversation, all talking together but, as it were, concealed, absent; recorded voices, mechanical enthusiasm and exhilaration . . . 'Bhuvanji, I could also produce the hard grating sound of drawing room conversation; you've no idea what a reservoir I have of that stale fluid. But I didn't ask your time for that.' Then she added gravely, 'Actually there are two sides to me—one natural, full of character, free; the other civilized and characterless . . . 'Why do civilizations fall into decay? It's because the virile natural character gets buried under the domesticated, cultured one—the individual becomes characterless. He no longer creates, he decorates . . .' Rekha said suddenly, 'Bhuvanji, I would like to know you only through my healthy, natural, free side—I want to keep you in contact only with that side of me. But honesty requires that I not conceal the other side from you.'³⁴

Bhuvan belongs outside this civilizational complex; his science, the logic of his thought, preserves him from being caught up in its social mores: 'No, I don't think you are like that. You—perhaps science has saved you. Or—' Rekha laughed—'should I say you have not become so civilized yet.'³⁵ Civilization, middle-class domesticity, and culture are intertwined; they stand for hypocrisy, make-believe, they hamper life, virility, creativity. Civilization hollows out time itself. As Rekha tells Bhuvan in the Carlton Hotel restaurant, deserted in the late evening: 'Civilization is like a gigantic waiting room,' said Rekha. 'Cafes and restaurants are there to pass the time—the means to fill a

---

³³ ND, 112.
³⁴ Ibid.: 112–13.
³⁵ Ibid.: 113.

vacuum. But waiting for what? Time between what and what? Nobody knows. Beyond the vacuum there is another vacuum.'[36] The people who constitute this civilization are vacant, themselves little more than ruins. It is as if Chandramadhav subscribes to Rekha's assessment of the civilized when, in speaking of himself, he finds himself playing on the many meanings of 'ruin'.[37] In the letter he writes to prepare the grounds for his proposal of marriage to her, he asks her to come to the Lucknow Coffee House and go with him to the Old Residency, where 'we shall sit amongst the ruins and talk . . . For Rekha, I have remained a ruin till now. You too are a ruin, but when we emerge from there we shall not be ruins any more; we shall have built a new, beautiful whole, a shimmering monument . . .'[38] Rekha dismisses this talk as the 'idiom of Delhi', a vacant play on words.[39] When they do meet in the Old Residency, the ruins are hit by a dust storm; his tears and her abrupt rejection follow. Rekha retreats to the Coffee House for a cup of coffee—a modern restorative at a modern site—and to read and muse over the letter he has handed her before she climbs into a train and moves on. City life, the hostel 'in this crowded Delhi', become more than ever associated with Chandramadhav's Delhi, Hemendra's Delhi.[40]

Hemendra is Rekha's husband, who has in the past humiliated and wounded her. Once, sitting atop a structure in the Jantar Mantar, he told her of the only relationship that had mattered to him, to a young man whom Rekha resembled; the resemblance was his only reason for marrying her. This is a memory which freezes her into a state of near immobility when she next visits the site with Bhuvan. It is as if the monument brings back a notion of ruin. Two ruins cannot

[36] Ibid.: 114.
[37] Rekha's critique of the city is echoed in Chandramadhav's thoughts about Lucknow and the Coffee House, Bhuvan's about Srinagar, after the abortion.
[38] ND, 99.
[39] Ibid.: 101.
[40] Ibid.: 192.

fuse to create a monument, just as moments of intense experience can apparently only fuse if the same sensibility, the same awareness, pervades the people who come together as friends or lovers. This is increasingly the case with Rekha and Bhuvan. Their relationship is one of 'interpersonal interpenetration', whereby 'more of the individual, unique attributes of each person, or ultimately all their characteristics, become significant.' The frame of reference for both then becomes 'a constant consideration of oneself in all possible situations. In other words, the information content of all communication is constantly being enriched by the ingredient "for you".'[41] The interpenetration of person, the participation in each other's being, form both the climax and the eventual termination of Rekha and Bhuvan's intimacy.

DOMESTIC INTERIORS AND PUBLIC PLACES

Rekha's married life has been one of abuse and loneliness. She indicates as much to Bhuvan. Focalized through her, the narrative provides memories of her life with Hemendra, not all of which she can communicate to Bhuvan. The private face Hemendra shows in the bedroom, reserving his public face, his social mask, for other occasions, finds ugly expression one night as he comes home. Seeing her reading in bed by the light of the lamp, for one moment he mistakes her for his long-lost friend and pulls her into a frenzied embrace. But he only has to hear her voice to release her as harshly. When she asks the meaning of this, he confesses, cruelly, impatiently: 'No, I might as well tell you—if only to rid myself of this daily nagging. Listen, I don't love you, nor have I ever. Nor will I ever.'[42]

Where domesticity is a combination of insecurity and ephemeral communication, joy—if any—can only be like a house built on sand. As Bhuvan and Rekha walk on a sandy islet off the banks of the

---

[41] See Luhmann [1982] 1988: 13, 21, 23. One can also 'participate in the other person's self-referential information processing or at least be able to adequately reconstruct it.' Ibid.: 24.

[42] ND, 120.

Yamuna, she is Miss Robinson and he her Man Friday. He builds a sandcastle for her, complete with garden, walls, a moat: 'As he worked, he kept up a commentary: That's the house—the forecourt—here we'll have a garden—we'll have to find some orchids to plant here—that's the boundary wall—this is where Friday is going to live—this . . .'[43] The castle is best demolished before a wave performs the operation, or other people find it and discover its magic: 'With a quick movement of his foot he levelled the sand houses and the walls. Then, stepping forward he shouted for the boatman. As they disembarked, he said: And thus Crusoe returned to civilization.'[44]

And in civilization there is no respite. The circuit of make-believe, suffering, abuse, make-believe, spirals on. The marital home, as we have seen, can afford no refuge to women such as Rekha. Intimacy and love cannot here endure in the constrictions of domesticity. In fact, domestic interiors have little space in the narrative, and the novel's departure from tradition is evident in part from the fact that wives and mothers play practically no role in it.

We glimpse another kind of domestic interior in Chandramadhav's house in Lucknow, where he has installed his wife Kausalya and their children. In one of the scenes he comes home to find time, a wife who has only known waiting and disappointment. And once again the man forces the woman into a tight embrace, taking her without her consent; she has no option except to acquiesce to marital rape.

> She knew that in the morning Chandra would look at her with the un-recognizing eyes of a stranger, which would then fill with sudden loathing . . . as for this—she does not know whether this means anything in itself; if there had been love, this too would have meant something, but perhaps when there is no love even this is something to be thankful for—but that look of hatred would poison even this . . . it would be better like this—that Chandra should rise in the morning and not see her or loathe her . . . Dust and ashes only, but the breath of hatred would blow even that away.[45]

[43] Ibid.: 125.
[44] Ibid.: 127.
[45] Ibid.: 198.

The dust and ashes represent a domesticity gone awry, grown stale, which Rekha herself invokes after the major catastrophe in the novel. She has aborted the child she was expecting, Bhuvan's child, and the abortion was done on an impulse, in a moment of fear and panic and lack of reassurance from Bhuvan. But in any case she sees no future in marriage and domesticity based on a 'love' which can prove so ephemeral, and linking with the uncertainty that the surgeon-violinist child she dreamed of may have had to face had he come into the world:

> 'I can bear no more, Bhuvan. It is not that the suffering is so great, it is that I am weary of fighting a battle which is futile, which can only end in utter futility ... Even supposing that we could have survived—that there had been a home, life together, that the surgeon-violinist could have come—what then? Supposing I were to die ten years from now, would it not be better that I died right now? That after ten years we should become indifferent and drift apart—it were a thousand times better that I die today.'[46]

These are radical notes, resisting merger into the idea of domestic bliss as the business of bringing healthy, bouncing children into the world during a period of nation-anticipation and nation-building. Yet bleak despair is not what powers the novel, but rather the release from it—and the language found for this release is unprecedented in the Hindi language. In the passionate storm of their love, neither Rekha nor Bhuvan is daunted by civilization, falseness, or confining domesticity.

There are spaces in the city, despite annoying persecution, and much more so in nature, where open, spontaneous communication can take place, where bliss, however ephemeral, can be experienced. A single line from W.H. Auden accompanies the play of private and public in emotional life in the shape that Rekha and Bhuvan

---

[46] Ibid.: 247. What Luhmann ([1982] 1988: 98) points out in the context of another novel seems particularly apposite here as well: 'Its [Love's] claim to completely individualized uniqueness can only give proof of itself in the exceptional, in the negative, in renunciation.'

experience it. A 'private' face is vulnerable, almost secret; to hide it is reflex. Whereas, in most social encounters in civilized society, in drawing rooms, but also in domestic situations—which are, in effect, private spaces—the 'public' face can provide protection. A public face can in private space disguise the truth, be almost a mask of evil, as in the case of Hemendra and possibly Chandramadhav. As against this, in the anonymity of public spaces private faces become less vulnerable; an exchange can occur which is not possible in private places. Rekha and Bhuvan meet in the Lucknow Coffee House, in a Delhi park; they hold conversations in railway carriages—'railway stations are my domain' Rekha says as they lean over the bridge which arches over and connects train platforms.[47] The movement possible within and the anonymity of these public places afford a certain safety. Here one's private face can be shown and seen unobserved. As Rekha says: 'This is perhaps another aspect of the matter of roots. In a moving train a person like me experiences a sense of freedom, whereas in any place suggesting stability I would only be aware of being a misfit and become uncomfortably mute. So please don't pay any attention to the things I say—they are just *en passant*.'[48] Though Rekha has little patience with those who come to coffee houses to feel the pulse of life, '(i)t is merely a whirlpool, a false movement', she herself visits them so that she can meet people spontaneously: 'A natural encounter between people—isn't that our only possible contact with the life of humanity? Apart from that, humanity is just a concept—an arid desert.'[49]

As she and Bhuvan converse in Qudsia Park on a later visit to Delhi—and are chased out by the nightwatchman, for this is after park hours—they escape from one part of the park to another. A smaller park to which they come is like a graceful monument, '(t)he smooth white trunks of the bottle palms on either side of the avenue were like columns supporting a canopy. The vagrant perfume of the queen-of-the-night met them every now and then. They skirted along

[47] Ibid.: 127.
[48] Ibid.: 34.
[49] Ibid.: 21–2.

the main avenue and strolled along a grassy lane. But the mood had changed.'[50] Yet another nightwatchman appears. They walk to the strip of grass between the two arches of Kashmiri Gate that serves as a traffic island, where one can safely sit for a while. It is here that Bhuvan quotes a line from a W.H. Auden poem, 'private faces in public places' which will be echoed with variations at several places in the novel:

> 'Isn't it odd,' said Rekha, 'in a city the only private places are in the middle of public roads!'
> 'Private faces in public places', quoted Bhuvan. Rekha sat down on the grass.
> 'Really?' said Bhuvan.
> 'Sure, if only to forget the frustration of having been chased out.'
> 'These are rightly called traffic islands,' said Bhuvan. 'Islands of rest between flowing streams of people.'
> 'Aren't they? You spend some more time with me and you'll begin to see islands everywhere.'[51]

Even as he accepts Rekha's notion of the island, Bhuvan inverts it. It is less a place which cuts off, more where one can find respite in the midst of flow, Shelley's green isles in a sea of misery. And yet Bhuvan remains insulated, afraid to make himself vulnerable and to open up the floodgate of feeling.

NATURE, PAIN, AND STRENGTH

Poems offer a mode of communication at a level deeper than prose and the protagonists cite them often. Bhuvan and Rekha can quote a stray line from a poem sure in the knowledge that the other will know the rest of the poem and understand the complex tangle of thoughts and feelings undergirding it. Lines from two poems by Lawrence and one by Eliot come to speak for Bhuvan and Rekha's relationship to each other. She has the upper hand in one case, being unafraid of intimacy and the pain it can bring along with joy. Bhuvan seems to

[50] Ibid.: 115.
[51] Ibid.: 116.

have the upper hand in the other as the one who can take—at least initially—decisions about a possible future together. This is signalled by Eliot's lines from the *Four Quartets*, which speak of 'wait and hope'. Bhuvan quotes two lines from the first of the two Lawrence poems in one of his initial meetings with Rekha:

> The pain of loving you
> Is almost more than I can bear.[52]

Lawrence's poem 'A Young Wife' gives the first inkling of his fear and the pain that the intensity of love can bring, of its incalculability, of the 'shadows in the sun', of which the poem also speaks, and of the night that lies looking up 'at the foot of each glowing thing'. Rekha can bear pain, Bhuvan had noted, when musing on her person: 'Perhaps Sartre—the eternal moment, the moment of eternal suffering . . . Rekha did seem to have an endless capacity for endurance—some inner strength to bear endless joy . . . The ultimate of joy, the ultimate of suffering . . .'[53] The unquoted lines of the poem lend significance to Rekha's reference to the joy, even in the shadows of the sun and in the night: in a later scene she speaks of 'That equal joy discover'. But does Bhuvan have this capacity?

However unarticulated in their actual conversation, social norms loom large as backdrop; Rekha and Bhuvan's relationship can have no legitimate place in the urban world, not even in the Westernized part of the city that they haunt. Rekha is both single and married; for Bhuvan to be with her can lead to social ostracism for both. For the moment, however, they cast all such considerations aside as they live together in the beautiful natural landscape of Naukuchia. The recklessness of this act is imaged by their reckless chase of the setting sun:

> The day was declining. Soon the sun would sink behind the hill. Suddenly Bhuvan said, 'Come, let's catch the sunset.'

[52] Lawrence 1993: 215.
[53] ND, 26.

They broke into a run, holding hands. The sun would set behind the hill; there were no clouds, only a glowing red ball would slip below the horizon to hide its nakedness. To see it sink, they would have to reach the edge of the hill first.

As they ran, Bhuvan said, 'Come on, Rekha, we have to race the sun.'

Rekha ran faster. Her grip on Bhuvan's hand tightened a little and began to drag; Bhuvan suddenly became aware she was out of breath and slowed down gradually, so as not to make it too obvious.

But the sun had set by the time they reached the bend of the hill. It was as if a quick hand had suddenly smeared the whole sky with dull paint.

There was light still, but it seemed diffuse and without a source, lost in the desert of the sky.

Bhuvan stopped and said, 'We lost.' . . . Rekha looked at the streak and said, 'But who can catch the setting sun?'

. . . A moment later her grip tightened again on Bhuvan's hand. 'But we haven't lost. The night has it own beauty. "That equal joy discover", Bhuvan.'

Bhuvan turned and caught hold of Rekha's free hand. For a moment he studied her face in the evening light. 'I do discover: I know that beauty too—you are the beauty of the blue-wrapped night. And in your hair are a million stars.'

'And you—you are the evening star,' said Rekha in a whisper. Very gently her hands drew him towards her.[54]

But Bhuvan's fear of the beautiful, its power and its potential for pain, is further intensified by this intimacy. When she comes to him in the night, his tears signal his fear of entering realms unknown: 'It's not a refusal, Rekha, not a rejection . . . it is profoundly beautiful . . . that, that should be ecstacy—I know . . . I believe—that is why I am scared . . . if it should not turn out—what is beautiful should be left alone—should endure—I didn't want to destroy what you have given me—don't want to risk it—it's too beautiful . . .'[55]

---

[54] Ibid.: 139–40.
[55] Ibid.: 142.

Rekha consoles him: 'But your tears—there's nothing unmanly about trying to protect someone from yourself . . .', gently interpreting the tears not as his reluctance to enter the relationship but rather as an effort to protect her from an act which can only bring social shame upon her.[56] In the end she helps him overcome this fear of experiencing intensity, to face the fact that there can be an unleashing of power outside his control.

When Bhuvan lands in Srinagar, on his way to Tulian to carry out his work on cosmic rays, and is accosted by the beauty of the lake-adorned city, he compares it to a woman loaded with ornaments sitting in the market place to offer her wares. He is reminded once more of the Auden poem, this time amended to 'public faces in public places',[57] almost as a prelude to his meeting with Rekha, and the transition to 'private faces in private places' because of the utter solitude of Tulian, where they live in tents open to the sky. Their coming together is expressed in lines from Solomon's 'Song of Songs', lines which Rekha had written in her little notebook that she had left with him when they parted, along with the blue sari she had worn when they chased the sun:

I rose up to open my beloved; and my hands dripped with myrrh, and my fingers . . .[58]

It is almost in these solemn tones that the narrator celebrates their union, focalized through Bhuvan, suggesting the pain of surrender and the pain yet to come. More important than the pain, the union is legitimized in an entirely novel way—not by Brahmanical ceremony, with bride and bridegroom circling a sacrificial fire which is witness to their marriage, but by the countless powers and divinities of the middle air: 'Let the sun bear witness. And the sky and the wind and the grass under one's feet and the rocks. And the countless powers and divinities of the middle air and of nameless planets . . . But there

[56] Ibid.: 145.
[57] Ibid.: 149.
[58] Ibid.: 159. Italics in the original.

is a truth that needs no witness except the pain of its own surrender, the countless agonies and possibilities hidden within, throbbing and incessantly active.'[59] Lawrence is echoed also via another poem which Rekha quotes to Bhuvan: 'Dark grasses under my feet/ Seem to dabble in me/ Like grasses in a brook/ Oh, and it is sweet to be/ All these things/ Not to be anymore myself/ For look— / I am weary of myself.'[60]

Even if nature cannot preserve them from a relapse into pain and misery, in it there can be moments of ecstasy.[61] 'The pain of loving' poem meshes with excerpts from the Lawrence poem entitled 'Admitted', with which the novel concludes. Its lines contain echoes of the pain of 'A Young Wife' but with a new inflection: the strength that a woman can give. And both are closely connected with nature. In what ways does nature then offer release from self and from pain?

In notes she leaves for Bhuvan to be read after her departure, Rekha invokes nature and God in one breath: 'Bhuvan, may I say one thing before I go? I am fulfilled. Even if I were to die now, I shall not have a grievance against God or against nature that I never knew any fulfilment. I shall go with gratitude—gratitude towards God, and—towards you, Bhuvan.'[62] What can nature as equated with God signify for Rekha and Bhuvan? There is little sense here of any kind of Vedantic or indeed pantheistic immanence of the divine, no sense that nature represents moral order or that it can be a regulating or guiding force. There is here an ethic of nature which goes well beyond the Hindi Chayavadi poets, beyond momentary melancholy and 'sweet, silent thought'. The sun, the evening, the blue-wrapped night, the evening star, the mountain sky, the winds, the rocks, the grass beneath one's feet—no protective, benevolent, or all-permeating power seems

---

[59] Ibid.: 162.

[60] From the short poem 'Non-entity'. Lawrence 1993: 194.

[61] Modernism explores 'new possibilities of sexual life . . . or even the wholesale rethinking of the relationship between the sexes or the relationship between mind and body . . .' See, Introduction in Lewis 2011: 3–4.

[62] ND, 165.

to reside in these forces. Instead, as the Lawrence poems show and encapsulate, the intense sentient perception of light and darkness, the colour, sound, and smell of flowers, water, and trees reflect a deeper awareness of experience. 'To be all these things', brings both depth and elevation, making it possible to plunge deeper into the self and release the force of feeling and perception inherent in it, while at the same time heightening and elevating it. The intensity of communication with nature is neither unconditional nor always available. 'But to be cut off from it is to fall into desiccation, emptiness, dulness, a narrow and shrivelled life, egoism, and cowardice.'[63] This is the vacuum that Rekha has spoken of when she compares civilization to a waiting room. When she speaks of her sense of fulfilment, however, she does

[63] The sentences and phrases cited are from Taylor [1989] 1996: 389, 445, and 491. Taylor offers a survey of the evolution of man's relationship to 'nature', particularly of post-Romantic views, which offers a possible entry into understanding the role nature plays in ND. According to Taylor, the Romantic view which saw nature as releasing an inner voice, true to itself and with full moral autonomy, was followed by an expressivist turn which saw man's inner domain 'as having *depth*, that is, a domain which reaches farther than we can ever articulate, which still stretches beyond our furthest point of clear expression.' Ibid.: 389. 'But along with an art of despiritualized nature in Realism and an art of the epiphanies of anti-nature, there is a third important form that the negation of Romanticism [Baudelaire, Mallarmé] takes in the nineteenth century, and that is an art which related to the wild energy of an amoral nature. This turn arises from the philosophy of Schopenhauer, not entirely in ways that he intended.' Ibid.: 441–2. 'In Mahler's Third Symphony we have one of the great expressions in music of Schopenhauer's theory of the will . . . Once again, as with Wagner and the young Nietzsche but even more markedly, Mahler seems to be saying that the development of the will through its fragmented phase was for the sake of this crowning achievement, in which we accede to the vision of oneness with the All.' Ibid.: 445. 'This idea of nature as a great reservoir of amoral force, with which we must not lose contact, is one of the important bequests of the post-Schopenhauerian period to twentieth century art and sensibility. We find echoes of it in a host of places, in Fauvism, Surrealism, D.H. Lawrence.' Ibid. It is Lawrence's vision of nature as an amoral but powerful force for releasing energies, which seems to find the deepest echo in ND.

not use similes, she does not *liken* herself to still waters; she becomes one with them. And yet, even as she surges towards Bhuvan, as the still water that reflects the sky, as she opens up to receive him, she does not melt into him, she does not become one with him.

> I was a body of still water; a lake, a pond, a little pool choked with weeds. You came like a stream and shook me, lit my hopes, bared me to the endless sky. Let me say it, Bhuvan, my body surged towards you as it never surged before. Every fibre of my being sought your touch, the touch of your hands, the hold of your arms, the warmth of your body . . . but in you I sensed a fear—no, not quite a fear. But a holding back, a restraint imposed from some far source . . . And it was the touch of this restraint that stilled the storm in my own being: the lake that I was found its normal surface again—a still surface, still water, closed unto itself. But, no, no! not closed unto itself, not covered again; it stayed open to the image of the sky.[64]

Though Bhuvan has not told her how he feels, it is the fulfilment of the moment she stresses as she tries to insulate herself against the lack of uninhibited reciprocation, the sense of not being securely lodged in his life:

> I have said again and again that there is no future; there is only an unfolding of the present, a culmination of its irresistible potentialities. I still feel the same. Once I merely believed it. Now it glows within me like a spark of experience. It is true and before this truth I bow my head . . .
>
> What is—let it be beautiful while it is, Bhuvan. When it ceases to be, may its ceasing be beautiful too . . .[65]

Bhuvan, the lake, the sky, allow Rekha to experience the unfolding of the present moment and beauty, even as she opens Bhuvan to realms of emotion which he had feared.[66]

---

[64] ND, 167–8.
[65] Ibid.: 169.
[66] As Luhmann ([1982] 1988: 25) points out of this particular moment of experience: 'The concept of love would nevertheless not be complete

Many months later, after Rekha and Bhuvan have separated—the understanding and misunderstanding between them too intense to become an everyday relationship—Gaura comes across lines that Bhuvan has marked in his copy of Lawrence's poems: 'A woman has given me strength and affluence. Admitted.' These indicate only a part of what the poem as a whole says, which once again completes the thoughts suggested. The unquoted lines invoke the fear that lies at the heart of love, love as an intense need, a hunger, 'more frightening, more profound/ than stomach or throat or even the mind;/ redder than death, more clamorous.'[67] Even when that hunger is stilled, there remains a lurking fear, of the vulnerability which the taking and giving entail, expressed in further unquoted lines from the same poem:

> She stood before me like riches that were mine.
> Even then, in the dark, I was tortured, ravening, unfree,
> Ashamed, and shameful, and vicious.
> A man is so terrified of strong hunger;
> And this terror is the root of all cruelty.
> She loved me, and stood before me, looking at me.

Rekha has in the meantime married the surgeon who treated her in the months that followed the abortion,[68] and Bhuvan and Gaura have come together. But nonetheless Rekha triumphs: 'she stood before me like riches that were mine.' And it is Bhuvan who must concede ground and admit that he was fearful, terrified, even cruel, that he was unable to reassure her in her moment of need. Little

---

if it were seen merely as a form of reciprocally satisfying action or as the willingness to fulfil wishes. Love initially colours an experience of someone's inner experience and thus transforms the world as the horizon of inner experience.'

[67] From the poem 'Manifesto' (Lawrence 1993: 262–8), which ends with the lines: 'We shall not look before and after/ We shall *be, now*/ We shall know in full/ We, the mystic NOW.'

[68] According to Nandkishore Acharya, Agyeya felt that Rekha had made a compromise with life by getting married after all. Oral communication, 1 September 2012.

wonder that the author himself gives Rekha prime position in his narrative; she towers above the others.[69]

'BE STILL AND WAIT WITHOUT HOPE'

Poems, then, punctuate and define Bhuvan and Rekha's conversation, serving as expressions of the sensuous, experiential depth of their encounter, as also its uncertainty. They anticipate their eventual understanding of each other and the contradictions inherent in their own attitudes. After her departure from Tulian and Srinagar, Rekha's notebook jottings show Bhuvan verses, this time from *Four Quartets*, which reflect Rekha's state of mind, her dilemma. If moments are unconnected, if indeed there is no future but only the present, what can waiting signify?

> I said to my soul: 'Be still and wait without hope.'
> For hope would be hope for the wrong thing,
> Wait without love, for love would be the love of the wrong thing.
> There is yet faith
> But the faith and the love and the hope are all in the waiting.[70]

The verses that follow make matters even clearer:

> Wait without thought, for you are not yet ready for thought;
> So the darkness shall be the light, and the stillness of dancing.
>
> Whisper of running streams, and winter lightning.
> The wild thyme unseen and the wild strawberry.
> The laughter in the garden, echoed ecstacy
> Not lost, but requiring, pointing to the agony
> Of death and birth.
>   You say I am repeating
> Something I have said before. I shall say it again.
> Shall I say it again? In order to arrive there,

---

[69] Agyeya in *Ātmanepad*. Agyeya [1960] 2003: 35.
[70] *Four Quartets*. Eliot 1991: 175–90. Citation on p. 186; the following citation on p. 187.

To arrive where you are, to get from where you are not,
    You must go by a way wherein there is no ecstasy,
In order to arrive at what you do not know
    You must go by a way which is the way of ignorance.
In order to possess what you do not possess
    You must go by way of dispossession.
In order to arrive at what you are not
    You must go through the way in which you are not.
And what you do not know is the only thing you know
And what you own is that you do not own
And where you are is where you are not.

After the ecstacy of encounter, of a momentarily blissful lack of rational thought, to get anywhere one must yet go through ways which are not ecstatic, and be content with dispossession and lack of knowledge, with a state of being at a place where one is not yet at the place one could have wanted to be. In the days that follow, Bhuvan's state of mind reflects this mistiness of mode, without knowledge of its own being, with no thought of what could follow and what could be asked of him.

Bhuvan repeats these lines, they serve almost as a refrain when he visits Rekha in Srinagar, in the apple orchard where she has now found work. He has received news that that the surgeon/violinist is on his way. He recalls the scene of their impossible chase for the setting sun. No impossible missions now. He would be content to watch the sun on the apple ripening in the evening sunshine. He recalls once more the lines

    ... There is yet faith
And the faith and the love and the hope are all in the waiting ... .[71]

But it is precisely faith which will desert both at the moment of their calamity, though at the end of the novel he finds himself echoing these lines once more, along with the images of islands and the river of time, though the waiting will now have to do with Bhuvan and

[71] Ibid.: 216.

Gaura: 'He was certain and he would wait, as Gaura would wait. For waitings too are islands of stillness, of frozen time in the endless river of time, without beginning and without end.'[72] It is as if Rekha, with her image of islands in the stream, will continue to determine the course of this relationship as well. The strength to approach Gaura comes to Bhuvan at Rekha's prompting and he recognizes that he owes it to her.

'MY INNER LIFE IS ABSOLUTELY MINE'

Why then was it not possible for Bhuvan and Rekha to come together? Could Bhuvan not recognize Rekha's vulnerability as a woman married but bearing another man's child, her solitude in this situation alongside her unwillingness to compromise? Bhuvan clearly does not reckon with her categorical stance and the inner freedom she so fiercely protects.

There is no simple way of understanding the impasse that Bhuvan and Rekha's relationship reaches within a matter of months. Bhuvan has left the pregnant Rekha and Srinagar with a promise that he will return within days. In his absence Rekha has received ugly, threatening letters from Hemendra, instigated and encouraged by Chandramadhav. In a moment of panic, Rekha aborts her child—with disastrous and long-term consequences for her mental and physical health. In her understanding, Rekha undertakes this drastic measure to protect Bhuvan from scandal, while Bhuvan blames her for the unilateral decision. He ultimately comes to recognize his part in the process and speaks of it, not to Rekha, but characteristically almost, to Gaura, many months later.

The crisis in their relationship, however, sets in well before the abortion and has to do with Bhuvan drifting into a situation without realizing its consequences, for he has compromised her as much as she has compromised him. Rekha finds it unacceptable that Bhuvan

---

[72] ND, 355.

should offer to marry her only *after* he finds out about the pregnancy. 'And what you are saying should not be a consequence but a cause. Only then could one accept, only then could one consider it.' And with that she seems to slip out of Bhuvan's grasp—perhaps also of the narrator's, for she cannot be obtained again. When he tries to persuade her, though as yet in a muffled way, saying that there are other things to think of, she

> . . . smiled wryly. 'Aren't there? And it is because there are other things to consider that this can no longer be considered. This can be thought of only when it is the one and absolute thing, unrelated to anything else.' . . . 'But Bhuvan, you are looking at things with society's eyes. There is nothing wrong in that view, nor is it irrelevant; but that is not the decisive view. Any decision—any solution which ignores the individual will be wrong—it will be hateful.'
>
> She was silent for a moment, then lowering her eyes, she continued, 'It could be that my thinking has been warped from the very beginning—but it has been that all through. My action—that society should regulate my social acts—that is right; but my inner life—no. That is mine—absolutely mine. Mine—which means the private domain of every individual.'[73]

But can inner life be separated from social acts? This remains an unanswered question. Faced with this dilemma, it is Bhuvan's turn to retreat, to not respond to her despondent letters once she decides to go her own way. When he does write, it is to express his belief that they had reached some kind of climax over the intensity of their love and the pain inherent in it. He seems to refer to the pain consequent upon the abortion here:

> 'Love can always die—immortal in one sense, it is always most vulnerable in another. But if that would have happened some time in the future, it would not have been because of the child—the reason would have existed in ourselves . . . that body of experiences together, Rekha—that comes between us like a wall. We shall meet, but meet only across such a wall; shake hands, but as if through a frame; see each other but as if

---

[73] Ibid.: 220.

set in this frame—you from this side, I from the other . . . Rekha, I still love you as much, but . . .'[74]

Though he says expressly that he cannot blame her, in fact he has done just that and Rekha says as much in her hurt response. Only much later does Bhuvan consider his part in the catastrophe, when he speaks of it to Gaura. He tells her, and in English, not Hindi, as if to establish some distance between what he says and himself, that Rekha had loved him more than anyone else, and 'I loved her. We were to have a child. I killed him.'[75] And reverting to Hindi, he admits, 'I see that I should not have left her alone, for then perhaps she might not have lost confidence—I . . .'[76]

But does Rekha's vision of civilization—of urban middle-class life and its constraints, with fulfilment restricted to brief unplanned moments—take over the entire novel? What of the collective that Bhuvan speaks of early in the novel?

CIVILIZATION AND SCIENCE

Though Rekha's civilizational critique remains the dominant frame of the novel, the other big issues of the time are also addressed in parallel frames: nationalism and the espousal of a national culture, and at considerable length the politics of the major intellectual movement of the time, the left-leaning Progressive Writers' Movement.

The only glimpse of nationalism provided is in the course that Gaura's life takes under Bhuvan's explicit direction. He tells her to get her college to stage a modern Hindi play, Jayshankar Prasad's *Dhruvaswamini* (1933), rather than a Sanskrit classic, Kalidasa's *Malavikagnimitra*, which she had in mind. This is surely an indication of the nationalism associated with developing contemporary Hindi literature and drama, rather than seeking recourse to the past. And it is Bhuvan who encourages her to find a life in the arts, to stay with classical Indian dance and music as she begins to train in the South,

[74] Ibid.: 272.
[75] Ibid.: 305.
[76] Ibid.: 308.

rather than settle prematurely for an arranged marriage. But this nationalist streak is restricted almost entirely to her person and her education; it seems to have no wider implications.

The Progressive Writers Association (PWA) is summarily dismissed. It is represented almost solely in the person of Chandramadhav. And Bhuvan's critique of his tortured, self-doubting existence sets the tone. Chandramadhav's own musings seem partially focalized through Bhuvan, presented almost as self-caricature, which spills over into the perception of the narrator. The writers and intellectuals associated with the PWA meet at the Coffee House in Lucknow, 'a few nondescript writer-journalists', an English lecturer, an Urdu versifier, an assistant editor of a Hindi daily and other such 'prominent literary figures'—faceless individuals, who can only hide behind the 'class' adjective which they attached to every substantive.[77] In his final communications with Bhuvan, Chandramadhav accuses him of following class interests even in his science. These faceless individuals make grandiose plans, of convening a World Writers' Conference in Lucknow. Not surprisingly, Chandramadhav ends up joining the Communist Party, rising to prominence in the ranks of the PWA. Bhuvan, in a letter to Gaura, dismisses Chandramadhav and his ilk in a few words: 'They shirk the responsibilities of their status but do not want to renounce the privileges they enjoy because of it. As I see it, they will remain unreliable till some major frustration disables them for good . . .'[78]

The emphasis on the freedom of the individual, the challenge Rekha poses to society at large and her express defiance of it, provide a polemical antithesis to the Progressives of the day. And the tone of the novel as a whole seems to defy the heart of the agenda that the PWA has set itself: 'We believe that the new literature of India must deal with the basic problems of our existence today—the problems of hunger and poverty, social backwardness and political subjection. All that drags us down to passivity, inaction and unreason we reject

---

[77] Ibid.: 195.
[78] Ibid.: 322.

as reactionary. All that arouses in us the critical spirit, which examines institutions and customs in the light of reason, which helps us to act, to organize ourselves, to transform, we accept as progressive.'[79] This is not the collective that Bhuvan speaks of, or the responsibility that he claims.

In his letters to Gaura, he speaks of his view of civilization, the inherent value of which he does not question. Rather, he sees it as something which must be preserved and defended. He speaks of civilizational affinity not only with Europe—this affinity is not racial, which attribute he sees as a 'betrayal of mankind'—but also with the Middle East. He speaks of the centuries of cultural contact and exchanges with these regions, seeing little of value in the new notion of Asia much vaunted in Japan as well as India.[80] Nationalism for him recedes when facing the fascist challenge to mankind at large. When the first Japanese bombs fall on Indian soil, he joins the British army:

> It was necessary to defend man's reason against man's inhumanity. All the means at the disposal of inhumanity had been made available by science: so the greatest challenge was now for science. It had either to prove its power for good or be destroyed forever. Science was both a philosophy and a technology; barbarism had adopted the latter while disowning the former, but if civilization (sabhyatā) had any meaning, it was under an obligation to vindicate the former—to vindicate philosophy and to re-establish its domain over technology. 'I do not see how I can kill or assist in any kind of killing; but if there is a job which I regard as necessary, I cannot pass it on to someone else only because it is a dirty job which I find hateful. I must recognize that it must be equally hateful for all—for all civilized people—and therefore, it is a duty, the equal duty of all.'[81]

In Bhuvan's words there may well be a reflection of Sartre's ideas in *Existentialism is a Humanism*—on individual freedom as

---

[79] From the Amended Manifesto, Calcutta, 24 December 1938, text in Pradhan 1979: 21.
[80] ND, 293.
[81] Ibid.: 326.

connected to the notion of freedom for all[82]—as well as of M.N. Roy,[83] but there is also an almost uncanny echo of another important voice of the period. In the Introduction to his *Discovery of India*, published in December 1946 in India, Jawaharlal Nehru affirms his belief in the power of science to save humanity. Conceding its destructive power if it becomes disconnected to moral discipline and ethical considerations, Nehru yet believes in the spirit of man and his capacity to survive present challenges:

> Yet I am convinced that the methods and approach of science have revolutionized human life more than anything else in the course of history, and have opened doors and avenues of further and even more radical change, leading up to the very portals of what has long been considered the unknown. The technical achievements of science are obvious enough, its capacity to transform an economy of scarcity into one of abundance is evident, its invasion of many problems which have so far been the monopoly of philosophy is becoming more pronounced. Space-time and the Quantum Theory have changed the picture of the physical world . . . Man no longer sees nature as something apart and distinct from himself. Human destiny appears to become a part of nature's rhythmic energy.[84]

Or again, perhaps the very progress of science, unconnected to and isolated from moral discipline and ethical considerations, will lead to the concentration of power and the terrible instruments of destruction

---

[82] 'When I affirm that freedom under any concrete circumstance, can have no other aim than itself, and once a man realizes, in his state of abandonment, that it is he who imposes values, he can will but one thing: freedom as the foundation of all values . . . And in thus willing freedom, we discover that it depends entirely on the freedom of others, and that the freedom of others depends entirely on our own.' Sartre [1946] 1974: 48.

[83] Roy speaks frequently of 'science', rarely as technology, more often as philosophy or as equated with 'reason'; thus for instance in the following, when speaking of the principles of the newly founded Radical Humanist Party: 'How often have we declared that we practice politics as a science; that our party knows no authority, that it places reason above faith?' Roy 1946: 66. I am grateful to Nandkishore Acharya for drawing my attention to this work.

[84] Nehru 1946: 20.

which it has made, in the hands of evil and selfish men, seeking the domination of others—and thus to the destruction of its own great achievements. Something of this kind we see happening now . . .

The future is dark, uncertain. But we can see part of the way leading to it and can tread it with firm steps, remembering that nothing that can happen is likely to overcome the spirit of man which has survived so many perils. Remembering also that life, for all its ills, has joy and beauty, and we can always wander, if we know how to, in the enchanted woods of nature.[85]

Human destiny is here linked to the rhythmic energy of nature—M.N. Roy's 'law-governed universe'—both of which have been invaded by man's scientific spirit of inquiry. But science has now become unconnected with ethical considerations; this is also Bhuvan's agonized reaction at the onset of war. The links need to be forged again in order to overcome the present catastrophe. Nehru seems to be suggesting that this can be done by discovering again the beauty of nature and drawing strength from it: thus, Rekha's 'nature' and Bhuvan's 'science'. In the face of disaster, destruction, and wanton evil, there is a need to preserve sanity and to forge relationships with those whose innocence has survived— for Bhuvan this has come to mean Gaura, not Rekha. It is in Nehru's words, then, that we find the link between science, nature, and beauty, which though suggested, remains unarticulated in the novel.[86]

CROSS-COMMUNICATION, AND CONCLUSION

The action of the novel plays itself out in the years between 1932 and 1942, and at the end of it we leave Bhuvan in the jungles of Burma. Though Hiroshima and Nagasaki loom and are almost anticipated in his words on the destructive potential of science, the atomic

---

[85] Ibid.: 22–3.

[86] Agyeya's close relationship to Nehru in these years is testified not only by the short Foreword Nehru wrote to his collection of English poems, *Prison Days and Other Poems* (1946), but also in his coeditorship of the Hindi festschrift for Nehru on his sixtieth birthday, *Nehru Abhinandan Granth* (1949).

explosion is a thing of the future, though not of the period in which the novel was finally written and published. Bhuvan yet ends with hope, bypassing the challenges that Rekha has posed.

Clearly, then, the two frames of reference we spoke of can only partially coincide. Rekha's frame of reference, her critique of civilization, particularly of the city and middle-class hypocrisy, her emphasis on the moment and on the self as an island, her express recourse to nature as a resource, her unwillingness to compromise, all remain peculiar to her and determine her destiny. Bhuvan takes up Rekha's citations from poems, her images colour his perceptions, but he has set out his own frame of reference to Rekha early on. After the initial conversation, however, he breaks off the discussion with Rekha, too drawn into her sphere to be able to counter it in his own terms. In his letters to Gaura he evolves his alternative view of civilization as climaxing in science, 'man's greatest achievement', though now disastrously unconnected with ethical consideration. The two frames intersect only in his worldview. His vision of science as the possible saviour of mankind, which he maintains firmly but is left struggling with at the end of the novel, is unshared with Rekha and leaves her largely untouched.

The narrative thus begins and ends with Bhuvan. Rekha is his road to self-discovery, to intensity of experience, to strength. He enables her, in turn, to find fulfilment and open up in a way that she has yearned for but not experienced before. In spite of the narrative ending with Bhuvan on the war front and his reflections on the fragility of civilization, however, it is the experiential moments with Rekha that remain etched in the memory of the reader, the intimacy in the wild, in the mountains, at the lake. Thus it is that the first frame, set by Rekha and the poems she and Bhuvan clothe their ideas in, dominates the novel, an innovation in novelistic form which uses all genres (as Bakhtin had said, though he had not included the poem). The novel ends with an echo of her words. There is no sense of 'the tying up of all narrative strands, of "closure".'[87] There is the hope and

---

[87] Childs 2000: 23.

the wait, but also the uncertainty. This can also mean that one can be left alone at any stage and revert to being what one is, an island in the stream—like Rekha herself, who, even in her marriage with her surgeon, remains alone.

This is the modernist condition. Agyeya's poem 'Confluence', in his first collection of poems (which was in English), best sums up the intimacy and the distance of Bhuvan and Rekha's relationship and perhaps even Bhuvan and Gaura's:

> All the June daylong
> We have wandered
> Held hands
> Hung over the wonder of being near
> Like blue dragonflies
> Droning over bracken
> Beside a mountain tarn . . .
>
> But now, as the blue-green twilight fades
> We have receded
> Withdrawn in unformed apprehension
>
> Is communion only
> A
> Confluence of solitudes?[88]

REFERENCES

'Agyeya', Sachidanand Hiranand Vatsyayan. 1946. *Prison Days and Other Poems, by 'Agyeya'*. Foreword by Jawaharlal Nehru. Benares: Saraswati Press.
———. [1951] 1980. *Nadī ke Dvīp*. Allahabad: Saraswati Press.
———. [1960] 2003. *Ātmanepad*. Delhi: Bharatiya Gyanapith.
———. 1980. *Islands in the Stream*. Translation of *Nadī ke Dvīp* by 'Ajneya'. Delhi: Vikas Publishing House.

[88] Agyeya 1946: 86. I am grateful to Nandkishore Acharya for drawing my attention to this poem as a possible extension of what Agyeya explores in his novel.

Bakhtin, M.M. 1981. *The Dialogic Imagination. Four Essays by M.M. Bakhtin*, ed. Michael Holquist, trans. Caryl Emerson and Michael Holquist. Austin: University of Texas Press.

Childs, Peter. [2000] 2008. *Modernism*. Second Edition. London, New York: Routledge.

Eliot, T.S. 1991. *Collected Poems, 1909–1962*. Orlando: Harcourt, Inc.

James, Henry. 2011. *The Art of the Novel. Critical Prefaces by Henry James*. Introduction by R.P. Blackmur, new Foreword by Colm Toibin. Chicago and London: University of Chicago Press.

King, Anthony D. 1973. *Colonial Urban Development: Culture, Social Power and Environment*. London, Henley, and Boston: Routledge and Kegan Paul, 1976.

Lawrence, D.H. 1993. *Complete Poems*. New York: Penguin Books.

Leavis. F.R. [1955] 1964. *D.H. Lawrence: Novelist*. Harmondsworth: Penguin Books.

Lewis, Pericles. 2011. *The Cambridge Companion to European Modernism*. Cambridge: Cambridge University Press.

Luhmann, Niklas. [1982] 1998. *Love as Passion: The Codification of Intimacy*. Translated from the German by Jeremy Gaines and Doris L. Jones. Stanford: Stanford University Press.

Manjapra, Kris. 2010. *M.N. Roy: Marxism and Colonial Cosmopolitanism*. Delhi: Routledge.

Nehru, Jawaharlal. 1946. *Discovery of India*. Calcutta: The Signet Press.

Nehru Abhinandan Granth Committee. 1949. *Nehru Abhinandan Granth, a Birthday Book Presented to Jawaharlal Nehru, Prime Minister of India, on Completion of His Sixtieth Year, November 14, 1949*. Calcutta: V. More.

Oldenburg, Veena Talwar. [1984] 2001. *The Making of Colonial Lucknow 1856–1877*, in *The Lucknow Omnibus*. Delhi: Oxford University Press.

Pradhan, Sudhi. 1979. *Marxist Cultural Movement in India: Chronicles and Documents (1936–47)*. Calcutta: Ms Santi Pradhan.

Roy, M.N. 1946. *New Orientation. Lectures Delivered at the Political Study Camp held at Dehra Dun from May 8th to 18th 1946*. Foreword by Philip Spratt. Calcutta: Renaissance Publishers.

———. 2004. *M.N. Roy: Radical Humanist. Selected Writings*. Compiled by Innaiah Narisetti. Amherst, New York: Prometheus Books.

Sartre, Jean-Paul. [1946] 2007. *Existentialism is a Humanism*. Translated by Carol Macomber. New Haven and London: Yale University Press.
Shelley, Percy Bysshe. 1954. *Selected Poems*. London and Glasgow: Collins.
Tagore, Rabindranath. [1929] 2006. *Shesher Kobita: The Last Poem*. Translated by Anindita Mukhopadhyay. Delhi: Rupa and Company.
Taylor, Charles. [1989] 1996. *Sources of the Self: The Making of the Modern Identity*. Cambridge, Mass: Harvard University Press.
Varma, Archana. 2011. 'Ālok huā apnāpan ko jīte hue: *Nadī ke dvīp*', in *Pūrvagrah*, Agyeya Special Issue: *Agyeya par ekāgra*, October 2010–March 2011.
Williams, Raymond. 1989. *The Politics of Modernism: Against the New Conformists*. London, New York: Verso.
Yadav, Rajendra. 1997. *Upanyās: Svarūp aur samvedanā*. Delhi: Vani Prakashan.
Zaehner, R.C. 1969. *The Bhagavad-Gītā with a Commentary Based on the Original Sources*. Oxford: Clarendon Press.

6

Culture Wars and a Cult Novel

THE 250-ODD-PAGE NOVEL *Gunahom ka Devata* (The God of Vice; hereafter GD) by the 23-year-old Dharamvir Bharati was first published in 1949. The action it depicts took place a little before that year, in the quarter between spring 1947 and summer 1948. Bharati (1926–1997) was to write two more works of enduring significance, the almost surreal novel *Suraj ka Satvan Ghora* (The Seventh Horse of the Sun; 1952) and the play *Andha Yug* (Blind Age; 1954), both secure in very elevated positions within the modern Hindi literary canon. But GD suffered a different fate. Though it became a cult novel for the Hindi-reading youth of North India and has appeared in countless editions, its very popularity has made it an object of suspicion among literary critics. Bharati himself came to regard the novel as a youthful sin.

What significance did GD have at the time it was published and why does it remain important even now, even if differently?

THE INDIVIDUAL IN SOCIETY

It is a modernist novel deeply marked by its time. The years before Independence made for radical changes of many kinds—in political beliefs, in life-styles, in ways of being young, and in the forms and goals of ambitions among the young. The resistance to the rise of Fascism in Europe, the participation of left-wing writers and artists in the Spanish Civil War, and nearer home the 1942 Quit India movement, the devastating Bengal famine—the most intense and vital literary movements of the time reflect these concerns. The Progressive Writers Association held its first meeting in Lucknow in 1936. Premchand delivered the last major address of his life here. It was from this as yet small but already pan-Indian movement that the Hindi Progressive Writers, Pragativadis as they called themselves, derived their legitimacy. A very broad spectrum of people with broadly progressive, left-inclining views came together under its banner. If Shivdan Singh Chauhan, their first and foremost ideologue, was also one of the eight founder-members of the Allahabad wing of the Communist Party of India, it was Jawaharlal Nehru who wrote the foreword to Chauhan's book on the Spanish Civil War, *Raktaranjit Spen* (Bloodstained Spain; 1938). The relatively fluid situation of the late 1930s and early 1940s was to change radically by the end of the Second World War and the onset of the Cold War. The literary camps that formed and the battles in the Hindi literary world as they emerged thereafter mirrored the Cold War and were largely centred in Allahabad. They were fought in books and pamphlets, but most of all in little magazines that appeared and rapidly disappeared. From at least 1946 the Hindi Pragativadis came increasingly to regard themselves as an organ of the Communist Party of India, which, according to the many who began to be edged out of it, received directives straight from the Soviet Union. Certainly, after 1945, Soviet Russian literature in English translation began to pour into India.

The difference between the fluid situation of the early 1940s and that at the end of the decade can be seen in the positions that Shivdan Singh Chauhan and Dharamvir Bharati took in their respective literary-political treatises on Pragativad. Shivdan Singh's work came out in 1946, though the essays that made up the collection went back some years. Bharati's book on Pragativad appeared in 1949, the same year as GD. The treatise and the novel both signalled what would become Bharati's departure from the Pragativad camp; the two works could also be seen as mutual explications of each other. So it is important to discuss these two programmatic works before looking at the novel and the lives of two young people in a colonial bungalow in Allahabad's Civil Lines. Their life-style belongs partly to an older world and only partly to the modern and progressive, and therein lie the contradictions which result in the tragic conflicts in their lives.

Shivdan Singh Chauhan wrote the essay from which his book *Pragativad* derives the title, in 1941. His definition of the term was generous: 'With Pragativad or Progressiv-ism, I mean those writers who accept Marxism in one form or another or feel in sympathy with it.'[1] To make his arguments he quoted primarily from American and British leftist authors: Joseph Freeman (1897–1965), Upton Sinclair (1878–1968), James T. Farrell (1904–1979), and Christopher Caudwell (1907–1937), though also from Lenin's *What is to be Done*. It was true, he admitted, that Marxism came from the West, but ideas and societies change with time, and they assimilate ideas from elsewhere, as they have in past centuries—the Sufi interaction with Bhakti traditions, for example. It was not in formalist or photographic social realism that Progressives believed. 'Realism' they understood to mean a specific point of view about life, one which could no longer be articulated by older styles.[2] For literature was not merely a passive reflection of society, it was analytic, and an instrument of/for change.[3] Regarding the vexed question of the place of the 'individual' in Progressive Literature, he was to be one who could actively experience change (*gati*) in society, and recognize that it was the movement of society, rather than a person's, that inspired social change. However, Chauhan conceded, it was only from the dialectical relationship (*dvandatmak pranali*) between individual, society, class, and tradition, that life as a whole could emerge (*sampurna jivan*) in literature, where the particular would become the general and the general particular.[4]

But Chauhan also sounded warning notes of a kind that intensified. Social Realism was not by itself adequate as a criterion of literary

[1] Chauhan 1946: 12.
[2] Ibid.: 5.
[3] Ibid.: 4.
[4] Thoughts from the essay 'Sahitya ki Parkakh' (1948) cited in Agrawal 2006: 82–3.

merit, aesthetic concerns also mattered.⁵ And in his 1939 essay 'Bharat ki jan natya-shala', included in his 1946 volume, Chauhan became the first of the Progressives to also propose that it was important to lay the foundation of a people's theatre that 'fulfilled the spiritual (*adhyatmik*) needs of the people.'⁶

The opposing literary camp, as yet without a name, Chauhan saw as constituted by those who supported 'Art for Art's Sake'. They would later come to be known as the Prayogvadis (Experimentalists).

Bharati's *Pragativad: Ek Samiksha* (1949) heralded a departure radical enough from conventional Progressive thought to force his instantaneous exclusion from the ranks of the elect in the Progressive camp. Yet he begins with a solemn avowal of belonging: 'Progress (*pragati*) is my honour (*iman*), the youth of my pen, but the truth I witness within me, to put *that* forward fearlessly is my duty.'⁷ There are two definitions of *pragati*, he tells us, a received or accepted one and a generous one. Generous is the one that helps human civilization and culture to grow. Accepted is the one that has been prescribed as adhering to the Marxist life-view (*jivan-darshan*).⁸

Though he cites Chauhan and another Hindi writer along with a couple of well-known British socialist writers and thinkers—among them Christopher Caudwell and the novelist Ralph Fox—the majority of Bharati's sources are Soviet Russian: well-known writers such as Gorki, but also anthologies, surveys, and thematically focused books such as Flores Angel's *Marxism and Literature*, published as early as 1945. This difference between the British and American orientation of the 1930s and the Soviet orientation of 1940s Pragativad is worth noting. The Cold War has set in.

According to Bharati, Pragativad came to India when it had run its course elsewhere in the world. In his detailed analysis of the

⁵ Ibid.: 21.
⁶ Cited in Agrawal 2006: 73.
⁷ *Bhumika*, in Bharati 1949b: 17.
⁸ Ibid.: 21.

relationship of the Party to literary creation and writers in the Soviet Union, Bharati is at pains to show that there was no single position to which one could refer; there had been many experiments. If things seemed to have become more inflexible for a time, by 1932 a more generous vision began to be propagated. If Stalin were *now* to be driven back into more rigid positions, it would be solely because of U.S. aggression.[9]

The questions Bharati poses are: How far should literature follow the directives of the party? And, can a politically bound literature ever really flourish?[10] In the course of his 200-page work he makes several points. First, that in art the mixing of classes is more significant than a focus on class struggle alone.[11] Thus, writing of middle-class concerns can be entirely legitimate. It is the perspective that matters. Second, that the Soviet Union has overcome the narrow vision which sees the national past as forgettable, therefore pride in the past is entirely legitimate.[12] The Soviet Communist Party is *for* Russia, whereas the Indian Communist Party is not for India, for whomever else it may be.[13] A country with a long history should draw energy from its own particular past in order to face the new, and experiment with it; and therefore the need both to turn back to history as much as to look to the future. The Urdu Progressives have understood the need for bold experiment well. Any language could be proud of the techniques employed by writers such as Ahmed Nazim Qasimi, Krishanchander, and Ali Sardar Jaffrey.[14] As we can see, Bharati makes free use of the dreaded word 'experiment' without any qualms.

Third, there needs to be literary space in progressive literature for the depiction of romantic love and emotional life. Literature can well depict how a lack of balance in matters emotional and relating

[9] Ibid.: 99.
[10] Ibid.: 93.
[11] Ibid.: 57.
[12] Ibid.: 65, 67, 72.
[13] Ibid.: 101.
[14] Ibid.: 108.

to discipline can become self-destructive.[15] Cromwell's puritanism in England and that of the Arya Samaj in India militated against the depiction of love and other gentle emotions. The Hindi Pragativadis are the latest example of this kind of puritanism.[16] But Lenin had loved Pushkin, who was born in a feudal age and died in a duel defending the honour of his exceedingly beautiful, exceedingly rich, and exceedingly foolish wife.[17]

Fourth, Marxism accepts that it is man who makes his circumstances (*paristhiti*). He changes society and while changing society is himself changed. But can man change the external world without first changing his inner world? This is the place where Marx refuses to give answers. Fifth, and this is where the Indian resolution to the conundrum comes in. The power which has made for the regulation of the mental world of man and inspired the highest external change has been spirituality (*adhyatma*). Not escapist spirituality, not traditionalist, but that which gives strength to human beings and inspires them to break through deadlocks, to accumulate courage and strength. 'Our spirituality,' Bharati proclaims, 'should be action-oriented . . . in the temple of the new age, the icons of Ram-Krishna, Jesus, will need to be installed next to Marx, only then will both aspects of human society, the inner and outer, find full evolution and an unwaveringly progressive life-view (*jivan-darshan*) appear before us, and only then will we be able to ready a frame for the world to come, in which there will be no exploitation, no bloodshed, no hatred, and no poverty.'[18]

Bharati distinguishes between dharma, which is progressive, has given man strength, and has supported agitations to change the world; and *majhab*, which insists on hidebound ritual and tradition and leads the superstitious astray.[19] Lenin and Stalin resisted *majhab* and the decadence of the Orthodox Church, and refused to link the state with it. Yet the USSR offered protection for freedom of faith. But

[15] Ibid.: 77.
[16] Ibid.: 77–8.
[17] Ibid.: 90.
[18] Ibid.: 121–2.
[19] Ibid.: 125.

Indian—and by that he means Hindi—Progressives have forgotten that all cultural progress in India was connected to the Buddha and Krishna.[20] As support for his thesis, Bharati cites Gorki: 'We have split our mind and heart into separate segments, and this has been the root cause of all conflict.' He adds: 'I am convinced that Gorki would have found the resolution (*shaman*) for this conflict in Indian *Vaishnavata*, Vaishnavism, where god loves the devotee rather than stand in judgment on him.'[21] As we will see, the last two passages, Gorki's and his own, Bharati puts into the mouth of the novel's heroine at a particularly climactic moment in his tale. In the midst of chaos and unhappiness in her life, she turns to Vaishnavata; and though it cannot finally save her, at that moment in time it offers her solace.

Bharati's defiant cry at the close of the work proclaims once more that the artist is a mental slave to no-one,[22] and that revolution and progress are not the patrimony of any one party.[23]

In asking for the reactivation and legitimation of domains that stood outside party control, Bharati was going several steps further than Chauhan. He was pleading for the legitimacy of depicting middle-class concerns, romantic love, and spirituality in a progressive work. The novel that appeared the same year was the creative articulation of just this stand. The place of love and marriage in the life of the individual could be a part of progressive thinking if viewed from the right perspective; they could provide the balance, fulfilment, and inspiration needed for individual life to be socially responsible and creative. But they could also be a source of deviation and decay, as is the case in this modernist novel, where certitudes hold only for a while. And neither the progressive creed nor spirituality can save the two main protagonists from the course that their passions take.[24]

---

[20] Ibid.: 128.
[21] Ibid.: 134.
[22] Ibid.: 137.
[23] Ibid.: 162.
[24] As Childs ([2000] 2008: 16) notes, 'Modernism has, therefore, been universally considered a literature of not just change but crisis.'

With which we come to the question of the changes taking place in middle-class life-styles in urban India in the late 1940s. The move of Indian families to the classical Civil Lines bungalow or bungalows in similar surroundings necessarily meant departures from social patterns of living arrangements in older urban centres. We know from Anthony King's classic work on the topic that

> The bungalow was invariably situated in a large compound, an area of marked territory which, in turn, was located at a distance from other buildings or places of settlement. The compound . . . was an enclosed space either leased, bought or appropriated by representatives of an incoming, 'invading' society from the indigenous inhabitants of the land . . . In fact, the compound was simply an extension of the bungalow's internal space, an outdoor room fulfilling a variety of social, political, cultural, and psychological needs. Thus the bungalow was in direct contrast to the courtyard house in the 'native city'; . . . [where a] 'central courtyard allowed the penetration of light and air; as the houses were three or four storeys high and there were closely clustered, cellular-structured buildings all around, the lower rooms were dark and cool. Activity in this courtyard house was centripetal: movement was inwards, towards the courtyard. In the bungalow, it was centrifugal, outward, on to the verandah, and further into the compound.[25]

By the end of the nineteenth century, King says, 'The bungalow and the [racially and culturally] segregated environment in which it existed was, however, not just a physical and spatial form but also an attitude of mind, institutionalized in Public Works Departments and lasting long after colonial rule.'[26] An observation in another invaluable work on the bungalow confirms it 'may have had a fixed address, like, say, 20 Albert Road, but when the residents moved, it moved with them. The Bungalow was a way of life, and while it lasted, it was portable.'[27]

The question then was about the cultural change which began from the first half of the twentieth century, when Indians began to move

[25] King 1984: 34–5.
[26] Ibid.: 59
[27] Mehrotra 2007: 26.

into Civil Lines bungalows. King says: 'To put it briefly: just when where, how, and for what reasons did members of a rising middle class abandon traditional behaviour, stop sitting cross-legged on the floor, eating with their fingers, sleeping on roll-away mattresses, living in traditionally designed houses in the ancient cities and villages and move into Western-style "bungalows", adopting, in the process, the chairs, dining tables, cutlery, tableware, bedroom suites and "sofa-sets" with which the houses of contemporary middle class Indian are filled?'[28] Traditional Indian houses, as we know, are made up of rooms with multiple functions.[29] Moving into a bungalow or being brought up in one means adopting, even if partially, a modern life-style and at least some of the social intercourse and attitudes that went with it.

This draws us back to the city depicted in the novel. Like almost all towns and cities that were not actually founded by the British, Allahabad had an older town and the newer British section, the Civil Lines and the Cantonment, which together are said to have been the largest in British India. It was also known for its university. The actor Saeed Jaffrey says that 'In the mid-Forties Allahabad University was considered the best in India.'[30] The two young people at the centre of the narrative are both students here. The novel opens with a young Chander strolling in the city's famous Alfred Park, though he lives in a rented room in the crowded inner city. As the Hindi writer Gyanranjan puts it:

> A town really cannot be divided into two equal halves, but if Allahabad were to be divided, Mahatma Gandhi Marg, or Canning Road, as it was called, would be on the one side and the Grand Trunk Road on the other. The beautiful affluent, glitzy Allahabad is quite distinct from the poor and crowded older town of the Grand Trunk Road. The two halves are as different from each other as the water of the Ganges is from the water of the Yamuna. One is muddy brown, the other is green.[31]

---

[28] King 1984: 50.
[29] Ibid.: 51.
[30] Jaffrey [1998] 2007: 219.
[31] Mehrotra 2007: 312.

Illus. 20: Civil Lines Bungalow, Allahabad

Illus. 21: Allahabad University

'The Hindi writers of the Old Town,' as Chris Bayly has called them, had vernacular education and had little or no access to the Civil Lines.[32] The opening passage of the novel is a poetic tribute to the contradictions the city contains, contradictions reflected in the novel's characters:

> If people still believe in city or village deities, I would say Allahabad's reigning god is assuredly a romantic artist. The city's layout, proportions and life-style are so unfettered; everywhere you look, there's a pure, clean openness. It has lanes that are narrower than Banaras' alleys, and roads wider than Lucknow's streets. Allahabad's Civil Lines can match towns like Yorkshire and Brighton but it's mohallas are worse than filthy swamps. The climate is varied, there is no sameness, no sense of balance . . . Truly, Prayag's presiding deity seems to be a free-spirited artist exiled from the groves of heaven, whose creation is rich with threads of every hue.
>
> During the autumn-winter months, and in the weeks between Basant and Holi, the city is even more beautiful than nasturtium and pansy flowers, more fragrant than the perfume of mango blossoms. Whether it is Civil Lines or Alfred Park, the shore of the Ganga or Khushru Bagh, a breeze—like a playful nymph—teases the flower buds and waves alike . . .[33]

But the old and new city also came together at times, and this is what made Allahabad modern and exciting for many. Dharamvir Bharati, originally from Shahjahanpur in north-western UP, came to study in Allahabad in the early 1940s. He lived in the heart of the old town, in Atarsuiya, along with Shivdan Singh Chauhan and other prominent leftists. But he had regular access to the bungalow life-style and Civil Lines. In writing about the time immediately after the publication of GD, but presumably also describing the time during its writing, when he was engaged in his PhD research at the University of Allahabad, Bharati tells us: 'In the breaks between

---

[32] Bayly 1975: 214.

[33] GD, 21. This translation is taken from Poonam Saxena's fine rendering of the novel in English (2015: 3). The other translations in this chapter are mine.

doing my research, when I used to take my old, broken bicycle and set out, the most pleasurable refuge was the splendid bungalow of my friend Amalendu Ghosh. Wide stretches of green lawn, flowers in blossom, and behind the bungalow, the dense shade of trees. We used to sprawl on the chairs set out in the open. The *khansama* would bring us tea and potato chops and we would plunge into those tales told the world over in almost all circles of friends between adolescence and youth.'[34]

The owner of the bungalow in the novel is Dr Shukla. Well-known economist from the Political Science Department in the university, but already working for the Government Psychological Bureau, he is a bundle of contradictions. In his public life he sees caste and religion as no barriers to social intercourse; in his personal life caste observances—Brahminical rules of purity and pollution—are still intact. When he eats *kaccha khana*—unfried, and by implication easily polluted food, for instance—he abandons Western clothes and dons a silk dhoti in order to remain pure. We are reminded once again of Prakash Tandon's observation about the contradictions inherent in modern life within a modern house: 'In its own way the house was like the British bungalows in front and grand-uncle's house at the back.'[35] One set of beliefs inhabit the front of the bungalow, another the back. Dr Shukla's beliefs, modern and traditional at the same time, also internalized by the young people he watches over, make for the central tragedy in their lives and, by extension, his.

Dr Shukla has virtually adopted the brilliant young economist Chander Kapur as his son. As Khatris, Kapurs are a scribal-cum-trader caste. Chander is engaged in doctoral research; he writes excellent English and has a bright future before him. Chander is a patriot, though not an activist, focused instead on doing good in the world by doing ground-breaking research in economics, though he knows the limits of materialist thought. He is an out and out

[34] Bharati [1976] 2000: 71–2.
[35] Tandon [1961] 1968: 38.

socialist (*samajvadi*), he has great integrity but is also an individualist (*vyaktivadi*). Thus, he belongs at the intersection of the progressive and experimentalist camps, perhaps mirroring the author's own position. Though an orphan and from a relatively poor family, Chander is something of an aesthete; he is elegant to the point of being a dandy. Bharati was translating Oscar Wilde at the time he wrote the novel, and we see traces of his style and fictional motifs everywhere.

Dr Shukla's daughter Sudha is the sole family member living with him in his bungalow. Her mother died when she was three; she has been brought up by her widowed Bua (father's sister) in a nearby village. She was sent to her father at thirteen; the village had begun

Illus. 22: College Girls 1940s, from family album

objecting to her being still unmarried. She was a wild child, tamed somewhat by Chander, who took charge of her education. There was mutual *adhikar aur akarshan* between them—a claim over each other and an attraction—but neither was aware of its nature, which was pure as the morning breeze in autumn. When our narrative opens, Sudha is in college, in the final year of her BA; no longer a rebel, she runs the household, having taken charge of her father's life and that of Chander. They have a teasing, bantering relationship; she has cultivated little ways to irritate Chander. The carefree, uncomplicated life of youth, their pranks, and their growing awareness of each other as young adults provide the charm and pleasure of the first pages of the novel, perhaps the first of its kind in Hindi.

Chander and Sudha move freely through the book-lined study where Dr Shukla spends most of his time, the garden—the story begins in early spring—the roof-top terrace, even Sudha's bedroom. It is a brother–sister relationship which acquires other dimensions as Sudha grows older. Their speech inflects the narrative, creating overlapping character zones which surround their person, provide their perspective, and propelled by their emotions and thoughts drive the narrative forward. This idyll, their charmed life together, which includes Sudha's friendship with Geysu, daughter of a cultivated Muslim family and classfellow in college, provides the foil for the sorrow and melancholy that will follow.

Binti, Sudha's cousin from the village, joins them in the bungalow at a later stage. Binti is a rural beauty, practical and pragmatic, intelligent and quick to learn. She tilts her head when she talks and pulls at the corner of her sari when embarrassed. Considered unlucky—her father died upon her birth—and always cursed by her tyrannical mother, Sudha's Bua, she has been brought up to be meek and submissive. Life with mother has been hell, she is eager to marry and escape it. She becomes a steady presence, a constant companion to Sudha, but most of all to Chander, changing radically during the course of the novel.[36]

[36] GD, 103.

LOVE WITHOUT MARRIAGE

The vexed issue of inter-caste marriage is first brought up when Dr Shukla suggests to Chander that there should be fresh scientific study and analysis of India's *jati* order. Chander responds casually: Why bother, isn't it on the verge of collapse? All restrictions regarding commensality (*roti-beti*) will be over in another two generations. Dr Shukla responds impatiently. Social (cultural) correspondence is the most important thing about marriage. Brahmin will not do well with Baniya. But Chander asks: Why look at it only from the caste point of view? Marriage and the choice of partner are also individual matters (*vyaktigat*) and mental equilibrium in marriage is surely more important than *jati* considerations? Dr Shukla is firm: Love marriages have not proved successful. Chander insists: But not where there is true love. Dr Shukla thinks this is romantic nonsense.[37] This rigidity about inter-caste unions and the ensuing crisis provides the substance of the narrative.

When her marriage to a progressive, politically active young Brahmin is proposed, Sudha reacts with stormy defiance. It is to happen at the end of that summer, the irascible Bua from the village insists. The love she and he have for each other, Sudha tells Chander, is purer than fraternal love (*rakhi ka sut*), so why can't she simply go on looking after her father and never marry? A deeply conflicted Chander raises the issue of inter-caste marriage and betrayal of the faith placed in them by Dr Shukla—a first suggestion of the danger of incest. For in the family's eyes theirs has been a sibling relationship,[38] besides which Chander outlines what is essentially a dizzyingly idealist project:

---

[37] Ibid.: 52.

[38] Nikhil Govind has pointed to the recurring incest motif in two other classic Hindi novels, both written earlier than *Gunahom ka Devata*, in Jainendra's *Tyagpatra* (1937) and Agyeya's *Shekhar: Ek Jivani* (1941–4). Up to a certain age, there is a great deal of freedom in sibling-like relationships (2014: 4–5, 119). Premchand's *Nirmala* (1927) is also a case in point. The love of a young stepmother for her husband's eldest son forms the central conflict of the novel.

'I understand how you feel, Sudha. Your heart (*man*) has told me, what it didn't tell you. But Sudha, did we come into each other's lives only to weaken each other and did we soar to celestial heights and hear the music of the soul (*atma*) only to transform it into wedding music?'³⁹ Sudha is no ordinary girl; does she want the world to see her as commonplace, sentimental? Distance and pain elevate one, he says by way of persuasion.⁴⁰ They won't find such a great match again so easily. Theirs is to be a love without marriage. And with this he sets into motion the experiment with various configurations of that explosive trio—love, sex, and marriage. Need all three be realized in the same union? An extraordinarily bold theme for the times.

Meanwhile, Pamela or Pammi de Cruz enters their lives as a freelance typist who works for Dr Shukla. She is from an Indian Christian family. Her maternal grandfather was a well-known archeologist, a Maharashtrian who married a Kashmiri Christian girl and so had to convert to Christianity. She is a girl of twenty-three, some years older than Chander. She lives with her brother Bertie in Rose Cottage.⁴¹ Very attractive, with tea-coloured skin, short hair, French perfume, blouse and skirt, painted nails, cigarette-smoking, easy-going, with a familiarity of manner, though she does not allow those she does not like to get familiar with her. She is no ordinary Christian girl, Chander notes (*Sadharan isai chokari nahim*).⁴² As an Anglo-Indian, Pammi belongs in a liminal world, neither English, nor Indian; sexual transgressions become possible with her. She is Hindustani, she tells Chander, but Hindustanis don't like to interact socially with

---

³⁹ GD, 113.

⁴⁰ Ibid.: 115.

⁴¹ Allahabad had its own Anglo-Indian colony; a cluster of Anglo-Indian cottages built in the English style, a part of which has survived the ravages of time. I am grateful to Arvind Krishna Mehrotra and Alok Rai for accompanying me to this idyllic though rundown area where the cottages still stand. Saeed Jaffrey recalls that 'Allahabad in those days had a huge Anglo-Indian community and most of the men worked in the railways. So there was a railway colony with lovely bungalows and a club with a large dance hall, and monthly balls.' Mehrotra 2007: 320.

⁴² GD, 40.

Illus. 23: Anglo Indian Cottage, Allahabad

her. Christian, Anglo-Indian society she doesn't like. Besides, she is divorced, she married for love but it did not work, it was sexually exploitative, so she mixes with no-one. She has been looking for a friend for four years and has now found one in Chander.

These four young people, Sudha, Chander, Binti, and Pammi, inhabit a world of their own, not entirely anchored in the traditional and so far removed from the older generation, here represented by Dr Shukla and intermittently his sister, that there is almost no communication between them. What are the moral standards that they set themselves in their fast-modernizing world where caste matters less and less, where marriage is a bond that does not necessarily contain desire?

Bharati has written an oft-cited essay on 'Modernity, that is, the Consciousness of a Crisis' which provides an entry point to our narrative.[43] All ages, he tells us, have regarded themselves as

[43] The essay was originally a part of the collection entitled *Pashyanti* (1969). It is now available in *Dharmvir Bharati Granthavali*, vol. 5: 476–89.

modern, but presently there is a sharper consciousness of the all-pervasive difference from the past—in religion, philosophy, science and knowledge, art, language, in all fields more generally.[44] It is not a simple question of westernization. The so-called difference between East and West is part of the mistaken notion propagated by the West itself during the colonial period. The two are complementary, for human nature is one.[45] Science has shown that the universe functions according to its own laws, not that of some creator, not even as a machine but as a brain. Science also frees mankind from superstition, gives everyone a sense of freedom, sameness, and fraternity. Man has become the centre of the universe but there is a strange hollowness to his being. What is the crisis? The source of moral values is undecided (*Naitik mulyom ka srota anishchit hai*).[46] Man has evolved not from the divine but from an animal existence, in his struggle for existence the survivor is the victor. There is no other measure to decide on values, with the result that all values have been devalued (*avamulyan*). The more victorious man has been *vis-à-vis* nature, the more he has lost himself. Existentialism has refused to recognize any stability of values; each person is to decide these for himself.[47] Thus, man has found himself isolated and alone. Industrial capitalism has made a commodity of literature, which has, additionally, come under the patronage of a state that tries to bind the author to its directives. Thus, between the three—the loneliness in the crowd, the commodification of literature, and the insistence that all moral values are to be guided by the state, there has arisen the sense of a crisis which is not that of literature alone. Though Nietzsche and Marx saw the evolution of man as part of an optimistic, positive development, and there were multiple themes of resurrection in literature after the First World War, Mayakowski's suicide and the mysterious death of Gorki in a communist camp and the circumstances of Lorca's death in the free

[44] Ibid.: 477.
[45] Ibid.: 480.
[46] Ibid.: 482.
[47] Ibid.: 483.

world have put a question mark on the formerly blind optimism of literature. Though Bharati ends his essay on an optimistic note, seeing a special place for literature in exploring the interiority of man and thus helping to restore values that reside within, the essay as a whole points rather to the crisis in moral values than to any reassuring restoration of them. This double-edged tone, of a moral crisis and the spiritual redress that proves to be no redress, is echoed in the novel as Chander is left to explore his moral options in the situation he has at least in part created for himself.

DEFIANCE: SEX WITHOUT LOVE OR MARRIAGE

When Sudha marries and goes away—in the winter of that year, 1947, Dr Shukla also leaves for Delhi—leaving Chander alone and bitter, he starts a relationship with Pammi which promises sex without love or marriage. Led by Bertie, Pammi's half-mad brother, to believe that sex is all that girls want, Chander finds a kind of fulfilment in his attachment to Pammi. The open sexuality of Rose Cottage is entirely different from the hushed, euphemistic, and reverent tones elsewhere in the novel when the subject is addressed. The inhabitants of Rose Cottage operate according to self-created rules. It is here, in this liminal Anglo-Indian world, that Chander meets his own freed self.[48] One day, still glowing from his meeting with Pammi, he discusses his newly won wisdom with Binti and asks her opinion: 'I thought until now that love and sex were two different things, I believed in love and abhorred sex, now both seem the same to me, I feel a kind of aversion for life. What do you think, Binti?'

She can hardly discuss this with him, she says, for she is quite illiterate. But she knows for sure that 'So much study is no good' (*Itna parhna-likhana accha nahim hota*).[49] It's because he and Sudha read too

---

[48] I am grateful to Gautam Choubey for drawing my attention to the out-of-bounds sexuality of Rose Cottage.

[49] GD, 175.

much that their thoughts are askew. Things in the village are different, where sex is not taboo. Every boy and girl there understands it and so are not upset over it. Girls put on weight after marrying. When Chander laughs at her simplicity, she explains yet more pragmatically that 'all this' is considered as natural as eating and drinking. There isn't such a to-do and secrecy about it. Girls before marriage . . . apparently even she.[50] Though Sudha was different, she kept to herself, read, and picked flowers from the lotus pond. Binti can tell him all this because she has faith (*vishwas*) in him, even more than in Sudha. This just confirms Chander's worst suspicions. Love is just glorified. Sex is all that girls want. He loses all trust, even in Sudha.[51] Scenes of unbearable unhappiness and suffering ensue. Chander is increasingly cruel to Sudha, his effort to degrade her, even to physically molest her, make him the god of vice that gives the book its title.

Back in Allahabad, alone in the bungalow, Chander meets Sudha's great friend Geysu.[52] Though not explicitly mentioned once, it is clear that Independence and Partition have taken place; there is talk of refugees. Chander finds out from her that Geysu's cousin Akhtar, who was to marry her, has chosen her younger sister Phul instead. She has now sworn never to marry. She has trained as a nurse at the Dehradun Maternity Centre; she'll work in some hospital. Her reaction to Chander's—that if he were in her situation he would marry again and get revenge against Akhtar—provides the beginning of the turning point in his life: 'Phooey, Chander bhai, revenge, flight, revulsion, man has never improved himself through these, nor ever will. Revenge and revulsion are expressions of weakness. And if I were to take revenge, against whom would it be? The very person for whom, in moments of solitude, I would give up my life (*sadake parti hum*)? How can that be? (*Yah kaise ho sakta hai*).[53] If one can spend a day without one's beloved, why not a lifetime? In the end

[50] Ibid.: 176.
[51] Ibid.: 177.
[52] Ibid.: 202.
[53] Ibid.: 205.

he would be hers. She had, in fact, drawn inspiration from Chander. Love without marriage is possible, apparently. This of course is the very thing Chander had tried to do and having tried to do it had been filled with negativity. Chander does reprimand himself briefly but chooses to ignore his inner voice. He bounces back to his old ways, though with a difference, with pangs of conscience.

The narrator steps in at this point to tell us it would be unjust to Pammi to see her as only thirsting for sex. She has deep compassion for Chander.[54] Chander does not want to hurt her either, but Pammi feels the difference that has crept into their relationship. As she explains in the letter she leaves in his hands before she drives away: 'The craving you felt for me has turned into pity for me . . . you only feel pity for me, a gratitude, and Kapur I won't accept that. Forgive me, even I have some self-esteem (*svabhiman*).'[55] Pammi returns to her husband, he will forgive her. In short, sex is housed in marriage again. 'This moment comes in the life of every woman, that's why, perhaps, Hindus attach more significance to marriage than to love.'[56] She advises him to marry a simple Hindu girl and not fall into the trap of some female intellectual who claims to love him.

THE MIRROR SCENE: SPIRITUALITY AS POSSIBLE RESOLUTION

The Muslim (Geysu) and the Christian (Pammi) girls' cumulative effect on Chander leads to the mirror scene, reminiscent of the much more fatal scenes in *Dorian Gray*. It is with this that the final section of the novel begins. As Chander gets ready to go to the cinema and looks into the mirror, his shadowy image speaks to him, baring his soul, telling him all the things he knows but will not face up to. He argues with it, but it talks back. Sinner, fallen man, characterless (*Papi, patit, charitrahin*). Collect a few more girls, Pammi, Binti, Sudha. Bertie was mad, but he didn't know how to bite like a mad dog.

[54] Ibid.: 209.
[55] Ibid.: 212.
[56] Ibid.: 214.

> 'You God with distorted limbs. He is selfish who cannot rise above himself. A single breath of yours has been more important than the storm raging inside someone else. You shoved Sudha in an oven in regard for your heart. You didn't shirk from using Pammi, even though you were aware of the disturbed state of her mind. You accepted intimacy with Binti, even though you didn't love her, and then you disdained both . . . and you say you are not selfish. Bertie may be crazy but he is not selfish.'[57]

This is a new moral code for men which does not allow them sexual freedom while reserving all the puritanism for the women. But the really important lines, something that Sudha will also echo, are these: 'First, you negated society and focused on your individual self as the centre of your exertions (*sadhana*). You then negated the individual . . . And so you were able to bring to fruition neither the love of humanity in your life, nor that of Sudha.' If one were to acknowledge, the voice goes on, that there are problems in the worldview that propagates the love of humanity at large—an indirect shot at the Pragativadi view—even a partial belief in it could lead one to accomplish something. 'Even if we acknowledge that you suffered some pain with Sudha's love, *you* could still have built something on the basis of its significance in your life. One takes on the journey of life. Hindrances, difficulties, make one wise, mature one's soul. Have you become any the more mature?'[58]

Chander argues with the image in the mirror, what is he do, is he to abandon his way, break his personality? The mirror image reprimands him again:

> 'Again the same negation and destructiveness . . . The knocks one receives on the way and the troubles one encounters make one's personality more mature, they mature the self. Has that maturity come to you? No. I know you want to negate even me now. You want to silence my voice. Self-defence has now become your profession. How dangerous you are. You . . . still . . . want . . . to disregard even me now' (221).

[57] Ibid.: 219.
[58] Ibid.: 220.

The episode breaks off abruptly and we find Chander back in Allahabad. It is early summer, 1948. Sudha is to visit the Allahabad bungalow with her husband Kailash, who is being sent to Australia on a cultural delegation by the new Indian government. He will be leaving Sudha with her father in Delhi while he is away. Chander works himself into a frenzy of expectations and good resolutions before their arrival. There is moisture in the air. Rain in May and green everywhere. At the railway station, he sees Sudha is ill and ailing. Later, her husband Kailash has a heart-to-heart talk with Chander. Though she has a character of gold, though everyone in the family loves her—her devotional exercises (*puja-path*) make her a special favourite of her mother-in-law—he confesses he did not get what he wanted by marrying her. When Sudha and Chander finally converse, she explains, it is not puja that she performs, just the recitation of the *Gita*, the *Bhagavata*, and sometimes from the *Sursagar*. She puts her new religiosity in a pragmatic context: 'The Hindu household is like a prison; if religion were not there to provide subterfuge, the prisoner does not so much as have permission to fast so that she can be released from life. I get some pleasure (*sukh*) from fasting as subterfuge.'[59] But even this subterfuge has helped her acquire faith (*vishwas*): 'I used to wonder why women are so devoted to worship rituals, then I saw why—the Hindu woman is so helpless, she receives so much insult, contempt, and disdain from husband and son that she would become a beast if it weren't for her worship. It's what has allowed the Hindu woman to remain elevated (*umcha*), to hold her head high.'[60]

In reading all these works, she has slowly regained her faith. She sees lack of faith as sin, and quotes a half verse from the *Bhagavadgita*: *samsayatma vinashyati*. The doubting soul perishes. In all these devotional works, she has found a very attractive symbol of love—Krishna. And so she finds a way to merge herself with Chander, safely sublimated to the status of the love god. 'I am a segment of your

[59] Ibid.: 231.
[60] Ibid.: 233.

atma, separated from you in this birth. But I will circle around you always and like the moon, continue to revolve in circles around you.'⁶¹ Then follows another verse from the *Bhagavdgita*: *Sarvadharmen parityajya, mamekam sharanam vraja* (Leave aside all other dharmas, seek refuge in me alone). Here we have, spelt out for us, Bharati's point about the place of progressive spirituality in Indian life, of its role in providing ethical inspiration and stability. It was as such that it had to be integrated in Indian Pragativad.

Though Sudha's situation is not the same as Geysu's, her love is reciprocated. But, like Geysu, she can find a way to live her love without marriage. She does reproach Chander, however, about his relationship with Pammi. Chander reacts with arrogance and bitterness: her love and Pammi's sensuality are two sides of the same coin. But, Sudha tells him with her newly acquired wisdom, she is not speaking of the ethical and the unethical (*naitik, anaitik*). Her scales for weighing bad and good are different. (*Meri pap aur punya ki tarazu hi dusri hai*). Her god is kind, he does not stand in judgement; he tries to persuade a person to understand his weaknesses and he speaks of forgiveness and of love. She doesn't consider bodily desire a sin.

> 'Bodily desire (*pyas*) is as pure as the worship of the soul (*atma ki puja*) . . . The atma articulates itself through the body and the inclinations of the body, the disciplining of the body happens through the atma. He, who separates atma and body is broken into pieces by getting enmeshed in the fearful storms of the mind. Chander, I was your atma. You were my body. I don't know how we were separated. Without you, I was left to become subtle atma alone . . . and without me, you became just body . . . When you writhe in pain on this shore of the *Vaitarani*, the river that forms the bounds of hell, I'll writhe on its other shore.'⁶²

Sudha does not content herself with this sublimation. She also upbraids him about his goals in life. He has no stability (*tumhare charitra mem kahim sthayitva nahim*).⁶³ He says, he will be stable now;

⁶¹ Ibid.
⁶² Ibid.: 234.
⁶³ Ibid.: 236.

he has seen that without her he doesn't remain human, he becomes an animal. He thought she had become absorbed in her married life, and the disinterest she expressed in marriage in his presence was feigned. In the momentary mental vacuum that followed, Pammi's brother Bertie became his philosophical guru. He also found real solace in Pammi's embrace and her submission washed away his bitterness. Sudha says she can't bind him, since she is not free herself. But she suggests that he marry Binti. He rejects this roundly. He recognizes, as he tells her, that one stage in his life is over.

Where now, what to do now? She repeats what the mirror had told him. He has fought the battle with himself. Now it's the turn of the battle with the outside world. Chander's individuality is flawed, it can mend itself by turning to bringing about social good—this, we may recall, is part of Bharati's individualist version of the Pragativad creed. And she will find fulfilment through him. Luhmann sees this kind of love as corresponding 'to the old "passive" concept of passion, according to which love culminated in a *loss of identity* and not, as one would think nowadays, in *gain* in identity.'[64] So, Sudha takes solace in a regressive notion of love and loss of her individual identity. If the tale had ended here, it would have seemed a conventional enough resolution. But this is a modernist tale. And Sudha speaks also of her own suffering, of *giving up* on herself, of the hell of physical intimacy with her husband. Thus for Sudha sex without love is not possible in marriage. As if to confirm the trauma this has been for her, Kailash tells Chander at parting that Sudha is pregnant. She goes to her father and Binti in Delhi, but within a matter of weeks she is taken seriously ill. Chander reaches Delhi in time to see her, to hear her call out in agony to him. The complications of the pregnancy kill her in the most painful way possible. It is in some ways a willed death.

CONCLUSIONS AND OPEN ENDS

The idyll in the Allahabad bungalow is finally over. The Central Government in Delhi has been beckoning for a while; Dr Shukla has

[64] Luhmann [1982] 1998: 63–4.

arranged for a position in the Department for Refugees for Chander. Chander is a socialist; he does not believe anything has changed now that the Congress is ruling instead of the British. This was the position most progressive thinkers of the time took. We are told that he likes his slow life in the university. But with Sudha's words in mind, he prepares to leave.

In a 1954 essay, Shivdan Singh Chauhan writes ruefully about the tight-lipped creed of both literary camps—progressive and experimentalist—to regard Independence as false and to deliberately ignore it.[65] 'And such was the dogmatism (*duragrah*) of the variousisms (*matvad*) that the incidence of receiving independence and the eight years after that, passed without their taking any note of them.'[66] In spite of responding to the magnetic pull of the centre and becoming witness to the vast changes that took place thereafter, both camps chose not to speak of it.

Sudha has not been able to take her bungalow existence and the freedom it afforded to her husband's home. It is the fate of very few

Illus. 24: Nehru addressing the nation, 15 August 1947

[65] 'Svadhin bharat men hindi sahitya ki gatividhi' published in *Sahitya ki samasyaen* (1959: 133), cited in Agrawal (2006: 98).

[66] Cited in Agrawal (2006: 96).

girls to take the centrifugality of their existence in a semi-Westernized father's bungalow house with them. And Sudha's life ends tragically.[67] Chander and Binti come back to Allahabad only to immerse Sudha's ashes in the rushing waters of the Sangam. In the sacral context of the Sangam of the Ganga and the Yamuna, the narrator speaks of Prayag rather than Allahabad.

Jeth dashhare ke din, phul, sangam, sham.[68]

The tenth day of the lunar calendar in *jeth*, in June, the bones, the Sangam and evening.

Chander is impatient and aggressive with Binti, venting his despair on her. He almost pushes her into the river. She steadies herself and screams at him. He apologizes: it will never happen again. The ashes are scattered in this scramble, he gathers some and fills the parting of her hair with the ash and kisses the spot. His lips are coated with ash. They must carry on, he tells her.

Ganga ki laharom mem bahta hua rakh ka samp tut-phut kar bikhar chuka tha aur nadi phir usi tarah bahne lagi thi jaise kabhi kuch hua hi na ho.[69]

The ashes flowing in the river like a snake had broken formation and scattered, and the river was flowing again as if nothing had ever happened.

And thus, finally, Allahabad, presaging the transition to another world, to Delhi with its officialdom, though the glories of its university, its Civil Lines, would last for at least another decade.

Novels don't necessarily have definitive readings and in this one there is no real closure. As I read it, Sudha's death underlines both

---

[67] A very valid point was made at the presentation of this paper at Delhi University (14 November 2012), by G. Arunima about the fact that Sudha is punished: she must die because she is pregnant, almost illegitimately so, and pregnant women must either lose their children, as Rekha does in *Nadi ke Dvip*, or they themselves must die.

[68] GD, 259.

[69] Ibid.: 260.

Illus. 25: Sangam, Allahabad

the intense desire and the near impossibility of successfully unifying sex, love—the new kind of romantic love which Binti has trouble understanding—and marriage. The quest has probably never ended, but its very intensity, its struggle to come to terms with the politics of its time, may be what has made the novel of enduring interest. Its positioning as a cultural manifesto of sorts, as expressing the progressive creed in an individualist strain, has long been forgotten.

Goethe (1749–1832) was only twenty-four when he wrote *The Sorrows of Young Werther*.[70] It became the rage in Europe; we have only to think of the spate of suicides that followed Werther's act of despair. It created an impact far beyond anything the author, even in his wildest moments, could have dreamt of. It was a novel he was both proud and ashamed of in his later years. Bharati was surely similarly placed when he looked back on this particular novel in the context of his life's work.

---

[70] First published in 1774, the revised edition appeared in 1789.

REFERENCES

Agrawal, Purushottam. 2006. *Shivdan Singh Chauhan*. Delhi: Sahitya Akademi.

Bayly, C.A. 1975. *The Local Roots of Indian Politics: Allahabad 1880–1920*. Oxford: Clarendon Press.

Bharati, Dharmvir. 1949a. *Gunahom ka Devata*, in Bharati 1999, vol. 1, *vide infra*.

———. 1949b. *Pragativad: Ek Samiksha*, in Bharati 1999, vol. 5, *vide infra*.

———. 1969. 'Adhunikata athava samkat ka bodh', in *Pashyanti*, in Bharati 1999, vol. 4, *vide infra*.

———. 1999. *Dharmvir Bharati Granthavali*, ed. Chandrakanta Bandivadekar. Nine volumes. Delhi: Vani Prakashan.

———. 2015. *Chander and Sudha: A Story of Middle-class Life*. Translated from the Hindi by Poonam Saxena. Gurgaon: Penguin-Viking.

Chauhan, Shivdan Singh. 1946. *Pragativad*. Muradabad: Pradip Karyalaya.

Childs, Peter. [2000] 2008. *Modernism*. Second Edition. London and New York: Routledge.

Govind, Nikhil. 2014. *Between Love and Freedom: The Revolutionary in the Hindi Novel*. London, New York, Delhi: Routledge.

Gyanranjan. 2007. 'Vagabond Nights', in Mehrotra 2007, *vide infra*.

Jaffrey, Saeed. [1998] 2007. 'From an *Actor's Journey* (1998)', in Mehrotra, 2007, *vide infra*.

King, Anthony. 1984. *The Bungalow: The Production of a Global Culture*. London: Routledge and Kegan Paul.

Luhmann, Niklas. [1982] 1998. *Love as Passion: The Codification of Intimacy*. Translated from the German by Jeremy Gaines and Doris L. Jones. Stanford: Stanford University Press.

Mehrotra, Arvind Krishna. 2007. *The Last Bungalow: Writings on Allahabad*. Delhi: Penguin Books.

Tandon, Prakash. [1961] 1968. *Punjabi Century: 1857–1947*. Berkeley, Los Angeles: University of California Press.

Wilde, Oscar. [1890] 2011. *The Picture of Dorian Gray and Three Stories*. Lexington, KY: Tribeca Books.

7

On the Rooftops of Agra

AGRA IS SYNONYMOUS WITH the Taj Mahal. The once prosperous Mughal city is now little more than a drab backdrop for the marble monument; its once famous colleges have receded almost entirely from the public imagination. To recall the vibrancy of its intellectual climate in the 1940s and 1950s I first turn here to two little-known novels of the period.[1] Their two young authors, born in the densely populated inner city, caught the spirit of the times in their respective early novels. In them the violence of the war in Europe and South East Asia sends ripples through university campuses as much as through the more traditional sections of Agra's residential and commercial quarters. And the students of the day register the social and political changes in the air as much as do conservative seths leaning on bolsters (*gav takias*) in their old-style shops. The novels mirror the cultural clashes, conversations, and conflicts between different sections of the city as well as those within families

---

[1] I thank Rajendra Yadav for drawing attention to these two novels, as also his insight into the cultural opposition between the two sides of Raja Mandi. I had a series of meetings with him: on 14 October 2012, 11 December 2012, and 26 December 2012. He helped me understand the environment of the haveli he lived in, of the layout of Agra, the literary climate of his times, and the camp formations that were both stimulating and destructive. Most of all, he helped me understand his novel in its context. To my great regret, I was not able to complete this piece in his lifetime. He asked about it shortly before he passed away on 28 October 2013.

and individuals. We begin with glimpses of the city provided by these novels in order to understand the specific constitution of the city of Agra, with its grand Mughal past, its subsequent decay, and the modernity reconfigured there by the British in the early nineteenth century, when it was used as their base in place of Delhi with its more immediate Mughal presence.

SCHISMS IN THE CITY: BAZAAR TALK AND COLLEGE LIFE

The first novel, *Seth Bankemal* (1940/1941) by Amritlal Nagar,[2] consists of a series of reflections, encapsulated in monologue, by a sharp-witted and lively Seth of that name, on the manners and customs of his times. The second novel, *Gharaunda* (Little House; 1941/1942) by Rangeya Raghav, is a coming-of-age tale woven around the lives of a group of students, male and female, at Agra's St John's College, reputed in its time as one of the best in the United Provinces.[3] The generational and ideological conflicts mirrored in the two novels in many ways reflect the social difference between the two parts of Raja Mandi, the commercial-residential quarter in the heart of the town, which is where the novel is set. One section of the Mandi is progressive; it borders on the campus colleges and its restaurants are the scene of conversations among intellectuals of the day. The other section is traditional; it contains the seats of the seths, bankers, and merchants, who resist change; and in its residential quarters live the seths' traditional families.

Herein lived also Rajendra Yadav. Though born and brought up in a traditional haveli, Yadav crossed over into the modern section of town when he visited the campus to attend college. He was reared

---

[2] Published first in 1955, the edition available today (2011) has been published by Rajpal and Sons; all quotations are from this edition. I thank Sharad Nagar, the writer's son, for providing all kinds of information about this novel.

[3] All quotations from the present edition, published in 2008 by Rajpal and Sons.

thus in a mixed milieu, that of the bazaar which lined his home and the campus which offered entry into the modern world. *Gharaunda* and *Seth Bankemal* form the ground as it were, from which would spring Yadav's *Sara Akash* (The Vast Sky), the novel on which this essay focuses, the first version of which was written and published in 1951.

Raja Mandi lies in a part of Agra deeply marked by the changes that set in after the 1857 uprising.[4] For improved access to the densely populated inner city, where sedition might brew, the British—as in Lucknow and elsewhere in North India's urban centres—cut a broad road which ran right through it. This was Drummond Street, also known as Thandi Sarak or Cool Street, because of the shade of the trees which lined it (now Mahatma Gandhi or MG Road). To the east of this road were the famous colleges of the city, Agra College, established as early as 1823, St John's College, established in 1850, the Medical College, and not too far from these the Rajput College (now Balwant Rajput College).[5] The part of Raja Mandi that

[4] Lucy Peck tells us in her guide to the city that Raja Mandi and neighbouring Gokulpura may have had a mixed heritage because of their location between two modern sections of the city: 'This area connected the Civil Lines to the north with the cantonment to the south. It is far more heterogeneous than the other two areas, containing as it does some large neighbourhoods of traditional urban development. This is probably because, while the Civil Lines and the cantonment were firmly outside the outer walls of the city, the many educational and hospital buildings that form the majority of the colonial buildings in this area were built here, inside the old walls where there was still available open space reasonably close to the population they were meant to serve.' Peck 2008: 137.

[5] According to Neville (1921: 131) St John's College was founded by Protestant missionaries, its first site being near St John's Church, closer to the old city centre; it moved to its present site in 1914. In 1862 it was affiliated in Arts to Calcutta University, and in 1888 to Allahabad University. Its MA standard was recognized as early as 1893 and affiliation in law in 1895. Agra College is an East India Company foundation, originally based on the educational endowment made by the Maharaja of Gwalior to a local scholar. It was considered Agra's most prestigious college, famous for its

bordered Drummond Road was the only 'modern' quarter within the city, the Civil Lines and Cantonment lay on the North and South, respectively, of it. This part of Raja Mandi contained shops which displayed the newest goods from the West, and restaurants and cafes where students and the literati met. Behind this border zone stretched the rest of the *mohalla* (neighbourhood), consisting of havelis, one of them belonging to Yadav's family, and the older bazaar. Gokulpura, another traditional neighbourhood, adjoined this area; here was situated the original of the shop in which sat the Seth we will speak of shortly, selling his gold and silver lace (*gota-kinari*), holding court, discoursing freely on his own colourful past as much as on the scandals of the day. [6]

Seth Bankemal (hereafter SB), a 112-page novella, consists of sixteen scurrilous monologues fired off by the lively Seth in the general direction of the young Agra-born short story writer, a 'modern' seeking a living in Bombay, who savours with ironic delight the Seth's wit and the colour of his bazaar speech, the celebrated *Dilli-Agra ki Boli* that had much earlier gone into the making of modern standard Hindi. The monologues revolve around the exploits of the Seth, now turned sixty-eight, looking back on forty years of adventure in the company of his rollicking friend, Parasnath Chaube, then a strapping young wrestler.[7]

---

academic excellence all over North India till well into the first decades after Independence. It is today a university with over 12,000 students.

As Peck (2008: 129) tells us, a long walk from the Raja ki Mandi station area (towards Civil Lines) can take one to Balwant Rajput College, which was founded in 1890 as a school for Rajput boys to be run on modern lines. 'The main building is typical of the colonial Gothic style used a great deal in Agra . . . The covered double staircase to the first floor of the rear building is worth looking at.' Ramvilas Sharma, the noted Hindi critic, was Professor of English here.

[6] Raja Mandi, Gokul Pura, and their environs lay to the west of the Old City. Ibid.: 137.

[7] The conversations seem to have taken place in 1941–2, since Subhas Chandra's escape from house surveillance to Germany via the Soviet Union is mentioned as current news.

These are war years; the Seth is canny enough to see through the machinations of the British as well as the politicians mouthing communal propaganda to manipulate and control their constituencies. The past decades have seen so much change, technological and social: electricity, running water, the radio, phonograms, films, bicycles, but most of all Western education which, according to the Seth, has emasculated the now suited-booted boys, no longer ready to follow in their fathers' footsteps.[8] The worst affected are the girls. The Seth relates the incident of a young woman in the neighbourhood, a model of demure domestic behaviour who, barely fifteen days after being taken to the films by her unsuspecting father, proceeded to run away with a college boy, who was doing his BA in, what else, but English literature. 'And the songs they sing in the bioscope, as if the world is crammed full of love. Hey you idiot, if the world were so full of love-shove, would we have those cunning Gandhi-vandhi kind of Mahatmas running around the place? And will love fill your stomach, brothers?'[9] Public scandal had followed this elopement, leading to the usual train of events: police, law court, brazen behaviour by the girl who protested publicly that she was of age and would do as she liked. She was naturally left to rack and ruin as the boy turned his back on her. 'We are talking of the self-same India,' the Seth continues with feeling, 'where girls immolated themselves, they became *sati*s, where they were regarded as goddesses and worshipped. The wretches used to turn to ashes in those flames just to preserve their shame, but in this age these blasted creatures go to see bioscopes and turn into whores.'[10]

It is these young boys and girls that we meet in our second novel as we become privy to what the younger college-educated generation is thinking and feeling. *Gharaunda* (Little House) is the first novel by the prolific Rangeya Raghav (1923–1962). Raghav was at St John's College, studying for his last year of the BA when he wrote this novel,

[8] SB, 55, 103.
[9] Ibid.: 106.
[10] Ibid.: 107.

just as is Bhagvati, the wide-eyed village youth, prime protagonist of the novel, with whose entry into college the novel begins and with whose melodramatic decisions about life and love it ends. The plot, often meandering and convoluted, revolves around a group of young people, who befriend Bhagvati, students of St John's College—called Mission College in the novel.[11] The number of girls entering college has increased dramatically that year, changing the very tone of the college, as the principal's secretary laments: 'A hundred and twenty girls this year as match for two hundred and seventy-five boys. Enough is enough Sahib! Last year, there were just seventy-eight, before that fifty-seven.'[12] Mission College is not only teeming with girls, it is equipped with sophisticated science laboratories and a well-stocked library, disdainful English professors, and more malleable native ones. The full spectrum of contemporary political discourses is represented here: the slogans of the Indian National Congress, of Hindu right wing forces, Gandhian social service, Christian missionary invective, but also the views of the Communist Party of India, trendy amongst the progressively minded youth. Most of all, the campus is rife with discussion—about life, love, politics, the future of the nation-to-be—carried on in the Students' Union. The fervent nationalism of the preceding decades has receded. The four friends with whom Bhagvati associates seek worldly success rather than any kind of fulfilment in nation-building. Several social butterflies inhabit the scene: Lila Ray and her friend Lavang, glittering with surface anglicization; they drive their own expensive cars and move freely in society. There is wealthy Indira, also anglicized, but willing to be tutored by Bhagvati in classical India and classical Indian dance—Shantiniketan is mentioned, as also Uday Shankar. She will ultimately pair with him.

The provocative, almost cynical views of Indira and Usha, the dry

---

[11] The novel was written and published, apparently to some acclaim, while Raghav was still a student at the College. As to the date of its composition, internal evidence, such as the mention of the World War and the fall of France, suggests that it was begun at least in 1940 and completed shortly thereafter.

[12] Raghav [1940/1941] 2008: 5.

intellectual, on love and marriage, questioning conventional notions, are echoed in one form or another by most girls in college. Usha mocks Indira's love for Bhagvati:

> 'Your love will last only as long as Bhagvati doesn't bow his head before you. The moment he is defeated and extends his hand, you'll suddenly remember you are the daughter of a wealthy man and that not every man has the right to love you. In your case, it is about class-love. Would you dare marry Bhagvati?'
>
> Indira hardened. Her mouth had opened a bit, as if the heat of retaliation had distorted even her innards. Pressing back into the chair she said, 'So marriage is the climax of love for you? One can't love without marriage?'[13]

Much later another noteworthy conversation breaks yet more taboos. The words of daring are put into the mouth of Lila, a mindlessly westernized and thus morally suspect woman who nonetheless plays an important role in Bhagvati's life, for she is also prey to passion for our hero. She is speaking to Vir Singh, a man who is once again somewhat morally suspect, but given to reflection. Lila says:

> 'Woman has had her neck wrung repeatedly simply because she is called "mother". I've read in the *Mahabharata*, at one time women were as free as cows . . . The *Mahabharata* is considered the fifth Veda, but just as the four Vedas could not save woman from the hateful darkness of social norms, just so the ultimately submissive *Mahabharata*, for all its arrogance, could not save her . . . Man has trapped her in the web of satihood.'
>
> Vir Singh was startled. He had never thought that an Indian girl would dare speak such hard truths. But he said nothing. He just listened.
>
> 'Satihood says that sexual intercourse is sin, that is, the laws of nature are sin, that is, the *maya* dealt out by his god is sin, that is, that man is sinful, in that case the Puranas made by man are also the outgrowth of sin. Only look at the way England's puritans talk. They give the woman

---

[13] Ibid.: 25.

just one license—that you receive a single husband, like a single bicycle. Whether she cares for the man or hates him, she circumambulates the primal fire; she signs on to that [marriage] license with the blood drawn from her heart. This license means that against her will, she dances naked through the nights with him . . .'[14]

The social daring of the auctorial voice of the young Rangeya Raghav gets this far but goes no further, granting women like Lila extraordinary freedom of expression but no immediate satisfaction. Ultimately, it is the *sati*-like figure whom both the plot and society will reward. For our purposes, however, it is important to note that if on the one hand Seth Bankemal is holding forth on the ways of the modern woman, on the other hand this kind of discourse is also coursing through college campuses on the other side of Raja Mandi in early 1940s Agra. Regardless of the values that they have inherited and internalized, the young men and women on campus have begun to question the roles allotted to them by society, and to find the language to express these ideas and sentiments, not only in the poetic diction of novels such as *Nadi ke Dvip* but also in their everyday speech. The structures of feeling have undergone a major shift. 'One generation may train its successor, with reasonable success, in the social character or the general cultural pattern, but the new generation will have its own structure of feeling, which will not appear to have come "from" anywhere.'[15]

THE CULTURE OF THE CITY AND THE HINDI LITERATI

As elsewhere in the post-Mughal cities of North India (with the exception of Banaras, as we have seen), literary Hindi had a relatively shallow presence in Agra. This is worth keeping in mind because we noted when discussing *Pariksha Guru* that the early Hindi fiction-writers consistently invoked the origin of Hindi in the speech of

[14] Ibid.: 113ff.
[15] Williams [1961] 1965: 65.

Delhi and Agra, *Dilli-Agre ki Boli*. Notwithstanding the vicinity of the Braj area with its vivid poetry in the literary idiom that came to bear the name of the region, the high literary languages of the city, as would be expected of an erstwhile capital of the Mughals, had been Persian and later Urdu in its heyday. The British arrival in the city—Lord Lake's army took over the city in 1803—had brought with it much bustle and several new administrative instances and institutions. From 1836 till immediately after the uprising, that is, since 1858, Agra was the seat of the lieutenant governor of the North Western Provinces. The High Court, with its attendant offices, remained here till 1868, whence it was moved to Allahabad. From the 1830s there was increased missionary activity; both the American Presbyterian Mission and the Church Missionary Society were active in the region, producing a spate of tracts and school books in Urdu and in Hindi. The Agra Government set up its own press in the late 1840s; the Agra Book Society was established in 1835. Agra became one of the centres of publishing, particularly educational publishing. A number of lithographic presses, of which sixteen were owned and operated by Indians, were set up before 1850. They did job printing for the government, but also put out Urdu newspapers and journals. However, this did not initiate literary activity of any note in Hindi, nor is there any indication of the presence of a Hindi-speaking intelligentsia in the city.[16] The *sant*-discourse of the Radhasoamis, we may recall, was just beginning to create a stir in the mid-1850s. All said and done, Agra in the nineteenth and early twentieth century was far more an important centre of Muslim intellectual life and debate and of Urdu poetry.[17] Ghalib, as is well known, fled the city, but the poems of Nazir Akbarabadi (died 1830), beloved poet of the

---

[16] The Nagari script was used for school texts and Tulsidas' *Ramayana* was published as early as 1851. See Stark 2007: 52.

[17] Avril Powell has written about the intense debates of the Protestant Pietistic missionaries with a range of Islamic representatives, foremost the ulama, focusing in particular on the debates in Agra and Lucknow in the 1840s, culminating in the 'Great Debate' of 1854 in Agra. Powell 1993.

city, became part of popular life. Creativity in an explicitly Hindi discourse was slow in coming.

Though there was sporadic activity in modern Hindi publishing from the middle of the nineteenth century, it was only from the 1920s that it acquired critical mass. And even then, as Yadav himself points out in a perceptive essay, the leading citizens in any given North Indian city or town till well into the mid-century—whether lawyer, civil servant, professor, surgeon, or doctor—tended to be Bengali *bhadralok*. It was possible for Sharat Chandra Chattopadhyay (1876–1938), the most popular Bengali writer of his time, to set his novel *Shesh Prashna* (The Final Question; 1931) in contemporary Agra, without mentioning anything local (the Taj Mahal does crop up in one scene).[18] There were few Hindi intellectuals and authors worth mentioning even in the first decades of the twentieth century. Of the Hindi journals that emerged thereafter, there were *Samalochak*, *Yuvak*, edited by Ranvir Chauhan, and most noteworthy was a weekly, *Sainik* (Soldier), established by Krishnadatta Paliwal in 1925.[19] This was aggressively nationalist, attracting contributors who were becoming leading voices in the Hindi world, and from the 1930s also a series of distinguished editors, including Agyeya for a short period.

Rajendra Yadav provides a vivid picture of the intellectual and literary life of the city, alive and bustling by the late 1930s, in his memoirs. The times were tumultuous, politically and socially. The Indian National Army (INA) trials in the Red Fort in Delhi rocked the nation; the Indian Navy revolt in the last days of the War, and the mass meetings organized by Aruna Asaf Ali and Jayaprakash Narayan dominated the discussions of the day. The loose assortment of writers, poets, and intellectuals who had constituted the progressive camp

---

[18] Yadav 1997: 53. This becomes clearest in the short article on the history of the journals and newspapers of the city by Sikarwar (2011: 314-15).

[19] *Sainik* became a daily in 1939. The files of this journal would surely go a long way towards reconstructing the intellectual history of this period, as much as of literary life in the city.

was moving towards sharply marked polemics by the end of the War, with sparks flowing in all directions. The Hindi literati of Agra, as elsewhere in North India, were splintering into groups around figures who attracted their own following, with the student community splitting at the same time. Many who would go on to acquire a wider reputation lived in clusters in the same neighbourhoods in Agra.[20] The cosmopolitan Rangeya Raghav—novelist, aesthete, philosopher— formed one pole of attraction for students; those who were outward looking (*unmukta*) and creative migrated towards him. The more academically inclined were pulled into the circle surrounding Ramvilas Sharma (1912–2000), a brilliant young intellectual who lived in Nayi Raja Mandi for many years and taught in the English Department of Rajput College. His vitriolic pen, his articles in Amrit Rai's progressive journal *Haṃs*, systematically demolished, one after the other, the progressive claims of the famous Chhayavadi poet-turned-Progressive Sumitranandan Pant, of Rahul Sankrityayan, Rangeya Raghav, and Shivdan Singh Chauhan (the ideologue of the early Progressives discussed in the previous essay, on *Gunahom ka Devata*).

It was into this scene that Yadav moved, when he came to live in the family haveli in Raja Mandi, which had been in his family for generations, in order to study in the famous Agra College, then still in its heyday. The haveli would provide the setting for his most famous novel. It echoed the history of the city: Akbar's famous courtier Raja Todar Mal was supposed to have built it, it was said to have a tunnel connecting it to the Fort. Yadav's pigeon-flying uncle maintained a fleet of birds on a part of its extensive roof, even as he ran a shop

---

[20] The enormously talented and productive author Amritlal Nagar lived in Gokulpura, bordering on Raja Mandi, as did Rangeya Raghav. Others, Padmasingh Sharma 'Kamlesh', Ghanshyam Asthana, Prakash Dikshit, Rajnath, Rajendra Sharma and Yadav himself also lived there or in Rajamandi. Prabhakar Machwe was studying in Agra College. Rajendra Raghuvanshi, leading member of the Indian People's Theatre Association (IPTA), was incredibly active; making Agra rather than Delhi the centre of theatrical activity.

that sold wall paint on the ground floor of the building. Situated thus in the heart of this intersection of old and new, Yadav was fortunate enough to remain in active communication with both sides of the literary and intellectual divide, the politically progressive as well as the literary-creative. Sharma and his cohort provided intellectual stimulation while Rangeya Raghav was a close friend; he designed the cover for Yadav's second book. The 1940s and 1950s were heady decades and it seemed as if Agra was all set to become one of the intellectual citadels of the day. But Ramvilas Sharma's destructive pen would eventually wreak havoc in the Hindi literary community, particularly in Agra. As Yadav put it, 'We felt very fired up at the time and had no idea then for how long this process would lay Agra waste' (*Us samay badi uttenjana lagti thi aur tab koi anuman nahim tha ki yah silsila Agra ko kab tak ke liye banjar banake rakh dega*).[21]

In the meantime, Yadav had embarked on a long and successful career, eventually acquiring a lasting reputation as a member of the movement that came to be known as the *nai kahani* (new short story) movement.[22] He would also emerge as its most vocal theorist. '*Nai kahani*,' according to him, 'saw the individual with his background (*pithika*) and context (*parivesh*), it was an attempt to see him in his social reality.'[23] Projected as a new kind of realism, harking back deliberately to Premchand rather than to its immediate predecessors, Agyeya or Jainendra, the *nai kahani* movement was a modernist rather than a modern enterprise, the confident social reform tones of earlier storytellers, such as those of Premchand himself and even Yashpal, having given way to the kind of open-ended doubt we saw in *Nadi ke Dvip* and *Gunahom ka Devata*. Focused more on inner rather than external events, this generation of writers seemed to be questioning all received notions, even reformist ones, gravitating towards universalist rather than nationalist or even regional ideas,

[21] Yadav 2001: 58-9.
[22] And later still, as the very active and creative editor of Premchand's journal, *Haṃs*, which he revived so successfully.
[23] In Yadav 1988: 45.

subscribing rather 'to the delights and dangers of rootlessness and the relationships between cosmopolitanism and global capitalism.'[24]

To which we would add global socialism. This might not have been the genealogy that the *nai kahani* writers themselves acknowledged, they resisted Agyeya, Jainendra, and others who immediately preceded them, but they were their successors and therefore impacted by many of the same literary currents, social forces, and political events, even if with a temporal gap—the Second World War, Hiroshima, the Cold War, the Existentialists, the Russian classics that Soviet propaganda let loose upon the rapidly forming Third World,[25] and, nearer home, Partition and Independence. The *nai kahani* writers, including Mohan Rakesh (the subject of the next essay), did not belong to the same generation as Agyeya or the much younger Bharati. But even though they resisted Agyeya, even though in their work there was no reference to 'nature', their habitat being rather the urban, there were considerable overlaps in their thinking. The *nai kahani* writers were also concerned with interiorities, in exploring notions of the self and the fine web of relationships with spouses and partners rather than the social and political conflict encountered in *Karmabhumi* and *Jhutha Sach*, and the narration of events in chronological order. This, however, did not mean that they remained unaffected by the politics of the day.

As Yadav's first novel shows, the new nation was struggling to find its feet, the first general elections with universal adult suffrage—a monumental enterprise—would be held in the winter of 1951–2. The debates in the newly elected parliament regarding the long awaited Hindu Code Bill would be discussed in the Press as much as in coffee houses and private conversations. The projected changes in the position of daughters and wives, of women moving into the profes-

[24] Lewis 2011: 2.

[25] Rajendra Yadav attended the Progressive writers meeting regularly (it used to be held nearby in Gokulpura) and read Russian writing voraciously: Tolstoy, Dostoeyevski, Gogol, and most of all Chekhov, whose short stories and plays he also translated. Interview, 26.12. 2012.

sional world in various capacities, affected the *nai kahani* writers and the characters that peopled their imagination. And, not surprisingly, under these changed circumstances the very structures of feeling changed.

MARRIAGE, INDIVIDUAL AMBITIONS, AND LIFE IN THE HAVELI

Sara Akash (The Vast Sky; 1960) is set in the heart of Agra, in a haveli in an unnamed *mohalla* very like the writer's own in Raja Mandi. The first version of this two-part novel was written in 1951, to be revised and published in its final form under the present title almost ten years later. It was written, Yadav recalls, after the runaway success of his long short story *Khel Khilaune* (Games and Toys), published in Agyeya's avant-garde journal *Pratik* (which ran from 1949 to 1952–3). A first person narrative set in the late 1940s, *Khel Khilaune* is a story filtered through two male perceptions, that of the narrator, whose sister wishes to study further but is being pressed into marriage, and that of his beautiful young woman friend, to whom he was devoted and who was similarly pressed into marriage. Academically brilliant and progressive, with multi-faceted talents, with eyes as deep and boundless as the open sky (*khula akash*),[26] this young woman was married against her will and forced into a life of mindless luxury and mundane domesticity. Suffocated and deeply unhappy, she doused herself with kerosene and set herself on fire within months of her marriage. The ambition, as much as the newly discovered talents, of such educated young women was tearing the social fabric of family life with new claims. These young women were attractive to many and sympathetically viewed by the young men who related their tales; their tragedy lay in the fact that within the confines of marriage these very men turned conservative and often broke their will, just as, in the short story, a child playing with a china Buddha figure ultimately shatters it to bits.

[26] Yadav 1980: 89.

As Yadav relates it, after the success of *Khel Khilaune* Agyeya asked him for another story of the same kind. This second attempt grew into a novel published under the title *Pret Bolte Haim* (Ghosts Tell their Tale) in 1951, which received bare critical notice at the time.[27] The novel was shot through by the same theme as the short story. Its frame had been inspired by the advent of the radio, a medium newly becoming popular in urban households, from which unembodied, ghostly voices seemed to emerge at odd times of the day. The author imagined the voices of the young protagonists of his novel—a man, his sister, and his wife—driven by rigid family structures to an early death, speaking from the world beyond, as radio voices almost, to tell their stories. Though surreal in its frame, the stories are all too real, grounded in a harsh everyday from which the young man, ambitious but unable to find employment, eventually escapes into suicide. The women had also escaped into death, driven by family violence; the sister had suffered a dowry death, the wife had been forced into satihood—in both instances it was death by fire.[28] Agyeya asked the

---

[27] Yadav 2001: 60. *Pret Bolte Haim* was published by Pragati Prakashan, run from an M.P.'s house—35 Ferozeshah Road, New Delhi, to be precise. It carries a long personal introduction, which begins with a description of the arrival of the radio in the neighbourhood and its eager adoption by the author's brothers, who construct so many receivers that the sound carries to every room of the house, disembodied voices which intrude into the routine of everyday life and dislocate the day. This remarkable beginning is put into brackets, but it forms the frame of the narrative and determines its mode. The second important incident is the eyewitness account of the remains of a youth who committed suicide by throwing himself in front of a train. The young writer, who is studying for his exams, is haunted by the head rolling on the rail tracks, severed at the lower lip from the rest of the body. The story of the young man who did not speak to his wife for nine years is that of a friend. Thus, much personal reminiscence, as yet only partially processed, is woven into the story.

[28] I am grateful to Sanjeev Kumar for drawing my attention to Balwant Kaur's perceptive article (2014), which notes that Rajendra Yadav mentions a similar incident in Gwalior at the time. Kaur remarks on the replacement of the surrealist frame of the first version by the realist (*yatharth*) of the

young author to drop the verbose beginning and end, with which request Yadav stubbornly refused to comply at the time.

Almost a decade later, in 1960, he did precisely that: drop the radio frame, drop the violent end of husband and wife, though not that of the sister, and publish the now tighter version under the title *Sara Akash*. The poet Ramdharisingh Dinkar's (1908–1974) rousing lines, heralding the break of the new nation's dawn, inspired the title of the reworked novel:

> O soldier, take fearless leave, all future history is yours
> The stars of the new-moon night grow dim; the vast sky is yours

Yet, when the vast sky figures in the novel, it is as a last resource, its vastness offering succour to those crammed in the tiny dark rooms of the haveli in the narrow lanes of the inner city. The slim novel attracted immediate notice; it was to be made into a film by Basu Chatterjee, acclaimed, in its turn, as the first of a new wave in Hindi cinema.[29] It captured a deeply poignant moment in the history of the individual, of young Samar, caught in a tight web of relationships—to a wife, the

---

final one. My own reading is that the realism of this later version moves in the modernist direction rather than the 'modern' of the first. There cannot be any simple resolutions to the dilemma faced by the young protagonists, through whichever version we look at their emotional crises. It is noteworthy that the women's perspective remains filtered through that of the young man connected to them in both versions.

[29] Kathryn Hansen's review of the film as relating to the novel provides some sense not only of its impact and of its focus but also of the aspects the film chose to stress, that of family relationships and the reasons why the several members of the joint family persecuted Prabha. It concentrated on the first part of the novel and concluded with the scene on the roof, introducing yet another angle to view the action, now transported into the late 1960s/early 1970s: '. . . an intriguing critique of the popular Hindi film and the powerful, even stunning effect it exerts upon its youthful audience. While the germ of this theme is present in Yadav's novel, Chatterjee has developed it much further, using techniques of juxtaposition and overlapping of sound unique to the film medium.' Hansen 1981: 19.

extended family, community, and nation—but isolated in his attempt to discover and realize his potential within the possibilities offered by the social and political frames of his specific time and place.

The meagre income of the elder of the three brothers, bolstered somewhat by the father's scanty pension, is barely sufficient for the survival of the eight-member family, to which is being added Samar's new bride. It already supports the elder brother's wife, small child, his parents, his two brothers who are both still studying, and a sister seeking escape from a tyrannical marriage. The family can only pin its hopes on the income that Samar and eventually also his much younger brother will generate once they complete their studies.

Samar is rebellious and resistant. As the first person narrator he is also the protagonist, the narrative being focalized entirely through him. This first person narrative gives him a voice and the possibility of maintaining 'the traditional fiction of a narrator who must appear more or less to discover the story at the same time that he tells it.' And of recording 'the perceptual activity of the character contemplating: of his impressions, progressive discoveries, shifts in distance and perspective, errors and corrections, enthusiasms or disappointments etc. A contemplation highly active in truth and containing a whole story.'[30] Samar's inner life and changing relationship to wife and family comprise the first part; the events in the second part are dotted by extensive discursive sections that enter his emotional life and inflect his reactions, thus making them a part of his consciousness and, mediated through him, that of his wife Prabha.

The novel presents two visions of the nation and personal destiny as linked with it. The first vision reflects the nationalist myth of the 1950s, of surging ahead, of nation-building shot through, in our case, with militant RSS rhetoric of self-sacrifice and achievement. Being a man, proving one's mettle, gaining recognition, and winning a place in society, is closely coupled with Hindu nationalist aspirations. Eventually, the two identities, the erstwhile nationalist and

---

[30] Genette 1980: 67, 102.

Illus. 26: Sangh Drill

the Hindu communal, merge to galvanize a weakening enthusiasm for the nation.[31]

The second is less a vision, more a perspective coloured by the disillusionment which had set in by the early 1950s and gathered force

---

[31] Cf. Balibar: 'To grasp the deepest reasons for this effectiveness [nationalistic feeling], attention will turn then, as the attention of political philosophy and sociology have turned for three centuries, towards the analogy of *religion*, making nationalism and patriotism out to be a *religion*—if not indeed the religion—of modern times. Every national community must have been represented at some point or another as a 'chosen people'. Nevertheless, the political philosophies of the Classical Age had already recognized the inadequacy of this analogy, which is equally clearly demonstrated by the failure of attempts to constitute 'civil religions'. By the fact that 'state religion' ultimately only constituted a transitory form of national ideology (even when this transition lasted a long time and produced important effects by superimposing religious on national struggles) and by the interminable conflict between theological universality and the universality of nationalism ... to understand why national identity, more or less completely integrating the forms of religious identity, ends up trying to replace it, and forcing it itself to become "nationalized".' Balibar 1991: 95. Its quasi-religious character

by the 1960s, of a nation disintegrating and barely held together, of social structures struggling out of older moulds, of men as well as women on the verge of questioning the claims of the nation, Indian-Hindu civilization, and the family. The second part of the novel unfolds this vision, and to some critics it has seemed to have been superimposed upon the older vision, which had apparently provided the original creative impulse.[32] In my reading, the two are closely interwoven; one would be incomplete without the other, for the second part of the novel systematically dismantles the worldview and belief systems of the first and is the necessary complement to it. The conflicting worldviews of the two sections of Raja Mandi represent the ideologies of two generations, that of the older, caught in a time warp, of the world depicted so wonderfully in *Seth Bankemal*, that uses satire as a tool, as a double-edged sword, the serrated edges of which saw at the old as much as the new. And that of modern youth, as reflected in the sharp intellectual debate and the discussions tearing though the campus, the cafés and hostel rooms, of Agra's famous colleges, as represented so vividly in *Gharaunda*.

The first part of the novel is titled 'The First Half: Evening, The Ten Directions, without Answers'. As it opens, the camera zooms in to focus upon Samar, left alone for a moment. There is commotion

---

makes nationalism, particularly when it seems to be losing its hold on people's imagination, more than amenable to being hitched to religion again, to being hyphenated with it.

[32] Vishwanath Tripathi in his otherwise moving and astute essay on the novel goes so far as to say: 'The first part of *Sara Akash* is a long short story. In filming just this part, Basu Chatterjee sealed it as a short story. The fact that the second part is just Samar's story doesn't make it into a novel. Samar is here a completely different character, struggling with a completely different problem. In the first half, he is a Premchand character. In the second, he is not even an Agyeya, Jainendra Kumar, Ilachand Joshi character; he is a character stemming from some foreign existentialist thinker. The situation is a realist one, the characters are non-realist.' Tripathi 2011: 167. As I have tried to show, the novel is a modernist one, not completely tied to a realist mode. It is self-reflexive and open-ended.

elsewhere—flames in the house opposite, smoke issuing from its windows, a young wife has immolated herself. While in this house, a marriage has taken place and a youth dreams of deeds of future glory:

> Never have I to forget that I have to become someone, someone before whom the world will bow, a single word from whom will be a command to the nation, who can free Mother India from the bonds of foreign infidels. India is the country of great men. The blood of Rana Pratap and Shivaji flows in my veins, I have not to put it to shame. It's we who have to keep going, to keep alive their tradition, to maintain the flow which protects their *samskriti*, culture. We are the youth (of today). Even to this day, there are a thousand Buddhas, Mahavirswamis, Krishnas and Ramas within us. We have to awaken them and bring them forward. It is our strength which will bear forth Hanuman, Bhima and Bhishma today. I continue to stand steadfast by my oath of observing lifelong celibacy, even today . . .[33]

This *brahmacharya* has no connection with Gandhi's notions of satyagraha. Samar is a member of the right wing RSS. The foreign infidels may have left the country, but the motherland still needs protection. The nation claims the individual. As Lydia Liu has noted, 'In order for the nation-state to claim the individual in some "unmediated" fashion, the individual must be "liberated": in the first place from the family, clan, or other traditional ties that claim his or her loyalty.'[34] This nationalist sense of needing to abstract himself from his family, however uncomfortable at times, stays with Samar through the course of the narrative, albeit in changing forms. He is in his second year of college and the day he speaks of is a very special one, for his wedding has just been celebrated. His dreams of glory seem destined to be shattered by the demands of mundane domesticity. The visions of ascetic militancy will persist into the next months, to be juxtaposed with a hope not entirely to be suppressed,

---

[33] Yadav [1960] 2000: 21.
[34] Liu 1995: 90.

of companionate marriage. Now that marriage has been foisted upon him, he muses even at the beginning, he has at any events to complete his MA, which means another four years of college. But if he stays away from his bride for this period, what will she do, where will she live? He is straining to cultivate himself; perhaps she can be of help: 'Someone was saying she is very educated, very intelligent. Can't my whole point of view be explained to her? Suppose, sometime in the future, we have to lead a domestic life, this period could prepare us for that. I should look at her face at least.'[35] Prabha, the new bride, is a matriculate; this is unusual in her social set-up. A wife need not always be a hindrance; can Rama's power (*shakti*) be separated from Sita's? Had Rajput wives not sent their husbands into battlefields? There is hope that she will support his ambition if he is able to keep his vow.

This hope is rudely shattered as he enters the nuptial chamber. Prabha is not on the bed, huddled and waiting. She is standing as if glued to the window and remains standing, her back turned to him. She doesn't greet him, doesn't make as if to touch his feet: so much for educated wives, they are arrogant and unbending. Incandescent with humiliation, he flees her presence, so there is no consummation of the marriage, which is scandalous. He is confirmed in his resolve never to speak to her, she will have to fend for herself.

The joint family watches these goings-on with consternation. The tide turns against Prabha who, adding insult to injury, has brought the family very little by way of dowry. Samar's parents are shocked by her ways. True, she works in the house obediently and silently, but her ways are not theirs: she refuses to observe purdah. She cooks with a watch tied around her wrist. No wonder the first meal she serves Samar and the family is over-salted. But watch or no watch, the burden of taking care of the household now falls heavily on her. Samar holds fast by his resolution, a complex mix of the resolve to retain his ascetic, RSS-driven *brahmacharya* ideology and resentment

---

[35] Yadav [1960] 2000: 21.

of Prabha's proud hold of herself. He ignores her existence altogether; he has no sense of when she wakes up, when she goes to bed. The illiterate and less attractive elder sister-in-law schemes against her. The classic joint family situation—breaking in the youngest entrant into the family, who is naturally placed at the bottom of the pecking order—makes for a series of exercises in patience for Prabha, hard work and toil calculated to drive her to breaking point. The family disenfranchises her in various ways, such as by reading her letters before handing them to her.

The only support Prabha finds comes from Munni, the married sister who lives with them, a more or less abandoned wife bound to a wastrel—a scoundrel of a whoring husband. One day, Munni's husband turns up to fetch her; the family holds council. Munni's pitiful cries can't save her. Munni's place is at the side of her husband, good or bad, and she leaves, shedding bitter tears. Prabha is left entirely alone now. The haveli structure, with its web of small and often windowless rooms opening into each other and then onto a series of courtyards—the centripetal heart of family life where all is observed, all discussed and regulated by the women of the family, bolstered by the men—leaves little space for manoeuvre. There is little to no room for withdrawal, solitary rumination, or intimacy.

On the roof or out of the narrow windows of the house that looks out on the narrow lanes of the city, Prabha gazes in despair at the sky. Samar is privileged enough; he can retreat into his tiny study which opens onto the rooftop and the vast sky. The rooftop is a special place, it adjoins other rooftops, allows a bird's eye view of other courtyards, a space that makes possible many kinds of freedoms in summer, winter, even the monsoons. In searing summer nights the family lines up its beds here, and in the severe North Indian winter one can sun oneself in the afternoons; in the kite-flying season boys run across it unspooling kite string, pigeon flyers house their birds here. Prabha seeks refuge here as often as she can legitimately escape family scrutiny, or thinks she can. One day, Samar overhears his parents' cruel remarks

Illus. 27: Raja Mandi Lane, Agra

about this alienating habit. She even takes the daal platter to the rooftop to pick over and clear the debris from the lentils, says his father. Washes her hair in the winter sun. How will she flirt with the neighbours if she doesn't sit there, says his mother, it's a mercy she hasn't run away with someone. Just the other day Pandeji's elder daughter eloped with a boy from the *mohalla*, says her husband. We ought to be grateful for all that these educated girls neglect to do, the mother says to the *bhabhi*, Samar's sister-in-law, who never fails to put in a good word for her sister-in-law.[36]

Samar and Prabha are all the same luckier than most young couples. Through and in spite of the turmoil of joint family life,

[36] Ibid.: 83.

the anxieties and jealousies, they find their way to each other and to companionship. It is with their tearful union on the roof, under the moonlit sky where Samar discovers her—a shadow in white, cowering against a wall and crying—that the first part of the work ends: on the rooftop.

INTIMACY, SELF-EXCLUSION, AND INDIVIDUAL ENDEAVOUR

The very title of the second part of the novel, 'The Last Half: Morning, the Ten Directions, Question-torn', suggests the quandaries Samar and Prabha face as they wake up into their golden dawn. Samar, focused on his newly found relationship, has little time now to go to the *bauddhik*, the regular discussion sessions of the RSS, though the indoctrination takes time to erode. The young couple often retreat into the intimacy of Samar's room. The romantic love that so many couples, educated by novels and now also films, find after marriage,[37] is viewed with downright hostility by the family, which wants no rupture of its tightly controlled structure. The couple's intimacy is similarly viewed by the rest of the family. 'Life in older, locally dense social systems was characterized by complex networks of relationships which blocked any self-exclusion by individuals, as also a "private life" or any retreat into a closely paired relationship. One was expected

---

[37] Cf. Raychaudhuri: 'Romantic love appears to have flourished more after marriage than as a pre-marital emotional experience leading to happy union. There is plentiful evidence to prove that a new intensity of emotion in conjugal relationship, for which there is little precedent in the pre-modern past, was now a part of the bhadralok's life experience. The greater intimacy made possible by the household set-up of the bureaucrats and professionals in urban and suburban areas, new sensibilities generated by a complex set of circumstances and the expectations informed by exposure to romantic literature, western and Indian, all contributed to an ambience of romance in marriage... Bankim's description of playful to intense attachment and his confession of his immense debt to his wife are all parts of a vast body of available documentation bearing on a new feeling for one's partner in marriage.' Raychaudhuri 1990: 86.

to share one's life with the community that was the family and live within an inviolable framework of understanding shared by all.'[38] One after another, the problems the couple face demand some resolution. Samar's decision to study further is barely tolerated and that too, only because he has taken up paid employment in a typesetting unit and his meagre income means some support for the sorely pressed family.

All that happened to Prabha was observed and communicated to us by Samar, filtered through his fantasy, and later his perception. He himself wonders later: she was an educated woman, didn't she have ambition, visions of her own personal destiny?[39] Here at last we hear Prabha's own voice, for she has now begun to speak to Samar:

> 'I have a class-fellow.' Forgetting all else in her enthusiasm, she began to tell me about her college friend Rama, winding up with, 'When I went home this time, she was asking me all kinds of things about you. We used to be the naughtiest girls in class. She is a very close friend of mine. We used to think to ourselves, we'll never marry, we'll study a lot and then go to villages and teach women there. Sometimes we thought we'd take light baggage and tour all of Hindustan on foot and keep a detailed diary. We'd meet all kinds of new people in towns and villages. We'd make plans to learn how to fight with knives and sticks to protect ourselves from bad characters and wild animals. And, sitting there, talking, God knows what other plans we made. Our families and friends would get really annoyed with us when they heard us chatter on so endlessly. But that only made us want to tease them the more.'[40]

Gandhian ideals of village uplift were current and legitimate enough for girls in the 1940s. What of these plans now? Prabha has blurted out her dreams, but she adds hastily, 'Forget all I've said. All I want now is that you study a lot. I'll do whatever you tell me.' The

---

[38] Luhmann [1982] 1998: 32.

[39] A pained Samar now admits that Prabha's letters are opened with his knowledge and tacit collusion and that the letters only reached her if they were passed by the family censorship board. Yadav [1960] 2000: 116.

[40] Ibid.: 138.

family's dire financial needs make it clear enough that Samar cannot really continue his education. Should Prabha become a *mastarni-vastarni*, a teacher, in some school, in order to support him? Samar breaks out in panic, 'Don't you breathe a word of this to anyone. If this reaches mother or *bhabhi*, there will be such a storm that the commotion on the day you cooked with your wristwatch strapped on will pale in comparison.' Later, rummaging in her trunk, he comes across her books: *Lives of Great Men*, Gandhi's *Autobiography*, a conduct book for women, and Premchand's *Rangbhumi*.

But Prabha wants more than just to ameliorate the lot of her fellow countrymen. In a long letter to Rama, which was never posted, she also expresses her dreams of companionate marriage and a life of prosperity in a bungalow in an urban setting: 'My husband will be a professor, or an official somewhere, the manager of some big firm. Just he and I, there'll be just the two of us, not the noise and clutter of mother-in-law, brother-in-law, nieces and nephews, no one at all. There'll be a big fat building, of the most modern kind. Wherever I see a piece of furniture I like, I adorn my dream house with it. Paint, colour, polish, curtains, here an evergreen *mehndi* hedge encircling a lawn, there a tennis and badminton court. Three or four servants.'[41] The epistle is a common enough device to allow a character to speak and enable the reader to get an unmediated glimpse of her most intimate thoughts. Here it is her vision of domestic love, set in a European-style bungalow, the dream of an inner-city girl for escape to a wider, more generous space: '. . . the influence of the bungalow, understood as a separate, single-storey, single-household dwelling is that, in contrast to these multi-household forms, it is a form of dwelling, usually owned by its inhabitants, with no one living above, at the side or below. It is also a "modern" form of dwelling for a Western-type nuclear family, or in some cases only one generation of it, in contrast to the more "traditional" dwelling forms associated with the extended or joint family.'[42] Prabha's books will probably

[41] Ibid.: 118.
[42] King 1984: 3.

remain locked in her trunk, her dreams have already been entirely subsumed in Samar's. She will look to him for guidance and do as he says, trying to balance the increasingly violent demands of the family with those of this new emotional allegiance.

HINDU DHARMA, CIVILIZATION, AND THE UNDIVIDED HINDU FAMILY

What makes this novel unusual is its own reflection upon itself and it is with this that the second part is also concerned. The second is less compact than the first; the narration of Samar and Prabha's gradual discovery of each other's emotional life, their ventures into creating their own future, and the ensuing family violence is punctuated by regular reverie and discussion.

Samar's meeting with Shirish early in Section Two and their conversations, which he communicates to Prabha, break the narrative, making for its self-reflexive tone; they serve as a commentary on family life and the nation, a critique and an analysis which Samar and Prabha gradually internalize. No more euphoria, no new break of dawn for the nation; instead, urban struggles for survival. Samar is plagued by doubt as he tries to establish his claims. What place can individual ambitions have *vis-à-vis* Hindu society (*samaj*), Hindu dharma, Hindu culture (*samskriti*), and the Hindu undivided family? Shirish soon begins to function as Samar's alter-ego, the voice of reason and progressive thinking—once again the voice of the Pragativad (discussed in the previous essay), or the voice of the other side of Raja Mandi. Samar first meets Shirish at the employment office, where he has gone to look at job postings to find some kind of work. A clean-shaven, fair skinned gentleman with unoiled hair, wearing spotless white pyjamas and a muslin kurta so fine that his vest peeps through, we learn later that he is a clerk in a government office, earning well enough, Rs 150 per month. Shirish sizes up Samar with a single glance, addressing him mockingly as 'Svayamsevakji'. His few comments on the political situation penetrate deep into Samar's consciousness. The solemnity on the faces of the leaders of the country is hypocritical and masks their absolute selfishness: they promise jobs that never materialize. Samar's dream of becoming someone 'solitary and great' begins to fall apart. 'From Dayanand to Shivaji, Rabindranath Tagore, Gandhi and Jawaharlal, which one of them hasn't figured as an idol for me?'[43]

Shirish turns out to be the cousin of whom his close friend Divakar has spoken so often—thus he is addressed as *bhai* (brother).[44] At their second meeting emerges the tragic tale of Shirish's sister, who has fallen into such a state of depression that she has had to be confined in a mental asylum. She was married at the age of eleven or twelve and proved too uneducated for her husband. As things stood before the new Hindu Code Bill, a daughter once married had no legal way back into her natal home except if she were abandoned or widowed. Hearing her tale, Samar felt he was speaking of the plight of his own sister Munni. Shirish Bhai was waiting for the Hindu Code Bill to be passed so that he could procure a divorce for her and get her remarried. Samar is shocked to the core. Does Shirish Bhai consider divorce, and the right of the daughter to inherit a part of her father's property, legitimate? Would it not weaken fraternal feeling within the family if daughters and sisters started staking their claims to property?[45] Samar voices many of the parliamentary debates over the Bill, regarded as a radical intervention in the existing Hindu social code—which presupposed natural affection within families sufficing for property matters rather than a legal securing, papering over the fact that natural affection worked invariably to the advantage of patriarchs and men.[46] Shirish Bhai's argument, that she would no longer have to depend on her brother's goodwill in order to have a

[43] Quotes from 114 and 115 respectively.
[44] Ibid.: 121.
[45] Ibid.: 123.
[46] Madhu Kishwar has recorded the often sentimental tenor of the debates when the Hindu Code Bills were introduced, which covered the reluctance to enact a legal measure favouring the daughter. Thus, Pataskar, the law minister, in parliament: 'But, as I have been always saying, I have got at least better faith in human nature, and I think the father ... will have equal regard for the son and the daughter ... After all, it is much better to leave it to the

roof over her head and that she could obtain a living of some kind, leaves Samar unconvinced, though images of Prabha and Munni swim before his eyes. All the ideals of Hindu womanhood, he argues, all those Hindu traditions such as *sati* will disappear entirely. Shirish Bhai's response is sharp: 'Don't call wasting away and dying under compulsion the forbearance of the Indian woman and then venerate it. Just two names, Sita and Savitri, extracted out of the thousands of years of history of crores of people. I ask you, shouldn't we bow down with shame when we invoke Sita's name? First we inscribe our banners with the names of innocent women inflicted with inhuman suffering—inflicted and massively stigmatized—and then we proceed to venerate them.'[47]

Samar has lived with the current stereotypes. He asks, in all innocence, if Shirish doesn't see Hindu dharma as the best in the world? Shirish Bhai's response begins to jolt him out of his complacency. Here, in fact, two worldviews, two variants of the modern, the Hindu traditional and the enlightened secular, confront each other:

> I see that you remain quite remote from the advancing world. Shriman Samarji, no one has even an inkling of this Sangh language of yours beyond the Arabian Sea. The world is making atom bombs and hydrogen bombs while you continue weeping for your cow-dung civilization. Have you ever tried looking carefully at other civilizations and cultures before waxing bombastic? . . . rivers of milk seem to have flowed through your country once, and no doubt it rained gold too, but yours are now the most ignorant people, and your religion the most unscientific of any.[48]

Samar can only respond weakly: 'It has never been our aim to centre ourselves on these external things. Which is why we have never attacked other countries or cried *jihad* to spread our faith over the

---

judgement of the father and I think he is bound to exercise it in a fair and equitable way.' Kishwar 1994: 2157.

[47] Yadav [1960] 2000: 125.
[48] Ibid.: 125-6.

world. We have always aimed for spiritual peace and progress.' Shirish Bhai scoffs at this—You have not attacked because you never had the strength—while admitting he may be talking too much. In the gaps between the meetings and conversations with Shirish Bhai, further incidents in family life propel the narrative forward: humiliations suffered by Prabha and Samar, Samar's hot-tempered attempts to assert himself and the routine backfire, the short reprieve when he finds work as a typesetter, which then eases the family's financial problems and makes possible his enrolment in a Master's programme.

At the next meeting with Shirish Bhai the discussion revolves around Hindu civilization (*sabhyata*) and culture (*samskriti*), large, overarching themes that undergird notions of self, woman, and family. Celebrating them is escapist and defeatist (*palayan*, *parajay*), a way to avoid facing responsibility. Samar cannot resist asking: What of tradition, what of history (*itihasa*) and myth (*purana*), the absolutist claims of which Shrish Bhai proceeds to demolish:

> 'We can't refuse to look this truth in the face. While men died of hunger and disease, your Indian culture was harping on about the prosperity of mankind. While roasting women and shudras like kebabs and feasting upon them, we continued to shout slogans about the equality of all human beings . . . Our greatest problem is that we don't have our own history. I don't know whether other people have their own true (*sachcha*) history or not, but what we have is not history, it is myth (*Purana*). There is such a mixture of poetry and history in our myths that it is very difficult to extract the facts out of them . . . It isn't hidden from anyone that each age views history and myth in the light of its own conditions and problems. And it breaks and bends things to suit these, so not only does it explicate them anew, it breathes new life into old outfits.'[49]

Shirish Bhai doubts whether, in fact, *any* nation or people possesses history. History always comprises newly configured facts and new interpretations of these. What he seems to be asking for, then, is not that history and myth be done away with, but that they be re-

---

[49] Ibid.: 141.

configured. The impression Samar carries away with him is both sobering and heart-warming. Shirish Bhai is the first person, more knowledgeable than he, who has taken the trouble to talk to him with such warm intimacy (*atmiyata*).

The reorientation Shirish Bhai is undertaking has method, it unfolds serially, almost step by step from larger to more specific themes. At the next meeting the discussion narrows down to focus on the problems Samar is most immediately facing. What does the individual do in face of the claims of the joint family? Should he sacrifice his ambitions, not study further, and simply take up a modestly paid clerk's position in some office in support partly of himself and partly of his family? In Prabha's acute analysis: 'The real problem is that we have very lofty dreams. Our map for the future is so entirely different.'[50] When Shirish Bhai asks whether he loves Prabha, Samar is puzzled, he hasn't learnt to regard his emotional attachment to his wife in this light. He seems neither to have been looking to choose his own partner nor for a marriage based on romantic love. He flounders; he doesn't have a name for what he feels for her. Is it regret, or pity for the compulsions she has to live with? He can only answer evasively. She it is who has ambitions for him, who is encouraging him to study; without her he would have given up long ago. As he walks on with Shirish Bhai through the dark streets in the moonlit night, he thinks of her. Wherever he is on such nights, he sees Prabha, on the roof terrace, a shrunken figure crouching there, 'or to be honest, weeping'.[51]

Shirish Bhai is forthright in his views: 'this joint family tradition will simply have to be broken.' It is no longer a financially viable or sustainable institution. Sentimentality (*bhavukta*) holds the family together, but there is little other than a surface unity, for beneath the smooth exterior exist several smaller conflicting units, leaving no space for individual development. The tensions and skirmishes of everyday life leave no room for the expansion of intellectual and

[50] Ibid.: 158.
[51] Ibid.: 168.

mental capacities. Break free and separate yourself if you want to remain alive is his message.

Samar is awestruck by Shirish Bhai's analytical skill and daring. These are thoughts that will soon filter through to Prabha on the roof terrace. She listens attentively and finds them acceptable, but Samar confesses he can't entirely subscribe to them; they seem to him immensely self-seeking (*ghor svarth*).[52]

'This is exactly what I told him, Prabha. I said, what you are saying seems right, but my soul does not agree. Ultimately it seems like extreme egotism. Then he talked for a long time about the soul and *samskaras*, deeply ingrained cultural traits. He says there is no such thing as a soul. Habit, influences, tradition, imitation, all these put together make for the *samskaras* taking hold of the mind. These *samskaras* prevent us from doing anything new. And we think it is our soul holding us back . . .'[53] Deeply internalized values are part of an ideological edifice not easy to topple. Even if the Hindu Undivided Family were not an anthropological or sociological reality everywhere in India, for colonial as much as for post-colonial law, it still represents the bedrock of Hindu society and its legal core.[54] And where it existed as a social reality, it could be merciless in its will to survive change. When Samar asks Shirish Bhai what he believes in, given that he opposes so much, Shirish Bhai laughs—he believes, he says, in all that remains after you leave out God, dharma, the soul, and *samskaras*. 'Which means you believe in nothing, Shirish Bhai,' Samar says. Shirish Bhai's response is that he merely believes in moving forward, grasping the new.[55]

That evening, as he throws buckets of cooling water on the roof terrace, it is as if he is pouring out the agitation and restlessness to bring about change in his era (*yug badalane ki kubulahat aur*

[52] Ibid.: 177.
[53] Ibid.
[54] See Lucy Carroll's lucid and brilliant article on the subject: Carroll 1991. As Patricia Uberoi points out 'for the family is not a mere unit of social structure but a cultural ideal and a focus of identity.' Uberoi 1993: 36.
[55] Yadav [1960] 2000: 179.

bechaini). Shirish Bhai has systematically dismantled the claims of cherished institutions and moral authority. In his very first meeting with Samar at the employment office, his remarks suggest that the nation-state has hoodwinked its youth. In their conversations thereafter—which punctuate Samar's many family clashes—he shows that the exalted position of Hindu women is largely theoretical; in practice the only hope of improving their lot is the promised Hindu Code Bill making divorce a possible solution for unhappy unions; legalizing the separate right of daughters in their fathers' property; allowing for a married daughter's retreat into the natal home in instances of marital disaster—a legal right rather than an act of charity. Hindu civilization could not sustain nationalism's exclusive claim on the individual, the kind Samar had originally wanted to uphold; it had little to show for itself in the modern age except decay and an uncritical valorization of the past. And finally, the loyalty and protection promised by the undivided Hindu family came at a terrible cost to individual growth. It was an enlightened humanism, socialist in its orientation, which Shirish Bhai implicitly preached, and an increasingly impressed Samar summed up his views for Prabha: 'Whether Hindu, Muslim or Christian, in this age, man doesn't need any religion. Only one religion is needed today—humanity.'[56] Enlightenment logic, as against the claims of Hindu civilization in its new-old guise, represented for Samar in the very structure of his family. How was Samar to operate this logic in his particular set-up, negotiate his way through so intricate a web and claim space for himself—what was to be the mediating instance?

TOGETHER YET ALONE: THE DILEMMA OF THE INDIVIDUAL

Samar intends resigning from a temporary job he has found. He is being underpaid and exploited. Prabha is being swallowed up by the

---
[56] Ibid.: 194.

women's world of bangles and ritual fasting. Then comes a telegram: Munni has expired. Samar hands it over to his father with an unnatural laugh. 'Here it is, written out, Munni is dead. What is not written out clearly is that Munni was killed . . .'[57] Like the young wife of the first scene in the novel, whose suicide was willed by the family, Munni's death seemed willed by hers. The opening and the end of the novel are marked, then, by the death of young women. Munni's fate could so easily have been Prabha's.

However, leaving the tyranny of the joint family also means leaving its shelter. At the close of the novel Samar is standing at the railway station, waiting to board the train which will take him to what he sees as the last day of work. A train from Delhi rolls in, he has thoughts of escape. Should he board it? Where is identity to be found; is it best to wipe it out; should Samar throw himself before the train? A series of images circles before his eyes, his own head rolling on the railway line, boarding a liner departing from Bombay harbour, heading for the big wide world, becoming a sadhu in Haridwar, the abandoned Prabha in ascetic robes bathing at the ghat, a notice in the newspaper saying his mother is very ill, he is to come home. 'Now the train behind had also started to move—two trains creeping off in two opposite directions. It seemed to me as if I was standing on a fast revolving potter's wheel as someone inside me kept repeating—leap down . . . climb up! Leap down . . . climb up! I looked up agitatedly and I saw . . . the vast sky above me was also beginning to tumble into the same revolution.'[58]

Whichever option is chosen, the questions remain: What of the family, what of the nation? Can either provide fulfilment of one's mission here on earth? 'The modern self,' as Lydia Liu has pointed out in the context of the early novel in China, 'is never quite reducible to national identity.' Its 'incongruities, tensions, and struggles' can pull asunder all cohesion.[59] The creation of the modern nation-state

---

[57] Ibid.: 250.
[58] Ibid.: 193.
[59] Liu 1995: 82.

and the volunteer forces of the Hindu Right have loosened the old bonds of the joint family and the clan. Both nation and communalized Hinduism ask that more narrowly defined identities—of *sampradaya* (sect) and *jati* (caste), of locality and region—be given up or at least become secondary, one in the name of the nation, the other in the name of religion. Both ask individuals to opt out of primary obligations to family and the socio-religious structures they are implicated in, and pledge allegiance first of all to the nation or to the communal organization that promises them self-realization and fulfilment. In what ways is the one, nationalism, intrinsically different from the other, communalized religion? Two faces, then, of late modernity.

However, once these constricting but also protective layers—in Samar's case of nationalism as mediated through his Right Wing Hinduism—are peeled off, what remains? Yadav saw hope in the removal of the blockages to free choice: 'till such time as there is free choice (*chunav*) in the joint family, girls behind windows looking out on narrow and filthy lanes will continue to gaze at the "vast sky", boys will continue to drift aimlessly (*bhatakte rahemge*) in offices, parks, and streets, they'll keep clashing with themselves, with the sky as their sole witness. This story of two utterly lonely people will remain true as long as the time between them does not begin to move.'[60] The sonorous ending of the first version of the novel had been dire but also hopeful: The three young people who spoke as voices from the beyond derided themselves for their inability to cope. They spoke in a chorus. They mourned the state of society, their own dead bodies, which were dead even as they lived. But they concluded on an optimistic note, still possible at the start of the 1950s, proclaiming a new dawn after the apocalypse:

> Today, from this radio of the ghost world, we proclaim that we will descend into pens, pervade minds, and swim in veins and arteries. We will ask unceasingly for new bodies . . . give us new form, we won't stay in these graves, we won't wander about restlessly . . . because the rays of

[60] Yadav [1976] 2010: 205.

light are bursting forth, we are beginning to recognize each other, we are no longer afraid of the light.

He, who has begun to create us from his revolutionary feet of destruction, we must dance with him, because he is Shiva, the eternal, and we are ghosts.

This is the Broadcasting Service of the Ghost World.[61]

But, as the later version of the novel shows, the release from the constricting bonds of the joint family, of communalized religion, of an idealized nation, also poses a dilemma—a modernist one. The young man is left standing at the railway platform, contemplating suicide or escape. The intersection of the old and new has not brought release or relief to Samar. '(R)aised to the level of the universal myth this intense, singular narrative of unsettlement, homelessness, solitude and impoverished independence' may be true not only of 'the lonely writer gazing down on the unknowable city from his shabby apartment.'[62] It may also serve to describe the fate of Yadav's hero—unsettled, solitary, torn, gazing in despair at railway tracks.

REFERENCES

Balibar, Etienne and Immanuel Wallerstein. 1991. 'The Nation Form: History and Ideology', in idem, *Race, Nation, Class: Ambiguous Identities*. London, New York: Verso.

Bhandari, Mannu. 2008. *Ek Kahani Yah Bhi*. Delhi: Radhakrishna Prakashan.

Carroll, Lucy. 1991. 'Daughter's Right of Inheritance in India: A Perspective on the Problem of Dowry', in *Modern Asian Studies*, 5/4.

Genette, Gérard. 1980. *Narrative Discourse: An Essay in Method*. Trans. Jane E. Lewin. Ithaca: Cornell University Press.

Guha, Sumit. 1998. 'Household Size and Household Structure in Western India c.1700–1950: Beginning an Exploration', *Indian Economic and Social History Review*, 35.

Kaur, Balwant. 2014. '*Sara Akash* mem Ghum Pretom ki Awaz', in *Naya Path*, 27/4, October–December 2013.

[61] Yadav [1960] 2000: 306-7.
[62] Williams 1989: 34.

King, Anthony. 1984. *The Bungalow: The Production of a Global Culture*. London: Routledge and Kegan Paul.

Kishwar, Madhu. 1994. 'Codified Hindu Law: Myth and Reality', *Economic and Political Weekly*, 13 August.

Hansen, Kathryn. 1981. 'Hindi New Cinema: Basu Chatterji's *Sara Akash*', in *South Asia: Journal of South Asian Studies*, N.S. 4/1, June.

Lewis, Pericles. 2011. *The Cambridge Companion to European Modernism*. Cambridge: Cambridge University Press.

Liu, Lydia. 1995. *Translingual Practice: Literature, National Culture, and Translated Modernity—China, 1900–1937*. Stanford: Stanford University Press.

Luhmann, Niklas. [1982] 1998. *Love as Passion: The Codification of Intimacy*. Translated from the German by Jeremy Gaines and Doris L. Jones. Stanford: Stanford University Press.

Nagar, Amritlal. [1955] 2011. *Seth Bankemal*. Delhi: Rajpal and Sons.

Neville, H.R. 1921. *Agra: A Gazetteer*, Volume 8 of the *District Gazetteers of the United Provinces of Agra and Oudh*. Allahabad: Government Press, United Provinces.

Peck, Lucy. 2008. *Agra: The Architectural Heritage*. Delhi: Roli, The Lotus Collection.

Powell, Avril. 1993. *Muslims and Missionaries in pre-Mutiny India*. Richmond, Surrey: Curzon Press.

Raghav, Rangeya. [1940/1941] 2008. *Gharaunda*. Delhi: Rajpal and Sons.

Raychaudhuri, Tapan. 1999. 'Love in a Colonial Climate', in *Perceptions, Emotions, Sensibilities*. Delhi: Oxford University Press.

Sahni, Bhisham, Ramji Mishra and Bhagavati Prasad Nidaria. [1976] 2010. *Adhunik Hindi Upanyas*, Volume 1, Delhi: Rajkamal Prakashan.

Sikarwar, Bachan Singh. 2011. 'Agra ke Akhbar,' in *Samagra Agra*, ed. Pranvir Chauhan. Delhi: Book Shelf, Publication Division of Knowledge Evolution Media (KEM) Pvt Ltd.

Stark, Ulrike. 2007. *An Empire of Books: The Naval Kishore Press and the Diffusion of the Printed Word in Colonial India*. Ranikhet: Permanent Black.

Tripathi, Vishwanath. 2011. 'Dampatya Prem ka Nayapan', in *Pakhi*, Rajendra Yadav Special Issue, 3/12, September.

Uberoi, Patricia. 1993. 'Introduction', in Patricia Uberoi, ed., *Family, Kinship, and Marriage in India*. Delhi: Oxford University Press.

Vanita, Ruth. 1994. *Strangers on the Roof.* Hindi translation of *Sara Akash.* Delhi: Penguin Books.

Yadav, Rajendra. 1952. *Pret Bolte Haim* (Ghosts Tell their Tale). Delhi: Progressive Publishers.

———. [1960] 2000. *Sara Akash.* Delhi: Radhakrishna Prakashan.

———. [1976] 2010. 'Ek Antarang *Sara Akash*', in *Adhunik Hindi Upanyas*, vol. 1, ed. Sahni, *et al.*

———. 1980. *Meri Priya Kahaniyam.* Delhi: Rajpal.

———. 1988. 'Kahani: Nai Kahani Tak,' in *Kahani: Svarup aur Samvedana*, 3rd Edition. Delhi: National Publishing House.

———. 1997. 'Hindi Pradesh aur Vaicharik Samkat,' in *Upanyas: Svarupa aur Samvedana*, Delhi: Vani Prakashan.

———. 2001. *Mud, mud ke dekhta hum . . . (lagbbhag atmakathya)* (Memoirs). Delhi, Patna: Rajkamal Prakashan.

Williams, Raymond. [1961] 1965. *The Long Revolution.* New York: Harper and Row.

———. [1973] 1985. *The Country and the City.* London: The Hogarth Press.

———. 1989. *The Politics of Modernism: Against the New Conformists.* London, New York: Verso.

8

Culture, Claustrophobia, and the New Capital of the Nation

*A*MDHERE BAND KAMARE (Dark Closed Rooms; 1961) by Mohan Rakesh (1925–1972), well-known Hindi dramatist, short story writer, and novelist, is about the struggle of artistically inclined middle-class protagonists to realize their ambitions in the first decade after Independence.[1] Almost documentary in character, it embodies an extreme form of realism. The effort to create real time and space is such that exact dates are provided for certain events and precise addresses noted.[2] It has been argued that 'All realist fiction gives itself authority by asserting a privileged relationship with reality.'[3] It is the 'real' that the author himself stresses in explicating his own stand concerning the process of writing. In speaking about the *nai kahani* (new story) movement, of which he was as much a foundational part as Rajendra Yadav, Rakesh takes pains, in an

---

[1] A translation of the novel into English by Jai Ratan has been published under the title *Lingering Shadows* (Delhi: Hind Paperbacks, 1969). I have not been able to procure a copy. I cite above with page numbers from the 1997 reprint of the Hindi original. All translations that follow are mine.

[2] Thus for instance we are told that the main protagonist, Harbans, leaves Delhi on 31 January 1951. When the narrator Madhusudan comes to Delhi, he meets Harbans again on 13 October 1959, after an interval of almost nine years.

[3] Cited in Liu 1995: 110.

interview with Carlo Coppola, to point out that the reality he and his cohort tried to capture in their stories was different from earlier forms in Hindi literature. The real was no longer to be a medium for an idea; rather the idea, if there was one, was crystallized through the reality itself.[4] Further, that the reality reflected was that of the urban middle class from which most writers in the movement stemmed; and that this middle-class mentality was so all-pervasive, so strong in its aspirations and frustrations, that it was also shared by those above and below.[5]

It was in the cities that Rakesh saw the reality of what he was trying to depict most densely presented: 'The conflict of the forces [influencing life] can be experienced everywhere—though much more sharply in urban life, since it is towns which are the chief centres of conflict, and of these again, more so the bigger cities. If our works do not reflect the accurate pulsation of this conflict, they do not represent reality.'[6] The novel is set, then, in Delhi and focuses on Panjabi protagonists, one of whom, Madhusudan, is the first person chronicler of their tale. His own life story only enters the narrative towards the end of the novel.

New Delhi is still primarily a city of bungalows and bureaucrats, with large pockets of refugees from West Panjab uneasily connected to the Walled City, recovering slowly from the violence of 1947 and moving southwards into new settlements such as Defence Colony, towards which the more prosperous families go. Muslim families in the havelis of the old city and in the less affluent housing on the periphery

---

[4] Rakesh 1973: 16.

[5] Thus Rakesh in the interview with Carlo Coppola: 'Most writers do come from the middle class. I think that if a man like myself were to try to write about the life in a village around Delhi or life in the Punjab, he would be trying to play a trick on himself, because that would not be part of his experience. Most writers today not only come from the middle class, they come more specifically from the urban middle class; those from the rural middle class have also been urbanized, for the most part.' See Coppola 1973.

[6] Rakesh 1975: 35.

of the old city have been driven out, the space thus vacated overrun with refugees. As *Jhutha Sach* in its second part depicted so graphically, the refugees have changed the very character of the city.[7]

The novel is focused not only on the lives of its protagonists but also on their participation in the process of creating a self-consciously national culture, largely based in the 'classical' past as this is constituted in the first decades after Independence in the national capital. Both practitioners and patrons of the arts are being defined anew, and once again the courtesan—this time *in absentia*—crops up in this context. Dance as an artistically developed form, both in the north and south of the country had been regarded as her domain. With what impunity could middle-class women embrace it? What space did middle-class bohemian life forms have in this new-old city? On what soil did they evolve and how, if at all, did they connect to the culture of the Old City, since New Delhi was created without roots in immediate Indian history?[8] As Mohan Rakesh says enigmatically

---

[7] As discussed in my Introduction, another cataclysmic event was the post-1857 cleansing which changed the demography of the Walled City. In one account of the post-1947 changes, 'Delhi had a population of perhaps 9.5 lakh (950,000) in 1947 (9.18 lakh in the census of 1941). At Partition, 3.3 lakh Muslims left Delhi, leaving about 6 lakh people (Hindu, Muslim, Sikh and others) behind. Nearly 5 lakh non-Muslim refugees arrived at the same time, making the balance of the new (refugee) inhabitants and the older city inhabitants very much on par. Even in 1951, by which time the capital had expanded considerably in size (the population of 17.44 lakh marking a 90 per cent increase on the 1941 figure), Partition refugees (not including the local Muslims) still accounted for 28.4 per cent of the total population of the city. In more ways than we generally acknowledge, politically, culturally and even demographically, the Delhi of the 1950s and after was a "Partition" city.' Pandey 2001: 122. 'September 1947 was a month of terror for Muslims: tortured days . . . when rich and poor, young and old huddled together . . .' Ibid.: 128. The quotation is from Azad 1988: 228–30.

[8] Anthony King has shown how, when New Delhi was settled, residential areas were allocated on criteria of race, occupational rank, and socio-economic status, resulting in the formation of entirely new communities which then re-created their own culture. Status in the city was marked by the social area allocated. King 1976: 244–51.

in the few words which form a preface to the novel and point to its manifold agendas:

> What should a preface contain? An introduction to the novel? An account of my own perspective? But if the perspective has to be recounted in the preface, why would I need to write the novel? And as for introducing the novel, I can't think of what to call it — a sketch of contemporary Delhi? The autobiography of journalist Madhusudan? The story of Harbans and Nilima's inner conflicts? Somewhere in the air the Koh-i-nur shimmers. The *qissa*, tale, of that Koh-i-nur? I really can't decide which. You alone can resolve the issue, once you've gone through it. And if you also can't resolve it either, then hand over the problem to someone else, follow my example and distance yourself from it.[9]

In this brief preface Mohan Rakesh refers to a tale which is inserted halfway through the narrative, of a dancing girl in the last days of the Mughal empire: 'Somewhere in the air the Koh-i-nur shimmers. The *qissa* of that Koh-i-nur?' The Koh-i-nur is the legendary diamond which was carried away, robbed, looted, along with the *takht-e-taus* (the Peacock Throne) by Nadir Shah of Persia when he invaded Delhi in 1739. A beautiful dancing girl at the Mughal court in Delhi had captivated the heart of Nadir Shah. Pleased with her dancing, he had told her he would grant her a wish; she wished that she be left behind in her beloved Delhi and not be transported to Faras (Persia) along with the *takht-e-taus* and the rest of his booty. And so she remained while the rest was carried off:

> The Koh-i-nur is leaving for Faras. The aged Takht-e-taus is leaving for Faras. Elephants, horses and horse-riders are going to Faras. Slave girls and slaves are going to Faras. *Dance and music are going to Faras.* Nadir regrets that he is unable to take Delhi's Lal Qila and other monuments to Faras. If it had indeed been possible, he would have torn them out of their foundations and taken them to Faras. Ghazani shall become Delhi . . . And Delhi? A vast mausoleum, where along with human beings,

[9] Rakesh [1961] 1967: 8.

the corpses of art and culture will lie rotting in the bazaars. So that, for generations, people can remember Nadir Shah was here once.[10]

The aged *takht-e-taus* had felt itself grow heavy; somewhere between Kabul and Ghazani it became metal and stone alone. That something which used to stir within him, which was tender and alive, where had it gone? Was the spirit of the *takht-e-taus* killed too as it hovered around Chandni Chowk, or was it left behind somewhere in the vicinity of the Delhi Gate while the *takht* itself left Delhi? Art and culture were leaving Delhi: what would come in their stead? The story of Harbans and Nilima and their ambitious search for a life in the arts was partly a response to this last query.

FIRST VANTAGE POINT ON THE CITY

Qasabpura on the periphery of the Old City. Madhusudan, the poet-narrator of the novel, lives in Qasabpura, a lower-middle-class residential area on the periphery of the walled city. When Partition happened, the owner of the house, the old sitar player Ibadat Ali Khan, abandoned it to flee to Lahore with his young daughter Khurshid, but finding no sense of home there he returned after an absence of just three months.[11] He suffers his first heart attack on finding there

---

[10] Ibid.: 213, emphasis added. As Blake notes: 'The degradation of the city in the 1750s elicited some of the finest poetry of the language from two of the greatest Urdu poets. Mirza Muhammad Rafi (1730–80), pen-name Sauda, was the son of a prosperous merchant who had migrated from Kabul to Shahjahanabad. Born in the city, Sauda remained there until 1757, when he left for Farrukhabad. Muhammad Taqi Mir (1722–1810), pen-name Mir, was born in Agra and came to Shahjahanabad the year before Nadir Shah's invasion. Returning to Agra for several years, he came back to Shahjahanabad and resided there from 1740 to 1760 and from 1772 to 1782. Both witnessed the fall of the city to Nadir Shah and the devastation that followed and for both it was the fall of a whole civilization. This experience inspired a new genre of Urdu poetry. The *shahr ashob* (ruined city) genre was a lamentation over the fate of a city.' Blake 1991: 165.

[11] The sitar had a special connection with Delhi. Miner says the first mention of the instrument occurs in *Murraqqa'-i-dehli*. 'By the third quarter of the century the name appears in Hindi poetry, such as in the *Nadirat-i-*

is no space for him in his own house. The house had been given as a gift to his great-grandfather or some faraway ancestor by the Mughal court, and his descendants have been living in it ever since. Ibadat Ali is a professional sitar-player; it was a profession his ancestors had also followed, the medal which Emperor Jahangir had given his ancestor Imitiaz Ali was still safe in his protection.[12] But now he is barely tolerated there, even less so Khurshid, his fiercely proud and defiant daughter; he has retired to the upper storey of his house and lives there, besieged by belligerence. He sometimes plays the sitar at night; it is the sole trace of culture in the raucous neighbourhood. Its hauntingly beautiful notes drift towards Madhusudan, tossing sleeplessly in his narrow, airless room at the back of the house. Qasabpura, for all its squalor, has the vitality of community life, of social networks created on the neighbourhood sidewalks.[13] The

---

shahi of Shah Alam and the *Hammir raso* of Kavi Jodhraj, and in European travelogues, the earliest European reference found so far being a 1777 letter . . .' Miner 1993: 32ff. It probably came to India from Persia by way of Kashmir. More than one version of the instrument existed by the end of the eighteenth century. Its adaptability to a wide spectrum of musical contexts was a characteristic throughout. By the 1830s it was known for solo performances as well as dance accompaniment. By the mid-nineteenth century it had evolved into a sophisticated solo instrument. In urban India it captured the popular imagination and was taken up by many amateurs. By the late nineteenth century there were a number of instruction manuals on playing it. Severe reprisals by the British after 1857 drove master musicians out but the instrument did not disappear with them: in the early twentieth century the author Hasan Nizami affirms that 'the traditions of Delhi did not stop completely . . . even through the bullets of 1857 the esthetes of Delhi did not give up their pleasures.' Ibid.: 129.

[12] Rakesh [1961] 1967: 17.

[13] 'The social structure of sidewalk life hangs partly on what can be called self-appointed public characters. A public character is anyone who is in frequent contact with a wide circle of people and who is sufficiently interested to make himself a public character. A public character need have no special talents or wisdom to fulfil his function—although he often does. He just needs to be present and there need to be enough of his counterparts. His main qualification is that he is public; that he talks to a lot of different

culture of the old city has deserted it; that which remains is decaying. It is this Qasabpura, newly resettled with refugees from western Panjab, which forms the middle ground between the declining culture of the old, and the Planned New, which is New Delhi.

The main occupant of the house of Ibadat Ali is a lower-middle-class Panjabi couple, known as the Thakur and Thakurain; they rent the rooms to Madhusudan and his friend. The Thakurain, a cheerful, somewhat worn but warm-hearted woman in her thirties, has a daughter of seven or eight who later plays a role in Madhusudan's life; at this stage she remains nameless. Madhusudan himself is a man of letters, a poet who has tried his luck in Bombay and retreated back into provincial Amritsar whence he came, to then try his luck again in Delhi. He is confused, puzzled, and bedazzled by Delhi, or at least as he imagines the new city to be from the vantage of his shabby back room in Qasabpura, near Basti Harphul Singh in the Sadar Bazaar area. To reach Qasabpura from Connaught Place, when Madhusudan misses his bus, means passing through Kath Bazaar, a red light area in those days. The images that this area conjures up have much to do with his past memories of dancing girls. It is this connection between dance and dancing girls of which he is inadvertently reminded every time he is accosted with the ambitions of women in the performing arts. Madhusudan's sphere of existence in 1951 is restricted to his lodgings in Qasabpura, his place of work in the editorial office of *Iravati*, a Hindi literary magazine, and the periodic extension of this world into the brightly lit world of New Delhi.

Madhusudan strains towards achieving the self-confidence and assurance of the men and women he meets regularly in the Coffee House,[14] who debate and discuss each other's lives, issues of art, abstract art, realist art. The Coffee House is the scene of many

---

people. In this way, news travels that is of sidewalk interest.' Jacobs [1961] 1989: 55ff. The Thakurain is clearly one such character. She plays a key role in Madhusudan's life late in the narrative.

[14] The Coffee House was first situated opposite Queen's Way, renamed Janpath; later in the Theatre Communications Building.

encounters and discussions brought to life in sharp detail later in the novel. Madhusudan registers in shocked detail the Anglicized ways of the writer-painter couple who befriend him; they are Harbans and Nilima, the prime protagonists of the tale as it unfolds. They live in a house in Hanuman Road, just off Connaught Circus.

The narrative revolves around two love triangles. The tale of the first triangle is primary, it occupies three quarters of the novel and is played out in the new city, though initially observed from the old city; Harbans and Nilima are its chief players, with Nilima's sister a shadowy third. The story of the second triangle, of which Madhusudan himself forms a part, crops up in the last quarter of the novel and in many ways replicates the course of the first triangle, eventually taking the main character back to the old city, coming full circle

Illus. 28: Connaught Place, New Delhi 1950s

in a way both conclusive and inconclusive, with many threads left hanging in the air.

SEEKING NEW SPACES: LIVES IN THE ARTS AND THE FIRST TRIANGLE

Harbans Khullar is a professor of history in a Delhi college. For Madhusudan, of the people he meets Harbans is 'the most significant person of that circle' (*us dayare ka sabse mahatvapurna vyakti*). He finds, when he first meets Harbans in Bombay, a man of wide interests and learning who can hold forth almost in one breath on literature, politics, dance, foreign missionaries, Chekhov, Dostoevsky, Leonardo da Vinci, Picasso, Uday Shankar, Pandit Nehru, and the Bishop of Lahore, and speak with equal ease about mysticism, cubism, and Kathakali. He has radical views which surface, unexpectedly, destructively, when he can no longer handle the cultural pretensions of those who wield actual power in the world he seeks to inhabit: these are the days of the Cold War, ideologies determine location in the camps that divide the literati. Harbans is also a novelist in the making, he is writing a novel about the mental conflicts of one Ramesh Khanna, who yearned to marry a girl for years, and once married to her yearned to free himself from her. Actually, he says, the novel is about himself. His prime anxiety concerns the language of the novel:

> 'I have been trying to write for a long time, but', he shrugged his shoulders hopelessly, 'I feel unable to write . . . I can't understand what I want. There's something I feel intensely but—but when I try to write, I find myself unable to do so. If I begin to write in Hindi, I feel I should be writing in English. And when I write in English, I feel that the idiom of that language escapes me. I feel a strange helplessness, as if I am bound tight in some straitjacket which won't give way even if I try a thousand times to break through it. And I don't understand whether I want to write, or do something else.[15]

[15] Rakesh [1961] 1967: 55.

Still, at this stage he is optimistic: 'As far as language is concerned, I can have someone put it right afterwards. It is my great tragedy [he uses the English word] that I know no language properly, neither Hindi, nor Urdu or English. None of these languages can be called my own.'[16]

The novel Harbans is writing consists of a sheaf of unlinked sheets, some half-written, some in Hindi, some in English, some with chapter titles, some without chapter titles, a novel without a beginning and presumably without an end. Obviously for him there is no pre-existing literary corpus which can serve as a reference point or model. The idiom he seeks has to be coined, in Hindi as much as in English. Or can it only be a mix of both? What recognition can it find, what readership can it create? His wife Nilima mocks his efforts to write. Harbans wants to go to England, though with uncertain goals, either to do a PhD or to write a novel. Will this solve his language problem?

This is more starkly also the predicament Madhusudan faces in his personal and professional life. Where will men such as Harbans and he find space, forum, and forms for what they are seeking to articulate? Clearly, Rakesh's novel could itself have only been written in Hindi—how else could it convey the discomfort of moving from one comfortably hybrid linguistic universe (Urdu-Hindi-Panjabi) into another, from the vernacular universe into the more cosmopolitan world of English?

Harbans' cultural confusion reflects the Indian language situation. With the foundation of the nation's capital in Delhi and declaration that Hindi would serve as the first official language of the nation—English, officially the second, still remaining the unofficial first—Hindi publishers and writers began to congregate in the capital. However, there was no tradition of Hindi writing in Delhi. The Walled City had been the cradle of Urdu writing and culture. The new city had no writing culture to speak of. The newcomers from Panjab, many

---

[16] Ibid.: 60.

with a strong Arya Samaj link and thus an allegiance to Hindi, such as Mohan Rakesh himself, formed a vital part of the literary scene in Delhi. Yet with all that, was Hindi destined to remain confined to the periphery of the New City? The decisions that the prime protagonists eventually take in their lives will signal the defeat or at the least the marginalization of the vernacular universe in Delhi's 'national culture'.

Harbans' wife who had refashioned herself as Nilima, concealing her old-fashioned name Savitri, represents the prototype of the modern woman. She wears jeans when at home in her house behind Connaught Place, the shopping heart of New Delhi. She has modern gadgets in her house. Harbans and she soon acquire a record player. She smokes; she addresses her husband without the honorific. She is free of speech and talks quite openly about her ambitions to Madhusudan, as well as of her conflicted relationship with Harbans. She is a reluctant artist, wielding a careless brush; Harbans has persuaded her to paint rather than dance. She had wanted to become a Kathak dancer, she had one highly acclaimed performance in Sapru House (the capital's centre for concerts and recitals) behind her, but Harbans made her switch to Bharat Natyam, which had by then acquired a classical pedigree and could, with comfort, be regarded as *the* national dance form.[17] Kathak, undergoing a similar process, remained somewhat suspect, too linked to dancing girls and courtesans for middle-class comfort.

A sideways glance at attitudes to dance may be relevant here, being fairly closely connected with Nilima's trajectory in the novel. To my knowledge, there has been no extended study of the 'classicization'

---

[17] Rukmini Devi Arundale (1904–1986) first 'discovered' and then modified and aestheticized and made amenable for modern upper-caste performance the *sadir* dance of the courtesans of South India. See 'Rukmini on Herself' in Ramani 2003: 1–69 for her own account of it, and Soneji 2012 for an account of the form as it existed prior to this adaptation, in both private salon and temple performance; the memory of its heterogeneous origins endures into the present.

of Kathak, which evolved as part of the courtesan culture of North India. The process, however, has been recorded by Joshi 1989 in a valuable biography of the dancer Leila Roy (1899–1947). Roy was an upper-class, half-English, half-Bengali woman who helped to shape dance in its modern incarnation, as it came to be practised on and off-stage, chiefly by upper-caste women, but also men. Her life could conceivably have struck a chord in writers such as Mohan Rakesh, though this is speculative and I have no evidence that he knew of her. Roy grew up in Calcutta and learnt to play the violin so well that she gave public concerts. She was intrigued by the 'nautch' form when she first saw it performed by two professional sisters who had learnt it from the famous gurus Kalka and Bindadin Maharaj. Her marriage to a high-standing naval officer, Captain Sahib Singh Sokhey, took her to Bombay. She was exposed to and inspired by what she saw of Bharat Natyam in Baroda. Roy decided to train rigorously in Kathak with Guru Pandit Sitaram Prasad of Calcutta, who tutored her privately. In 1934 she made her first public presentation of *Krishna Leela*, inspired by Vidyapati's Vaishnava *Padavali* and choreographed for the modern stage in the Opera House in Bombay under the auspices of the Swatik League and Swadeshi League. The form was thoroughly 'classicized', the costumes were inspired by seventeenth-century Rajput paintings, the stage decor was created by the art historian Karl Khandalawala. Thereafter, Roy took the stage name Madame Menaka. She continued her training under Lacchu Maharaj (second son of Kalka Maharaj and nephew of the legendary dancer and teacher Bindadin). Her troupe was called Menaka Indian Ballet. It toured Europe and Southeast Asia over 1935–8. Engagements poured in: Geneva, Lausanne, Montreux, Luxembourg, Germany (where they stayed for six months, performing at the Berliner Volksbuehne; they were present at the Olympiad held in Berlin in 1936 and won three prizes out of the thirteen awarded at the Olympiad), Brussels, Holland, Scandinavia, Eastern Europe, Western Europe; in London there were 750 performances. The themes of her stage productions were Sanskritized, as also the titles. There was even a film appearance in *Die Tiger von Eschnapur* and rave reviews all over. Upon her return there was a public reception in Bombay. She established a school for young boys and girls, but this was not a success, and World War II prevented further tours in Europe. Menaka's failing health prevented further activity; she died after a painful illness in 1947. Her article 'Dance in India'—published in September 1933 in *Sound and Shadow*, a now defunct journal from Madras—provides a good view of the ancient pedigree sought for it as also its projection as a 'national' form:

> It is true that dance even more than other arts in our country is in a state of decay and neglect but there is no doubt that it had reached a very high state of artistic development and refinement. You have only to look up the ancient texts to see that the essential elements laid down centuries ago have not been surpassed anywhere even today for their high standards. Though the art of dance is decadent and the public appreciation is quite uncritical, all is not lost. There are still to be found very capable exponents of the traditional technique and if we must have a dance revival, we must learn the traditional techniques from these masters and must not be misled by self-styled authorities on Indian dance . . . The 'Kathaka' dance was danced in the ancient times by women of the highest families. Mythologically it is attributed to Parvati, who is supposed to be its first exponent . . . It must express the life and emotions of our nation and not be mere ethnographic posturing. We must make it live again and it is only through hard and conscientious work that one can even hope to make that attempt.[18]

In a way, we have come full circle in our narrative trail, from the courtesan Suman in *Sevasadan*, in the teens of the twentieth century, who distanced herself from dance and music to reclaim the respectability she once had as a housewife, to middle-class women's endeavour from the 1930s to reclaim dance as an artistic form. When Nilima discloses to Madhusudan that she had wanted to dance, Madhusudan involuntarily recalled a book his father had written when he

---

[18] See Joshi 1989: 43 and 59.

himself was growing up in Amritsar. It was called *Var vadhu vivechan*; he translates the title himself into English as 'A History of Dancing Girls in India'. It could never find a distributor; he himself had seen only one copy of it before it disappeared. He also recalls going with this father to dance performances in respectable homes, though no other children within the all-male audiences were present on such occasions:

> And I remember that Pitaji had taken me along to a couple of functions where there had been dance performances. It is likely that he and his friends had formed a society, which used to invite a famous dancer from elsewhere and organize a performance for her. The dance was performed at the place of some friend or the other. Thirty to forty people, at most, would collect to watch the performance. I must have been eight or nine years old. I can't say why Pitaji took me along. Perhaps he did not want me to remain indifferent to such matters. Or perhaps he wanted to impress his friends with the fact that he treated his son as an equal. At the age of twelve he had sent me off all alone to sightsee in Mathura and Agra. But it could also be that he wanted to be seen coming out of such functions accompanied by his son, so that no one could point a finger at him. At all events, one thing is certain, that in those days, it did not enter my head that there was any thread connecting these dance performances with the kothas, [brothels] of Kanjariyomwala Bagh.[19]

And in the next sentence, almost, he tells Nilima that he did not know she had already had a dance recital at Sapru House. His association of dance with selling the body, however, is deeply ingrained. Dancing was connected to a stigmatized profession from which it was in the process of emancipating itself. His father had always hurried him through the Kanjariyomwala Bazaar in Amristar. But they had also been different times: the dance and culture which had flourished under the patronage of the courts and the connoisseurs of the upper classes had since disappeared, leaving behind only the stigma attached to the profession. Where can Nilima find legitimation for what she is

[19] Rakesh [1961] 1967: 52.

trying to do, where can she find validation, authenticating instances? For a middle-class performer, acclaim, it seems, can only come from outside the country.

Meanwhile there is Nilima's beautiful sister Shukla. She attracts any number of men—artists and intellectuals who hover around Harbans and Nilima. There are not many women in the coffee house. Nilima and Shukla bask in the glow of attention they provoke whenever they turn up there. But Shukla's relationships are dictated by Harbans. She is entirely fixated on him, as Nilima discloses to Madhusudan: 'The fact of the matter is that she really looks up to Harbans. Harbans has also spoilt her no end with his affection and she considers everyone else inferior. When I tell Harbans that he is ruining the girl's life, he turns around and berates me. If this girl marries someone, it will be because Harbans tells her to. And if Harbans tells her to remain a spinster all her life, she'll remain a spinster all her life.'[20] Harbans himself radiates a sense of uncomplicated ownership and responsibility for her. She will find a partner only in his absence, as Nilima confides to Madhusudan. These encounters are abruptly terminated when Harbans leaves for London in 1951. As things stand, he and Nilima seem unable to help themselves when they are with each other, even as they cannot cut loose from each other and make something of themselves when they are not together. He asks Nilima to join him after a while; it is the year 1952. Madhusudan also leaves Delhi, and loses track of the couple's life.

SECOND VANTAGE POINT: THE LOFT IN WEST DELHI

Madhusudan comes back to Delhi after nine years. He has abandoned writing poetry in Hindi and the entire Hindi world and turned to English, the silent victor in the many language debates in the country. Madhusudan has worked for a newspaper in Lucknow and is established enough as a journalist to be the political reporter for an English newspaper, the *New Herald*; later, his political views being

[20] Ibid.: 57.

too outspoken and even critical, he is asked to become the Art and Drama critic of the paper and play his role in creating the capital's culture. His world slowly opens onto newer vistas. He has shifted his location from the periphery of the Old City to West Delhi to a *barsati* in Anand Parbat.[21] He now lives at a height which affords a panoramic view of the city, both old and new, providing the novel with a sketch of Delhi, as promised in the preface. The area he sees is the densely populated Karol Bagh, filled with refugees:

> Half of Delhi could be seen from the windows of the room in which I lived. The barsati atop the two-and-a-half storey house built at a height on Anand Parbat was like the bastion of a sentry. All around the Rohtak Road area, people had constructed little rooms out of the barsatis in which mostly clerks, journalists, teachers, and other professionals lived, those who could not get accommodation in houses because they were single, those who could not pay the full rent for an apartment. So heedlessly did the hot dry winds of summer and the icy winds of winter blow through these barsatis that the= people living in them grew rapidly anxious to marry as quickly as possible and become reputable citizens.[22]

Coming home late at night and not being able to find sleep, he would gaze out of the window. From his West Delhi rooftop, he had a panoramic view of the urban landscape; in laying it out, he seemed to mark his own position within it, with a sense of wonder, of belonging as much as of estrangement, of finding as much as of losing himself.[23]

---

[21] *Barsatis* became a popular mode of existence for the young and the bohemian. The classic *barsati* novel of the period is *Ek Chithara Sukh* (A Tattered Joy; 1979) by Nirmal Verma (1929–2005), also a member of the *nai kahani* group.

[22] Ibid.: 201.

[23] As discussed earlier in the essay on *Jhutha Sach*, 'In 1947 Delhi lay mainly within the old city wall. Lutyens' New Delhi was outside it, southwards at one extreme; and the old Secretariat complex and civil lines outside it, northward, at the other . . . Sadar–Paharganj, Karol Bagh–Patel Nagar, Civil Lines–Subzimandi and West Delhi form the main resettlement areas of refugees. These colonies have acted as independent nuclei for further extension. They remain like islands, self-contained, yet are drawn into the

I used then to wander up and down the roof terrace for a full hour or gaze out of one of the three windows of the barsati at the dense clusters of light, strewn so widely. The farthest clusters are settlements such as Tilak Nagar and Rajouri Gardens, which have come up only in the last years. A little removed from them one could glimpse the lights of Palam Airport. If one shifted a little to the left of Palam, one could see the seductive lights of that glittering township which is known by the name of Chanakyapuri or Diplomatic Enclave. The eye roves over Chanakyapuri to then focus a little nearer home, because the incline of the hillock does not allow them to wander farther in that direction. On this side there is the Karol Bagh area, the borders of which join Patel Nagar on the one side and on the other side Pahar Ganj and Sabzi Mandi. To look farther afield than Karol Bagh I have to leave one window and go to the other. I can only guess at the location of Connaught Place. The areas around Ajmeri Gate, Asaf Ali Road and Darya Ganj can also not be seen from my window. I go to the third window and try to make out the locations of Kashmiri Gate and Chandini Chowk. Chandini Chowk used once to be called the heart of Delhi. Has the heart of Delhi also been dislocated and does it beat somewhere else now? And where in this length and breadth is that 'somewhere else'?[24]

Not so far from Palam Airport are the new centres of power, the embassies and high commissions. They play an active role in

---

mainstream of Delhi life. These colonies are each equipped with a market place, a shopping centre, a temple and a gurdwara, a bank, a police station, a school, a post and telegraph office, a taxi stand, a cinema and in certain cases, a swimming pool and a terminal bus depot. The houses are usually not multi-storeyed or spacious. On the main roads there are larger houses, but within the colony single-storeyed houses predominate and further on are the small houses of low-income groups. Daily needs are met in a market which is usually at the centre of each colony . . . people in these colonies have tried to recreate their former lives. Walking in these areas one feels as though one were in the Dev Samaj, Krishan Nagar, or Ram Nagar colonies of Lahore. As these colonies expand, their well-to-do inhabitants move out to healthier and more select localities—like Golf Links, Vasant Vihar, Greater Kailash, Ring Road, New Friends Colony and Defence Colony.' Datta 1986: 442–50.

[24] Rakesh [1961] 1967: 202.

the cultural life of the city. A great deal of 'national' culture finds its authentication here. Is this the new heart of the city? Or is it in Connaught Place, which Madhusudan can only imagine in the impenetrable darkness, dotted with restaurants? Many of them have become his haunts, the Coffee House, La Bohème with its dark interiors, the classy Gaylords; the owners of many of these are refugees from Lahore. There are also new cultural centres and concert halls near Mandi House, envisaged as the cultural core of the new city, a place Madhusudan calls Delhi Kala Niketan, Sapru House, the AIFACS building.

But so many lives are left untouched by this cultural life. His editor sends him to the 'slums' to report on lives there; he goes to Qasabpura, now an object of study. His editor, anglicized and liberal, speaks to him, pulling at his pipe: 'Behind the lives on these streets, there is the life people have in their small homes. Who knows what kind of lives in how many dark and narrow lanes lurk behind this glitter and bustle. There a new city is fast constructing itself. Behind it is an old city which is collapsing slowly.'[25]

> Where, indeed, does the heart of Delhi beat? In its enormous workforce? Those on cycles, going to their humble desks in offices, as much as those going in their cars to the more affluent locations, to their banks and business concerns, to the corridors of power in North and South Avenue, and in another direction, to Chanakyapuri, the home of the diplomats: Somewhere in the air a *koh-i-nur* shimmers.
>
> Early every morning, thousands of cycles emerge from the different settlements of the city to return, tired and worn, to the same bastis again. Hundreds of cars, from an old 1902 mobile to a Dodge Kingsway of the sixties, dart hither and thither: Hardinge Road, Sundar Nagar, Chanakyapuri, North Avenue, South Avenue, Janpath, Rajpath, Old Mill Road, Parliament Street, Connaught Place, Connaught Circus.
>
> Each person the rival of another. Each engaged in warfare with the other. For each his house his Ghazni, his citadel . . .[26]

[25] Ibid.: 200.
[26] Ibid.: 213.

A MODERNIST CULTURE IN THE MAKING: THE COFFEE HOUSE

In this breadth and anonymity, the place where people come again and again and acquire known faces is the Coffee House—what the narrator calls the *adda* or regular meeting place of *paramhams*, the 'ascetics of utmost sanctity',[27] people who have reached enlightenment or at least claim to have.[28] Rakesh draws a satirically vivid picture of the cultural life of the capital as centred in the Coffee House. The 'ascetics of utmost sanctity' form their own clusters, have their own affinities.

The first group is composed of journalists whose talk turns around scoops, politics, and scandals. Another group comes from varied walks of life, the common factor being the use of the Coffee House as meeting ground: these include Sundar Juneja, Distribution-in-Charge of a soft drinks concern called the Vita Rose Company; and Shyam Malhotra, a life insurance agent who can quote from Sahir Ludhiyanavi and Faiz Ahmed Faiz; Jaydev, or 'Dirty Engine', who works in the sanitation department; Bhadra Sen, a real estate agent; Chaudhary, who has odd jobs as broker, insurance agent, contractor,

---

[27] McGregor [1993] 2003: 604.

[28] Rakesh [1961] 1967: 214ff. 'Adda could thus become a space for the practice of literary cosmopolitanism by members of the middle or lower-middle classes ... The democratization, as well as a certain social radicalism, of this particular sort of adda may be seen in the fact that there was nobody's parlor available to them.' Chakrabarty 2000: 198. As we saw, the Coffee House also played a role in *Nadi ke Dvip*; the novel's heroine had no parlour, no home to receive and converse with friends. The history of the Coffee House, in Hindi novels alone, set in Lucknow, Allahabad, and Delhi, remains to be written. Delhi could, by virtue of its many displacements and dislocations, have no continuous culture of conversation, idle or otherwise, through the first half even of the twentieth century. Apparently the Urdu poets working for All India Radio frequented the Coffee House between 1942 and 1945. There was also the Carlton Cafe at Kashmiri Gate, where Bengalis and Kayasths converged. After Independence they would have drifted to the new Coffee House near Connaught Place, mentioned above.

and passport expert. One finds oneself in the thick of the professional middle class.

It is the third group which is of greatest interest, the art circle, again formed of many sub-circles: there are those who sit in family cabins and have serious discussions about problems and issues in the theatre: does commercial theatre have a future in Delhi, can the literary theatre gain a footing as commercially viable theatre, will the government scheme of establishing auditoria in various parts of the country succeed? Will the theatre of the future be entirely symbolic? What place do music and dance have in the theatre? A few young women are also included; they don't quite know how they fit or how appropriate their being here is. They discuss the acting and staging of plays, many with Sanskritic titles, perhaps in an attempt to classicize theatre: *Chandragupta, Vikromavarshiya, Lalit Madhava, Veni Samhara*, but also *Mughal Darbar* (Mughal Court), and *Rangdar Shishe* (Coloured Glasses). The reigning authority is a dramatist who goes on a foreign tour every four months and adds something cutting or corrective every once in while.[29]

The second sub-group is formed of writers, poets, and critics: their conversation usually turns around new literature—*nai kavita* (new poetry) and *nai kahani*; they discuss what *nai* can mean, whose work is newer and whose not. There is a sense of breaking new ground and dismantling the old. The clusters of poets and writers who make up these groups talk about a 'new consciousness', the term is used in English, and once again the question is whose consciousness is genuinely new and whose only for show. Only one person in the group is neither writer, poet or critic. This is Janak Sukhadia from Calcutta. He pierces a hole in the balloon that is new consciousness. He can't understand the phenomenon: what is this bird, is this just a new trend set up to dupe the world, why did he not discover it when he read the works of these writers, most of which he never felt like reading. People shake their heads when he gets up and leaves after

---

[29] No doubt caricatures of real-life people, the allusions are lost today.

his little outburst. But most agree with him. It is to this group that Harbans belongs.

A third sub-group consists of a single person, the art critic Gajanan, who sits at a table in lonely splendour. For twenty years, he had made it his business to make and break reputations. People seek him out, he shuns most, they are only out to achieve their own individual happiness, which in Gajanan's cynical opinion amounts to little more than the search for social status—again the use of the English term. Madhusudan avoids him.

An old Urdu poet hails Madhusudan, his gestures are unsteady; he is already intoxicated. He wants to talk to him seriously about something he has read recently in a Hindi book:

> 'Does Mother India only live in villages; doesn't she ever come to Delhi?' And when Madhusudan laughs and evades this question, he says: 'Look, this is not a laughing matter, ever since I've read that she lives only in villages, I've been wondering: Does she never come to Delhi, or did she go back to the villages, because the air here didn't agree with her? And if she doesn't live in the capital, then who is the person who lives here? Is she India's step-mother? And that old Rajput,' he pointed to a poster hanging on the wall, 'where does his mother live? Does she never write to her son and ask that he call her back to Delhi? My mother writes to me every eighth day.'[30]

Madhusudan glances up at the poster, an old Rajput face with a froth of white beard and a cup of hot coffee proclaiming '[t]his beautiful coffee and this beautiful face, both are Indian'—an oblique reference to official culture's utter disregard for the urban, the middle class, and the modern.

The men and women in the Coffee House articulate everyday urban concerns, the politics and policies emerging from the capital but also the issues faced by the middle classes seeking expression of their own issues, and of the literary and artistic trends becoming evident in their midst. There is a heady conviction of a culture in the

---

[30] Rakesh [1961] 1967: 221.

making, of modernist art forms even then in the process of creation. The Hindi language literati discuss the newly born theatre, provided for the first time with urban venues and official state patronage with the formation of the National School of Drama in 1959. They discuss the *nai kavita* which crystallized in the mid-1940s, for the first time deploying non-metrical forms reflecting the cadences of the spoken word, and experimenting with form as much as with language and meaning; they speak of *nai kahani* which took shape in the 1950s, with Mohan Rakesh, Rajendra Yadav, and Kamleshwar as its centre. But these primarily urban forms set in urban landscapes are in many ways at odds with the general direction of state support. They are, as the Urdu poet so astutely notes in his complaint, not the concern of Mother India. Modern literature in the Indian languages, of which Hindi is just one, though placed in a position of some privilege, is left without a rudder. Bharat Mata looks only to the rural, to folk-art. This burgeoning middle-class culture, with all its aches and pains, its tenuous ties to the rural, is not what is going to find consecration in the 'national culture' which the capital is seeking to conjure up in the shortest possible time.[31]

[31] Bourdieu (1993: 121) has noted the relationship between various instances of consecration, between agents of production, reproduction, and diffusion: '(1) There are institutions which conserve the capital of symbolic goods (academies, museums, learned societies and the educational system); (2) the institutions which ensure the reproduction of agents of "cultivated disposition" who have the power to grant cultural consecration. The lector-position he or she occupies within the system of production and circulation of symbolic goods represent the ambivalent relationship between producers of scholastic authority . . . and (3) organizations which are not fully institutionalized, literary circles, peer groups . . . who award cultural consecration . . . All in all, however, intellectuals and artists occupy a dominated position in the field of power. Artists and especially professors coming from the petite bourgeoisie are most directly under the control of the state. The state [neo-orientalist in our case] has the power to orient intellectual production by means of subsidies, commissions, promotion, honorific posts, even decorations, all of which are for speaking or keeping silent, for compromise and abstention.' Ibid.: 124–5.

PERFORMANCE AND AUTHENTICATION FROM WITHOUT

On 13 October 1959, Madhusudan meets Harbans again in the crowd milling around Janpath, as Queen's Way is now called. Through conversations with Harbans and Nilima he is transported to the grey urban landscape of London, the desolation of lodgings where their Indianness, the unfamiliar, pungent smell of their cooking, make for hostility with the landlady, where the washing hangs wetly in the apartment, money is scarce, and the sense of loneliness and isolation overwhelm all else. The novel does not in fact move to Europe, to London or Paris, where a great deal of the action of past years takes place; the narrative mediates a sense of these cities through the two protagonists. The letters Harbans writes to Nilima, to which Nilima allows Madhusudan access, provide Harbans' point of view. Harbans reverts to calling her Savitri, and asks her to write to him in Hindi, reflecting perhaps nostalgia, perhaps an urge to be more intimate; or it could be that he does not consider her English good enough for the purpose. His letters discuss and analyse their relationship. Thus, from London—as is typical for this novel, a specific address is given: 31 Bunns Lane, Mill Hill, London, NW7—he writes of his ambition for her: 'I want to see something in you, so beautiful, that I can claim it with my whole person, without having to lose a word over it. I want to see the kind of completion (*purnata*) in you which also fills my interior and startles me, awaking such passion that my whole being is absorbed in it.'[32] As Luhmann has pointed out, this self-absorbed individuation, which seeks at the same time to find its complement in that of a partner, endangers the very nature of the union founded on the principle of complete merger and complete differentiation.[33] Though Harbans has given up his opposition to her artistic ambitions, so that the merger would seem possible, he gives fresh instructions to mould her at the same time: 'Go on doing what you want and

---

[32] Rakesh [1961] 1967: 99.
[33] Luhmann [1982] 1998: 38.

go in whatever direction you like. I'll say nothing to you now; will say nothing to you ever. I have no right to say anything. It would be good if you were to write your letters only in Hindi now because your English makes my head buzz.'[34] He is not only giving her fresh instructions on how to conduct her correspondence with him, he is further demeaning her by not allowing her to use the hierarchically more powerful language.

While Harbans is away, Nilima, defying his wishes, has spent a year in Mysore to learn Bharat Natyam. Harbans, meanwhile, is not able to get his PhD, nor has he written his novel. Instead, it is Nilima who has found the first real forum for her dance, her first real 'cultural consecration' and the first sustained authentication—abroad.

In London she accosts the famous dancer Uma Dutt while doing odd jobs at the Indian High Commission. Uma Dutt's dancing partner Urvashi has suddenly decided to return to India and Nilima takes the opportunity to step in and accompany the troupe on its tour through Europe. Harbans decides he will support Nilima, he will forget himself while helping her to evolve her personality and realize himself through her; he ultimately agrees to become the manager of the troupe. He seems unable to stop managing her life for her. For him, Nilima's dancing will be made somewhat respectable in the capitals of Europe. Harbans and she will go from Paris to Madrid and back again, from Paris to Bonn, from Bonn to Geneva, to Bern, and then on to West Berlin. But Harbans will soon recoil from what he sees. He is inexperienced, unused to commercial dealing; the tour is a disaster. There are a series of mishaps. In relating this experience to Madhusudan, he reflects bitterly: What can art mean to these people? Catering to their expectations means prostitution of another kind:

> Theatre, impresario and audiences. The commercial aspect of the world of art. There would be a fight with the impresario one day, the next day the theatre manager would decide to simply withhold the money owing to them. Without understanding each other's language, we would fight

[34] Rakesh [1961] 1967: 94.

long battles. Bharat Natyam does not mean dance there, it's just entertainment. Like the rope trick. India (*Bharat*) means elephants, snakes, and the rope trick. Indian dance is just one more link in that chain. It is all entertainment: *bhava, abhinaya, mudra,* emotion, performance, posture. Kathakali is the dance of puppets. Advertisement is the most important part of that show. The new impresario always talks about publicity.[35]

Harbans will leave the troupe in a huff, dragging Nilima along with him. Left alone after being unable to fulfil his ambitions and disregarding Nilima's success, he speaks of his sense of claustrophobia thereafter, of being stuck in a dark room without windows, of not being able to move out: 'What happened after that [Nilima's arrival] allowed no ray of light to remain in my life. I have been adrift in pitch darkness since then; I see no light at the end of the tunnel. It seems to me that I have been locked in a cell for life detainees and that I will be left to stamp my feet in it for the rest of my life.'[36]

This is the darkness at the heart of the narrative: a fumbling, an inability to fulfil ambitions. He feels stifled, his writing, which seeks to articulate his sense of being, seems adrift in a world with no mooring. He seems unable to articulate what it is that he seeks. At the same time he will not allow Nilima the means to find her artistic fulfilment; he does not even see merit in her endeavour.

Back in Delhi, Harbans and Nilima carry on their lives in an over-furnished house in Defence Colony. Nilima's sister Shukla, married to Surjit, lives next door and keeps an eye on Harbans' needs, while he chooses to ignore her existence; he hates Surjit. There is no older generation in this modernist novel of frustrated couples, no mention of an extended family house with a courtyard, no children, no sense of a rooted past, just the newly forming nuclear family in modern housing in a Delhi disconnected from the culture of its own Mughal past, groping for a sense of direction in Nehru's India.

[35] Ibid.: 159.
[36] Ibid.: 133.

Nilima takes Madhusudan for a walk to a still green area, Okhla, in the white winter sunshine of January: they come upon a signboard pointing to *Gram Joga Bai ko, Sahi Ram Marg* (Joga Bai's village, the right way to Rama);[37] they take this path. She confides in him: 'You are as much my friend as you are his (Harbans'). At least that's how I regarded it in those days.' In the semi-rural setting of Okhla she relates the tale of her escapade in Paris, the effort to free herself from 'old and antiquated *samskaras*', deeply ingrained cultural traits. In the course of her work with Uma Dutt she came to know the Burmese dancer U Ba Nu. She stayed on in Paris with him for three anxiety-ridden days. She considered quite seriously whether she could lose herself in an unfamiliar country amidst unfamiliar people and spend the rest of her life there? She describes how she and U Ba Nu wandered through Paris together, boulevards, parks, the Seine, the theatres, they all seemed like a vast museum to her and she the only visitor. She did not want to return to the hotel, every uninhabited room was like Harbans' house. Then, in a final burst of anxiety, Nilima does run back to Harbans. She is still afraid he will not accept her once he finds out. She remembers the fate of the women left behind in Pakistan after they rejoined their husbands. But then, like all Rakesh's couples—most famously the one in his last play, *Adhe Adhure* (Neither Half nor Whole, 1969)— she and Harbans can neither live with each other nor live without each other.[38] This is how London and Paris are portrayed, at one remove, as part of a related experience. They

[37] Ibid.: 170.
[38] For an analysis of the play, see Dalmia 2006: 130–6. The main woman protagonist, who, perhaps not surprisingly, is also called Savitri, is presented in an extremely unsympathetic light, counterposed to the bedraggled figure of a long unemployed husband. As against Nilima with her glamour and her artistry, she is a working woman, whose income supports her entire household. She is shown as impatient, easily riled; the children complain, are unruly and neglected. She has dared to have a series of men friends, she is held responsible for most ills in the family. There seems to be no family space for her, however vital the money she brings in.

provide an escape; fast expanding Delhi, modernizing partially and painfully, remains the primary site.

Though Harbans and Nilima return to India together, they are culturally still at odds with themselves, with each other, and with the world. Harbans has taken up work with an unidentified intelligence agency. Nilima remains ambitious, continuing to seek ways of legitimating her dance and finding avenues of recognition. Meanwhile, as she tells Madhusudan later, Shukla has married Surjit. He is as tall and broadly built as Harbans and Harbans himself once thought highly of him. Shukla discovers his past—that he is already married—once she is in a physical relationship with him. She weeps bitterly, thinking of Nilima and Harbans in faraway London. Surjit marries her on 17 May 1955, a day before the Hindu Marriage Law is passed, making bigamy illegal. However, the triangle—Harbans, Nilima, Shukla—carries on much as before despite Shukla's marriage.

They live in a world torn by the Cold War. The narrative registers President Eisenhower's visit to India between 9 and 14 December 1959. Eisenhower and Nehru talk to each other about a possible threat posed by China. India is walking a tightrope between two blocs, the West, regarding itself as the Free World, and the socialist

Illus. 29: President Eisenhower at a public reception at the Ramlila Grounds, Delhi, 1959

countries behind the Iron Curtain; a young nation is seeking to find its moorings, politically as much as culturally. What does this mean for the artistic couple at the heart of the narrative?

THE SECOND AUTHENTICATION: THE ROLE OF THE POLITICAL SECRETARY AND THE SECOND TRIANGLE

Back in Delhi, Nilima has continued to search for a public forum for her dance. As we have seen, in the Delhi of 1959 there are new players; the cultural landscape has changed radically. The national academies for music and drama, for art, for literature, have come into existence, though they are not mentioned explicitly in the novel and play no role in the narrative. But there are foreign cultural agencies, attached to the embassies and high commissions, not only as the new patrons and funders of art but as legitimating institutions. If in 1951, dancing seemed still rooted in the older courtesan culture, by the end of the 1950s, courtesan culture and the elite connoisseurship it asked for were things of the past; there are areas of the city reserved for prostitution without the arts. The old, decaying courtly culture represented by Ibadat Ali has disappeared into oblivion. Ibadat Ali has no connections in contemporary Delhi. There are other internationally recognized stars-in-the-making. Dance forms in their new 'classical' guise have national, and with that international, aspirations. Patronage is dispensed by the Delhi Kala Niketan and the foreign cultural agencies, and awarded to the select few that they choose to favour.

There is the slightly sinister figure of the Political Secretary of an unspecified embassy who hovers on the horizons of both Nilima and Harbans. The Political Secretary seems a composite figure representing both sides of the Iron Curtain.[39] Harbans drags Madhusudan to his

[39] There was no homegrown modernist art in Delhi, as there had been through the 1940s in Bombay. See Dalmia 2001. Resisting nationalist attempts to mould art, Rudolf von Leyden, art critic of *The Times of India*, said in the Republic Day Supplement of the paper on 26 January 1950: 'An official art policy which demands direction by force or persuasion will hardly

spacious house with a sprawling terrace, with wall-to-wall carpeting in a subdued grey in the living room, into which one can sink luxuriously. The assembled company includes Nilima, as also the Gulatis, a 'socializing' couple. The Political Secretary is busy that evening, baiting a pair of modern artists seeking patronage, uncertain of their wares. The one has a series of abstract paintings, which please no-one, but no-one dare exhibit ignorance or distaste as they are viewed in succession; the other artist has canvases with figures in garish colours and landscapes. In the Cold War clash of cultures, abstract expressionism, as it was called, was seen as representing the Free World, with New York and the United States in the lead.[40] Figural art, social realism, was the domain of the Soviet Union.[41] The two artists thus represent the two sides of the Iron Curtain. The Political Secretary asks them to find titles for the paintings, and they indulge each other,

---

be successful in developing a vigorous contemporary art. Good art is the true language of any given time in history and is made in free imagination of the artists. If you tell him that he must paint like somebody else or paint only approved subjects as per schedule, he will not give you art that is going to live . . . And so one cannot really be happy about the scholarships awarded last year by the Central Government although as a first sign of official patronage they were welcome. They laid down the condition that the recipient must spend three months in an (approved) village. Apart from the fact that the red tape attaching to such a condition has prevented (at least in Bombay) the payment of scholarship more than four months after they were announced, one must doubt whether anything can be achieved by such enforced rustication. If an artist feels deeply about the village and its life, he will want to go and work there in any case; if he does not he will be wasting his time and public money. Too strong an emphasis on nationalism in art is also a danger that might lead to isolation of the artist. The best art has always taken from the running streams of creative work.' Ibid.: 286. Dalmia writes of the reluctant purchase by the national art academy of a modernitst painting, *Zameen* by M.F. Husain (1955). Ibid.: 106.

[40] See Guilbaut 1983 for a careful study of the process by which the United States came to play a leading role in the world of art after World War II, in particular chapter 5.

[41] See Clark [1981] 1985 for the term Social Realism, with its many ramifications, in the Soviet Union.

play games, 'a play, of which the Political Secretary is the hero.'[42] He and his wife can play at connoisseurship merely on the basis of their power to dispense favours, offer positions in cultural institutions, and send people abroad on tours and scholarships. Harbans is recognized as an authority of sorts; at the same time, he is constantly put in his place: if nothing else, he is accused of being jealous of his wife. Madhusudan is plainly mocked; he is told to look out that he does not become as difficult as the previous Art and Drama critic of the paper, that he does not begin to play power games. What the narrator seems to be showing is the blatant cultural insensitivity of the white man even in independent India, patronizing, conscious of his power to create and destroy and secure art in India based on his presumed knowledge of the European art scene.

The Political Secretary offers Harbans the possibility of organizing a seminar on 'World Culture' and present a paper on Indian art after the Mughal period, broad sweeping themes which treat Indian art ahistorically and a-contextually. Harbans reacts with as much revulsion as he had in Europe. But the Political Secretary is much more interested in Nilima—as Nilima is in him. She has a Bharat Natyam performance choreographed to a Northern devotional song coming up under the auspices of the Delhi Kala Niketan; this is to be her first major performance after her foreign tour, and she considers it crucial for her career. There has been much tension at home about this. Harbans sees Nilima as prostituting her talent, as self-seeking. But Harbans is sent off, all the same, with two booklets of the most expensive tickets to the Political Secretary, which at the last minute,

---

[42] Rakesh [1961] 1967: 243. Mohan Rakesh was very aware of the Cold War and of writers and artists who sold out to one or the other side in the battle to win them over. As he said in his 1972 interview with Carl Coppola: 'To my mind, it seems that this country has been a chess board for quite a long time between the United States' ideologists and the USSR's ideologists. I mean, it was actually in the chambers of New Delhi that the game was being played, and many of the intellectuals here were being made pawns in the game.' A writer had to be committed, Rakesh's own commitment was broadly Leftist, but not anchored in any particular ideology. Coppola 1973.

he refuses to deliver. We will come back to the reasons why he does not do so later, when we discuss why Harbans dissociates himself from Nilima's ambitions. Without the promised supply of tickets, the embassy contingent stays away, and Harbans himself stays away in frustrated rage. Nilima's performance cannot turn out to be other than a disaster.

> It was not so much a Bharat Natyam performance, it was much rather the drama of her own conflict with herself. Each time the dancer faltered, it was the musical accompaniment which seemed to hold her up. Her eyes were glazed, perhaps because of the tranquillizer, or because of the tension she had suffered through the day, or for a reason larger than both these. All the while, looking at her, it seemed to me that she was thinking of something very faraway, something which kept coming back to gnaw at her, even though she kept pushing it away. What was that faraway thing? Did it have something to do with the empty chairs in the front row, or her own domestic life with Harbans, or the dawning realization that if she were not to make the best of the opportunity given to her at the age of thirty-four, then . . .?[43]

Nilima is exhausted and cannot quite conceal it. She barely manages to hold her posture till the end. There is thin applause. The following day, most reviews are either mildly enthusiastic—some commend her being a Northerner dancing a Southern dance to the lyrics of Northern *sants*—or plainly bland. Sushma Srivastava, the famed art critic of the *New Delhi Times*, is patronizing. Only the critic Gajanan is outright in his critique. Nilima leaves her husband. There is domestic turmoil. And political turmoil: violence in the Congo, in Algeria, in Laos.

Harbans has shut himself in his study, he is drinking uncontrollably, an anxious and caring Shukla hovering over him, blaming her sister for deserting him, but knowing all the while that in the end the two could not and would not stay away from each other. Nilima will indeed return to the ailing Harbans, to cook for him and care for him.

---

[43] Rakesh [1961] 1967: 305.

The triangle will reform itself: Harbans, the demanding intellectual male, the ambitious, artistic Nilima who seems to have abandoned all hope of a career, and the compliant and domestic Shukla, filling in the gaps of Nilima's domesticity.

CULTURE AS A BUFFER ZONE: THE DISSOLUTION OF THE SECOND TRIANGLE

Towards the end of the narrative, Madhusudan—who has primarily been a participant-observer, a narrator—enters the action of the novel. The focus shifts to his love relationship, which as it evolves replicates the first triangle with some variation. The young girl from his days in Qasabpura will become the Shukla-equivalent in his life. We had met her as the seven- or eight-year-old daughter of the Thakurain, whom Madhusudan looks up in order to write a story for his paper about this neighbourhood. She is now a girl of marriageable age and the Thakurain is an impoverished widow, cursing the longevity of Ibadat Ali, the sitar player. Madhusudan writes his story about the neighbourhood, which prompts the municipality to send a team to clean it up, driving away the vegetable vendors from the sidewalks. The imminent threat now: the houses which are falling from sheer disrepair, including the Thakurain's, are to be torn down. He finds this out when the Thakurain turns up at his place indignantly, accompanied by her daughter. She proposes that he marry her daughter, to the surprise and embarrassment of all concerned. And when he rebuffs her gently, she bursts out: 'Why don't you say clearly that if you were to marry, you'd marry a *balkati sonpari* [a golden fairy with bobbed hair]!' The daughter, Nimma, stands up proudly to go, and he is reminded of Khurshid's pride and rage in the old days. This is the image which will stay with him.

Meanwhile, he has become involved with the art critic Sushma Srivastava. She is a woman of wide influence, very westernized. The first extended meeting with her takes place in the newest restaurant in Connaught Place, the dark and exotic La Bohème. She is self-assured, impatient, imperious, her name is being coupled increasingly with

Madhusudan's, whom she clearly desires as a partner. Her views about life are decisive, individualistic, an irritant for Madhusudan. There is a final encounter in her room in Constitution House, where she tries to seduce him. She mentions being offered a three-year position in the Political Secretary's country. The first warning bells ring for him. Her independence conjures up uneasy associations. He rejects Sushma mercilessly, just when she begins to let him know how vulnerable she is, in spite of her declared independence of being. The images that Madhusudan once again recalls when recoiling from intimacy with Sushma are of the Kanjariyomwala Bazar in Amritsar, and childhood memories of swine wallowing in filth.

There is then, disqualification, even condemnation of ambitious modern women, of both Nilima and Sushma, by the two main male protagonists, Harbans and Madhusudan, each time from morally high grounds: they are regarded as women who pander to the prostitution of Indian culture by the West. The final disclosure and denunciation of the result of this pandering comes from Harbans.

He tells Madhusudan that the Political Secretary has offered him a very good position, the post of Secretary in the newly formed Bharatiya Samskriti Kendra (Indian Cultural Centre), which has fallen vacant. How can the Political Secretary of a foreign embassy be offering something which 'promotes Indian art and culture? There is nothing in their programme which is even distantly connected to politics in any way,' Madhusudan protests. Harbans hangs his shoulders disconsolately and says:

> You are a journalist, so you know what 'buffer state' means in politics. This kind of 'buffer state' also has a meaning in the field of literature, art and culture. It is the task of the Indian Cultural Centre to see that litterateurs and artists are maintained as just such a buffer state, so that, if nothing else, at the least, they don't go over to the other side. From the political point of view, that is surely not of little significance. That's why they are funding the English weekly magazine *Culture*,[44] that's why they

[44] The reference is surely to a specific journal, perhaps *Thought*, which was

send a couple of people on trips abroad each year. These are all measures to keep the buffer state intact. That's why the name of a certain person can be useful in one way, that of another can be useful in another way, that's why they reach out to them. Why do you think they are offering me the position of Secretary of the Indian Cultural Centre?[45]

He indicates that he is important for these people precisely because he works for an intelligence agency. He also brings up Sushma Srivastava's name: he used to go around with her once, thinking it was an intellectual relationship, until he discovered that she was getting a new house built for her father in Karnal. He knew their financial situation. When he asked her how her father came about this wealth, she merely pressed his hand and said that one did not ask such questions. Madhusudan's world is shaken to its very foundations. Visions of his future life with Sushma rise before his eyes: a house in Defence Colony or Jor Bagh, a beautifully maintained garden, flowers, garden chairs, and book-lined walls, dimly lit lamps, conversations about the classics in the dark corners of La Bohème.[46] This is followed by a vision of the two-roomed house in which the Thakurain lives with her daughter Nimma. Nimma sitting on a broken *modha* (wicker seat), a cup of tea in her hands, tea leaves swimming in it as she casts a scared look at her mother. It is clear that Sushma does not stand a chance either, she too has prostituted herself to foreign pimps of culture, and as with Shukla in Harbans' case, there is Nimma now to think of.

Spending the night in Harbans's house, while Nilima is still away, on the one hand, Madhusudan thinks of his own loft in Anandparbat:

> The same coming home alone every day and knocking at the door. The owner's wife opens the door with the same suspicious look in her eyes, takes hold of her daughter by the arm and sends her in. Climbing up

---

brought out from Delhi from the late 1940s, but it is now impossible to be certain which journal is meant.
[45] Rakesh [1961] 1967: 243.
[46] Ibid.: 323.

the steps, I don't feel like entering my room. Entering, I don't feel like tidying away anything. Standing near the window, I see the layout of the city, spreading out into the distance. The trains pass the Sarai Ruhela station one by one. The spirit wandering in the dark moans every now and then. From the room I go to the terrace, from the terrace to the room.[47]

Back in the room in Harbans' house, Madhusudan flips through the disconnected chapters of Harbans' manuscript. 'Why haven't the worms eaten up these papers all these years? It is nonsense, sheer nonsense. I ought to throw these papers into the fire . . .' and then, going through the disjointed titles and reaching the last, unnumbered chapter, he thinks, 'Non-chapter—what will the end be?'

Madhusudan speaks with the moral authority of the narrator when he tells us that he finds Harbans' disjointed novel-writing venture unacceptable, though it is the thing that seems to matter the most to Harbans himself. So, just as Harbans disqualifies Nilima, Madhusudan disqualifies Harbans. Meanwhile, his own editor is beginning to find Madhusudan's reporting too poetic, too partisan. For one reason or another, the men seem to be failures at what they do, while the women's efforts to reach what they want are disregarded or blocked by the men. It seems almost like the last straw when Madhusudan's offer to write a feature on the control some foreign embassies exercise over cultural institutions elicits a caution from the editor against wading too deep in troubled waters. These are politically sensitive themes, he warns. In the end, Madhusudan opts out of the complications of a life that seems uncontrollable to him by trying to find a simple solution to his relationships. He ends the narrative by taking a taxi to Qasabpura. 'Which pur?' the taxi driver asks. Old Delhi has receded in more ways than one from the world of New Delhi with its bureaucrats and embassies:

'Basti Harphul Singh,' I said and relaxing a little, slid further down the seat. 'Basti Harphul Singh?' The Sikh driver thought this over a bit and

[47] Ibid.: 324.

asked, 'Where's that, Sahib?' 'Barah Tuti Bazaar' I said irritably. The Sikh driver started the car. It jerked into motion and I took a quick look at the diary on my lap to make sure that it was still there. The taxi crossed the Chelmsford Road Bridge and reached Qutub Road. I took a deep breath and feeling a little lighter in my heart, slid further down the seat.[48]

The taxi is going from New Delhi to the promise of Nimma and the community life which Qasabpura still holds, of extended families, of neighbours who meddle in each others' business and thus betoken a caring, of whatever kind. Madhusudan has decided to revert to the world from where he came, not actually to go back to the old city or revalidate it but rather to pick up a piece of it and integrate it into the new. At the same time, he is attempting to reject the *adhunikta* (modernity) that Sushma represents and the world that she brings with herself. Is this a desperate bid to reverse time? Has the reader, propelled to think in another direction, been left hanging in mid-air after all in relation to Madhusudan? With his provincial background, he seems more stable than Harbans, though his journalistic endeavours remain largely unappreciated. Meanwhile, Harbans carries on floundering in his unfinished novel. The language question remains unresolved, it is not as if his writing stint in London led to a resolution. His modernist project remains abandoned, incomplete. The men are repeatedly shown as unsuccessful in their effort to artistically or professionally articulate what they observe and feel. Yet it is the women who suffer real violence, and at the hands of men. Nilima and Sushma's attempts to occupy public space, to garner success by getting authentication for their efforts from outside, are regarded unsympathetically by Harbans, but, more importantly, by the narrator. And none of the characters, each struggling in his or her own way, is portrayed as likeable, warm-hearted, or generous. We are allowed insight into their thought and action, but no closeness.

Writing some years later, Mohan Rakesh recorded his own very modernist anxiety regarding the processes of change underway, of

---

[48] Ibid.: 330.

novel writing under such circumstances and of the dilemmas of the individual: 'Old traditions are being abandoned while new traditions remain unable to evolve. Within single individuals there simmers an awareness which finds no opportunity for collective upsurge. The present is available to us in this disordered context. Why is it not possible to depict this in today's novel: beyond the given context, our experience as witnesses of the rapid pace of history, all that we see, all that we experience, the way we want to live, the way we are living?'[49] The older moral ethos no longer holds lives together; a newer one has not yet replaced it. The frustrations of *Amdhere Band Kamare* seemed to Rakesh one way in which he could show the truth of existence as he saw it—darkly. He was representing a particular moment in the life of the nation's capital, 'a sketch of contemporary Delhi', as he had tentatively proposed in the opening statement of his novel. Caught in the web of the burgeoning cultural scene in Delhi with its newly evolving national culture, its uncertainty about the present, its paucity of patronage for the modern, its reliance either on government funds which stressed the importance of classical and folk culture or on foreign cultural agencies—driven in their turn by the rigid ideologies fostered by the Cold War—the contemporary writer and artist was left without dependable orienting grids. On surer ground was all that betokened the past. Tapati Guha-Thakurta has noted the 'resounding absence' of the modern in the grand show of pan-Indian art put up at the Government House in winter 1948.[50]

---

[49] Rakesh 1967: 189.

[50] As Guha-Thakurta notes about the spectacular art exhibition of 1948, there was 'one resounding absence: the absence of the "modern" in the spectacle of India's art heritage. Such an absence becomes easily naturalized in the event (as even in my essay), as the attention veers predominantly on celebrated notions of "history" and "heritage" that halt the narrative of India's achievements well before the "modern" age. So, when we return to the scene of the 1948 exhibition in New Delhi, we find ourselves entirely in the grips of an art-historical past: a past that effectively dislodges the present in staking its singular civilizational claims over the nation's art.' Guha-Thakurta 1997: 90.

The upshot of which, in the decades which followed, as the artist Gulammohammed Sheikh has put it, meant that '(t)here is false consciousness of both the tradition as well as the modern . . . And, in fact, unless the distinctions are made, we may, by evoking the tradition, be abusing that as well—even while we muddle through the modern without coming to terms with it.'[51] Muddling through the modern in relation to the arts, dance, and political and cultural reportage—this is what Rakesh's novel has caught the spirit of so well: New Delhi in the 1950s, Shahjahanabad, its older now disjointed part, the once proud Mughal city of a once powerful empire, now the capital of the new-born nation, struggling, in a very modernist narrative, to find its way into the modern.

REFERENCES

Azad, Abul Kalam. 1988. *India Wins Freedom: The Complete Version*. Madras: Orient Longman.
Blake, Stephen P. 1991. *Shahjahanabad: The Sovereign City in Mughal India, 1639—1739*. Cambridge: Cambridge University Press.
Bourdieu, Pierre. 1993. *The Field of Cultural Production: Essays on Art and Literature*. Edited and introduced by Randal Johnson. New York: Columbia University Press.
Capetti, Carla. 1993. *Writing Chicago. Modernism, Ethnography, and the Novel*. New York: Columbia University Press.
Chakrabarty, Dipesh. 2000. 'Adda: A History of Sociality', in *Provincializing Europe: Postcolonial Thought and Historical Difference*. Princeton and Oxford: Princeton University Press.
Clark, Katerina. [1981] 1985. *The Soviet Novel: History as Ritual*. Second Edition with a new Afterword. Chicago: University of Chicago Press.

[51] *Journal of Arts and Ideas*, March 1991: 40. As Kumar Shahani put it: 'This blinding of contemporary art has been encouraged by the state . . . the deflecting of the idea of Indianness utterly to a feudal-tribal context with the subterfuge of associating all that is modern with the non-Indian, basically western . . . This kind of Indianness or Bengali-ness or Marathi-ness, is completely on the surface, and the more on the surface it is, the more "Indian" it is accepted as.' Ibid.: 38.

Coppola, Carlo. 1973. 'Interview with Mohan Rakesh', in *Journal of South Asian Literature,* Special Issue, Mohan Rakesh, ed. Carlo Coppola, 2–3/9.

Dalmia, Vasudha. 2006. *Poetics, Plays and Performances: The Politics of Modern Indian Theatre.* Delhi: Oxford University Press.

Dalmia, Yashodhara. 2001. *The Making of Modern Indian Art: The Progressives.* Delhi: Oxford University Press.

Datta, V.N. 1986. 'Punjabi Refugees and the Urban Development of Greater Delhi', in *Delhi through the Ages: Essays in Urban Hisory, Culture and Society,* ed. R.E. Frykenberg. Delhi: Oxford University Press.

Guha-Thakurta, Tapati. 1997. 'Marking Independence: The Ritual of a National Art Exhibition': *Journal of Arts and Ideas,* 30—1. December.

Guilbaut, Serge. 1983. *How New York Stole the Idea of Modern Art: Abstract Expressionism, Freedom, and the Cold War.* Translated by Arthur Goldhammer. Chicago: Chicago University Press.

Joshi, Damayanti. 1989. *Madame Menaka.* Delhi: Sangeet Natak Akademi.

Jacobs, Jane. [1961] 1989. *The Death and Life of Great American Cities.* New York: Vintage Books.

King, Anthony D. 1976. *Colonial Urban Development: Culture, Social Power and Environment.* London: Routledge and Kegan Paul.

Lefebvre, Henri. 1991. *The Production of Space.* Translated by Donald Nicholson-Smith. Oxford: Blackwell Publishing.

Liu, Lydia. 1995. *Translingual Practice: Literature, National Culture, and Translated Modernity—China, 1900–1937.* Stanford: Stanford University Press.

Luhmann, Niklas. [1982] 1998. *Love as Passion: The Codification of Intimacy.* Translated by Jeremy Gaines and Doris L. Jones. Stanford: Stanford University Press.

Mantri, Ganesh. 1992. *Rajdhani Kalchar.* Delhi: Satsahitya Prakashan.

McGregor, R.S., ed. [1993] 2003. *The Oxford Hindi–English Dictionary.* Delhi: Oxford University Press.

Miner, Allyn. 1993. *Sitar and the Sarod in the 18th and 19th Centuries.* Edited by International Institute for Traditional Music, Berlin. Wilhelmshaven: Florian Noetzel Verlag.

Pandey, Gyanendra. 2001. 'Folding the National into the Local: Delhi 1947–1948', in *Remembering Partition: Violence, Nationalism and History in India.* Cambridge: Cambridge University Press.

Rakesh, Mohan. 1967. *Parivesh*. Varanasi: Bharatiya Jnanpith Prakashan.
———. [1961] 1997. *Amdhere Band Kamare*. Delhi: Rajkamal Prakashan.
———. 1975. *Sahityik aur Samskritik Drishti*. Delhi: Radhakrishna Prakashan.
Ramani, Shakuntala. 2003. *Rukmini Devi Arundale: Birth Centenary Volume*. Tiruvanmiyur, Chennai: The Kalakshetra Foundation.
Soneji, Davesh. 2012. *Unfinished Gestures: Devadasis, Memory, and Modernity in South India*. Chicago: University of Chicago Press.
Sundaram, Vivan. 1991. 'A Tradition of the Modern'; and in the discussion thereafter with Kumar Shahani and Gulammohammed Sheikh. *Journal of Arts and Ideas,* March, 20/21.

Epilogue

Looking Backward, Looking Forward

Through their attention to detail, their minute documentation of shifts in structures of feeling, novels are often a record of social history in ways that social history itself is not. What I have attempted in this book is to juxtapose eight major novels, more or less in chronological order, to show these shifts—their character and general direction. To review them, finally, let us take a big step back into the late nineteenth century, when the novel form first crystallized in Hindi, and then move gradually into the mid-twentieth century: 'For how could we come to understand a genesis, the genesis of the present, along with the preconditions and processes involved, other than by starting from the present, working our way back to the past and then retracing our steps?'[1]

The focus of my inquiry has been relatively wide and has depended on the data each novel has offered. I have taken note variously of the history of the North Indian city, particularly after 1857; of the precise location of the narrative in a given city; of house forms and neighbourhoods; of the state of education and newly founded colleges; and of the political and literary discourses of the period. The volume of such information has been uneven because it has depended on what each novel made available. Instead of attempting a summary of all that has been discussed, when retracing my steps here I will focus on what is possibly the most salient thematic link across these novels: the difficulties that women face in the social spaces they inhabit, and

---

[1] Lefebvre 1991: 66.

what they themselves say when they speak. The relations of power depicted in these novels show women as most vulnerable, as those that register change most acutely, as those that react most sensitively to the process of modernization and to shifts in the cultural climate of a particular place and time. They start out with major handicaps—their financial dependence is almost always crippling. But they are spirited and educated, they challenge the assumptions of a given narrative and come to dominate it in spite of the male narrator—often, in fact, to his chagrin. They register the contradictions of modernity even as they reflect the dilemmas of the modernist conundrum in the changing social environment offered by the cities of North India.

My focus has by no means been entirely on women; I set out with no feminist agenda. I focus upon them in this Epilogue because their voices best exemplify the change in the newly emerging Hindu middle classes which came into prominence after the decimation of the Muslim elites of the region after 1857, and even more so after Partition. The process of modernization, of forging nationhood, could only be very different from what happened, for instance, in colonial and post-Independence Calcutta and Bombay. The two metropolises were literally stamped out of nothing by the British. The early, intense, even intimate, contact with Western culture offered conditions for modernization which were entirely absent in the North, both Hindu and Muslim.

There is a vast amount of scholarship on Bengal, on the woman question and its treatment in fiction and autobiographical writing by women, particularly by Tanika Sarkar,[2] but also by Rimli Bhattacharya;[3] there are also very significant works on western India: I am thinking, amongst others, of Rosalind O'Hanlon and Meera Kosambi.[4] This is not even to touch on other parts of the subcontinent, particularly in the South, which had its own peculiar social set-ups, its own range of caste structures, its own venerable literary traditions.

[2] Sarkar 1999, 2000, 2009.
[3] Bhattacharya 1988.
[4] Metcalf 1990; O'Hanlon 1994; Kosambi 2007.

Even what I offer for North India is by no means a complete picture. I have not touched on the wealth of literary material in Urdu, on which, amongst others, Barbara Metcalf, Gail Minault, Aamir Mufti, and Rakshanda Jalil have expended much labour.[5] My project, then, has been neither comprehensive, even as far as the North is concerned, nor comparative, taking into consideration the many neighbouring modern Indian literary traditions. I have tried more to redress the balance in the scholarship—to take stock of what happened in Hindi, with its early claim to the stature of national language but shallow historical presence in most North Indian cities (the exception being Banaras)—than restate known facts and reinstate Bengali and Marathi once more in their positions of primacy.

Juxtaposed below are some of the things I have said about these eight novels, interspersed with the words of the women, sometimes reported, sometimes direct, claiming rights, expostulating or merely expressing the intensity of a given moment. This is less to provide a history of the social space available to women, more to view the range of positions they come to occupy.

In a climactic scene of Shrinivasdas' *Pariksha Guru*, we visit Madanmohan in his prison cell in colonial Delhi. Rich, shallow, and spoilt, living in luxury in the heart of Chandni Chowk, he has led an idle life up to this point, impervious to the sage advice of his friend, the lawyer Brajkishor. Madanmohan has lived extravagantly, he is the prototype of the shallowly westernized and self-indulgent young man, whereas his wife has stepped straight out of a conduct manual for women: she has all the Victorian virtues of a good and thrifty housewife and of a loving and caring mother who carefully supervises the education of her children:

> With so little expense has she made such excellent domestic arrangements that Madanmohan is spared all labour at home. When she has leisure, she does not sit idly gossiping about other people and chattering about jewels and jewellery, she practices reading and writing, embroidery and

---

[5] Minault 1998; Mufti 2016; Jalil 2014.

drawing pictures, etc. . . . The children are very little but while playing she teaches them the basic moral principles and, though unaware, by increasing their knowledge of things she stimulates their natural capacity for knowledge. But she does not burden their minds; there is no hindrance to their innocent play and laughter.

As much as the nation, the new merchant and the professional man need the other half to efficiently manage the domestic sphere, so the author has provided her with the requisite character:

> In relation to her husband, Madanmohan's wife was truly affectionate, well-wishing, a companion in pleasure as well as in pain, and obedient. Early on, Madanmohan held her in great affection. But when he began to keep the company of friends such as Chunnilal and Shimbhudayal, the addiction of dance and music entrapped him into raptures over the false airs and graces of the courtesans . . . His poor, simple, able wife began to seem rustic to him. For a while things were kept secret, but how can there be pleasure in the flower of love after the worm has entered it?

But even Madanmohan's excess has limits, and life eventually catches up with him. Spending an unpleasant night in a debtor's prison, he casts back to thoughts of his string of ingratiating friends, now indifferent to him; he thinks of his wife, a model of virtue, and of his neglect of her. We witness the transformation in his character as he faces his own inner demons in that dark night: menacing shapes seem to loom over him, heaviness weighs him down. Overcome by the surrounding terrors, he faints, to wake up with his head in the lap of his wife, her hot tears bathing his face. Brajkishor has sneaked her into the prison cell. The expected reconciliation and promises of change follow. The world around him is calling upon young merchants like him to contribute to the wealth and well-being of his country, to rise to the challenge of nationhood. But Madanmohan's wife remains almost wordless, her person entirely subsumed to the needs of her husband. Nonetheless, a new interiority, even if short-lived, and a new sense of domesticity have entered the Hindi novel in the late nineteenth century, in a narrative otherwise stiff and unbending, as precursors to much that will unfold in the novels of Premchand after a gap of a few decades.

The faceless wife of *Pariksha Guru* as much as the courtesans who hover on the horizons of Madanmohan's life become the unforgettable Suman of Premchand's *Sevasadan*. She is the daughter of a Brahmin police officer who is caught taking a bribe, so unskilled is he in the art. In her dowry-less state, vital, vibrant Suman has been married off by an unfeeling mother to an older and relatively poor man. Feeling caged in the confines of her small airless house in the narrow lanes forking off Dal Mandi—the glamorous courtesan quarter of Banaras—Suman becomes aware of the privileges enjoyed by Bholi, her courtesan neighbour. Bholi is less beautiful and less musically talented than she is, but the rich and powerful of the city court her:

> Suman sat there for a long time, trying to disentangle cause from effect. Finally she came to a conclusion: Bholi is independent while I'm shackled. Her warehouse (*dukan*) is open and sees a rush of clients, mine is shut, so no one stands and waits. She isn't bothered by barking dogs; I'm scared of social censure. She isn't in purdah, while I am. She chirps freely as she hops from branch to branch, I cling to just one. It is shame, the fear of ridicule, which makes me the servant of another.

These are bold insights: a wife is no better than a prostitute; she also sells herself—though to just one client. Circumstances will force Suman to abandon her enforced wifehood and set up shop as a courtesan, to then acquire overnight fame in the bazaar of beauty. In an age of high nationalism, however, the voice of social reform will also seek her out there in the shape of a voluble activist, Vitthaldas.

> Vitthaldas: Now that our greatly revered Brahman ladies are treading the primrose path of dalliance, there can be no stopping our decline. Suman, you're responsible for the Hindu *jati* having to lower its head.
>   Suman answered earnestly: *You* may think so, no one else does. A few gentlemen have just left after listening to the *mujra*. They were all Hindus, none of them seemed to have lowered heads. They seemed glad that I'm here. Besides, I'm not the only Brahmani in the Mandi; I could

name a couple of others of very high families straight off whose kinfolk were unwilling to take care of them; they came here from a sense of helplessness. If the Hindu *jati* isn't in the least ashamed of itself, how long are frail women like us going to continue protecting it?

Suman's cry from the very heart of the city is that of the nation's women. She is victimized in yet another instance, as social reform also sweeps through the Municipality Board, to which Indian members are now nominated. It is in communal terms that an increasingly polarized Board will argue for and against the removal of courtesans from the centre of the city to its outskirts, though the Board's divisions turn out to be actually generational rather than religion-based. The older generation pays lip service to reform while wishing to go on with traditional ways; the younger members of the Board, earnest professionals who belong to the new world of the up and coming middle class, are ready for reform. They will prevail, the relocation will come into effect and Suman, persuaded to give up her profession, will become head of a cheerless institution for the education of courtesans' daughters. We are at the dawn of Gandhi's age. The high-spirited and defiant Suman will be left a wan, wistful figure at the end of the novel, all resistance beaten out of her. We are told that the nation expects sacrifices of its women, but what does it give them in return? We are left with ambivalent messages: the lot of the courtesan is shown to be actually better than a housewife's. Social reform, though necessary, reforms at the wrong end; it is a cheerless business. Ostensibly, all is as it should be at the end of the novel, yet it is not a happy end.

Given the opportunity, the education, and the social standing, neglected wives can find other avenues to gain recognition, as this age gives way to another. Premchand's *Karmabhumi*, his penultimate novel, is also set in Banaras, now a city of colleges and street action. Sukhada, its heroine, is the wife of Amarkant, a college student, the son of a conservative merchant. They live in Bulanala, a wealthy commercial neighbourhood. In wilful defiance of his father, Amarkant takes, as so many others of his kind, to the world of Gandhian politics. The nation forms the reference point for the series of agitations that follow. He leads the movement to alleviate the punitive legal action faced by Munni, a Rajput woman raped by a white soldier in a field outside the city. Crazed by her experience, she has avenged herself by killing a white man. There is a wave of public sympathy for her and eventually the court exonerates her of murder. Amarkant has played a leading role in the agitation for it. But his real battle is with his wilful wife Sukhada, in which he sees himself as a losing partner. Sukhada dominates not only the relationship but also the narrative. She has a large airy room, furnished in a modern way, with tables, chairs, and books. Prints of paintings by Dhurandhar and Ravi Varma adorn the walls. She reads, occupies herself with her recreations, she seems to do no housework.

In resistance to her and his father, Amar, now in love with Sakina, a poor Muslim girl, defies his family and leaves home. At least in principle, a Hindu–Muslim match is held out as a possibility, though it does not in the end take place. The scene of action shifts to another battle: Dalit temple-entry. Amar's father leads the upper-caste resistance to this measure. It is Sukhada who springs into action as she becomes witness to the ensuing violence in the city, her strong will now harnessed to a social cause:

> Sukhada didn't get into arguments. She was a self-willed woman. The pride that had made her luxuriate in comfort, that had kept her from contact with inferiors, that had prevented her submitting to anyone, now suddenly welled up (*utsarg*) and spilled over. She leapt out of the house in a frenzy, put herself in front of the police, and admonished those who were running away: 'Brothers, why are you running off? This is not the time to escape, it's time to come out and bare your chests. Show them how you can sacrifice your life for dharma. Only those who fight for dharma get to God. Victory is never for those who run off.'

Sukhada faces bullets herself, several Dalits are killed, and finally the doors of the temple are thrown open. The city almost deifies her. She is the very personification of the new woman, educated, self-confident, propelled into a leadership role which she will fulfil again later and even go to prison for, when she tries to retrieve land appropriated by the rich for the housing of the poor, leading a popular agitation in the process.

When Amarkant has left the city for a mountain village, it is in strident feminist tones that Sukhada confides to Sakina: 'He betrayed me. I can't pamper a guttersnipe. If I were to run off with another man, would he try and persuade me to go back to him? Maybe he'd come back to break my neck. I'm a woman and a woman's heart is never too hard, but I won't pamper him, to my dying day I won't.' As she says to Dr Shanti Kumar, Amar's professor in college and political mentor: 'I ask you shamelessly: What right has a man who does not fulfil his obligations towards a woman expecting a woman to fulfil hers? You are truthful, so I want to ask you this—were I to avenge myself tit for tat on account of his behaviour with me, would you ever forgive me?' And Sukhada once more to Sakina: 'If he was hungry for love, so was I hungry for it. What he wanted of me, I also wanted of him. If I couldn't give what he wanted, why did he, in his turn, react rebelliously? Was it because he is a man, and if a man wants to, he can treat a woman like his shoe, but it's a woman's dharma to remain looped around his feet?' The narrator allows these statements to stand without contradiction. Like Madanmohan, Amarkant, cast into prison for inciting peasants to withhold revenue, will learn to face himself at last: 'He had no steadiness, no discipline, no [real] aspiration. There was arrogance (*dambha*) in his service, intoxication (*pramad*), ill-will (*dvesha*). It was this arrogance that made him disregard Sukhada. Instead of attempting to get to the truth that dwelt in that woman of comfort, he rejected her. His outer eye covered the inner.'

Sukhada and Amarkant come together at the end. Premchand shows both the tensions of marital relationships and the power battles, as much as he shows reconciliation and compromise. But he cannot bring himself to glorify the submission of a woman to a man's will. His women are too strong to melt into their partners. Sukhada holds her own till the end, claiming victory over her husband. And once again the narrator does not contradict her.

Another decade and a half, and we find the Sukhadas of the world, even those of less affluent circumstance, going to college themselves. We have moved to Lahore, that most cosmopolitan of North Indian cities, where Hindu, Muslim, and Sikh live side by side, though in increasing tension. The fervent nationalism of the Quit India movement of 1942 is giving way to the more pressing communal issue. The first volume of Yashpal's epic *Jhutha Sach* (1958, 1960) moves both quickly—as political and personal events pile up—and slowly, dwelling on each month and sometimes day, through 1947, the year of Independence and Partition. As we have seen, it narrates primarily the story of Tara and of her brother Jaydev Puri as they negotiate the politics of the times and their own destinies. They live in a congested house in the fictive Bhola Pandhe ki Gali, in the walled inner city of the Hindu quarter, and are constrained by all the social limits set by their surroundings. The second volume spans the first decade after Independence and moves to a Delhi filled with refugees.

In Lahore, campus life has opened the doors of freedom. Spirited Sukhada has become Tara, who falls in love with a fellow student, Asad Ahmad, though she has been engaged to be married to Somraj, of her own Khatri caste, for two years. As Tara protests to her mother, who wants to arrange a meeting with a girl being proposed as a match for her brother Puri: 'What kind of a meeting is that? No conversation of any kind. Nowadays, people meet each other several times before they get engaged, they continue to talk to each other.' Her mother scolds her: 'this is not engagement, this is illicit love (*ashnai*). This can happen in houses in Anarkali, Gawal Mandi, and Mall Road. What'll people in the *gali* and neighbourhood say if they hear of this?' The *gali* ethos links the private to the public with unerring immediacy; it recognizes no privacy. And thus it is that it comes to rule the lives of the novel's protagonists. Puri is in love with Kanak, an affluent Brahmin girl, portending a match intolerable for her family, who live in affluent Gawal Mandi. 'If her life is becoming too heavy for you, I can carry my sister's burdens,' Puri tells his mother. 'There is no match between her first division and a boy who was caught copying something in his exams.'

Yet there is no support of brother for sister, once Puri learns of Asad's existence in his sister's life. The city is in flames, the affluent begin to leave the city. In this turmoil Asad declines to come to the rescue of a desperate Tara, citing Communist Party discipline—which does not allow for cross-religious marriages in these troubled times—as reason. An unwilling Tara is forced to marry. Beaten by her husband for supposed infidelity on the wedding night, she is saved further humiliation by arson in the city and the flames leaping up the stairs.

Her defiance has left her defenceless, it has cast her into the helplessness and victimhood that the times have brought upon women. She flees down the street, is caught by another brutal man, and raped. She wonders: 'What have I done wrong, for what am I being punished? For not wanting to marry Somraj? Or for going with Asad? Am I not even free to kill myself?' Neighbouring Mehar says the next morning: 'The bastards fight each other but they defile the bodies of women (*mitti kharab karna*).' Tara's body is a symbol of that of women at large, Hindu or Muslim, during the entire bloody process of Partition.

In a city that has now become part of Pakistan, a series of terrifying ordeals follow, the last of which consists of imprisonment with others, equally destitute, in a house in Shekhupura. Stripped of part of their clothing, half-starved, the women are imprisoned in an abandoned house. The old city of Lahore with its shared religious culture, its aspirations, its tales of personal strife, has ceased to exist. In the new nation, beginnings are tough. But, the educated and the capable have new chances. As Tara observes, Partition has also freed women: 'A lot was destroyed during Partition, but the solid layers of earth with which society was smothered have been cracked, as if an earthquake has burst open the walls of a prison, freeing those inside—even if they have been injured in the process. Many perished, many never recovered from their injuries, but Panjabis are a vital lot, they seem to have fallen on their feet.' Over the succeeding years, elections will be held, lives rebuilt. Tara becomes a high-standing official in the central government in Delhi, later happily married to an older mentor from her Lahore days. Her life finally settles into a relatively staid course. Yashpal's narrative plunges into the depths of human experience by retaining a studied dryness while representing scenes of utter degradation.

Yashpal could have touched the heights of human emotion but desists. The articulation of such emotion appears in Agyeya's *Nadi ke Dvip*, where capable, resourceful Tara becomes Rekha, educated, sensitive and, like all the women we have met so far, spirited. She is able to articulate joy, fulfilment, the experience of beauty in nature, as much as its opposite: the claustrophobia of city life and incomplete recognition of the needs of her emotions and inner life.

Agyeya's novel, set in an earlier period than *Jhutha Sach*, i.e. in the late 1930s and early 1940s, scales emotional heights never encountered in any of the previous novels. We move from the modern to the modernist perspective, to a 'new literature that was rebellious, questioning, doubtful and introspective but confident and even aggressive in its aesthetic conviction.'[6] The most powerful scenes in the novel take place in the mountains: in the wild beauty of Naukuchia, a tiny hill station in lake-dotted Kumaon, and on the banks of Lake Tulian, high up in Kashmir. Bhuvan and Rekha spend their time in a Dak Bungalow and in tents, the freedom and openness of these places being juxtaposed with the claustrophobia of North Indian cities of the 1930s. Delhi and Lucknow appear as cities of the period between 1932 and 1942.

Moving from native state to native state, wherever she can find a position as a girls' tutor, without a permanent home and a drawing room to bolster her position, Rekha is always on the move, in trains, railway stations, waiting rooms, her meeting places with friends and acquaintances either a coffee house, or park benches and river banks. She emanates both strength and vulnerability:

> 'Then, I suppose, I am like the Tree of Knowledge—the Upside-Down-Tree—my roots adrift in the sky. But please don't think I am complaining.'

[6] Childs [2000] 2008: 20.

The train had started. At the next station Bhuvan said again, 'If a person like you wanders around, it must be by choice—it's difficult to credit it being out of necessity. And wandering by choice is a reflection of inner strength.'

Rekha laughed. 'The inner strength comes from the wandering, Dr Bhuvan! Because when there are no roots to hold the soil one has to draw sustenance from elsewhere to survive while drifting in the air. Wandering by choice? Yes, I suppose you might call it that; because one has chosen not to be crushed into the dust, not to be lost in the dark abyss—one has chosen to struggle for survival.'

Rekha is both single and married; to be with her can lead to social ostracization for both. For the moment, however, they cast all such considerations aside as they revel by the lake at Naukuchia. When she speaks of her sense of fulfilment, Rekha does not use similes, she does not *liken* herself to still waters, she becomes one with them. And yet even as she opens up to receive Bhuvan, she does not melt into him, she does not become one with him. Theirs is a new language of desire:

> I was a body of still water; a lake, a pond, a little pool choked with weeds. You came like a stream and shook me, lit my hopes, bared me to the endless sky. Let me say it, Bhuvan, my body surged towards you as it never surged before. Every fibre of my being sought your touch, the touch of your hands, the hold of your arms, the warmth of your body . . . but in you I sensed a fear—no not quite a fear. But a holding back, a restraint imposed from some far source . . . And it was the touch of this restraint that stilled the storm in my own being: the lake that I was found its normal surface again—a still surface, still water, closed unto itself. But, no, no! not closed unto itself, not covered again; it stayed open to the image of the sky.

This ecstacy is counterposed to the despair that follows Rekha's abortion and Bhuvan's turning away from intimacy with her. But what stays with the reader is the beauty and the poetry, the daring and defiance in Rekha when she refuses Bhuvan's marriage proposal:

'But Bhuvan, you are looking at things with society's eyes. There is nothing wrong in that view, nor is it irrelevant; but that is not the decisive view. Any decision—any solution which ignores the individual will be wrong—it will be hateful.'

She was silent for a moment, then lowering her eyes, she continued, 'It could be that my thinking has been warped from the very beginning—but it has been that all through. My action—that society should regulate my social acts—that is right; but my inner life—no. That is mine—absolutely mine. Mine—which means the private domain of every individual.'

Tara could have said these words in *Jhutha Sach* had she had the wherewithal to express herself in such words within her environment. But that was not her, or indeed Yashpal's, idiom. After Agyeya, the Hindi novel was never the same again. A new idiom of personhood had been found.

A melancholy, lower pitched yet deeply moving language appeared in *Gunahom ka Devata*, an earlier novel covering a later period, i.e. the year of independence, 1947, and set far removed from the bloodshed of Panjab, in a Civil Lines bungalow within relatively peaceful Allahabad. The only child of her Brahmin family, Sudha, studying in Allahabad University and in love with Chander, a young Kayasth economist almost adopted by her professor father, is to be married off that summer. The love she and Chander have for each other, Sudha tells Chander, is purer than fraternal love; why can't she simply go on looking after her father and not marry at all? Intercaste marriage is a problem; marriage would betray Dr Shukla's trust in them both. Chander persuades her to marry and that starts of a period of intense suffering for both. Sudha leaves for her married home and Chander takes up a relationship with the Anglo-Indian Pammi. After a while, Pammi puts an end to it; she feels Chander is just using her.

It is Sudha and Chander's meeting towards the end of the novel which creates the emotionality that made *Gunahom ka Devata* a cult novel for generations of North Indian youth. Sudha is visiting

Allahabad with her husband. She is pregnant, as Chander will find out from her husband. To survive marriage, she has retreated into a life of religion. When Sudha and Chander finally converse, she explains, it is not puja that she performs, just the recitation of the *Gita*, the *Bhagavata*, and sometimes of verses from the *Sursagar*. She puts her new religiosity in a pragmatic context: 'The Hindu household is like a prison; if religion were not there to provide subterfuge, the prisoner does not so much as have permission to fast so that she can be released from life. I get some pleasure (*sukh*) from fasting as subterfuge.' But even this subterfuge has helped her acquire faith (*vishwas*): 'I used to wonder why women are so devoted to worship rituals, then I saw why—the Hindu woman is so helpless, she receives so much insult, contempt, and disdain from husband and son that she would become a beast if it weren't for her worship. It's what has allowed the Hindu woman to remain elevated (*umcha*), to hold her head high.' In all these devotional works, she has found in Krishna a very attractive symbol of love. And so she finds a way to merge herself with Chander, safely sublimated to the status of the love god. 'I am a segment of your *atma*, separated from you in this birth. But I will circle around you always and like the moon, continue to revolve in circles around you.'

She does reproach Chander, however, about his relationship with Pammi. Chander reacts with arrogance and bitterness: her love and Pammi's sensuality are two sides of the same coin. But, Sudha tells him with her newly acquired wisdom, she does not speak of ethical, unethical (*naitik, anaitik*) in her assessment of him. Her scales for weighing bad and good are different. Her god is kind, he does not stand in judgement; he tries to persuade, to understand his weaknesses, and speaks of forgiveness and of love. She doesn't consider bodily desire a sin.

> 'Bodily desire (*pyas*) is as pure as the worship of the soul (*atma ki puja*) . . . The atma articulates itself through the body and the inclinations of the body, the disciplining of the body happens through the atma. He, who separates atma and body is broken into pieces by getting

enmeshed in the fearful storms of the mind. Chander, I was your atma. You were my body. I don't know how we were separated. Without you, I was left to become subtle atma alone . . . and without me, you became just body . . . When you writhe in pain on this shore of the *Vaitarani*, the river that forms the bounds of hell, I'll writhe on its other shore.'

Chander's individuality is flawed; it can mend itself by working for social good. And she will find fulfilment through him. So Sudha takes solace in a sublimation of love, which means a loss of her individual identity as it merges into that of Chander. Yet she speaks also of her own suffering, of *giving up* on herself, of the hell of physical intimacy with her husband. Thus for Sudha sex without love is not possible in marriage. In spite of an older mode of suffering and its attempted sublimation, this is a new constellation: romantic love as seeking to culminate, find fulfilment, in marriage. If frustrated, it can turn into violence, to an almost willed death, as in Sudha's case.

This is not to posit a progressive crystallization of the notion of individual love through our novels, of desire leading to the expectancy of marriage, but rather to a zigzagging and uneven course in the evolution of romantic love and the freedom to express it, dependent on location in a given city, in class, in family, in time. Even as in life, so also in literature—the novel in turns anticipates and registers the subtle and not so subtle shifts in structures of feeling. With *Nadi ke Dvip*, along with the relative economic independence of the woman, the language of female desire came into being, a desire so intense that it could not be contained within marriage. With *Gunahom ka Devata* we have the same kind of desire, unfulfilled because of social constraints, the impossibility of inter-caste marriage turning on itself in violent self-destruction.

Shifting to another location, we find ourselves in a time warp. In the heart of Agra, as depicted in Rajendra Yadav's *Sara Akash* (1960), we have Prabha and Samar negotiating their way to each other under the watchful eyes of a traditional extended family. Prabha is mediated through Samar, who tells his story in the first person. His rigid right wing views and avowed austerity culminate in a rejection of his new bride. Educated, erect, willing to work, Prabha refuses to supplicate, so she remains silent through half the narrative. The haveli in the inner city of Agra, with a web of small, often windowless rooms opening into each other and then onto a series of courtyards, the centripetal heart of family life where all is observed, discussed, and regulated by the women of the family, bolstered by the men, leaves little space for manoeuvre. There is little or no room for withdrawal, for solitary rumination, for intimacy. Samar and Prabha are luckier than most young couples, all the same. Despite the turmoil of joint family life, its anxieties and jealousies, they find their way to each other and to companionship, and it is with the scene of their tearful union on the roof—under a moonlit sky, where Samar discovers her, a shadow in white, cowering against a wall and crying—that the first part of the work ends. Samar later recalls that wherever he happens to be on a moonlit night, he thinks of Prabha in just this position, cowering on a roof and weeping.

It is only when they speak to each other that we begin to hear Prabha's own voice:

> 'I have a classfellow.' Forgetting all else in her enthusiasm, she began to tell me about her college friend Rama, winding up with, 'When I went home this time, she was asking me all kinds of things about you. We used to be the naughtiest girls in class. She is a very close friend of mine. We used to think to ourselves, we'll never marry, we'll study a lot and then go to villages and teach women there. Sometimes we thought we'd take light baggage and tour all of Hindustan on foot and keep a detailed diary. We'd meet all kinds of new people in towns and villages. We'd make plans to learn how to fight with knives and sticks to protect ourselves from bad characters and wild animals. And, sitting there, talking, God knows what other plans we made. Our families and friends would get really annoyed with us when they heard us chatter on so endlessly. But that only made us want to tease them the more.'

Gandhian ideals of village uplift were current and legitimate enough for girls in the 1940s. What of these plans now? Prabha has blurted out her dreams but adds hastily, 'Forget all I've said. All I want now is that you study a lot. I'll do whatever you tell me.' So,

Prabha recedes, waiting, supporting, doing the housework, balancing the increasingly violent demands of the family with those of this new emotional allegiance. She accompanies her husband through his intellectual and emotional journey of discovery over a period when all that he has taken for granted—such as his certitudes about family, community, and nation—dissolve one by one, leaving him in the end with only his own uncertainty. The modernist ending, with a jobless Samar contemplating train tracks in a bid to either fly to a bigger city or to commit suicide, subsumes Prabha in his eventual fate.

Prabha becomes Nilima in our last novel, Mohan Rakesh's *Amdhere band kamare* (1961). The novel begins in the early 1950s in post-Partition Delhi. Madhusudan, the poet-narrator of the novel, houses in Qasabpura, a lower-middle-class residential area on the periphery of the walled city. Madhusudan registers in detail the anglicized ways of the writer-painter couple who befriend him: Harbans and Nilima, the prime protagonists. Harbans Khullar is a professor in a Delhi college. Well-read, articulate, he is trying to write a novel in Hindi. His wife represents the prototype of the modern woman. She has refashioned herself as Nilima, concealing her old-fashioned name Savitri. She wears jeans in her house on Hanuman Road, just behind Connaught Place, the shopping heart of New Delhi. She has modern gadgets in her house, including a record player. She smokes, she addresses her husband informally and talks quite openly about her ambitions to Madhusudan, and even of her conflicted relationship with Harbans. She is a reluctant artist, wielding a careless brush; Harbans has persuaded her to paint rather than be a Kathak dancer.

In a way, we have come full circle in our narrative trail, from the courtesan Suman in *Sevasadan*—who distanced herself from dance and music to try and reclaim the respectability she once had as a housewife—to a middle-class woman's endeavour to reclaim dance as an artistic form. The couple disappears from Madhusudan's life when they leave one after another for London. They meet again in 1959.

While Harbans is away, Nilima, defying his wishes, spends a year in Mysore learning Bharat Natyam. Harbans, meanwhile, is unable to get his PhD, nor write his novel. Instead, it is Nilima, now also in London, who has found the first real forum for her dance, her first real 'cultural consecration'. Here, while doing odd jobs at the Indian High Commission, she is able to join the troupe of a famous dancer, Uma Dutt. Harbans decides to support Nilima and realize himself through her; he agrees to become the manager of the troupe. In his perspective, Nilima's dancing is made somewhat respectable by being performed in the capitals of Europe, but there are a series of mishaps. Relating his experiences to Madhusudan, he reflects bitterly that their art can mean little to European audiences, and catering to their expectations is prostitution by another name. Harbans leaves the troupe in a huff, dragging Nilima along with him: it is as if she has no will of her own. Left alone after being unable to fulfil his ambitions and disregarding Nilima's actual success, he speaks of his claustrophobia, of being stuck in a dark room without windows, of not being able to move out. Nilima's success does not matter because he can find no intrinsic merit in her endeavours. But though this degree of male narcissistic chauvinism may seem excessive, it is not in fact all that far from the many similar instances of it in all our eight novels, making the varieties of patriarchy and aggressive male subordination of women a very clear thread through them all.

At the novel's end Nilima leaves her husband, but eventually returns to him, abandoning all hopes of a career. It seems that if she and Harbans cannot live with each other, they cannot live without each other either. There are two ways of looking at Nilima's success and failure: either as failure alone, or as a prelude to further forays made by others into the world of dance as an art form shorn of courtesan associations.

The changing position of women is one index by which I have read this process of change, of a modernization closely coupled initially with nationalism. For the women characters, as much as for the male, nationalism plays a formative role in the period leading up to Independence, in defining what is expected of them. We see this in our first three novels: thus the character portrayal of Madanmohan's dutiful wife in *Pariskha Guru*, through the expectation that Suman should forsake her successful life as a courtesan and take up her reformative role as head of an educational institution for the daughters of prostitutes. We accost nationalism in its full-fledged form in *Karmabhumi*'s Sukhada and her leadership of successful agitations for Dalit temple entry and housing for the poor. Nationalism has already begun to fade as an ideal in our fourth novel, *Jhutha Sach*, the novel of Partition. The nation is nothing other than bloodshed and violence, more a disaster than the fulfilling of a promise.

The modernist novels around the cusp of Independence and thereafter inhabit a more troubled emotional terrain. Rather than the nation, more universalist concerns occupy Rekha and Bhuvan in *Nadi ke Dvip*—nature, science, and civilization. Rekha sees the connection of human beings to each other as ephemeral and regards them as islands in a stream. Bhuvan hopes for the positive application of science in the contemporary world. But the Second World War has begun and mankind seems poised on the road to destruction. Can science save humanity?

Less clearly voiced are the international politics of *Gunahom ka Devata*, written amidst debates set in motion by the Cold War. Within larger humanist concerns, happiness and unhappiness are cast in an individualistic frame and coupled with finding fulfilment in the love of another human being: Sudha speaks to Chander of needing to turn to social good as a cure for self-indulgence and self-destruction. In this emotive setting, Independence happens in the distant background, almost as a non-event. There is the pull of Delhi as the centre in the work of nation-building, but it is given a rather slight weight by the narrative.

Nationalism figures in *Sara Akash* in another more troubling frame: Samar is a member of the RSS and believes in a Hindu nation. The nation as it has come into being is a corruption of the ideal; it is in the dismantling of his notions by his friend Shirish, and of other linked notions, that he acquires a better understanding of his troubled place in the world.

In our last novel *Amdhere band Kamare*, no ideal exerts a pull on its characters and the nation is a reality with no promise, particularly for those in urban India. The nation is not only still in the grips of Cold War politics, modern art forms are being created amidst the tensions provided by these pulls. Amidst all this uncertainty, Harbans cannot accept Nilima's ambitions and the narrator Madhusudan tries to bolt back into a traditional relationship with a young woman within a traditional set-up.

Modernization and even partial autonomy for women are linked to education, which, at the end of the nineteenth century and the beginning of the twentieth, is informal for women as much as men, as we see in *Pariksha Guru* and *Sevasadan*. Education acquires a formal cast only starting with the 1930s. College and university campuses figure in *Karmabhumi*, though in this novel only for men. In *Jhutha Sach*, possibly also in *Nadi ke Dvip*, women have access to it as well, though it is not clear that Rekha has enjoyed any formal education. By the time we get to *Gunahom ka Devata*, educational spaces are shared by women and men, but their consequences can for women be adverse. *Sara Akash* has Prabha's education regarded with hostility by her orthodox in-laws. There is no mention of a formal education in relation to Nilima in *Amdhere band Kamare*, and moreover she is regarded as ultra-modern by the narrator Madhusudan. Her husband Harbans is a professor, and though he does decry her use of English he makes no other disparaging comment about her education. Education is linked, however, to what characters expect from partnerships.

Through these novels, the notion of marriage changes with time. If it means companionship in *Pariksha Guru* and *Karmabhumi,* in *Sevasadan* it is a conventional relationship which seems riddled with faults, with women playing the subordinate role. In *Jhutha Sach*, women and men expect to be in love and choose their own partners, while in *Nadi ke Dvip* and *Gunahom ka Devata* marriage means a deeper, more existential relationship. We almost take a step backwards in time in *Sara Akash*, where, initially, there is more uncertainty regarding personhood and partnership. We see the woman character only through the consciousness of her husband, and her fulfilment in life is seen as entirely subordinate to that of her husband. Even more crucially, in *Amdhere band Kamare* marriage does not solve the problem of finding a meaningful existence for the individual; the struggle for meaning and self-fulfilment continues through marriage and beyond it.

As we journey through city space and time, we see through these fictions how closely intermeshed the public and the private are, how importantly the politics of the day are formative for the lives of women as much as men. Though we traverse nearly a century, there is no sense of linear progression from the less to the more emancipated; the lives of women remain troubled and contested. Ways of perceiving them become more complex as the art of the novel matures. We travel thus a long way from the simple husband–wife equation of *Pariksha Guru* in Delhi's Chandni Chowk; we take leave of spirited Suman in early-twentieth-century Banaras; resolute, defiant Sukhada in Gandhian Banaras; sturdy Tara in the inner city of Lahore and then post-Partition Delhi; the sensitive yet steady Rekha towards the beginning of the World War in Calcutta; a wildly passionate Sudha as she lies dying in the capital of newly independent India; a compassionate and resilient Prabha in her haveli in Agra; and Nilima left wistful in her Defence Colony flat in a fast modernizing Delhi at the end of the first decade of Independence. Though their sequence is chronological, and though perceptions change from the modern to the modernist in our last four novels, in a symbolic or literary sense all the troubled women they reveal coexist in modern North India. In the Introduction I delineated the terminal of our inquiry as the end of the period of Nehruvian nation-building. Today, fifty years on, looking at the state of affairs in relation to nationalism, urban change, cultural activity, and gender relations—the thematic core of our eight novels—it seems to me that one reason they continue to speak to us with such powerful immediacy is well conveyed by the French saying '*plus ça change, plus c'est la même chose*'. In many ways, the more things change, the more they tend to remain the same.

REFERENCES

'Agyeya', Sachidanand Hiranand Vatsyayan. [1951] 1980. *Nadī ke Dvīp*. Allahabad: Saraswati Press.

Bharati, Dharmavir. 1949. *Gunahom ka Devata*, in Bharati 1999, vol. 1, vide infra.

———. 1999. *Dharmavir Bharati Granthavali*, ed. Chandrakanta Bandivadekar. 9 volumes. Delhi: Vani Prakashan.

Bhattacharya, Rimli. 1998. *Binodini Dasi's My Story and My Life as an Actress*. Delhi: Kali for Women.

Childs, Peter. [2000] 2008. *Modernism*. London and New York: Routledge.

Jalil, Rakshanda. 2014. *Liking Progress, Loving Change: A Literary History of the Progressive Writers' Movement in Urdu*. Delhi: Oxford University Press.

Kosambi, Meera. 2007. *Crossing Thresholds: Feminist Essays in Social History*. Ranikhet: Permanent Black.

Lefebvre, Henri. 1991. *The Production of Space*. Translated by Donald Nicholson-Smith. Oxford: Blackwell Publishing.

Metcalf, Barbara D. 1990. *Perfecting Women. Maulana Ashraf Ali Thanawi's Bihishti Zewar*. Berkeley: University of California Press.

Minault, Gail. 1998. *Secluded Scholars: Women's Education and Muslim Social Reform in India*. Delhi: Oxford University Press.

Mufti, Aamir R. 2016. *Forget English: Orientalism and World Literatures*. Cambridge, Mass, London: Harvard University Press.

Premchand. 1996. *Premchand Rachanavali*. 20 volumes. Volume 2: *Sevasadan, Premashram*. Delhi: Janavani Prakashan.

———. 2006. *Premchand Rachanavali*. 20 Volumes. Volume 5: *Gaban, Karmabhumi*. Delhi: Janvani Prakashan.

Rakesh, Mohan. [1961] 1997. *Amdhere Band Kamare*. Delhi: Rajkamal Prakashan.

Sarkar, Tanika. 1999. *Words To Win: The Making of Amar Jiban: A Modern Autobiography*. Delhi: Kali for Women.

———. 2000. *Hindu Wife, Hindu Nation: Community, Religion and Cultural Nationalism*. Ranikhet: Permanent Black.

———. 2009. *Rebels, Wives and Saints: Designing Selves and Nations in Colonial Times*. London, New York, Calcutta: Seagull Books.

Shrinivasdas. 1964. *Shrinivas Granthavali*, ed. Shrikirishnalal. Banaras: Nagari Pracharini Sabha.

Yadav, Rajendra. [1960] 2000. *Sara Akash*. Delhi: Radhakrishna Prakashan.
Yashpal. [1958] 2000. *Jhutha Sach*. Part One: *Vatan aur Desh*. Allahabad, Lok Bharati Prakashan.
———. [1960] 2003. *Jhutha Sach*. Part Two: *Desh ka Bhavishya*. Allahabad: Lok Bharati Prakashan.

Index

Aaj, 154
Acharya, Nandkishore, 265n, 285n, 293n
Adhe Adhure, 391
Adhyatma movement, 71n, 78–9, 81n, 103, 304
Advani, Ram, 260n
Africa, 18
Agra, 1, 8, 17–19, 27, 30, 47, 57, 59–62, 71, 73–4, 77–8, 82, 88, 104, 328–30, 335–41, 420
"Great Debate" of 1854, 336
Agra, 61n
Agra College, 34, 330, 338
Agra School Book Society, 63, 336
Agrawal, Purushottam, 301n, 302n, 324n
Agyeya/Ajneya, S.H.V., 4, 5n, 14–16, 255, 256n, 262, 263n, 265n, 271n, 285n, 286n, 294n, 296, 313n, 337, 339–42, 346n, 416, 418; *see also* Vatsyayan, Sachidanand Hiranand
Ahmad, Nazir, 67–8
Akbar (emperor), 62, 78, 101, 206
Akbarabadi, Nazir, 336
Akbarnama, 62
Alam, Muzaffar, 78n
Alborn, Timothy, 102n

Aligarh, 47
Aligarh College, 68n
Allahabad, 1, 8, 15, 22n, 26, 30–1, 33–5, 47–8, 60, 63, 152n, 259, 300, 307, 309, 321, 323, 325
Allahabad University, 34n, 330n
Ambedkar, B.R., 155
Amdhere Band Kamare, 17, 36, 38, 42, 44, 366–76, 380–6, 388–402, 422–3, 425–6
American Presbyterian Mission, 63, 336
Amita, 235n
Anderson, Benedict, 36
Andha Yug, 299
Angel, Flores, 302
Anglo-Indian, 314–17
Ap ka Banti, 17
Ardhakathanak, 57, 62, 71, 73n, 74–81, 100, 103
Armstrong, Nancy, 7n
Arondekar, Anjali, 55n
Arundale, Rukmini Devi, 376n
Arunima, G., 325n
Arya Samaj, 20, 122, 132n, 203, 209, 304, 376
Asaf Ali, Aruna, 337
Asaf-ud-Daulah, 27
Ashk, Upendranath, 14n
Asthana, Ghanshyam, 338n

429

Auden, W.H., 276, 278
Aurangzeb, Emperor, 206
Austen, Jane, 18
Avadhi, 72–4, 86n, 118
Awadh/Oudh, 27–8, 30
Awasthi, Rekha, 154n
Azad, Maulana, 243n
Azad, Muhammad Husain, 25n, 368n

Babur (emperor), 62
Bacon, Lord, 85
Bakhle, Janaki, 140n
Bakhtin, Mikhail, 3, 4n, 7, 14, 122n, 126n, 143, 146, 261n, 295
Balibar, Etienne, 37, 345n
Balzac, 18
Banaras, 1, 11, 13, 20, 25, 31–3, 45, 47, 59–60, 88, 109, 111–17, 131, 132n, 150–5, 159–60, 163, 170, 176–7, 200, 215, 335, 408, 410, 426; see also Varanasi
Banaras, the Sacred City 115n
Banaras Hindu University, 152
Banaras Light Press, 47
Banker's Magazine, 102n
Banarasicharita/Banarasicharitra, 74, 103
Banarasidas, 57, 71–81, 83–4, 88, 99, 101, 103–4, 166
Banker (*sahu*), 69–70, 92, 166
Bareilly, 27
Bareilly College, 34
Bayly, C.A., 32n, 34n, 35n, 69, 70n, 75n, 142n, 309
Bazar-e-Husn, 109
Begum, Jahanara, 23
Belvedere Press, 48

Bengal, 2, 7, 38
  radicalism, 35
Bengali, 117, 143, 408
  bhadralok, 2, 337
Besant, Annie, 152
Bhadra, Gautam, 55n
Bhagavadgita, 48, 321, 419
Bhagavata Purana, 46, 58
Bhagwat, Neela, 141n
Bhagyavati, 59
Bhandari, Mannu, 17
Bharat Jiwan Press, 47
Bharat Natyam, 376–7, 389–90, 396, 423
Bharati, Dharamvir, 15–16, 256n, 299–300, 302–5, 309, 310n, 311, 315–17, 323, 326
Bharatiya Rashtriya Congress ka Itihas, 154n
Bhasin, Kamla, 229n, 238n
Bhatkhande, Vishnu Narayan, 140
Bhatt, Balkrishna, 56n
Bhattacharya, Rimli, 407
Bhumika, 302n
Blackburn, Stuart, 55n, 87n
Blake, Stephen P., 90n, 370n
Bombay, 2, 7, 31
Bombay Presidency, 140
Boner, Alice, 151
Bose, Subhas Chandra, 331n
Bourdieu, Pierre, 44, 387n
Brahmos, 212
Brajbhasha, 46, 73, 86n, 87n, 118
Britain, 18
British, the, 8–9, 19, 22, 62
  conquest of Punjab, 20
  post-1857, 23n, 38, 56, 371n, 406
Buddenbrooks, 18
Buddhism, 264n

INDEX

Butalia, Urvashi, 224n, 229n, 233n, 234n, 238n
Byron, Lord, 86n

CWMG, 156n, 168n, 191n
Calcutta, 2–3, 7, 31, 45, 60, 377, 426
Calcutta School Book Society, 45
Calcutta University, 35, 330n
Cambridge School, the, 19
Canning College (Lucknow), 30
Carroll, Lucy, 359n
Caudwell, Christopher, 301–2
Central Hindu College, 152
Central Hindu Girls School, 152
Centre for the Study of Social Sciences, Kolkata, 55n
Centre of South Asia Studies, UCLA, 55n
Chakrabarty, Dipesh, 384n
Chandra, Bipan, 19
Chandrakanta, 11, 117
Chandrakanta Santiti, 117n
Chatterjee, Basu, 343, 346n
Chatterjee, Bankimchandra, 2, 143, 351n
Chatterjee, Indrani, 41n, 99n
Chattopadhyay, Sharat Chandra, 337
Chaudhuri, Rosinka, 55n
Chaudhuri, Supriya, 55n
Chauhan, Ranvir, 337
Chauhan, Shivdan Singh, 300–2, 305, 309, 324, 338
Chesterfield (Lord), 86n
Childs, Peter, 256n, 268n, 295n, 305n, 416n
China, 37, 361, 392
Chitralekha, 124n
Choubey, Gautam, 317n

Christian College (Lucknow), 30
Chunder, Bholanath, 22n
Church Missionary Society, 63, 336
Clark, Katerina, 394n
Cold War, 9, 15, 17, 37–8, 40, 300, 302, 340, 374, 392, 394, 395n, 402, 425
colonial, 1–2, 9, 18, 28, 31, 34, 39, 46, 55, 63, 67, 111, 132, 154, 160, 196, 259–60, 316, 359, 407
Colvin, Sir Auckland, 34n
Colvin Taluqdars College, 30
communalism, 9, 30, 36, 127–8
  Hindi–Hindu, 26
  Hindu–Muslim, 127–8, 130–2, 196
  riots, 22, 206, 217, 227–8, 243n
  Urdu–Muslim, 26
  violence, 226–30, 241, 249, 367, 368n, 415
Communist Party of India (CPI), 300, 303, 415
Company Bagh, 23, 64
Congress Party, 35, 245, 248
Conte, Gian Biagio, 6, 103n
Coomaraswamy, Ananda K., 115n
Coppola, Carlo, 367, 395n
Cornwallis Code, 33
courtesans, 11–12, 25, 42, 75, 77, 98, 109n, 112–17, 132n, 134–6, 142n, 410, 424
  dance and, 368–9, 372, 376–9, 393, 422
  music and, 140–1
Cowper, William, 86n
Curzon, Lord, 35n, 167

Dada Kamared, 13n
Daedalus, 38n

Dalit, 181, 185
　social order, 187
　temple entry, 155, 160, 174–6,
　　184, 200, 412, 424
Dalmia, Vasudha, 20n, 55n, 56n,
　　60n, 81n, 86n, 94n, 109n,
　　113n, 391n, 393n, 394n
Daniélou, Alain, 151
Das, Shyam Sundar, 47
Dashakumaracharita, 73
Datta, V.N., 237n, 382n
Davis, Natalie Zemon, 79n, 80n
Dayanand Anglo-Vedic College, 30,
　　207, 209, 233
Dayanand Anglo-Vedic School,
　　203, 211
Delhi, 1, 8, 13–17, 19–20, 22,
　　25–8, 31, 49, 57–64, 82, 85,
　　88, 104, 128, 203, 207, 235,
　　247–8, 271, 273, 321, 323,
　　325, 336, 367–70, 376, 384n,
　　385, 402, 415
　Chandni Chowk, 18, 22, 64, 66,
　　68, 83, 91, 370, 408, 426
　Daryaganj area, 48
　Municipal Council, 84
　municipality, 26
　New Delhi, 48, 237, 241, 257,
　　372, 382–3, 400–3
　post-Partition, 205, 239, 422,
　　426
Delhi College, 27, 66–7, 92
Delhi Gazette, 22
Delhi Gazetteer, 63
Delhi Society, 67
Devi, Shivrani, 157, 164n, 165n
Devrani Jethani ki Kahani, 59, 104
dharma, 158, 160, 168, 164,
　　175–6, 178, 180, 198, 304,
　　322, 354, 356, 359, 412–13

Dharmayug, 14, 203n
Dhruvaswamini, 290
Dickens, Charles, 144n
Dikshit, Prakash, 338n
Dinkar, Ramdharisingh, 343
Discovery of India (Nehru), 19,
　　293
Don Quixote, 18
Dumas, Alexandre, 143
Dundas, Paul, 69n, 70n, 81n
Dyal Singh College, 212–13

East India Company, 22, 32, 330n
*East India Progress and Condition
　of India During 1917–1918*
　report, 130–1
East India Railway, 64
Eisenhower, Dwight D., 392
Ek Chithada Sukh, 17n, 381
Eliot, George, 181
Eliot, T.S., 261, 262n, 279
Engels, Friedrich, 154
English language, 27, 67

Farrell, James T., 301
Fascism, 39
Faizabad, 28
Fazl, Abul, 62
Flood, Finbarr B., 23n
Farooqui, Mahmood, 19n, 22n
Forman Christian College (Lahore),
　　207, 215
Fort William College, 45, 58, 87n
Four Quartets, 279, 286
Fox, Ralph, 302
Freeman, Joseph, 301

Gaban, 198
Gahmari, Gopalram, 11
Gandharva Mahavidyalayas, 140

INDEX   433

Gandhi, Mohandas K., 2, 154–7,
    195n, 241–6, 248, 353, 411
  Civil Disobedience, 152
  Gandhian views, 165, 167,
    174–6, 191, 195, 199, 412,
    421
  khadi, 168, 199
  Non-Cooperation Movement,
    153n
  Poona Pact, 155n
  Salt March, 153n
  satyagraha, 9, 191, 347
  untouchability, 9, 155, 174–6
Gaonkar, Dilip, 38
Garden Cities of Tomorrow, 212n
Gauridatta, Pandit, 59–60, 68
*General Principles of Inflection and
  Conjugation in the Braj Bakha*,
  59n
Genette, Gérard, 44n
Ghalib, Mirza Asadullah, 64, 336
Gharaunda, 329–30, 332–5, 346
Ghaziuddin's Madrasa, 27n, 67
Ghosh, Amalendu, 310
Girdhardas, 86n
Girti Diwarem, 14n
Gita Press, 48
Glover, William, 163n, 207n,
    209n, 211n, 212n
Godan, 12
Goendka, Jaydayal, 48
Goethe, Johann Wolfgang von, 5,
    326
Goldsmith, Oliver, 85–86, 97
Gorakhpur, 48
Gorki, M., 154, 302, 305, 315
Government College, 30, 207
Govind, Nikhil, 6n, 13n, 15n,
    172n, 250, 313n
Great Depression, 188

Growse, F.S., 82n
Guha-Thakurta, Tapati, 55n, 115n,
    402
Guilbaut, 394n
Gulistan, 85
Gunahom ka Devata, 15–16, 26,
    30, 36–7, 42, 299–300, 309–
    25, 338–9, 418–20, 424–5
Gupta, Narayani, 20, 22n, 23n,
    25n, 27n, 64n, 66n, 67n,
    84n, 129n
Gurukul Kangri, 203
Gyanranjan, 307

Hali, Altaf Hussain, 27
Halle University, Germany, 55n
Hamilton, Commissioner, 67
Hams, 154, 157, 158n, 255n, 338,
    339n
Hansen, Kathryn, 343n
Harischandra, Bharatendu, 32,
    46–7, 56n, 60n, 83, 94n,
    113, 117
Harishchandra's Magazine, 34n, 57n
Harivamsha, 85n
Harshacarita, 74
Hasan, Mushirul, 66n
Havell, E.B., 115, 116n
Hindi, 2, 20, 45–6, 48, 72, 82,
    209–10, 376
  anti-Hindi riots, 2
  as a language, 4, 234
  dialect-inflected, 16n
  modern, 3, 150
  national language, 2, 48, 210
  novels, 1–4, 6, 26, 31, 35, 55–7,
    85, 87, 99, 104, 112, 203,
    235, 256, 426; *see also* novel,
    Hindi
  spoken, 59

Hindi literature, 3, 7, 113, 239
  Bhakti traditions, 301
  canon, 7, 46
  chhayavadi, 7, 12, 256, 282, 338
  idiom, 61
  literati, 387
  moral (*niti*) tales, 85–7, 91, 94
  navin, 117
  periodisation, 9–11
  Pragativadi (Progressives), 15, 299–305, 320, 322, 324, 340n
  Prayogvadi (Experimentalist), 15, 302, 324
  styles, 84
Hindi Pradip, 56n
Hindi publishing, 44–9, 337, 375
  translations, 47, 117
Hindi Sahitya Sammelan (Association of Hindi Literature), 47–8
Hindi Upanyas Kosh, 56n
Hindu, 9
  caste ideology, 155, 354–5
  culture, 26, 225, 354–7
  Hindi, 1, 59–60
  middle class, 3
  Right, 17, 344–5, 362
  undivided family, 349–55, 358–62
  womanhood, 356, 360, 419
Hindu Code Bill, 340, 355
Hindu–Sikh culture, 31
Hindu Marriage Law Act, 44, 248, 392
  monogamy, 42, 44
Hindus, 26, 66, 209
Hindustan Republican Association, 204
Hindutva, 9

Hitopadesha, 85, 87, 94
Hosargrahar, Jyoti, 23n
Howard, Ebenezer, 212n
Hugo, Victor, 143
Husain, M.F., 394n

India
  1857 uprising, 1–2, 19n, 20, 22, 23n, 27–8, 31, 55, 63–4, 66–7, 128n, 257, 371n
  1905, 32
  Army Sanitary Commission, 128
  British, 2, 29, 31
  census, 112
  educated classes, 27
  Five Year Plans, 40
  Government of, 129–30
  High Court, 33
  Independence, 1, 9, 25, 31, 39, 223–4, 226, 246, 299, 318, 324, 340, 366, 414, 423
  Inter-Dominion Treaty, 233n
  Jallianwallabagh, 2
  middle class, 32
  modernisation, 2–3, 8, 22, 27, 407, 425
  nationalism, 1–2, 9, 11–13, 17, 36–7, 39, 99, 110, 160–2, 164, 167, 172, 188, 198, 209, 213, 234, 249, 268, 290–2, 333, 344n, 346n, 362, 410, 414, 424
  North, 1–4, 7–8, 31, 35–6, 42, 55, 71, 156
  nuclear family, 390
  Partition, 1, 9, 14, 20, 31, 36, 40, 48, 203, 205–6, 210n, 222, 224–6, 229, 233n, 234–8, 249, 318, 340, 368n, 370, 407, 414–15, 424, 426

Quit India, 414
refugee camps, 234–5, 237n, 239, 241, 368n
Royal Commission on Decentralisation, 130
secularism, 414
South, 2
"three language formula", 2
women's political rights, 156–8
Indian middle class, 11, 17, 32–4, 118, 159, 177, 200, 259, 271, 386
  characters, 177, 366
  contemporary, 307
  dance, 380, 422
  domesticity, 272
  English-educated, 29, 30, 35, 210
  Hindu, 3
  hypocrisy, 295
  lower, 43, 213, 222, 370
  modernising, 147
  morality, 127
  North Indian, 31, 35, 199
  urban, 256, 290, 367
  values, 200, 267, 303, 306, 367
Indian National Army, 337
Indian National Congress, 47, 170, 218, 248, 333
  Karachi session, 156
Indian Navy, 337
Indian Penal Code, 68n
Indian People's Theatre Association (IPTA), 338n
Indulekha, 90n
Islam, 209

Jacobs, Jane, 372n
Jaffrey, Ali Sardar, 303
Jaffrey, Saeed, 307, 314n

Jagaran, 154–5
Jahangir (emperor), 19
Jain, Nemichandra, 204n, 221n, 222, 238n
Jainism, 71, 74, 81n, 82n
Jalandhar, 236, 238, 248
Jalil, Rakshanda, 408
James, Henry, 261n
Jataka tales, 112
Jama Masjid, 28
Janavani Prakashan, 109n
Jaunpur, 57, 70, 72–3, 76–7, 88, 166
Jhansi, 27
Jhutha Sach, 14, 18, 25–6, 30–1, 33, 36–7, 43–4, 203–50, 340, 368, 381n, 414–16, 418, 424–5
Jinnah, M.A., 243n
Jones, Kenneth, 209, 212n
Joshi, Ilachand, 346n, 377, 378n
Journal of Arts and Ideas, 403n

Kabir (saint/poet), 48, 86n
Kadambari, 57
Kahler, Erich, 40n
Kaisar Bagh, 28
Kalidasa, 85n, 290
Kalsi, A.S., 56n, 61n
Kalyan, 48
Kalyan-Kalpataru, 48
Kamaleshwar, 16, 387
Kan, Kikuchi, 5
Kapur, Kalidas, 143–5
Karmabhumi, 13, 33, 35–6, 39, 42–3, 153–4, 158–93, 195–200, 213, 216, 340, 411–13, 424–5
Kashi ya Banaras, 150n
Kashmir, 242, 257

Kathak, 376–7
Kathakali, 390
Kathuria, Shailaja, 61n
Kaur, Balwant, 342n
Kaur, Bibi Inder, 237
Kavi, Raghunath, 47
Kaviraj, Sudipta, 38
Kavivachansudha, 83
Kayasth Pathshala, 35
Keshavdas, 46
Khadgavilas Press, 46
Khan, Sir Khizr Hayat, 217–18, 224
Khan, Sir Syed Ahmad, 68n
Khandalawala, Karl, 377
Khari Boli, 59, 73
Khatri, Devakinandan, 11, 61n, 117n
Khel Khilaune, 341–2
Khilnani, Sunil, 234n, 247n
Kinaram, Sadhu, 116
King, Anthony, 207–8, 306–7, 368n
King, Christopher, 47n, 64n, 66n, 165n
Kishwar, Madhu, 156n, 178n, 355n, 356n
Kosambi, Meera, 407
Krishanchander, 303
Krishna, Professor Anand, 132n, 151n
Krishnacharya, 87n
Krishnadas, Rai, 151
Kuch apbiti kuch jagbiti, 94n
Kumar, Jainendra, 6, 13–14, 145, 154n, 313n, 339–40, 346n
Kumar, Radha, 153n
Kumar, Sanjeev, 342n
Kumar, Udaya, 90n
Kurprin, Aleksandr, 145

Lahore, 1, 8, 14, 18–20, 26–7, 30–1, 34, 66, 163n, 203, 205–12, 217, 221, 227, 234, 236, 238, 240–1, 414–16, 426
Lahore Government College, 67
Lallujilal, 58–60, 87n
Lawrence, D.H., 261, 262n, 279, 282, 283n, 285n
Lath, Mukund, 71n, 73n, 74n, 75n, 76n, 78n, 80n
Lazarus Press, 47
Leavis, F.R., 7n, 261n, 262n
Lefebvre, Henri, 406n
Lelyveld, David, 68n
Lenin, Vladimir, 154, 301, 304
Lewis, Pericles, 256, 282n, 340n
Leyden, Rudolf von, 393n
Lishman, Frank, 152n
Liu, Lydia, 37n, 347, 361, 366n
Lives of Great Men, 353
Lodi, Sikandar, 61
Lok Bharati Prakashan, 203n
London, 7
London Missionary Society, 45
Lorca, Federico Garcia, 316
Low, D.A., 192n
Lucknow, 1, 15, 20, 27–31, 45, 47, 128–9, 153, 236, 259, 273
Lucknow University, 30
Luhmann, Niklas, 5, 41n, 274n, 276n, 284n, 323n, 352n, 388

MacDonald, Ramsay, 155
Machwe, Prabhakar, 338n
Madhuri, 153
Madras, 2, 7, 31
Mahabharata, 48, 85
Maharaj, Bindadin, 377
Maharaj, Kalka, 377
Maharaj, Lacchu, 377

Mahesh, Premchand, 49
Maila Amchal, 16n
Maine, Sir Henry, 129
Majithia, Dyal Singh, 212n
Malavikagnimitra, 2
Mangilal, Shri, 82n, 83
Mani, Preetha, 16
Manjapra, Kris, 267n
Manusmriti, 85n
Marathas, the, 62
Marathi, 117, 143, 408
Marx, Karl, 154, 316
    Marxism, 301–2, 304
Marxism and Literature, 302
Matiram, 46
Mayakowski, Vladimir, 316
Mayo College, 152n
McGregor, R.S., 56n, 384n
Medhasananda, Swami, 116n
Medical Hall Press, 47
Meerut, 27
Mehrotra, Arvind Krishna, 23n, 306n, 307n, 314n
Menaka Indian Ballet, 377
Menon, Ritu, 229n, 238n
Metcalf, Barbara, 407n, 408
Minault, Gail, 408
Miner, Allyn, 370n, 371n
Mir, Muhammad Taqi 'Mir', 370n
Mirat ul Urus, 67
Misra, B.B., 32
Mishra, Pratap Narayan, 47
Mishra, Ram Narayan, 47
modernity/modernism, 2–3, 8, 17, 19, 38–40, 43, 55, 58, 88, 94, 111, 132, 176, 222, 315, 329, 362, 401, 407
Mody, Sujata, 143n
Moradabad, 27

Moretti, Franco, 18n
Motichandra, 112
Mrigavati, 72
Mufti, Aamir, 55n, 408
Mughal empire, 8, 19, 71–2
Muir Central College, 35
Mukherjee, Meenakshi, 56n, 90n
Mukhopadhyay, Anindita, 262n
Mukhtar, Askad, 236n
Mukul, Akshaya, 48n
Muldas, 72
Munshi Naval Kishore, *see* Naval Kishore
music, indigenous, 118, 140–1
Muslim Evacuee Camp, 227
Muslim League, 217–19
Muslims, 9, 22, 25–6, 66, 336, 368n

Nadi ke Dvip, 14–15, 27, 29–30, 36, 38, 40, 43, 255–96, 325n, 335, 339, 384n, 416–18, 420, 424–5
Nagar, Amritlal, 116, 117n, 128n, 329, 338n
Nagar, Sharad, 329n
Nagari Pracharini Sabha (Association for the Propagation of the Nagari Script), 47, 150
Nahr-e-Bihisht, 23
Nai Kahani, 16, 340–1, 366, 381n, 385, 387
Nai Kavita, 15, 385, 387
Naim, C.M., 64n
Nanda, Debidas, 130n
Napier, Colonel Robert, 28
Narayan, Jayaprakash, 337
Narrative Discourse, 44n
Natak, 60n

National Book Trust, 49
National College, 204
National School of Drama, 387
Naval Kishore, Munshi, 45–6
Naval Kishore Press, 45–6
Nehru, Pandit Jawaharlal, 1, 19, 226, 243, 293–4, 300, 390, 392
Nehruvian
  era, 1–2
  vision, 9, 426
New Left Review, 43
Neville, H.R., 330n
Newman, Daniel M., 99n
Nietzsche, Friedrich, 316
Nirmala, 313n
Nizami, Hasan, 371n
North Indian cities, 19–20, 23n, 26, 44, 71, 128, 257, 330, 406–8, 414
North Western Provinces, 30, 33–4, 46, 63, 129, 336
North West Provinces Act, 129
notions
  existentialism, 265, 316
  family, 41
  marriage, 42, 262–3n, 312–13, 317, 319, 349–51, 358, 410, 412
  relationship, 42
  romance, 312, 319, 351, 358
  self, 42, 58
  sex, 316–19, 323
  sociality, 58, 410
novel, 3, 406
  Hindi, 1–4, 6, 26, 31, 35, 55–6, 85, 87, 99, 112, 203, 235, 256, 406, 426
  Indian English, 4

modern Hindi, 57
vernacular, 9

O'Hanlon, Rosalind, 407
Oldenburg, Veena, 20, 28, 128n, 259n
Omvedt, Gail, 155n
Oriental College, 30
Orsini, Francesca, 5n, 11, 13n, 41n, 47n, 48n, 55n, 58n, 64n, 66n, 152n
Oudh Municipalities Act, 129

Padmavat, 73n
Pairokar, 210, 214, 217
Pakistan, 219, 223, 225, 242, 244
Paliwal, Krishnadatta, 337
Paluskar, Pandit Vishnu Digambar, 140–1
Panchatantra, 85, 87n
Pandey, Gyanendra, 239n, 368n
Pant, Sumitranandan, 12, 338
Pariksha Guru, 8n, 10, 18, 31, 33, 36, 38–9, 42, 55n, 56–7, 60, 77, 81, 85–6, 88–102, 104, 335, 408–10, 424–6
Paris, 7, 18
Parsis, 140
Peck, Lucy, 330n, 331n
Pernau, Margrit, 67n
Persian, 3, 45, 60, 67n, 72, 74, 82, 86n, 97n, 336
Phillauri, Shraddharam, 59–60
Poddar, Hanuman Prasad, 48
Pope, Alexander, 86n
Powell, Avril, 336n
Pradhan, Sudhi, 292n
Pragati Prakashan, 255n, 342n
Pragativad: Ek Samiksha, 301–2
Prakash, Om, 48

Prakrit, 72
Prasad, Baleshwar, 48
Prasad, Dr Rajendra, 226
Prasad, Guru Pandit Sitaram, 377
Prasad, Jayshankar, 12–13, 151, 290
Prasad ki Yad, 151n
Pratik, 341
Prem Jogini, 113–14
Premashram, 159n
Premchand, Munshi, 2, 4, 11–14, 16, 25, 61, 103–4, 109, 117–20, 122, 123n, 124–5, 132, 133n, 134, 138n, 145–6, 153–61, 164n, 181, 184, 193–4, 198–200, 213, 215, 300, 313n, 339, 346n, 353, 410–12
Premsagar, 58
Pret Bolte Haim, 342
Prinsep, James, 112–13, 115n
Prison Days and Other Poems, 294n
Pritchett, Frances, 25n
Progressive Writers Association, 291, 300
    Urdu, 303
Progressive Writers' Movement, 290, 300, 302
Punjab, 20, 27, 129, 203, 207, 209–11, 418
    Government, 83, 217
    Panjabi, 375
Punjab University, 30
Punjabi Century, 208n
purdah, 156
Pushkin, Alexander, 304

Qasimi, Ahmed Nazim, 303
Qalam ka Sipahi, 153n

Queen's College, 150, 152, 159, 167
Quran, The, 86n
Qutuban, 72

RSS (Rashtriya Swayamsevak Sangh), 344, 347–8, 351, 424
Radhasoamis, 336
Radical Humanist Party, 293n
Rae, George, 102n
Raeside, I.M.P., 87n
Rafi, Mirza Muhammad "Sauda", 370n
Raghav, Rangeya, 329, 332, 333n, 334–5, 338–9
Raghuvamsha, 86n
Raghuvanshi, Rajendra, 338n
Rahul Sankrityayan, 338
Rai, Alok, 124n, 125n, 132, 314n
Rai, Amrit, 145, 153n, 154n, 338
Raidasis, 185
Rajgiri, Mir Sayyid Manjhan, 72–73
Rajkamal Prakashan, 48
Rajpal and Sons, 329n
Rajput College, 330, 338
Rakesh, Mohan, 16–17, 340, 366–9, 371n, 374n, 375–7, 379n, 382n, 384, 386n, 387–9, 391, 395n, 396n, 399n, 401–3, 422
Raktaranjit Spen, 300
Ram, Lala Shri, 84
Raman, Srilata, 269n
Ramayana, 85n, 111, 117–19, 336n
Ramcharitmanas, 45, 48, 74, 86n
Rangbhumi, 353
Rao, Velcheru Narayana, 57n, 72n, 81n
Rat ka Reporter, 17n

Ravidas, 185
Ray, Gopal, 9–11, 13–14, 56n, 59n
Ray, Rajat Kanta, 42n, 55n, 82n
Raychaudhuri, Tapan, 351n
religion, 69, 154, 345n
Renold, Leah, 152n, 153n
Renu, Phanishwarnath, 16n
Reynolds, G.W., 144n
Ripon, Lord, 129
Rospatt, Alexander von, 264n
Roy, Leila, 377–8
Roy, M.N., 265, 266n, 267, 293–4
Roy, Ram Mohan, 32
Rumi, Raza, 210n
Ruswa, 11

Saadi, 86n
Sadadarsh, 83
Sadana, Rashmi, 48n, 55n
Sahitya Akademi, 49
Sainik, 337
Samalochak, 194, 337
Sanskrit, 45, 48, 60, 72–3, 82, 114, 209
Santbani Pustakmala, 48
Sara Akash, 17–18, 37, 39, 44, 330, 341, 343–4, 346–63, 420–2, 424
Saraswati, 143
Saraswati, Dayanand, 209
Saraswati Press, 153n, 154n, 255n
Sarkar, Sumit, 19n, 153n, 189n, 190, 192n
Sarkar, Tanika, 407
Satyagraha in South Africa, 191
Saxena, Poonam, 309n
scripts
 Farsi, 72
 Hindi, 45

"Hindugi", 72
Kaithi, 45
Nagari, 11, 45, 58, 60, 97n, 336n
Schomer, Karine, 7n
Scrutiny, 262n
Senapati, Fakir Mohan, 98n
Seth Bankemal, 329–32, 335, 346
Sevasadan, 11–12, 25–6, 33, 36, 39, 42, 109–11, 118–27, 132, 134–47, 196, 198, 378, 410–11, 422, 425; *see also* Bazar-e-Husn
Shah, Bahadur "Zafar", 22
Shah, Wajid Ali, 22, 28
Shah Alam (emperor), 210n, 371n
Shah Jahan (emperor), 23, 62, 79, 90n, 207n
Shahani, Kumar, 403n
Shahjahanabad, 25, 63, 83, 403
Shaivas, 71, 74
Shakespeare, William, 86n
Sharma, Padmasingh "Kamlesh", 338n
Sharma, Pandey Bechan "Ugra", 13n
Sharma, Professor R.K., 74n, 103n
Sharma, Rajendra, 338n, 339
Sharma, Ramvilas, 103, 331n, 338–9
Sharqi, Sultan Husain Shah, 72
Sheikh, Gulammohammed, 403
Shekhar: Ek Jivani, 4–5, 15n, 255, 313n
Shesh Prashna, 337
Shesher Kobita, 262
Shingavi, Snehal, 160n
Shrinivasdas, Lala, 10, 56, 60, 68, 81–5, 87n, 88–9, 92n, 95n, 97n, 99n, 100n, 103, 408

INDEX

Shukla, Ramchandra, 56n
Shulman, David, 57n, 72n, 81n
Sikarwar, Bachan Singh, 337n
Sikhism, 209
Sikhs, 30, 227, 234
Simeon, Dilip, 242n, 244n, 245n
Simhavalokan, 204, 210n
Sinclair, Upton, 301
Singh, Bhagat, 204
Singh, Dhirendranath, 46
Singh, Gadadhar, 57n
Singh, Jagmohan, 47
Singh, Shiv Kumar, 47
Singh, Shri Shashank, 150n
Sisters, 236n
Sitaramaiya, Pattabhi, 154n
Six Acres and a Third, 98n
Smith, Thomas, 61n, 62n
Snell, Rupert, 71n, 74n, 79n
Sokhey, Captain Sahib Singh, 377
Sorrows of Young Werther, The, 6, 326
Sound and Shadow, 378
Spear, Percival, 26n
Spectator, 85
St John's College, 330, 332–3
Stalin, Joseph, 303–4
Stark, Ulrike, 45, 63
Stribodh, 85, 99
Subalterns, 19n
Subrahmanyam, Sanjay, 57n, 72n, 78n, 81n
Sufi poetry, 72–3, 80, 301
Sukhdas, 181n
Suleri, Sara, 206n, 207n
Sunita, 13
Suraj ka Satvan Ghora, 299
Surdas, Sant, 46, 118
Sursagar, 118, 321, 419

Swadeshi League, 377
Swatik League, 377

Tagore family, 32
Tagore, Rabindranath, 2, 143, 262
Tagore, Sourindra Mohan, 140
Tandon, Prakash, 208n, 210n, 234, 310
Tar Saptak, 15
Tarlo, Emma, 168n
Taylor, Charles, 37n, 58n, 199n, 283n
This is Not that Dawn, 204n
Thought, 398n
Tribune (newspaper), 204, 212n, 219
Tripathi, Suryakant "Nirala", 12–13
Tripathi, Vishwanath, 346n
Trivedi, Harish, 56n, 135n
Tulsidas, Sant, 45–6, 48, 74, 86n, 111, 118, 336n
Tyagpatra, 6n, 13, 313n

USSR (Union of Soviet Socialist Russia), 300, 302–4, 340, 394
Uberoi, Patricia, 41n, 359n
Umrao Jan Ada, 11
United States of America, 394
Urdu, 3, 20, 45–6, 60, 72, 82, 97n, 109–10, 234, 336
   Anglo–Urdu intelligentsia, 27
   culture, 67
   Hindi–Urdu belt, 34, 46
   Hindi–Urdu divide, 58–9, 154, 375

Vaishnavas, 71, 73, 82n, 305
Vallabha community, 73
Valmiki, 85n
Vani Prakashan, 48

Varanasi Sanskrit Yantralaya, 47
Varma, Archana, 255n
Varma, Balmukund, 150n
Varma, Ramchandra, 116
Varma, Ramkrishna, 47
Vatsyayan, Sachidanand Hiranand, 4, 5n, 14–16, 255, 256n, 262, 263n, 265n, 271n, 285n, 286n, 294n, 296, 313n, 337, 339–42, 346n, 416, 418; *see also* Agyeya
Vedalankar, Sharada, 59n
Verma, Bhagvaticharan, 124n
Verma, Mahadevi, 12
Verma, Nirmal, 17, 381n
Vicar of Wakefield, The, 86, 97
Viduraprajagara, 86n
Vinaypatrika, 86n
Vishnupurana, 85n

Watt, Ian, 82n, 88n
Williams, Raymond, 40, 42–3, 167n, 181, 206n, 256, 335n, 363n
women
  caste and, 124
  characters, 25, 36, 423
  constructs of, 5, 124, 342, 349, 357, 398
  dance and, 368–9, 372, 376–9, 393, 422
  education and, 61n, 85, 99
  language of, 59
  morality and, 111–16, 127, 135, 141–2, 240, 320
  nationalism and, 152, 155–7
  patriarchy and, 171, 173, 225, 334, 407
  rights of, 44, 156–7
  violation of, 224, 228–32, 233n, 234, 238–39, 415
  working, 267
Wood, Sir Charles, 129
World War II, 9, 15, 39, 300, 333n, 337, 340, 378, 424

Yadav, Rajendra, 8n, 16–17, 255n, 328n, 329–30, 337, 339–43, 347n, 348n, 352n, 356n, 359n, 362n, 363, 366, 387, 420
Yama: The Pit, 145
Yashpal, 4, 13n, 14, 16, 203–5, 210n, 229, 235, 236n, 239, 242n, 250, 339, 414, 416, 418
Young India, 156n
Yuvak, 337

Zaehner, R.C., 269n
Zameen, 394n
Zulaikhan, 236n

www.ingramcontent.com/pod-product-compliance
Lightning Source LLC
Chambersburg PA
CBHW070231240426
43673CB00044B/1756